# Learn Grafana 10.x

A beginner's guide to practical data analytics, interactive dashboards, and observability

**Eric Salituro**

BIRMINGHAM—MUMBAI

# Learn Grafana 10.x

**Group Product Manager**: Kaustubh Manglurkar
**Publishing Product Manager**: Apeksha Shetty
**Book Project Manager**: Kirti Pisat
**Senior Editor**: Tazeen Shaikh
**Technical Editor**: Rahul Limbachiya
**Copy Editor**: Safis Editing
**Proofreader**: Safis Editing
**Indexer**: Subalakshmi Govindhan
**Production Designer**: Ponraj Dhandapani
**DevRel Marketing Coordinator**: Nivedita Singh


First published: June 2020

Second edition: December 2023

Production reference: 1201123

Published by Packt Publishing Ltd.
Grosvenor House
11 St Paul's Square
Birmingham
B3 1RB, UK.

ISBN 978-1-80323-108-2

www.packtpub.com

*To my wife, Susan, for her infinite patience, support, and companionship. To my mother, Patricia, who introduced her son to so many books, yet never expected that he would someday go on to write one.*

*– Eric Salituro*

# Contributors

## About the author

**Eric Salituro** is currently a software engineering manager with the enterprise data and analytics platform team at Zendesk. He has an IT career that spans more than 35 years, over 20 of which were spent in the motion picture industry working as a pipeline technical director and software developer for innovative and creative studios such as DreamWorks, Digital Domain, and Pixar. Before moving to Zendesk, he worked at Pixar, helping to manage and maintain their production render farm as a senior software developer. Among his accomplishments is the development of a Python API toolkit for Grafana aimed at streamlining the creation of rendering metrics dashboards. He is the author of *Learn Grafana 7.0*.

# About the reviewers

**Chad Isenberg** has been working as a data professional since 2018 and is currently a data engineer at Zendesk. His experience and interests include analytics, data platforms, data quality, DataOps, and many other *data*-prefixed subjects. He is passionate about the data community and contributes articles and blog posts to platforms such as Medium and LinkedIn.

**Mahdi Karabiben** is a data engineer with over 7 years of experience working on petabyte-scale data projects. As part of Zendesk's core data team, he's currently leading multiple projects related to data quality and observability. Prior to Zendesk, Mahdi worked on building data platforms at FactSet, Crédit Agricole CIB, and Numberly.

# Table of Contents

# 3

# Diving into Grafana's Time Series Visualization 49

# Part 2 – Real-World Grafana

# 4

# Connecting Grafana to a Prometheus Data Source 79

# 8

## Surveying Additional Grafana Visualizations                                        201

# 9

## Creating Insightful Dashboards                                                     225

# 10

# Working with Advanced Dashboard Features and Elasticsearch    265

# 11

# Streaming Real-Time IoT Data from Telegraf Agent to Grafana Live    305

# 12

# Monitoring Data Streams with Grafana Alerts                            327

# 13

# Exploring Log Data with Grafana's Loki                                369

# Part 3 – Managing Grafana

## 14

## Organizing Dashboards and Folders    403

## 15

## Managing Permissions for Users, Teams, and Organizations    427

# Preface

Grafana is an open source analytical platform used for analyzing and monitoring time-series data. This second edition will help you to get up to speed with Grafana 10's latest features for querying, visualizing, and exploring logs and metrics no matter where they are stored. Along the way, we'll introduce key concepts and best practices in software development, data visualization, and application administration.

The book begins by showing you how to quickly install and set up a Grafana server using Docker. You'll become familiar with important components of the Grafana interface and learn how to analyze and visualize data from sources including InfluxDB, Telegraf, Prometheus, Logstash, and Elasticsearch.

We will cover many of Grafana's key panel visualizations, including **Time Series**, **Stat**, **Table**, **Bar Gauge**, and **Text**. You'll use Python to pipeline data, transformations to facilitate analytics, and templates to build dynamic dashboards. You'll explore real-time data streaming with Telegraf, Promtail, and Loki, as well as observability features such as alerting rules, PagerDuty, and Slack integrations.

As you progress, the book will delve into the administrative aspects of Grafana, from configuring users and organizations to implementing user authentication with Okta and LDAP, organizing dashboards into folders, and more.

By the end of this book, you'll have gained the knowledge you need to extract, transform, and load data; connect Grafana to time-series databases; build interactive dashboards; and leverage ad hoc data exploration for observability. Whether you are interested in visualization for data science or observability for your operations, this book will provide the launch pad for anyone looking to become proficient using a data visualization and observability application such as Grafana.

## Who this book is for

This book is for business intelligence developers, business analysts, data analysts, and anyone interested in performing time-series data analysis and monitoring using Grafana. Those looking to create and share interactive dashboards or looking to get up to speed with the latest features of Grafana will also find this book useful. Although no prior knowledge of Grafana is required, basic knowledge of data visualization and some Python programming experience will help you understand the concepts covered in the book.

# What this book covers

*Chapter 1, Introducing Data Visualization with Grafana*, provides a brief introduction to the use of data visualization in general and specifically in Grafana. We will then move on to installing a Grafana server onto your machine, using either a native installer or a Docker container. Launching the server and connecting to it with a web browser will also be covered.

*Chapter 2, Touring the Grafana Interface*, will explore the workings of the major UI components after you have launched and connected to the Grafana web application. We will look at the search bar, side menu, and **Home** dashboard.

*Chapter 3, Diving into Grafana's Time Series Visualization*, will dive into the **Time series** panel visualization for a closer look at how to work with the major components of the main Grafana visualization. After connecting to a test data source, we will also identify common panel components in preparation for working with other visualizations.

*Chapter 4, Connecting Grafana to a Prometheus Data Source*, will show you how to launch the Prometheus time-series database from a Docker container, load an actual time-series dataset, and query and visualize data in Grafana.

*Chapter 5, Extracting and Visualizing Data with InfluxDB and Grafana*, will show how to write a simple Python **Extract, Transform, and Load** (**ETL**) script to access data from a public data server and push it to InfluxDB. We'll also connect Grafana to InfluxDB and try out some more advanced query techniques.

*Chapter 6, Shaping Data with Grafana Transformations*, will introduce the concept of the Grafana data frame, and how the different Grafana transformations can shape query data. We'll also chain transformations into a more complex data pipeline.

*Chapter 7, Surveying Key Grafana Visualizations*, will see us use the **Table**, **Stat**, **Bar Gauge**, and **Gauge** panel visualizations to display our weather data.

*Chapter 8, Surveying Additional Grafana Visualizations*, will see us modify the Python ETL script to download earthquake data. We'll visualize the data using **Geomap**, **Bar chart**, **Histogram**, and **Heatmap** visualizations.

*Chapter 9, Creating Insightful Dashboards*, uses what we'll have learned about Grafana panel visualizations and some basic information design principles to create production dashboards for visualizing weather and earthquake data.

*Chapter 10, Working with Advanced Dashboard Features and Elasticsearch*, explores the powerful advanced features of the dashboard, including annotations, templating with variables, and dashboard linking, as well as techniques for sharing dashboards. We'll pull down public data from the city of San Francisco and use Logstash and Elasticsearch as the data source.

*Chapter 11, Streaming Real-Time IoT Data from Telegraf Agent to Grafana Live*, will present the first in a trilogy of chapters on observability by introducing the concept of real-time data streaming. We'll build a data pipeline to stream data from an **Internet of Things** (**IoT**) simulator using standard MQTT protocols and then use InfluxDB to send the messages to Grafana Explore.

*Chapter 12, Monitoring Data Streams with Grafana Alerts*, will show you how to take streaming data, monitor it for anomalies with alerting rules, and connect those alerts to a set of notification channels, including email, PagerDuty, and Slack.

*Chapter 13, Exploring Log Data with Grafana's Loki*, will complete the observability trilogy by showing how to capture observability metrics and logs with the combination of Promtail and Loki. We'll perform an ad hoc analysis with Explore to check for correlations between metrics patterns and logging events.

*Chapter 14, Organizing Dashboards and Folders*, will show you how to label dashboards and organize them into folders to make them easier to find. We'll also look at other dashboard features, such as starred dashboards, dashboard playlists, and the **Dashboard list** panel visualization.

*Chapter 15, Managing Permissions for Users, Teams, and Organizations*, will show you how to manage users, teams, and organizations, including access control and user addition and deletion.

*Chapter 16, Authenticating Grafana Logins Using LDAP or OAuth 2 Providers*, will show you how managers can connect Grafana user authentication to a variety of services. We'll authenticate using an internal LDAP server and use OAuth 2 to authenticate using external services from GitHub, Google, and Okta.

*Chapter 17, Cloud Monitoring AWS, Azure, and GCP*, will show how Grafana can provide monitoring support for a variety of services provided by major cloud platforms, such as **Amazon Web Services** (**AWS**), **Microsoft Azure**, and **Google Cloud Platform** (**GCP**).

# To get the most out of this book

In order to complete the majority of the exercises in this book, you will need to download and install Docker along with Docker Compose. For the examples in the book, we will be downloading and installing other software and datasets, including Grafana and Loki, so you will occasionally need an internet connection. You can download and install each software package independently, but our tutorial instructions are designed to work with Docker. We do that so that all software dependencies and network management can be encapsulated within the Docker container paradigm.

We will run a fair amount of software from the command line, so you should be comfortable with typing commands into a shell, such as **Bash** or **Windows PowerShell**. To access the contents of the book's GitHub repository, you will either need Git or an unzip application.

Having an interest in science in general and data science, in particular, will go a long way toward making this book interesting and useful. It would also be helpful to have some programming experience with a scripting language such as **Python**, but since all the code is included, you can run it directly from a clone of the book's GitHub repository. Some familiarity with relational databases will help you understand some of the terminology and concepts behind time-series databases.

| Software/hardware covered in the book | Operating system requirements |
| --- | --- |
| Grafana | Windows, macOS, or Linux |
| Docker | Windows, macOS, or Linux |
| Loki/Promtail | Windows, macOS, or Linux |
| Prometheus | Windows, macOS, or Linux |
| InfluxDB/Telegraf | Windows, macOS, or Linux |
| Elasticsearch/Logstash | Windows, macOS, or Linux |
| OpenLDAP | Windows, macOS, or Linux |
| Python 3.7+ | Windows, macOS, or Linux |

*Grafana is an application under constant development and revision, and as such, the depictions, descriptions, and illustrations in this book represent a snapshot in time and are current at the time of writing. By the time you read this book, features may have been added, altered, or deleted outside of our control. However, we believe any deviations from the book should be easily accommodated with only minor adjustments.*

It might also be helpful to use an IDE application such as **Microsoft Visual Studio Code**, or **JetBrains PyCharm**.

In order to follow along with the exercises in *Chapter 16, Authenticating Grafana Logins Using LDAP or OAuth 2 Providers*, you will need accounts with GitHub, Google, and Okta. To follow the exercises in *Chapter 17, Cloud Monitoring AWS, Azure, and GCP*, you will need to create an account with AWS, GCP, and Microsoft Azure.

**The examples and software in this book have not been validated for security reasons**. They require an external internet connection and leverage open source software under a variety of licenses, so if you intend to use any of this software within a security-conscious computing environment (such as in an education or corporate environment), it is highly recommended that you consult your local IT professionals in advance.

I hope to show with the examples in this book how easy it is to build simple data visualization pipelines with Grafana and today's open source tools. I also hope this book will inspire and empower you to seek out your own datasets to acquire, analyze, and visualize. Best of luck!

**If you are using the digital version of this book, we advise you to type the code in yourself or access the code via the GitHub repository (link available in the next section). Doing so will help you avoid any potential errors related to the copying and pasting of code. Each chapter folder includes dashboards, docker-compose.yml files, and a Makefile to help out when running some of the command-line tools.**

# Download the example code files

You can download the example code files for this book from GitHub at `https://github.com/PacktPublishing/Learn-Grafana-10`. Any update to the code will be updated in the GitHub repository.

We also have other code bundles from our rich catalog of books and videos available at `https://github.com/PacktPublishing/`. Check them out!

# Conventions used

There are a number of text conventions used throughout this book.

`Code in text`: Indicates code words in text, database table names, folder names, filenames, file extensions, pathnames, dummy URLs, user input, and Twitter handles. Here is an example: "Mount the downloaded `WebStorm-10*.dmg` disk image file as another disk in your system."

A block of code is set as follows:

```
FROM python:3
SELECT mean("value") FROM "temperature"
WHERE $timeFilter
GROUP BY time($__interval), "station" fill(none)
```

When we wish to draw your attention to a particular part of a code block, the relevant lines or items are set in bold:

```
listener 1883
allow_anonymous true
```

Any command-line input or output is written as follows:

```
% docker-compose down
```

**Bold**: Indicates a new term, an important word, or words that you see onscreen. For instance, words in menus or dialog boxes appear in **bold**. Here is an example: "Click on **Load Data | API Tokens**."

> **Tips or important notes**
> Appear like this.

# Get in touch

Feedback from our readers is always welcome.

**General feedback**: If you have questions about any aspect of this book, email us at `customercare@packtpub.com` and mention the book title in the subject of your message.

**Errata**: Although we have taken every care to ensure the accuracy of our content, mistakes do happen. If you have found a mistake in this book, we would be grateful if you would report this to us. Please visit `www.packtpub.com/support/errata` and fill in the form.

**Piracy**: If you come across any illegal copies of our works in any form on the internet, we would be grateful if you would provide us with the location address or website name. Please contact us at `copyright@packt.com` with a link to the material.

**If you are interested in becoming an author**: If there is a topic that you have expertise in and you are interested in either writing or contributing to a book, please visit `authors.packtpub.com`.

# Share Your Thoughts

Once you've read *Learn Grafana 10.x*, we'd love to hear your thoughts! Scan the QR code below to go straight to the Amazon review page for this book and share your feedback.

`https://packt.link/r/1-803-23108-4`

Your review is important to us and the tech community and will help us make sure we're delivering excellent quality content.

# Download a free PDF copy of this book

Thanks for purchasing this book!

Do you like to read on the go but are unable to carry your print books everywhere?

Is your eBook purchase not compatible with the device of your choice?

Don't worry, now with every Packt book you get a DRM-free PDF version of that book at no cost.

Read anywhere, any place, on any device. Search, copy, and paste code from your favorite technical books directly into your application.

The perks don't stop there, you can get exclusive access to discounts, newsletters, and great free content in your inbox daily

Follow these simple steps to get the benefits:

1.  Scan the QR code or visit the link below

https://packt.link/free-ebook/9781803231082

2.  Submit your proof of purchase

3.  That's it! We'll send your free PDF and other benefits to your email directly

# Part 1 – Getting Started with Grafana

In this section, you will gain a broad understanding of how to quickly set up a Grafana application server and use it to visualize data. You will also learn about Grafana's basic features such as the search bar, main menu, panel visualizations, and dashboards. Further, you will also take a deep dive into how to query data sources and graph the results with Time series panel visualizations.

This part comprises the following chapters:

# 1

# Introducing Data Visualization with Grafana

Welcome to *Learn Grafana 10.x*! Together, we will explore **Grafana**, an exciting, multi-faceted visualization tool for data exploration, analysis, and alerting. We will learn how to install Grafana, become familiar with some of its many features, and even use it to investigate publicly available real-world datasets.

Whether you are an engineer watching terabytes of metrics for a critical system fault, an administrator sifting through a haystack of log output looking for the needle of an application error, or just a curious citizen eager to know how your city works, Grafana can help you monitor, explore, and analyze data. The key to getting a handle on big data is the ability to visualize it.

But before we find out how Grafana gives you that ability, we'll need to cover a few basic concepts behind data visualization. Following that, we'll set up our own instance of Grafana, which will form the fundamental building block for the exercises that follow in later chapters.

The following topics will be covered in this chapter:

- Appreciating data and visualization – we'll take a brief overview of the data landscape and how visualization is useful

- Why Grafana? We'll look at what makes Grafana an attractive solution

- Installing Grafana – we'll install the Grafana application server and get it running

- Connecting to the Grafana server – we'll launch the Grafana application by connecting to the installed server from a web browser

Tutorial code, dashboards, and other helpful files for this chapter can be found in the book's GitHub repository at `https://github.com/PacktPublishing/Learn-Grafana-10/tree/main/Chapter01`.

# Technical requirements

Grafana is relatively easy to set up, but since it is a web server application, you will need to execute a few shell commands to get it running. For the purposes of this book, we will assume that you will access Grafana from the same computer that you installed it on. The following are the technical requirements for installing and running Grafana:

- Familiarity with the command shell

- A terminal application or an SSH to the machine where you plan to install Grafana

- Docker (in order to run Grafana from a Docker container)

Optionally, you will need to have the following:

- Administrator access to install and run Grafana from the command line, rather than in a Docker container

# Appreciating data and visualization

In the not-too-distant past, most of us consumed data pretty much solely via a daily newspaper—the financial pages, the sports section, and the weather forecast. However, in recent years, the ubiquity of computing power has immersed every part of our lives in a sea of data.

Around the clock, our built environment and devices collect innumerable amounts of data, which we consume. Our morning routine starts with a review of emails, social media posts, and news feeds on a smartphone or tablet, and whereas we once put down the daily newspaper when we left for work, our phones come with us everywhere.

We walk around or exercise and our phones capture our activity and location data via the **global positioning system** (**GPS**), while our smartwatches capture our vital signs. When we browse the web, every single interaction down to a mouse click is logged and stored for analysis. The servers that deliver these experiences are monitored and maintained by engineers on a round-the-clock basis. Marketers and salesforces continually analyze this data in order to make business-critical decisions.

On the way to work, our cars, buses, and trains contain increasingly sophisticated computers that silently log tens of thousands of real-time metrics, using them to calculate efficiency, profitability, engine performance, and environmental impact. Technicians evaluating these physical systems' health or troubleshooting problems often sift through an enormous stream of data to tease out the signs of a faulty sensor or a failed part. The importance of this data is globally recognized. This is precisely why data recorders are the most valuable forensic artifact after any transportation accident, and why their recovery generates such widespread media coverage.

Meanwhile, in the modern home, a smart thermostat dutifully logs the settings on a **Heating, Ventilation, and Air Conditioning** (**HVAC**) system, as well as the current temperature both inside and outside the house. These devices continually gather real-time weather information in order to make decisions about how and when to run most efficiently.

Similar to the systems at home, but on a much larger scale, nearly every building we pass through during the day collects and monitors the health of a number of key infrastructure systems, from air conditioning to plumbing to security. No amount of paper could possibly record the thousands of channels of data flowing through these physical plants, and yet the building management system aggregates this data to make the same kinds of simple decisions as the homeowner does.

Moreover, these examples represent only a drop in the ocean of data. Around the world, governments, scientists, NGOs, and everyday citizens collect, store, and analyze their own datasets. They are all confronted with the same issue: how to aggregate, collate, or distill the mass of data into a form that a human can perceive and act on in a few seconds or less. The response to this issue is effective data storage and visualization.

## Storing, retrieving, and visualizing data

For years, the basic language of data visualization was well-defined: using a chart, graph, histogram, and so on. What was missing was the ability to rapidly create these charts and graphs not in hours or days but in seconds or even milliseconds. This requires processing power that draws representations of thousands and thousands of data points in the time it takes to refresh a computer display.

For decades, only the most powerful computers could manage the processing power required to visualize data on this scale, and the software they ran was specialized and expensive. However, a number of trends in computing have converged to produce a renaissance in data acquisition and visualization, making it accessible not only to domain practitioners but also to technically proficient members of the general public. They are as follows:

- Cheap general-purpose CPUs and graphics GPUs
- Inexpensive high-capacity storage, optimized for physical size and maximum throughput
- Web standards and technologies, including JavaScript and CSS
- Open source software frameworks and toolkits
- Scalable cloud computation at affordable prices
- Broadband networking to enterprises, homes, and mobile devices

A common feature of virtually all of this data, that is, for each sample from a sensor or line in a log file, is the snapshot from an invisible ticking clock: a **timestamp**. A dataset gathered from these data points across a period of time is referred to as a **time series**. A stored object containing one or more time series is a **time-series dataset**. An application that can provide optimized access to one or more of these datasets is called, naturally, a **time-series database** (**TSDB**). While a whole class of NoSQL time-series databases, such as InfluxDB, OpenTSDB, and Prometheus, have sprung up, venerable SQL relational databases, such as PostgreSQL and MySQL, have added their own support for time-series datasets.

That's fine for storing and retrieving data, but what about visualizing data? Enter Grafana.

# Why Grafana?

While there are many solutions in the data visualization space, Grafana is proving to be one of the most exciting, exhibiting rapid growth in scope and features, broad options for deployment and support, and an enthusiastic community contributing to its future growth. Before going into the specific features that make Grafana an attractive solution, let's take a look at the criteria we might use to characterize a useful data visualization application:

Figure 1.1 – Grafana UI

For the purposes of this book, we will be looking at particular software applications that fulfill four major functions: exploration, analysis, presentation, and observability.

# Exploration

Quickly loading and displaying a dataset with the idea of identifying the particularly interesting features for deeper analysis, sometimes referred to as **drilling down**, is an example of *data exploration*.

Another common term for data exploration is **ad hoc analysis**. This refers to the nature of using data visualization techniques without a pre-defined analysis in place. Ad hoc analysis is useful for getting a *feel* for the data's characteristics, and whether any interesting patterns are discernable.

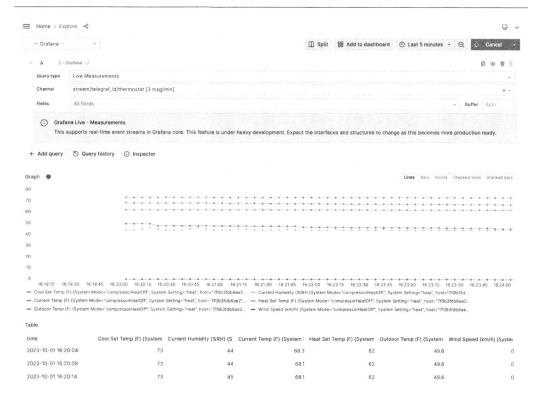

Figure 1.2 – Grafana exploration

In this book, we'll be frequently using the **Explore** feature of Grafana to perform just this sort of data exploration.

## Analysis

After we have examined our data, we may well want to *analyze* it. That is, we may want to quantify the data statistically or correlate it with other data. For example, we may want to see what the maximum value or average value is, or otherwise aggregate the data for a specific time range. We may also want to look at multiple datasets over the same time period to look for events that might be time-correlated.

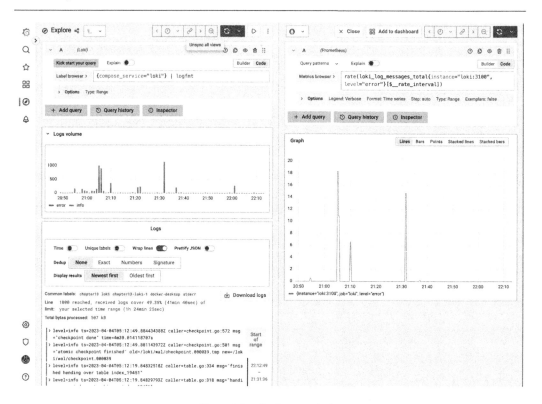

Figure 1.3 – Grafana analysis

Grafana contains several analysis features that we highlight throughout the book. We will also leverage Grafana's powerful transformation features to aid us in our analysis.

## Presentation

Once we have identified the data we are interested in, we will want to *present* it in an aesthetically pleasing manner that also gives the viewer clarity about what the data represents, in effect helping to tell a story about the data, which would be otherwise difficult to do without specific domain knowledge.

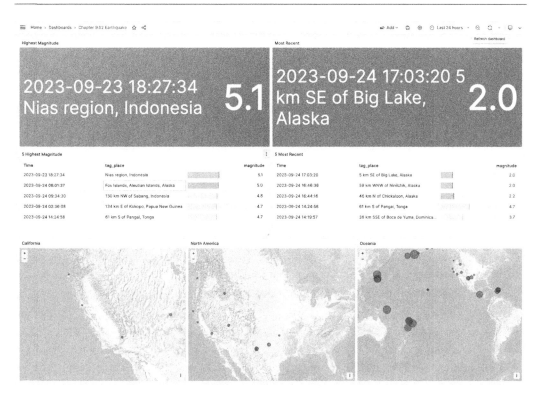

Figure 1.4 – Grafana presentation

Assembling panels into dashboards is a common Grafana workflow for presentation, and we will spend much of our time in this book covering not only how to construct dashboards to tell the story of our data, but also how to structure our data visualizations to be both clear and meaningful.

## Observability

Finally, we may need to observe the data over time, or even in real time as it may represent critical data. If the data crosses into a realm of concern, we may need to be notified immediately.

Grafana has extensive and powerful *observability* features, along with integrations for popular notification services such as PagerDuty. In this book, we'll learn how to build alerts to detect anomalies in our data, and how to craft appropriate notifications depending upon the severity of the alert.

## Choosing Grafana

While there are quite a few powerful data analytics tools on the market that fulfill these functions, Grafana has a number of features that make it an attractive choice:

- **Fast**: The Grafana backend is written in Google's exciting Go language, making it extremely performant when querying data sources or feeding thousands of data points to multiple dashboard panels.

- **Open**: Grafana supports a plugin model for its dashboard panels and data sources. The number of plugins is constantly growing as the Grafana community enthusiastically contributes to the project.

- **Beautiful**: Grafana leverages the attractive and powerful D3 library. Many of the popular dashboard tools, such as Datadog and Zabbix, can quickly generate beautiful graphs from thousands of data channels, but they only offer some limited control over the display elements. Grafana provides fine-grained control over most graph elements including axes, lines, points, fills, annotations, and legends. It even offers the much sought-after dark mode.

- **Versatile**: Grafana is not tied to a particular database technology. For example, Kibana is a powerful, well-known member of Elasticsearch's **Elasticsearch, Logstash, and Kibana** (**ELK**) stack; it is only capable of visualizing Elasticsearch data sources. This gives it the advantage over Grafana of a better ability to integrate Elasticsearch's analysis tools in its graphing panels. However, due to its plugin architecture, Grafana can support a variety of ever-growing data sources (at last count in 2022, over 150), from traditional RDBMs, such as MySQL and PostgresQL, to modern TSDBs, such as InfluxDB and Prometheus. Not only can each graph display data from a variety of data sources, but a single graph can also combine data from multiple data sources.

- **Free**: While they are very powerful tools indeed, Datadog and Splunk are commercial packages and, as such, charge fees to manage all but the smallest datasets. If you want to get your feet wet, Grafana is freely available under the Apache open source license, and if you do plan to run it in your enterprise, you can purchase tiered support.

These are just some of the criteria you might use to evaluate Grafana against similar products. Your mileage may vary, but now is a great time to be in the market for visualization tools. Grafana and its competitors each have their own strengths and weaknesses, but they are all very capable applications. Here's a short list of the few we covered:

- Kibana (`https://www.elastic.co/`)

- Splunk (`www.splunk.com`)

- Datadog (`https://www.datadoghq.com/`)

- Zabbix (`https://www.zabbix.com/`)

With this in mind, let's install Grafana.

# Installing Grafana

At its core, Grafana runs as a web server, and as such, it is not a typical double-click application. You will need to be comfortable with the command line and have administrator privileges on the computer you plan to install Grafana on. To download the latest versions of Grafana, check out `https://grafana.com/grafana/download`.

The Grafana application server runs on *nix operating systems (Linux, OS X, and Windows), and it can be installed locally on a laptop or workstation or on a remote server. It is even available as a hosted application if you'd rather not deal with setting up or managing a server application on your own.

In this section, we'll walk through the most typical installation options:

- Docker
- OS X
- Linux
- Windows
- Hosted Grafana in the cloud

Once you've completed the installation of your choice, proceed to the *Connecting to the Grafana server* section for instructions on how to access Grafana from a web browser.

## Grafana in a Docker container

The easiest and least complex installation method is to run Grafana from within a Docker container. Docker is available for all major platforms and can be downloaded by visiting `https://www.docker.com/`.

After installing Docker, open a terminal window and type in the following command:

```
% docker run -d --name=grafana -p 3000:3000 grafana/grafana
```

The percent (`%`) symbol is simply there to indicate we are typing in commands to an interactive shell such as `zsh` or Windows PowerShell. If you are cutting and pasting from the book, you'll want to leave out that symbol.

Docker will automatically download and run the latest version of Grafana for your computer's architecture. Bear in mind that since this basic container has no persistent storage, nothing will be retained if you delete the container. I suggest you run the container with a temporary volume so that Grafana's internal database will continue to exist, even if you destroy the container:

```
% docker volume create grafana-storage
% docker run -d --name=grafana -p 3000:3000  \
    -v grafana-storage:/var/lib/grafana \
    grafana/grafana
```

> **Note**
>
> The book and its tutorial examples were written for the macOS operating system, a POSIX-compliant OS that shares many similarities to Linux, including the shell. However, with a few syntax modifications here and there, Windows users should be able to use these same commands in PowerShell.
>
> For example, in the preceding command, you'll want to use the backtick ( ` ) in PowerShell for line continuation, rather than the backslash ( \ ).

I will proceed with Docker and its companion product Docker Compose for the purposes of this book as it will allow an almost turnkey installation experience, as all the necessary dependencies will be automatically downloaded with the container. It will also install in its own sandbox, so you don't need to worry about installing a stack of software that will be difficult to delete later. Finally, in future chapters, we will be setting up data sources using similar Docker containers, so managing the data pipeline as a combination of containers will be very consistent and straightforward.

## Make and Makefile

In the book's GitHub repository, you'll find a `Makefile` in each chapter directory. You can use it to streamline some of the common Docker commands. If you're not familiar with the `make` command or it isn't installed on your computer, you can still cut and paste many of the commands embedded in the `Makefile`.

While space doesn't permit a comprehensive introduction to the concepts that underlie `make`, here is a quick example of how to use it in concert with this book. The following is from the `Makefile` in the `Chapter02` directory of the book's GitHub repository:

```
up:
    docker-compose up -d --pull missing
```

On the first line, the word `up` before the colon ( : ) is referred to as the *target*. Anything following that colon is a *dependency*; there are no dependencies associated with the target. The second line is the *command*; there must be at least one command. For decades, the venerable `make` command and associated `Makefile` have been the backbone for building software, often with hundreds of complex dependencies. Nonetheless, for our use of `make`, we'll use it mostly as a notepad of shortcut commands. To use it, you simply run a `make` command from the shell:

```
% make <target>
```

`make` will first run any targets named in the list of dependencies, followed by the command(s) associated with the target. Run the following:

```
% make up
```

You are using `make` to run this equivalent command:

```
% docker-compose up -d --pull missing
```

There is no requirement to use `make` for this book; all the commands you need are in the text.

## Grafana for macOS

There are two options for installing and running Grafana for macOS:

- Homebrew
- Command line binary install

Using Homebrew is the simplest option as it wraps all the installation chores in a single command. To get Homebrew, visit `https://brew.sh/`. If you want more control over where to install Grafana, the command line option is a better choice.

### Homebrew

Homebrew does not ship as part of macOS, but you can easily install it:

```
% /bin/bash -c "$(curl -fsSL https://raw.githubusercontent.com/
Homebrew/install/HEAD/install.sh)"
```

To install Grafana via Homebrew, run the following commands:

```
% brew update
% brew install grafana
```

If you want to keep Grafana running even after a reboot, use the Homebrew `services` subcommand to launch the installed Grafana application as a service. You will first need to confirm `services` installation:

```
% brew tap homebrew/services
% brew services start grafana
```

### Command line binary install

To install via the command line, open a Terminal shell window and download the macOS distribution tarball, then untar it into the directory of your choice (replace `${GRAFANA_VERSION}` with the current version):

```
% wget https://dl.grafana.com/oss/release/grafana-${GRAFANA_VERSION}.
darwin-amd64.tar.gz
% tar -zxvf grafana-$GRAFANA_VERSION.darwin-amd64.tar.gz
```

Once you've untarred the file, `cd` into the directory and launch the binary by executing this command:

```
% ./bin/grafana-server web
```

## Grafana for Linux

While Linux comes in a number of flavors, each falls into one of two installation systems: yum for Red Hat-based releases or apt for Debian or Ubuntu releases. Typically, you download the binary and then run the installer on the package file. To get the latest Grafana binaries for Linux, visit https://grafana.com/grafana/download?platform=linux.

### Yum installation (Red Hat, Fedora, CentOS)

The installer for Red Hat distributions (CentOS, Fedora, and Red Hat) is yum. To download and install it (replace ${GRAFANA_VERSION} with the current version), use the following:

```
% wget https://dl.grafana.com/oss/release/grafana-%{GRAFANA_VERSION}.
x86_64.rpm
% sudo yum install grafana-${GRAFANA_VERSION}.x86_64.rpm
```

To start up Grafana, use systemctl:

```
% systemctl daemon-reload
% systemctl start grafana-server
% systemctl status grafana-server
```

To keep Grafana running even after a reboot, use the following:

```
% sudo systemctl enable grafana-server.service
```

### Apt installation (Debian, Ubuntu)

The installer for the Debian distributions (Debian and Ubuntu) is dpkg. To download and install it (replace ${GRAFANA_VERSION} with the current version), use the following:

```
% sudo apt-get install -y adduser libfontconfig1
% wget https://dl.grafana.com/oss/release/grafana_${GRAFANA_VERSION}_
amd64.deb
% sudo dpkg -i grafana_${GRAFANA_VERSION}_amd64.deb
```

To start up Grafana, use the following:

```
% systemctl daemon-reload
% systemctl start grafana-server
% systemctl status grafana-server
```

To keep Grafana running even after a reboot, use the following:

```
% sudo systemctl enable grafana-server.service
```

## Grafana for Windows

Installation for Windows is straightforward:

1.  Go to `https://grafana.com/grafana/download?platform=windows`.
2.  Download the latest MSI installer file from the download link.
3.  Launch the `.msi` file to install.

## Grafana Cloud

If you would rather not install Grafana on your computer, or you don't have access to a computer that can run Grafana, there is another option—Grafana will host a free instance for you. Free Grafana Cloud hosting provides very generous limits on the number of users, metrics, logs, and traces. To sign up for the hosted version, go to `https://grafana.com/get/` and select **Cloud**.

Now that you have installed and started up Grafana, let's have a look at the interface. Grafana is a web application, so we'll connect to it with an ordinary web browser such as Chrome, Safari, or Edge.

# Connecting to the Grafana server

Once you have installed and launched Grafana, open a browser page to access the Grafana application. It can be found at `http://localhost:3000`. If everything goes well, you should see a login page, as follows:

Figure 1.5 – Grafana login

Log in with the `admin` username with the password `admin`. You will then be prompted to change it to something more secure (which you can skip if you wish). Once you have logged in, you should see the base Grafana interface:

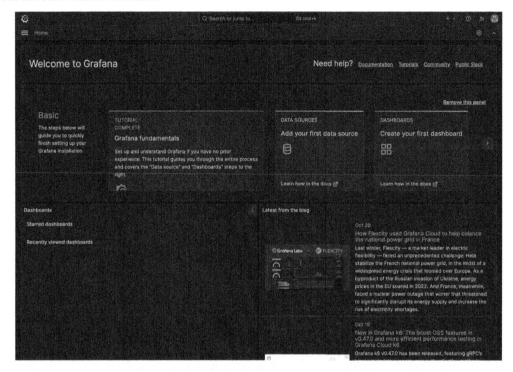

Figure 1.6 – Grafana home page

Great job! You've successfully installed and connected the Grafana application.

## Summary

Congratulations! Over the course of this chapter, we learned about data visualization and why Grafana is a powerful tool for data visualization. We also downloaded and installed Grafana. Finally, we launched the Grafana application from our browser, setting us on a learning path for future chapters.

In our next chapter, we'll take a tour of the Grafana interface and familiarize ourselves with its basic features. This will serve as a foundation for upcoming tutorial exercises. I'm looking forward to our shared journey!

## Further reading

The official Grafana documentation can be found on their website at `https://grafana.com/docs/`.

# 2

# Touring the Grafana Interface

By this point, you've successfully installed and run Grafana, so next, we're going to familiarize ourselves with the Grafana **user interface** (**UI**). In this chapter, we will take a general tour of the default **Home** dashboard, mostly concentrating on the sidebar menu. While you will spend the majority of your time interacting directly with dashboards and panels, you will find that the sidebar is a helpful navigation hub, providing both quick access to simple creation pages and links to more complex functions, including data source creation, **Explore**, alert management, and server administration.

> **Note**
> This chapter is intended to provide a (mostly) high-level tour of these major features. We will go into more detail about many of these features later in the book. I'll point out which chapters correspond to the topics covered. If you're already somewhat familiar with Grafana, this chapter should serve as a quick review and a point of reference.

Specifically, we'll cover the following topics in this chapter:

- Exploring the main Grafana UI components
- Introducing the Grafana search bar
- Identifying the UI components of the **Home** dashboard, including the title bar
- Diving into the Grafana main menu items and sub-items

## Technical requirements

Tutorial code, dashboards, and other helpful files for this chapter can be found in the book's GitHub repository at `https://github.com/PacktPublishing/Learn-Grafana-10/tree/main/Chapter02`.

# Exploring Grafana—the Home dashboard

After logging into the Grafana application, you should end up on the **Home** dashboard, as shown in the following figure. Here, I've annotated some of the key UI elements in the Grafana interface:

Figure 2.1 – The Home dashboard

The following are key UI elements located on the Home dashboard:

1. **The Grafana logo button**: This returns the user to the Home dashboard.

2. **Organization menu**: This allows you to switch organizations.

3. **Search or jump to…**: This searches for or jumps to various actions, pages, or preferences.

4. **Dashboard menu**: This adds or imports dashboards and creates alert rules.

5. **Help menu**: This links to documentation, support, and community pages.

6. **Grafana News**: This opens the latest Grafana blog posts.

7. **User menu**: This links to the user profile and preference settings or signs the user out.

8. **Menu toggle**: This opens the main menu.

9. **Add menu**: This adds panel visualizations, adds rows, or imports panels from the library.

10. **Dashboard settings**: This opens the settings for the current dashboard.

11. **Top search bar toggle**: This hides or reveals the search bar.

12. **Dashboards panel**: This is a dashboard panel containing favorite and recently viewed dashboards.

Grafana is structured around three main interactive UI components that together constitute its core functionality: **dashboards**, **panels**, and **rows**. The page in the preceding screenshot is really just another dashboard—specifically, the **Home** dashboard. A dashboard acts as a canvas upon which you can display one or more rows of panels in a grid-like arrangement. It also can serve, as in the case of the **Home** page, as a web page; you can bookmark it or share it with a simple URL. An entire dashboard can be imported and exported in JSON text file format, making it easy to share, save, or transfer to another version of Grafana.

The most useful and visible component of a dashboard is the *panel*. Panels implement a variety of *visualizations*, from generating graphs, organizing data into tables, and displaying useful text to simply containing a menu list of dashboards—which happens to be the kind of panel you see on the **Home** dashboard in the preceding screenshot. Panels are implemented via plugins in Grafana, so any capable developer can add to the variety of Grafana panels by creating new ones. An administrator can download and install interesting panels beyond those that ship with Grafana.

> **Note**
>
> While a panel is technically now a container for a visualization, historically, each type of panel was implemented as an independent code object. As of a few releases ago, the panels were re-engineered under a common architecture supporting multiple visualizations. For the end user, there is no real distinction between a panel and its visualization; thus, the terms can be used interchangeably.

In *Chapter 3, Diving into Grafana's Time Series Visualization*, we'll be taking a much closer look at what might be considered the canonical Grafana panel visualization—the time series panel visualization. Right now, let's take a tour of Grafana's dashboard UI.

# Introducing the Grafana search bar

There are two main UI components visible on the **Home** dashboard:

- Search bar at the top
- Dashboard below

Each dashboard UI is organized around two main components:

- A dashboard title bar containing the main menu
- Dashboard rows and panels

Let's start by taking a look at the controls on our **Home** dashboard. Depending upon the nature of the dashboard, you may see additional controls, which we will highlight later. For now, let's keep things simple by looking at the basic controls.

At the top of the interface is the search bar. This contains several navigational features. If you're familiar with older versions of Grafana, you will know that they were located in a side menu.

The portion of the dashboard that contains panels is the entire space below the title bar (as seen in *Figure 2.1*). The title bar contains the main side menu on the left and a set of controls on the right. The controls enable you to add new panels, open the dashboard's settings, and hide/reveal the upper search bar.

At the top of the Grafana UI is the search bar. The search bar contains a collection of controls that, in previous versions of Grafana, were located in other areas of the UI. These include the following:

- The **Home** button
- The **Organization** menu
- The search box
- The **Dashboard** menu
- The **Help** menu
- Grafana blog
- The **User** menu

We'll be covering many of these controls over the course of the book, so I won't go into much detail about them just now.

## Grafana logo

On the far left of the dashboard search bar is the Grafana logo icon. It serves as a home button for Grafana. Clicking on it will take you to the **Home** dashboard, which can be set in the preferences to be any specific dashboard.

Figure 2.2 – The Grafana logo

## Organization menu

Next to the **Home** button is the **Organization** menu. Grafana can be configured with one or more organizations, each having its own users, alert rules, and dashboards. We'll talk more about organizations in *Chapter 15, Managing Permissions for Users, Teams, and Organizations*.

## Search box

At the center of the search bar is the search box, an interesting multi-function control. Typing text into the box will activate the search function, listing out any matching links. Clicking on the box without typing will bring up a menu of shortcuts to special actions, pages, and preferences, as shown in the following figure:

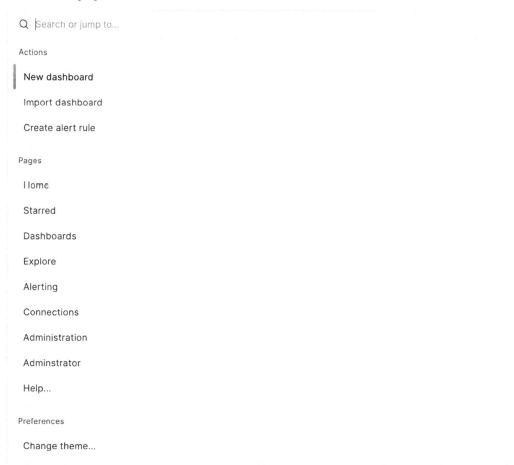

Figure 2.3 – The search box

## + (add) menu

Clustered on the right side of the search bar are several menu icons. The leftmost is the + (add) menu. Clicking on it allows you to create a new dashboard, import an existing dashboard, or create a new alert rule, the basic building block of Grafana observability. We'll look at creating dashboards in *Chapter 9, Creating Insightful Dashboards,* and we'll introduce alert rules in *Chapter 12, Monitoring Data Streams with Grafana Alerts.* Let's take a brief look at the menu items.

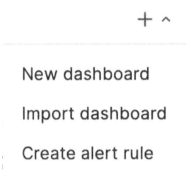

Figure 2.4 – Search bar add menu

These three options are simply shortcuts to actions that are normally accessed via the Grafana menu. Let's check them out.

### New dashboard

The **New dashboard** selection in the + menu is a shortcut to the **New | New Dashboard** selection on the **Dashboards** page. It creates a new empty dashboard containing instructions on how to add content to it. We'll look at the **Dashboards** page a little later on.

### Import dashboard

The + | **Import dashboard** selection is a shortcut to the **New | Import** menu option on the **Dashboards** page. Here is where you can import a previously exported dashboard. We'll talk about both the import and export of dashboards in later chapters.

### Create alert rule

This option is a shortcut to the + **Create alert rule** button on the **Alerting | Alert rules** page. We will discuss alert rules in this chapter a little later in the section covering the Grafana menu.

# Help

To the right of the divider bar is the **Help** menu button, as shown in the following figure:

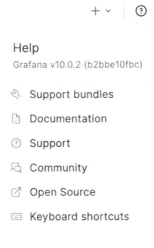

Figure 2.5 – The Help menu

Let's go over some of the more notable options.

## *Support bundles*

Support bundles are packages of useful debugging information primarily used by Grafana support. If you happen to run into a difficult issue and you open a support case, you may be asked to submit a support bundle along with your ticket.

Clicking on + **New support bundle** will open the **Create support bundle** page with a number of options for deciding what will be included in the bundle. Every option (with the exception of **Basic information**) is optional and may be omitted if you have any concerns about sending sensitive information.

Clicking on **Create** will create a bundle and add it to the list of support bundles where it can then be downloaded and attached to your support ticket or deleted by clicking on the trashcan icon.

## *Documentation*

Selecting the **Documentation** button launches a new web page in your browser and opens the Grafana documentation home page for the corresponding version of Grafana.

### Community

The **Community** option launches the Grafana Labs Community Forums website. The forum allows you to meet a community of other Grafana users and to share feedback with Grafana Labs about your product concerns and requests.

### Keyboard shortcuts

Selecting **Keyboard shortcuts** displays a pop-up window with a cheat sheet of keyboard shortcuts. The other three are links to Grafana community forums, technical support, and documentation.

## Grafana blog

To the right of the **Help** menu is a button that activates a Grafana Blog popup.

## User menu

Finally, on the far right-hand side of the search bar is the **User** menu.

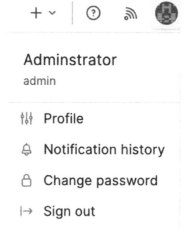

Figure 2.6 – The User menu

The **User** menu links to the settings pages for the current user, where you have options such as **Profile**, **Notification history**, and **Change password**. We'll take a look at these next.

## Profile

The **Profile** page serves a handful of functions.

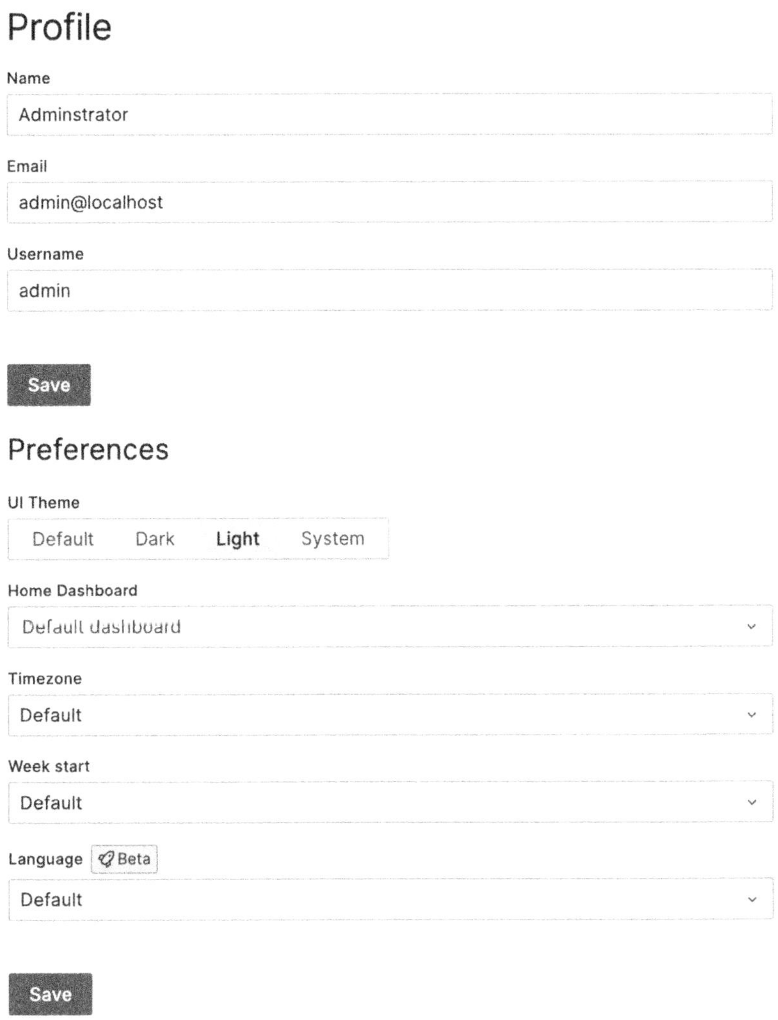

Figure 2.7 – User preferences page

User profile settings on this page fall into the following four functional groups:

- **Profile**: You can set or change **Name**, **Email**, and **Username**
- **Preferences**: You can set or change **UI Theme**, **Home Dashboard**, **Timezone**, and **Week start**

- **Organizations**: You can change the organization by clicking **Select Organization**
- **Sessions**: You can log out of the session by clicking on the red power button

Notably, going to **Preferences | Home Dashboard** allows you to reconfigure your **Home** dashboard to another one of your choosing.

### Notification history

The **Notification history** tab shows all of your notifications, which are mostly errors you've received. You can clear them out by selecting the message you want to delete (you can click the box at the top to select all of them) and clicking the **Dismiss notifications** button.

### Change password

You can change your password here. You'll need to authenticate with your old password and then enter the new one twice for confirmation.

### Sign out

**Sign out** logs you out of Grafana.

That wraps up our tour of the Grafana search bar. It's a relatively new addition to the Grafana UI, so expect it to undergo some revision with each numbered release.

## Expanding Grafana's main menu

The Grafana menu has been somewhat restructured in Grafana 10 compared to previous versions. Some items have been moved to other parts of the interface while others have been renamed. Many of the main menu items have additional submenu items that can be revealed by clicking on the disclosure icon. The state of the Grafana menu is kept even when it is hidden. A complete explanation of each item will not be provided here, but rest assured that we will cover most of them in later chapters of this book!

At the top level are the following Grafana menu options:

- Home
- Starred
- Dashboards
- Explore
- Alerting
- Connections
- Administration

The icons in this menu lead to some of the most common yet impressive features of Grafana. For example, from this menu you can do the following:

- Return to the **Home** dashboard

- Create and manage dashboards and folders

- Explore data sources in an ad hoc fashion

- Create and manage alert rules, contact points, and notification policies

- Configure data sources

- Configure users, teams, and organizations, download and install plugins, and create service accounts

As we tour the Grafana menu options, we'll also walk through some of the more significant submenu items. Space does not permit us to go through all of them in detail, but over the course of this book, we will revisit them with tutorial examples that demonstrate their utility. There's a lot to cover, so let's get started!

## Home

Figure 2.8 – The Home button

This one is pretty obvious: it launches the **Home** dashboard as the Grafana logo does.

## Starred

As you create dashboards, you'll undoubtedly have a few that you will want to return to one or more times from a set of your *favorites*. A list of your favorite dashboards is visible when you enable the **Starred** toggle. Clicking on the **Starred** menu item leads to the **Dashboards** page. To favorite a dashboard is quite simple: from any dashboard (except for **Home**), simply click the star icon that appears to the right of its name in the breadcrumbs:

Figure 2.9 – The Starred dashboard

Next, we'll go down to the **Dashboards** item, the first on our list of menu items that opens its own page. Many of the menu items have their own pages, and you'll also find that their sub-items have their own pages as well. You can reach those pages from the menu or from a list that can be found to the left of an opened page.

## Dashboards

Selecting the **Dashboards** menu item takes you to the **Dashboards** page. Clicking the toggle reveals submenu items for **Playlists**, **Snapshots**, and **Library panels**. Clicking **Dashboards** takes you to the dashboard management page where you can do the following:

- Search for dashboards by name

- Filter the list of dashboards by tags

- Create new dashboards or import existing ones

- Create dashboard folders and organize dashboards into folders

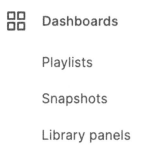

Figure 2.10 – The Dashboards menu

The page features a list of dashboards inside of their folders. If don't see all your dashboards listed, make sure the **Starred** filter is unchecked.

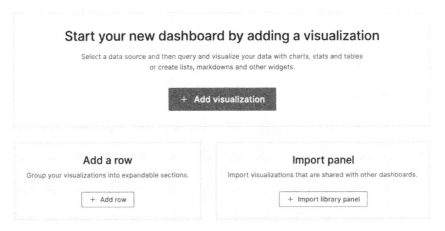

Figure 2.11 – The Dashboards page

You can also switch from icon view to a list view and change the sort order of the results. We'll be taking a closer look at the features of the **Dashboard** page in *Chapter 10, Working with Advanced Dashboard Features and Elasticsearch*, and *Chapter 14, Organizing Dashboards and Folders*.

On the right, the blue **New** menu creates new dashboards and folders and imports existing dashboards. Let's take a look at the three options: **New dashboard**, **New folder**, and **Import**.

### New Dashboard

As mentioned earlier, clicking **New** | **New Dashboard** creates a new empty dashboard containing instructions on how to add content to the dashboard. Try it out!

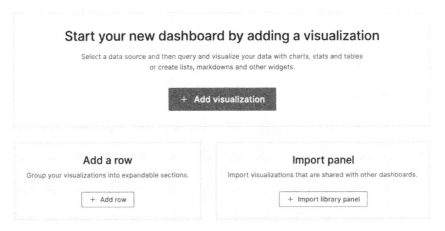

Figure 2.12 – New Dashboard

Comparing the new dashboard's title bar to the **Home** dashboard, you might notice some new icons in the top right:

Figure 2.13 – Dashboard buttons

Here are the basic functions of these buttons:

1.    Adds new visualizations to the dashboard.

2.    Saves the current dashboard.

3.    Dashboard settings.

4.    Sets the time range for the graph.

5.    Zooms the time range.

6.    Refreshes the dashboard.

7.    Sets the dashboard refresh interval.

You'll typically find the time controls (icons **4–7**) anytime you have a time series-based panel on your dashboard. We will go into more detail about the time series panel visualization in *Chapter 3, Diving into Grafana's Time Series Visualization*. Feel free to experiment with dashboard creation. Create a new dashboard and populate it with any number of panels. Until you hook up a data source, you'll be somewhat limited in terms of what you'll be able to display. If you accidentally delete your panel or convert it into a row, you can always create a new one with the **Add Panel** menu.

### Dashboard settings

At the upper right of the **Home** dashboard is a small gear icon that represents the dashboard settings button. Clicking on this button gives you access to a wide array of settings for the dashboard. Some of the main functions available on the settings page are as follows:

- **General**: General dashboard settings let you change titles, descriptions, folders, and so on

- **Annotations**: These are settings governing annotation queries

- **Variables**: These are template variables used in the dashboard and its panels

- **Links**: These are links to other dashboards and external sites

- **Versions**: These are revision controls for the dashboard

- **Permissions**: You can access the controls for the dashboard

- **JSON model**: This is a complete JSON description of the dashboard

We'll be taking an in-depth look at many of these Dashboard settings in *Chapter 10, Working with Advanced Dashboard Features and Elasticsearch*. Other dashboard settings will be covered in other chapters as the need arises.

### New folder

The **New folder** option in the **New** menu is a handy way to quickly create a folder so that you can group dashboards and keep things manageable:

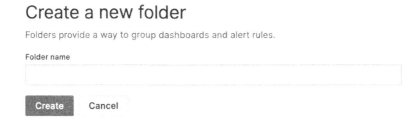

Figure 2.14 – Creating a new dashboard folder

You'll find that once you've created a handful of dashboards, keeping up with them on a **Dashboards** panel, like on the **Home** dashboard, can get pretty cumbersome.

### Import

Finally, the **Import** selection will launch the **Import** page. From here, you can import a dashboard stored at `https://grafana.com` or import a previously exported dashboard JSON file. This is one of the easiest ways to share a dashboard as a JSON file in in plain text format, and you can even send it in an email.

We'll now move on to the first of the sub-items in the **Dashboards** menu item: **Playlists**.

## Playlists

The **Playlists** sub-item takes us to the **Playlists** page, where you can create groupings of dashboards orchestrated to run in a particular sequence and for a specific amount of time:

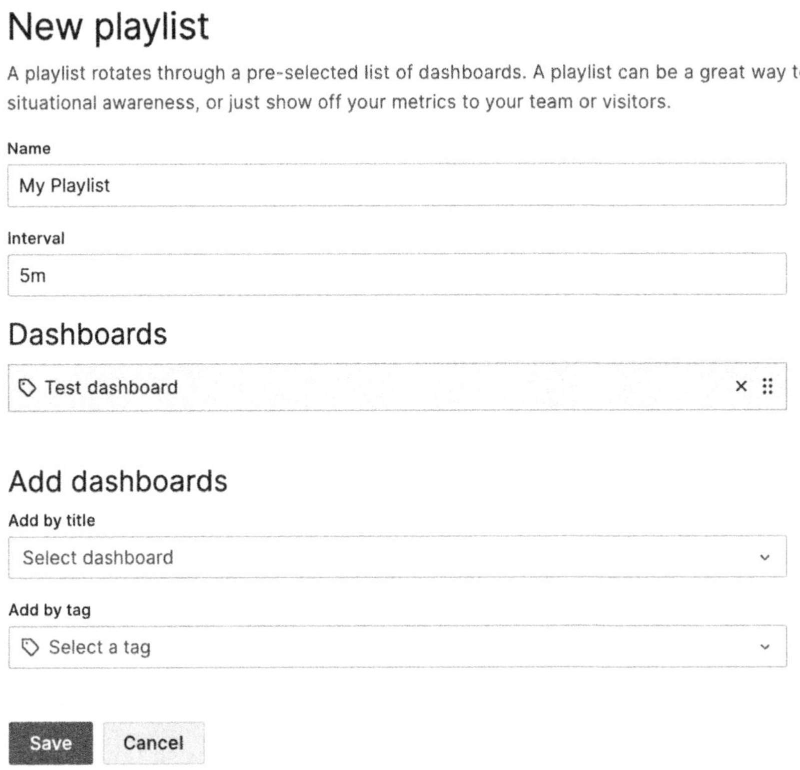

# New playlist

A playlist rotates through a pre-selected list of dashboards. A playlist can be a great way to build situational awareness, or just show off your metrics to your team or visitors.

**Name**

My Playlist

**Interval**

5m

## Dashboards

| ◌ Test dashboard | × ⠿ |
| --- | --- |

## Add dashboards

**Add by title**

Select dashboard ⌄

**Add by tag**

◌ Select a tag ⌄

Save    Cancel

Figure 2.15 – New playlist

Typically, you use playlists when you want to set up an automated Grafana-driven kiosk-type display. You can set up such a playlist in Grafana easily by taking the following steps:

1. Click on + **Create Playlist.**

2. Name your playlist.

3. Set the interval timing between dashboards.

4. Add the dashboards to the list, either by title or tag.

5. Click **Save.**

We'll continue down the list to the **Snapshots** sub-item, which can be found directly below the **Playlists** sub-item.

## Snapshots

The **Snapshots** page, also accessed via the **Dashboards | Snapshots** menu selection, allows you to capture the state of a dashboard in what are called snapshots:

Figure 2.16 – The Snapshots page

This displays your datasets, but there's no way to access the original data sources and queries. Snapshots are a great way to share a live dashboard in scenarios where you need to demo your dashboards offline or can't share access to your data sources.

Snapshots are created by clicking the share icon next to the dashboard name. A snapshot can be stored on your Grafana server or shared out to Grafana's hosted service at `http://snapshots.raintank.io/?orgId=2`.

The last of the sub-items under **Dashboards** is the **Library Panels** sub-item.

## Library panels

Library panels give you the ability to replicate a single panel across many dashboards, so rather than copying the panel from one dashboard to the next, an *instance* of the library panel is created, which the dashboard then references. When a change is made to the library panel, all instances make the change automatically.

From the **Library Panels** page, you can search for library panels by name or description. Clicking on a library panel brings up a dialog that allows you to navigate to any dashboard that references the panel. Clicking on the trashcan icon deletes the library panel.

# Explore

**Explore** is one of Grafana's most exciting features. It is a kind of data-driven scratchpad for exploring a data source prior to implementing it on a dashboard visualization. It is also well integrated with Loki, Grafana's system for logging exploration.

If you've ever worked with a dashboard-driven tool such as Grafana, you might have started with a dashboard, loaded up a graphing panel, fed it the data, and then messaged queries or time frames to look for patterns. What if you could do away with the overhead of building and configuring dashboard panels and go straight to the analysis? That is what **Explore** is for:

Figure 2.17 – Explore mode

**Explore** gives you a fullscreen panel, so you can immediately start exploring your data without concerning yourself with the panel or its appearance on the dashboard. With Loki, **Explore** takes things a step further. By integrating logging with your metrics, you can correlate metric indicators with significant logged events. If you've ever tried to troubleshoot a problem by repeatedly flipping back and forth between your graphs and logs, imagine working with them on the same interface!

We'll explore **Explore** and **Loki** in much more depth in *Chapter 13, Exploring Log Data with Grafana's Loki*.

## Alerting

As more applications grow and expand into the cloud, observability becomes a must-have. Grafana Labs has continued to make observability a key competitive feature. Here's a look at the items available in the **Alerting** menu:

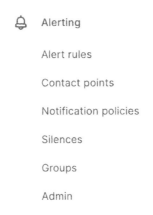

Figure 2.18 – The Alerting menu

Clicking on the **Alerting** menu item takes you to a page describing some of the important concepts of Grafana Alerting. It is a powerful and complex feature, and as such, we are only going to be able to touch on a few key aspects for now, but we will cover alerting in greater detail in *Chapter 12, Monitoring Data Streams with Grafana Alerts*.

### *Alert rules*

Alerting rules in Grafana are the mechanism for creating alerting *pipelines*, which begin with your data sources and end with an alert going out to a notification service of your choosing. There are four steps in creating an alert rule, and on the **Alert rules** page, you begin by clicking + **Create alert rule**:

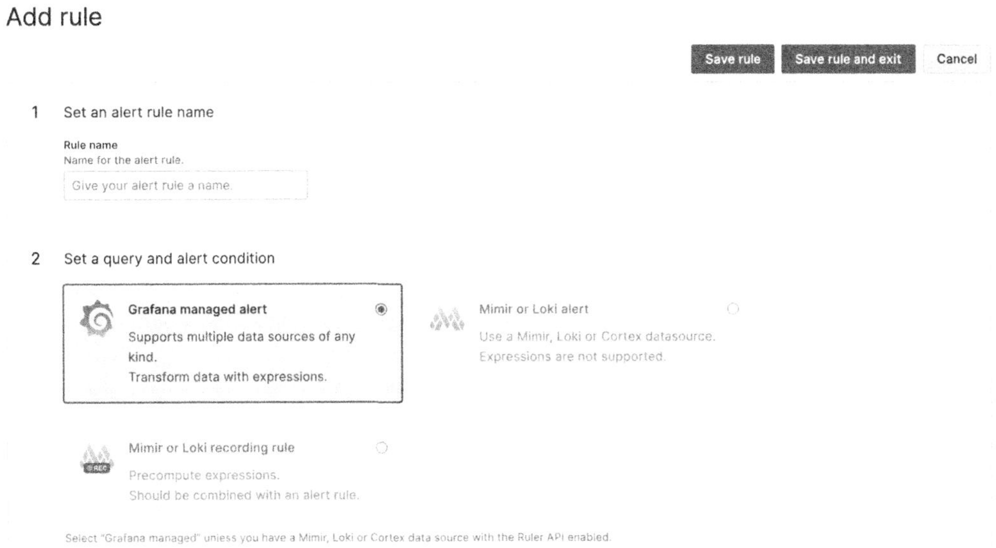

Figure 2.19 – Creating an alert rule

From there, the steps are as follows:

1.  Set an alert rule name.

2.  Set a query and alert condition for triggering an alert.

3.  Set alert evaluation behaviors to establish the alerting interval.

4.  Add details to your alert rule by setting the name and documentation for the alert.

5.  Set a label(s) for routing the alert to notification services.

Once you've created a rule, you can then manage it on the **Alert rules** page:

Figure 2.20 – The Alert rules page

You can search and filter alerts by data source, label, state, or type. For example, with just a couple of clicks, you can find all the firing alerts for a specific data source. As you can tell, as the number of alert rules increases, it becomes imperative to have a good labeling scheme so that you can keep your rules well-organized and manageable.

## Contact points

Once you've created an alert rule, you'll need to create alert messages and configure destinations for those messages. The **Contact points** page is where you define both **Message templates** and the **Contact points** for those messages. Grafana provides access to the powerful Go language templating system for embedding alert-specific content into the message body. Messages can then be sent to one or more services (such as an email service or Slack)which Grafana refers to as **contact points**.

### Notification policies

The **Notification policies** page is the switching center for Grafana Alerting. Here, **Notification policies** define how alerts are routed to various contact points. Notification policies can be configured to route certain alerts to specific contacts by matching against the alert label.

### Silences

There are times when you don't want an alert to fire, for example, during a maintenance window. Here, in the **Silences** page, you can silence one or more alerts for a specific amount of time. The alerts are matched by label, so you can silence alerts by their group name, their severity, or their label.

### Groups

The **Groups** page provides a simple interface for defining groups of alerts by label. As we saw before, an alert group can be simply a set of alerts with the same label. When you've identified a grouping, you can examine any alerts and their current states.

### Admin

The **Admin** page provides access to the configuration of the Alertmanager. An Alertmanager is a server responsible for orchestrating alerting services. By default, Grafana comes with the Prometheus-based Alertmanager. You can configure other external Alertmanagers for load balancing, security, or high availability. For the purposes of this book, we will be using the built-in Grafana Alertmanager.

At this point, it is to be expected that you find these features a bit overwhelming. Grafana Alerting is powerful and complex, but we'll go over the process of setting up an alert step by step in *Chapter 12, Monitoring Data Streams with Grafana Alerts*.

## Connections

Grafana is a *data-agnostic* application, meaning it is not built around a particular data format. Rather, connections between Grafana and various databases are abstracted behind a plugin architecture referred to as a **data source**.

 Connections

Add new connection

Data sources

Figure 2.21 – The Connections menu

### Add a new connection

Clicking on the **Connections** menu item leads to the **Add a new connection** page, which contains an extensive library of these data sources. From here, you can search for the data source that matches your needs.

The list is so extensive that not all the data sources listed ship with the version of Grafana you've installed. After selecting a desired data source, you may need to first install the data source plugin before proceeding to configure it.

Configuring and managing data sources is handled in our next sub-section: *Data sources*.

### Data sources

Setting up the data source connection that backs your graphs will most likely be your primary administrative function within Grafana. From the **Data sources** page, you can create any number of data sources from the available data source plugins:

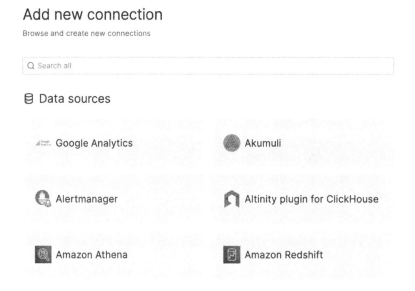

Figure 2.22 – Adding a new connection

To set up a data source, you will typically need to know at least a few things, such as the data source's server IP address and port, the correct authentication credentials to access it, and the name of the database on the server itself. There is one data source you can create that has no setup, as it is an internal plugin to Grafana. The TestData DB data source is a dummy data source that mimics the characteristics of a time series database with random data. We will use the TestData data source in the next chapter to get familiar with the Grafana panel before integrating it with a real data source.

We will take a detailed look at data sources in *Chapter 4, Connecting Grafana to a Prometheus Data Source*.

## Administration

The **Administration** page is Grafana's administrative command center. While you can certainly use Grafana as an application solely for yourself, it is also designed to work as a full-featured data visualization and observability application that can support hundreds of users. From the **Administration** page, you can do this and more.

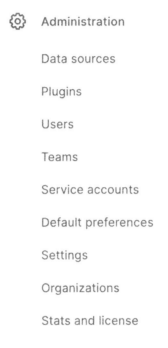

Figure 2.23 – The Administration menu

Clicking on the **Administration** menu item leads to a landing page for the submenu items. We'll go over the different options under **Administration**.

### Data sources

The **Data sources** page here is a copy of the one found under **Connections**. As such, you should assume that it will be eventually removed from this location. From here on, we will only refer to the **Data sources** sub-item located under **Connections**.

## Plugins

The **Plugins** page is an inventory page listing all the installed data sources and panel plugins. It also features a link to the plugins catalog on `https://grafana.com` where you can download and install more plugins:

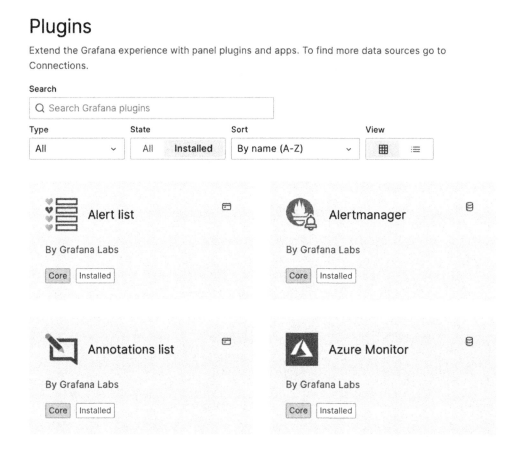

Figure 2.24 – The Plugins page

## Users

The **Users** page under **Administration** is where you can change any user's password, add them to various organizations, and even log them out of Grafana entirely. It's an important page for user management.

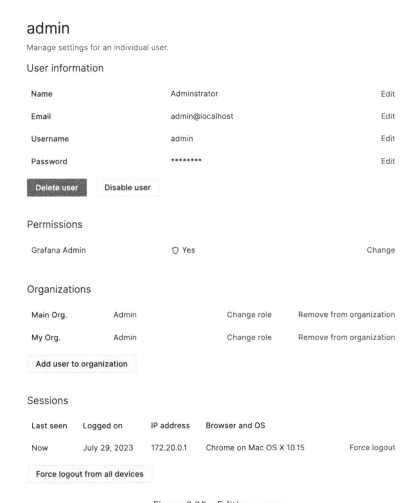

Figure 2.25 – Editing a user

Here's a summary of the different sections on the **Users** page:

- **User information**: This sets a user's name, email, username, and password and can also delete or disable a user
- **Permissions**: This enables admin permissions for the user
- **Organizations**: This adds users to organizations with specified roles
- **Sessions**: This reviews user logins and forces users to log out

Selecting **Administration | Users** takes you to the **Users** page. There are two tabs—one for all users and another only for those in the current organization. You can create or invite new users, set access levels for existing ones, or delete users entirely.

## Teams

Next to the **Users** tab is the **Teams** tab, accessed via **Configuration | Teams**. The concept of teams is primarily used to establish UI settings for an entire group of users. Simply create a new team and add users to it. Default UI settings can then be established for all members of the team. A team can have its own **Home** dashboard, UI theme, or time zone setting. This feature is useful if you are using Grafana to manage groups that want their users to have a tailored Grafana experience.

More information on both users and teams management will be covered in *Chapter 15, Managing Permissions for Users, Teams, and Organizations*.

## Service accounts

Service accounts provide a flexible mechanism for generating a random token to be used by software to access the Grafana API. Service accounts pair one or more tokens with a set of permissions called a **Role**. Multiple tokens with potentially different expiration dates can be associated with a single service account.

Here's an example in which I've created a new service account called `My Service Account`. The role for the service account is **Viewer**, which means it can only access dashboards and not edit them. I've also generated an eternal token, which could then be transferred to a developer or DevOps engineer for installation so that the application can access Grafana. Finally, I've established the permissions for managing this service account so that only one user admin has full admin permissions to not only edit or delete the service account but also to grant other users the permission to manage the service account as well.

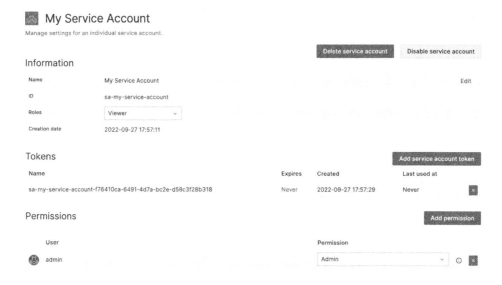

Figure 2.26 – Editing a service account

We'll be taking a closer look at service accounts in *Chapter 11, Streaming Real-Time IoT Data from Telegraf Agent to Grafana Live.*

### Default preferences

Selecting **Default preferences** under **Administration** sets the global interface parameters for an organization. Notably, here is where the default **Home** dashboard is set. In order to be eligible for designation as the **Home** dashboard, a dashboard must also be starred. Besides the **Home** dashboard, this is where the UI style (light or dark mode) and time zone are also set:

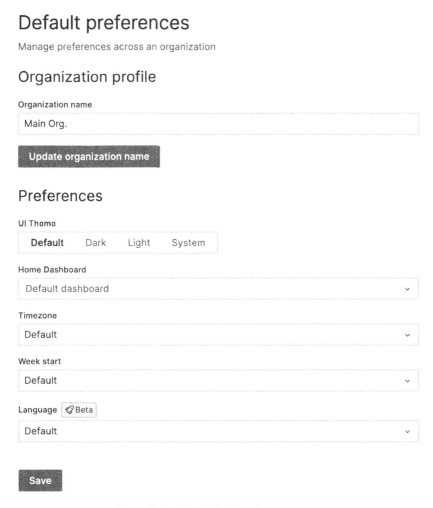

Figure 2.27 – The Default preferences page

### Settings

Clicking **Administration** | **Settings** opens a page displaying the current settings for the Grafana server configuration as stored in the grafana.ini file. It is beyond the scope of this book to fully discuss configuring the Grafana server via grafana.ini. If you want to learn more about how to configure the Grafana server, check out the documentation at https://grafana.com/docs/installation/configuration.

### Organizations

Organizations are Grafana's mechanism for supporting multiple independent Grafana sites from a single server. Each organization is completely independent of the others and has its own **Users**, **Teams**, **Service accounts**, and **Default preferences** settings. To set the preferences for another organization, you would first switch to that organization before making changes.

Creating or deleting an organization is simple:

- Click on the **New org** button to go to a page where you can set the name of the new organization

- Click on the red × button to delete an organization:

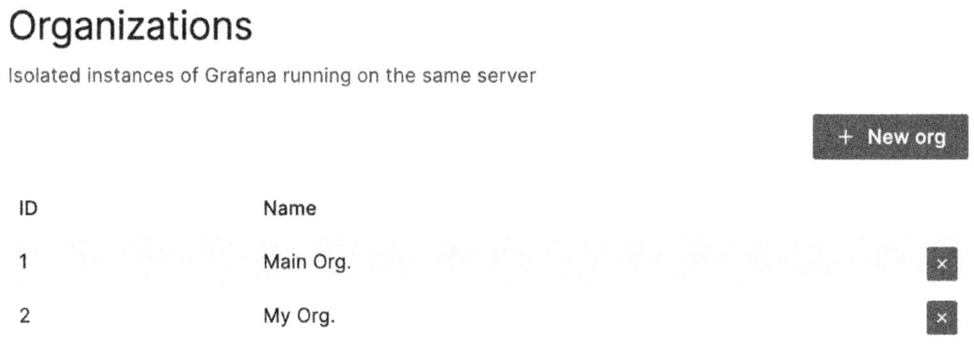

# Organizations

Isolated instances of Grafana running on the same server

| | + New org |
|---|---|

| ID | Name | |
|---|---|---|
| 1 | Main Org. | × |
| 2 | My Org. | × |

Figure 2.28 – The Organizations page

Once you create an organization, however, you will need to populate it with users before anyone can access it. For now, we will work solely within the default organization created for you when you installed Grafana; however, if you wish to find out more, *Chapter 15*, *Managing Permissions for Users, Teams, and Organizations*, will cover user and organization management in more detail.

*Stats and license*

If you want to get an idea of how many resources (from users to dashboards to alerts) have been created on your server, select the **Stats** tab on the **Server admin** page for a list of interesting statistics.

That does it for the Grafana menu! Take a breather before we round out the chapter by looking at the typical dashboard UI elements.

# Exploring the Grafana dashboard UI

Let's step back and look at a dashboard. It is divided into a title bar with several controls and a content area that contains our visualization panels and rows. We'll spend plenty of time talking about how to add and organize dashboard content. For now, let's become familiar with the dashboard's title bar controls.

## Grafana dashboard title bar

At the top of the dashboard is a title bar with the following controls:

- Grafana menu toggle
- Home dashboard breadcrumb
- Add menu
- Dashboard settings
- Search bar toggle

We've already introduced the Grafana menu located on the far left of the dashboard title bar. We'll now start with the breadcrumbs that indicate our dashboard page name and its position in the folder hierarchy.

### Breadcrumbs

While navigating from one page to the next or into dashboard folders, the breadcrumb interface provides a series of links to each level in the hierarchy. Situated to the left of the breadcrumbs is usually the **Home** dashboard.

### Add menu

The **Add** menu provides a quick interface for adding dashboard components such as new visualizations, rows, library panels, and (if you have cut or copied a panel) the clipboard panel.

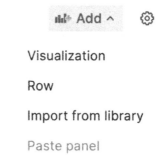

Figure 2.29 – The dashboard visualization Add menu

Click on **Add | Visualization** to create a new panel visualization on the **Home** dashboard or on a dashboard you've created. You'll find a time series visualization has opened and taken you to the **Query** tab, all set for you to start working with a TestData data source.

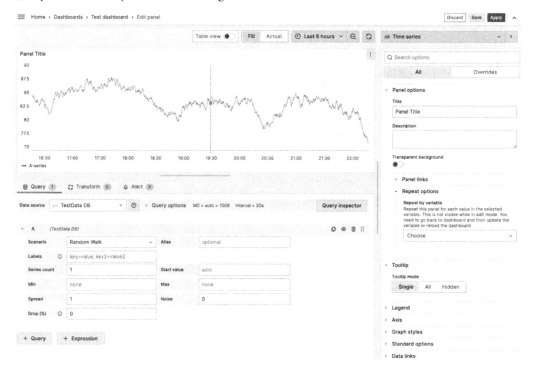

Figure 2.30 – Editing a panel

As you can see from the breadcrumbs in *Figure 2.30*, you're now on the **Edit panel** page for the panel. To get back to the dashboard, click on the **Home** breadcrumb. You should now see a simple graph of the random data you were just looking at in the panel editor:

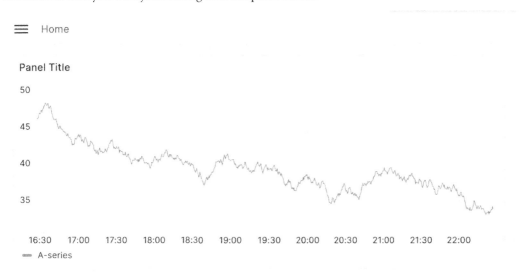

Figure 2.31 – Panel on the dashboard

The **Row** option in the **Add** menu, as the name implies, adds a row to the dashboard. Rows are both a simple divider for dashboard panels and a powerful structure for dynamically building a dashboard page. When you assign a special template variable to a row Configuration, Grafana will appropriately replicate each configured panel on that row to reflect the value of the template variable. We'll be taking a closer look at both rows and template variables in *Chapter 10, Working with Advanced Dashboard Features and Elasticsearch.*

## Dashboard content

We couldn't finish up without mentioning the most important part of the dashboard: the content area where data is visualized in panels. Directly below the dashboard title bar is where dashboard panels and rows are sized and arranged. Besides graphical data, panel visualizations can convey a wide variety of information, including textual and numerical data, spreadsheet-like tables, and even lists of dashboards. The current **Home** dashboard serves as a landing page for the Grafana application by default, but you can always change the **Home** dashboard to any one of your choosing.

# Summary

There you have it—a tour of the basic Grafana interface. We looked at the Grafana UI, identified key elements, and took a closer look at some of them, including the search bar, the Grafana menu, and the dashboard. Of course, we have barely scratched the surface and we've scarcely created a dashboard or visualization panel!

In *Chapter 3, Diving into Grafana's Time Series Visualization*, we will cover a key feature of the Grafana interface—the time series visualization. If you plan to do any graphing, you're going to be using the time series visualization. It's the most powerful and feature-rich of the panels available in Grafana, so we're going to spend the entire next chapter going over its interface. After that, in *Chapter 4, Connecting Grafana to a Prometheus Data Source*, we'll complete our introduction to Grafana's interface by looking at data sources and how they bring time series data to Grafana.

# 3

# Diving into Grafana's Time Series Visualization

We've now come to the chapter you've hopefully been waiting for – using Grafana to actually graph something. In this chapter, we will examine a basic object to query and visualize data – the panel. Within a single panel, you will find the ability to visualize data in a myriad of ways.

While there are a number of different panel visualizations to choose from, the most common one used to produce beautifully styled metrics is the **time series** (formerly **graph**) visualization. It is one of the most versatile panel visualizations, and on first viewing, it seems to have an intimidating set of features. Due to this, we will take a broad overview approach to the panel before diving into the details in later chapters.

Much like we did in *Chapter 2, Touring the Grafana Interface* in this chapter, we will break down the major UI elements that comprise a panel.

In this chapter, we'll cover the following topics:

- Touring the Grafana Panel UI, especially the time series visualization
- Generating test data series from the **Query** tab
- Modifying Grafana panel options
- Setting up monitoring using the **Alert** tab

The tutorial code, dashboards, and other helpful files for this chapter can be found in this book's GitHub repository at https://github.com/PacktPublishing/Learn-Grafana-10/tree/main/Chapter03.

# Touring the Grafana panel UI

Here is a typical Grafana panel in edit mode:

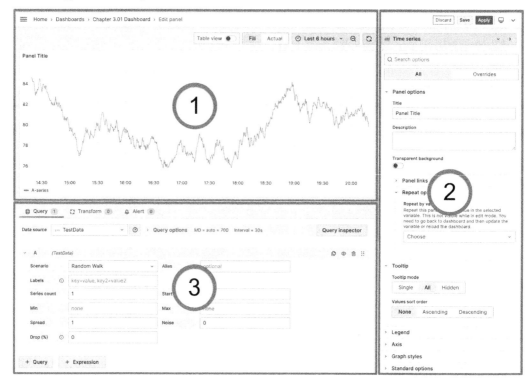

Figure 3.1 – The edit panel UI

The panel's UI can be broken down into roughly three main functional areas as demarcated in the preceding screenshot:

1. **Panel display**: A preview display and a time picker
2. **Options settings**: The panel visualization type, styles, and links
3. **Panel tabs**: Data query, data transformation, and alerting

Throughout this chapter, we will delve into each of these areas. First, we will look at the **Query** tab in the context of how to use it to produce graphed data. Then, we will explore how the various panel settings shape the look of the graph and how to set typical panel display features, such as a title. Finally, we will see how the **Alert** tab can establish monitoring rules for thresholds that, when exceeded, can trigger alerts. Of course, all of this is dependent on what we'll create first – a simple data source.

## Creating a simple data source

A Grafana plugin that supplies panels with data is called a **data source**. Obviously, if you want to set up a graph panel, you will need such a source for data, but what happens when you create a graph panel without specifying a data source? Fortunately, Grafana has thought of this scenario, and if you don't have even a single data source set up, the panel will still have something to graph – a built-in *fake* data source.

If you've already created a panel, you may have seen it graph a mysterious dataset that seems to come from nowhere. The data comes from a built-in data source, called **TestData DB**, which generates pseudo data under several **scenarios**. The default scenario is called **Random Walk**; it's useful for producing a fake dataset that resembles some real-world metrics, where each data point is a small, random deviation from the previous one. It generates a curve modulated with multiple frequencies of random noise. It maintains the same frequency characteristics at all timescales – that is, the data doesn't get noisier as you zoom in, so it is ideal for mimicking physically based metrics, such as temperature, stock prices, or population data.

Let's start from the **Home** dashboard to set up an actual data source that can produce a variety of fake data for us to work with:

1. Click on the Grafana logo or the **Home** option from the main menu to return to the **Home** dashboard if you're not already there.

2. From the main menu, select **Connections | Data Sources**.

3. Click **Add Data Source**.

4. Scroll down to **Others** and select **TestData**.

5. Accept the default name or enter a new one of your choice.

6. Make sure **Default** is set to **On**.

7. Click **Save & Test** to confirm that the data source is working.

If you're successful, you should see a banner with a green check mark, indicating that the data source configuration works. The **Settings** tab should look something like this:

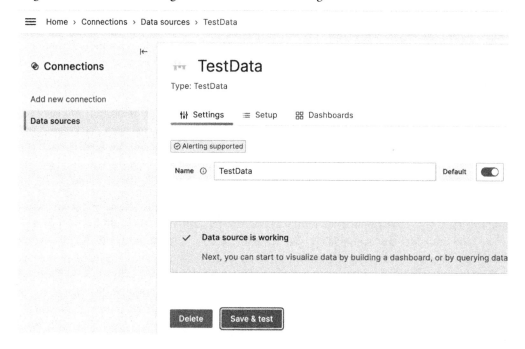

Figure 3.2 – Adding a TestData data source

You've now successfully created your first data source! You can now return to the **Home** dashboard using either the breadcrumbs or the main menu.

## Creating a graph panel

The next thing we need to do is to create a graph panel. By now, you've probably already created a few panels, so this should be relatively familiar. Let's start with a fresh dashboard so that we can keep things separate from the work we did previously:

1.  Go back to the **Home** dashboard.
2.  In the top search bar, select + | **New dashboard**.
3.  Click **Add visualization**. By default, you will have created a time series visualization panel.
4.  You will now need to select a data source, so select the **TestData** data source you created earlier.

Let's return to our dashboard and save our progress:

1.  Click **Apply** to save your panel changes and return to the dashboard.

2.  Click the **Save Dashboard** (disk) icon at the top of the dashboard to save the dashboard for future reference. It is a good practice to regularly save your dashboards.

3.  To go back and edit a panel visualization, click the three-dot menu button at the top right of the panel, and select **Edit**.

After completing this little exercise, the UI should resemble the following, which is not all that different from the first graph we created in *Chapter 2, Touring the Grafana Interface*:

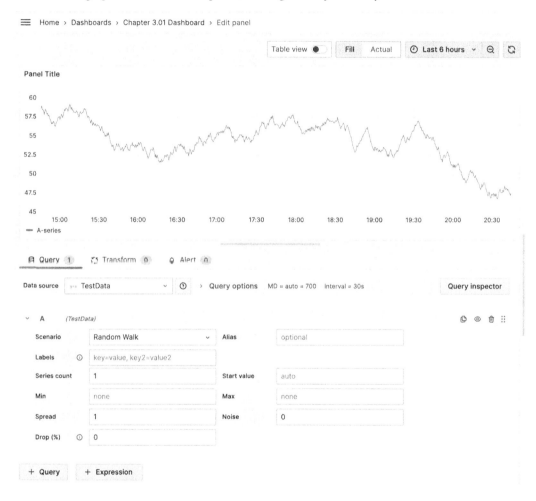

Figure 3.3 – Editing a new panel

Since you designated the new **TestData** as your default data source, any newly created panel will use this default as its data source. Don't worry – you can always set any panel to use another data source with a quick menu selection. Now that we've created our first data source, let's find out how to generate some data for the panel to visualize.

# Generating data series in the Query tab

Let's take a closer look at the **Query** tab, also called the Query Editor. To open a panel editor, click on the panel title and select **Edit** from the pulldown menu. If it isn't already selected, click on the **Query** tab to select it. The **Query** tab is where we assign a data source to the panel's queries. We'll take a closer look at the Query tab shortly.

With **TestData** set as the default data source, Grafana also sets up **Random Walk** to be the default query scenario, so we are now ready to go with both a data source and a scenario that produces the displayed dataset series.

Before we delve further into the **Query** tab, we should probably talk a bit about its purpose. Unlike some visualization tools that are designed to connect to a single data source, Grafana is data source-agnostic. The Grafana data source plugins are not only responsible for presenting the Grafana user with a simplified query interface but also for structuring the returned data in the form of a Grafana *data frame*, a generic object used in many of Grafana's panels.

Most Grafana users will find that, even with a graphical query UI, they can make pretty sophisticated queries. Where a more complex query might be cumbersome in the query UI, Grafana often provides a raw text editor mode to enter queries in the native query language of the data source. In later chapters, we'll work in both modes so that you can get a feel for the strengths of each mode.

Bear in mind that the data source query interface will not provide protection against dangerous queries, so if you're planning to use native queries, talk to your database administrator about creating a restricted account for Grafana data sources.

## What is a query?

Essentially, a query is a mechanism to extract a data series for display by a Grafana dashboard panel. The **Query** tab allows you to extract multiple queries from the same data source or a mix of multiple data sources. It can even reference a data source from other panels. Depending on the data source plugin, Grafana will convert the tab's queries into API calls to the data source server (such as a SQL statement to an RDBMS), retrieve the data in data frame, and then display some or all of it, depending on the current time range.

For now, we'll just use the current **TestData** as our data source so that we can concentrate on the different aspects of the graph panel interface. In the following chapter, we'll look more closely at how to query an actual third-party data source, rather than an internally generated one.

## Query tab features

Let's have a look at the main features of the **Query** tab. Depending on the data source, individual queries will differ, but the overall interface will be the same, as shown in the following screenshot:

Figure 3.4 – The Query tab UI

Here are the key features that have been identified in the preceding screenshot:

1. The **Data source** menu
2. **Query options**
3. The **Query inspector** button
4. The query
5. The duplicate query button
6. The query visibility toggle button
7. The **Delete** query button
8. Query order drag and drop
9. The + **Query** button
10. The + **Expression** button

We'll now examine many of these features, seeing how they work together to give you control over a data source query and the resulting data series.

### The Data source menu

The **Data source** menu is where you will select the data source for the panel. In general, a panel will usually contain queries from a single data source; the pulldown will present a choice from all the available data sources. However, if you do plan to combine data series from multiple data sources on a single panel, select the **Mixed** data source from the pulldown. You will then specify the data source for each individual query.

### Query options

Monitoring the value of a given point at a sample of time (called an **interval**) is critical to maintaining the proper visual representation of data. Next to the **Data source** menu is the **Query options** section, which contains the following options to configure how the panel handles the display of time series data:

- **Max data points**
- **Min interval**
- **Relative time**
- **Time shift**

**Max data points** controls the maximum number of data points that should be displayed, even if the time range is very wide. **Min interval** is used to set the smallest chunk of time or interval Grafana will divide a time range, in order to aggregate all the points in an interval into a representative data point. Setting the value to the frequency of each data point helps Grafana optimize the display of time series panels, especially when dealing with wide time ranges. For example, suppose your data is written to a Prometheus database once every minute (the *sampling frequency*); here, you would set **Min interval** to 1m. **Interval** shows Grafana's calculation for the time period represented by a single data point.

While the time range control at the top of the panel is used to set a global time range for all the panels on the dashboard, often, you would want to override the time range for individual panels. Perhaps you want to see a 1-hour, 2-hour, or 4-hour range for an individual panel. You don't want to have to keep flipping the time range multiple times so that you can replicate the panel three times, setting three different time ranges.

The **Relative time** setting is used to set the panel time range to one that's independent of the dashboard time range. The **Time shift** setting is useful for shifting the panel's time range to an earlier time by a specified offset from the current time. Using both the **Relative time** and **Time shift** settings has the effect of altering the width of the window of time displayed and/or moving the endpoint of that window back in time, relative to now.

To specify the time interval for **Min interval**, **Relative time**, and **Time shift**, use the following time abbreviations:

| Abbreviations | Time interval |
|:---:|:---:|
| Y | Year |
| M | Month |
| W | Week |
| D | Day |
| H | Hour |
| M | Minute |
| S | Second |
| Ms | Millisecond |

Table 3.1 – Time abbreviations

## Query inspector

The **Query inspector** button will open a text console, revealing the contents of the query that Grafana submits to the API. This is a very informative feature for a couple of reasons. If you are having trouble getting the results you want, **Query inspector** can give you an insight into how you might be making an incorrect query to the data source. Additionally, by viewing the actual generated query, you can determine how you might go about making it more efficient. A more efficient query can substantially improve the responsiveness of a Grafana dashboard, especially when it contains several panels.

## Query

The query is, of course, the central interface to derive a dataset. It can contain several components, depending on the data source. In the case of the **TestData** data source, it is simply a **Scenario** dropdown, allowing you to select from several different options to generate test data.

The **Alias** text field is used to give the dataset a name of your choosing. The data source will designate a name for each query, but that name is often not very descriptive, so adding an alias is a good way to document the contents of the query. In later chapters, we'll look at some tips on how to use the alias name to annotate the legend and create display overrides.

## Query controls

The query UI comes with a few control icons to manage queries:

- **Copy (pages) icon**: Creates a copy of the current query directly below it. This saves some time if you want to use the same query but display different aggregations, or change a single field (column).

- **Visibility (eye) icon**: Enables and disables the query.
- **Delete (Trash can) icon**: Deletes the query.
- **Drag and drop (dotted) icon**: Moves the query up or down and has the effect of changing the order of the datasets as they are displayed. This has a direct impact should you choose to stack multiple datasets (the **Display** section).

Next, let's discuss the query and expression options in more depth.

### + Query

+ **Query** creates a new query below the current one. This query will create a new dataset and display it along with existing queries.

### + Expression

+ **Expression** adds a new expression operation to your queries. These operations can manipulate the results of the query by performing math, filtering, reduction, and so on. Even more powerful operations can be performed by creating transformations found under the **Transform** tab.

Now that we have familiarized ourselves with some of the UI features in the **Query** tab, let's play around with some actual queries to see how they affect the panel graph.

## Duplicating an existing query

With this in mind, let's go back to our query. Since we got a query for free when we created the panel, let's create another one, just to see how it affects the display:

1. Confirm that you have selected the **TestData** data source from the **Data source** dropdown.
2. Click on the duplicate query icon. You should now see two queries, both with the **Random Walk** scenario:

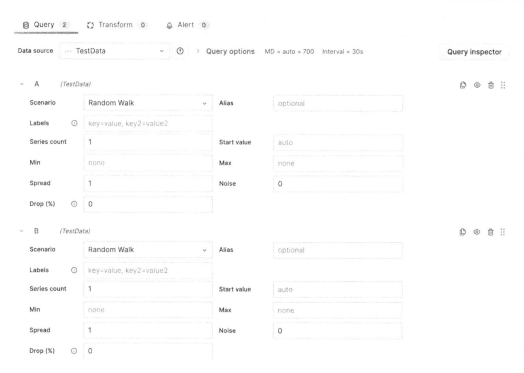

Figure 3.5 – Adding a second query

If you don't see two separate series representing the **A** and **B** queries, click the **Refresh dashboard** button (next to the time series drop-down menu).

## Transform

As I previously mentioned, right next door to the **Query** tab is the **Transform** tab. While it is beyond the scope of this chapter to go into detail about transformations, suffice it to say that this is an incredibly powerful Grafana feature. Imagine a data frame that holds your queries as a spreadsheet, with a column of data representing each query result.

Now, imagine performing all sorts of transformations on each column, with new columns containing the results of each transformation. Imagine performing various cleaning and filtering operations on your data. Imagine extracting new data from the existing columns or reducing the data in a column to a single aggregation.

Now that you have an idea of the power of transformations, have a look at some of the many transformation options available in the **Transform** menu. You'll see that some of them will not be valid for graph-type panels. Never fear – such transformations can be visualized in Grafana's **Table** visualization as well. In later chapters, we will leverage the power of **Transform** to shape query results into a more suitable form for our purposes.

Let's now move on to the **Panel** settings and see how we can use them to modify the look of our panel.

# Editing the panel settings

On the right-hand side of the graph display, you'll find the panel settings area, where you'll find a boatload of features to tailor the look of your panel, including changing the visualization entirely.

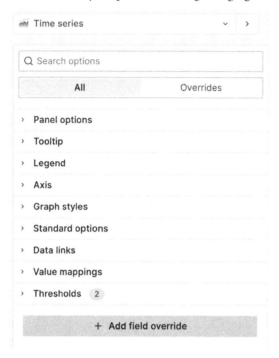

Figure 3.6 – Panel settings

The panel's myriad of options is available from one easily accessed column, with each one featuring a disclosure control so that you only need to see the options relevant to the task at hand.

## Selecting panel visualizations

The data frame architecture of Grafana allows for many graphs to be made from the same query datasets. The selection of a visualization serves as a quick mechanism to switch out the current panel visualization for a different one. Clicking on the **Visualization** tab reveals a list of possible visualizations installed in Grafana. Use the **Search** box to help filter down by name the number of panels in the listing.

There are so many Grafana visualizations now that it is well beyond the scope of this book to cover more than a small sample. In later chapters, we'll introduce other panel visualizations, but our primary focus will center on the **Time series** visualization.

Clicking on the **Suggestions** tab will show you some of the visualizations suitable for your data source query. If you have set up some reusable library panels, they can also be accessed from the **Library panels** tab.

Changing the panel will also alter the various options available, so you can try out various visualizations and adjust their unique options. Those settings are cached, so you can always switch from one visualization to another without losing settings. Experiment!

## The Panel options section

Starting from the top of the panel settings, the **Panel options** section is used for general panel settings, such as the title or description. As shown in the following screenshot, the **Panel options** section contains five settings in three groups:

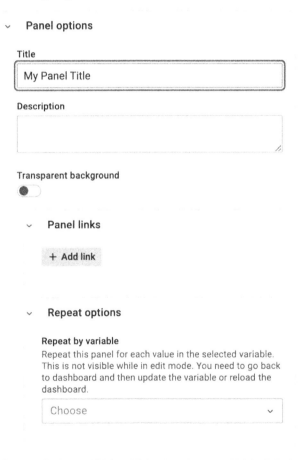

Figure 3.7 – Panel options

The first group gathers a few global settings for the panel:

- **Title**: This sets the panel's title on the dashboard. Setting the panel's title is obviously a good practice if you want to make it clear to yourself and others what the panel represents. Titles support variable substitution, and in *Chapter 10, Working with Advanced Dashboard Features and Elasticsearch,* we will look at how to use variables to automatically set parts of the title.

- **Description**: This sets the content of the panel's information popup. This information is displayed by hovering over the information icon (**i**) in the top-left corner of the panel. The **Description** setting also supports markdown formatting for attractive text styling, without the need for HTML editing.

- **Transparent background**: This increases the panel's transparency.

The next group deals with panel links, which are used to set up links from this panel to other dashboards, panels, or even data annotations. For instance, if you would like to add links from the panel to other resources, such as other panels, dashboards, or even other websites, you can use the **Panel links** section. Let's see how!

Clicking + **Add link** brings up a dialog box with three settings:

- **Title**: Contains the link text

- **URL**: Link to another resource

- **Open in new tab**

The link will appear at the bottom of the information (the **i** icon) popup if the panel's **Description** contains text; otherwise, the corner will display a link icon, and the link will appear when it's hovered over. This feature will be discussed in more detail in *Chapter 10, Working with Advanced Dashboard Features and Elasticsearch.*

The final group, **Repeat options**, is used in combination with template variables to automatically generate additional panels. Select a template variable from the dropdown to select the parameter to create the additional repeating panels. We will look at template variables and how to use them to dynamically create panels in *Chapter 10, Working with Advanced Dashboard Features and Elasticsearch.*

Let's try out a few of these panel settings to get a feel for how they alter our panel's display characteristics.

### Setting the panel title and description

Let's return to our panel and fill in these fields to give our panel a title and description. It's a good practice to set the title of your panels, as well as to provide a description, since it provides users with some context and documentation for the panel:

1. Fill the **Title** text field with `My Awesome Panel` or some other text of your choice.

2. In the **Description** textbox, add the following text (or something similar with some markdown tags):

```
### My Awesome Panel
This is where I'd like to make a description of my *awesome*
panel.
```

3.  Hover over the tiny **i** symbol in the top-left corner of the panel display to see your **Description** text in all its markdown-rendered HTML glory:

Figure 3.8 – The panel title

The **Panel options** section is one of the most important and most used sections; hence, it's placed near the top of the panel settings. Setting the panel's title and description provides key information for your users and other dashboard developers.

Let's move on to the following section, where we will configure the data point tooltips.

## The Tooltip section

The **Tooltip** section is designed to serve as a miniature legend that appears near any point that you hover over:

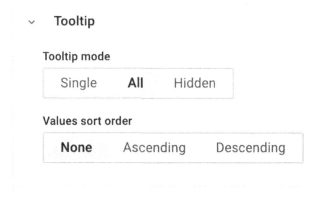

Figure 3.9 – The Tooltip settings

As you can see from the preceding screenshot, it has two settings:

- **Tooltip mode**: This sets how much content to display in the tooltip. The three modes available here are as follows:

  - **Single**: This only draws the value for the hover point

  - **All**: This draws the values of all dataset series on a single tooltip

  - **Hidden**: This hides the tooltip entirely

- **Values sort order**: This sets the order for the dataset. If you choose **All** in **Tooltip mode**, **Values sort order** will sort each series' point values (at the sample point) in **Ascending** or **Decreasing** order; if **None** is selected, it will order them by how each data series is specified in the **Query** tab.

## The Legend section

You've probably already seen the legend in action when you first set up the graph panel. The **Legend** options are mostly designed to control the placement of the legend, or its contents. Here's an image of the **Legend** section:

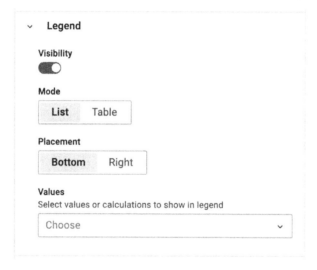

Figure 3.10 – The Legend settings

It contains four settings. Let's examine them:

- **Visibility**: This turns the legend on or off.

- **Mode**: This displays the legend as a list or a table. By default, the legend displays as a list. Switching the mode to **Table** arranges the entries and values in a more structured table format. In this mode, it also has a nifty spreadsheet-like column sort feature.

- **Placement**: This sets where the legend is displayed on the panel. **Right** places the legend off to the right, rather than at the bottom of the graph. If you enable the right-hand side placement, you can also guarantee a minimum width by setting the **Width** value.

- **Values**: This sets additional values to display along with the dataset label. Along with a label to describe each dataset, the legend can display a combination of nearly 25 different types of aggregations, including even the dataset values themselves. Simply select one or more from the **Values** dropdown. Typing in the **Values** box will filter the possible options. Clicking on the **x** symbol deletes a value.

## The Axis section

Moving on to the **Axis** section, note the options below the **Time zone** setting, which are mostly used to configure the *y*-axis display:

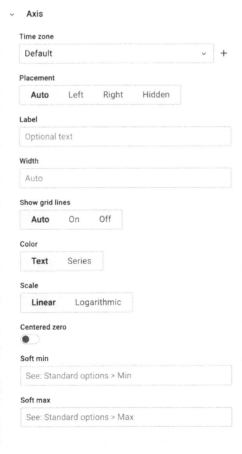

Figure 3.11 – The Axis settings

Here's a rundown of the **Axis** settings:

- **Time zone**: This sets the current time zone for the time axis
- **Placement:** This hides or places the *y* axis
- **Label**: This sets the label for the *y* axis
- **Width**: This sets the minimum width of the *y*-axis values
- **Show grid lines**: This turns on or off *y*-axis grid lines
- **Color**: This sets the color of the *y*-axis values and label
- **Scale**: This sets the scale for the *y* axis to either log or linear
- **Centered zero**: This centers the *y* axis on the zero value
- **Soft min/Soft max**: This constrains the limits of the *y* axis if there are no values

While most of these settings are relatively straightforward, let's look a little closer at a couple that might need explanation.

### Time zone

In the time series panel visualization, the *x* axis represents a series of time values, as set by the time picker at the top of the panel. The **Time Zone** setting adjusts the time values to correspond to another time zone.

For example, suppose you are looking at a series of metrics on a server in your local time zone, but you want to correlate them to some error logs that are timestamped in UTC. Setting the time zone to **Coordinated Universal Time** will set the displayed times on the *x* axis to UTC by offsetting them to the appropriate hours; technically, **Default** is UTC time adjusted to the local time zone. Bear in mind that the underlying data is not altered, just the times displayed on the *x* axis.

### Soft min/Soft max

While, in most cases, Grafana's defaults are quite suitable to display quality graphs, occasionally you have the need to offer Grafana some *hints* to help it along. In the case of **Soft min** and **Soft max**, the goal is to make sure your graph mostly shows data and not an empty space. Setting **Soft min** and/or the **Soft max** forces a setting for the top of the graph (**Soft max**) and bottom (**Soft min**), such that it won't scale the *y* axis any higher or lower respectively, unless there is data beyond the range of the **Soft min** and **Soft max** settings. Grafana will constrain the *y* axis up or down unless there are actual data values beyond those settings, hence the term *soft*.

# The Graph styles section

The **Graph styles** section is where you can make the most substantial changes to the appearance of the graph:

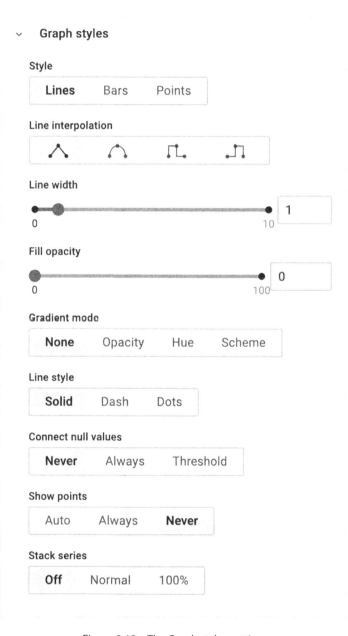

Figure 3.12 – The Graph styles settings

You have three choices of a graphic object to represent your data:

- **Lines**
- **Bars**
- **Points**

Here, you can decide which combination of bars, points, or lines to activate when drawing the graph. It is here that you should take care when choosing the drawing objects that best represent your data. For instance, if your data represents a set of sampled quantities, you may not want to use lines that imply the data is continuous. Likewise, if the data doesn't represent a measurable quantity, a bar may not be appropriate.

Once you have determined what object you want to represent your data, and depending on which objects you have enabled, additional options will appear. Let's look at these choices in further detail.

### Lines options

When you select the **Lines** style, the interface will present an additional set of options to give you control over how the lines should be drawn:

- **Line interpolation**: This connects data points with straight, curved, or 90-degree segments
- **Line width**: This sets the line thickness
- **Fill opacity**: This sets the transparency for the fill area below the lines
- **Gradient mode**: This sets a gradient for the fill area
- **Line style**: This sets the style of the line to solid, dashed, or dotted
- **Connect null values**: This sets whether missing values be connected
- **Show points**: This sets whether data points should also be drawn
- **Point size**: This sets the size of points when **Show points** are enabled
- **Stack series**: This sets how to stack multiple dataset lines

There are a couple of settings that bear further explanation.

### Fill opacity and Gradient mode

If you want to fill the area below the lines, you may also want to set how the area varies in color and opacity. Setting **Fill opacity** makes the fill area transparent (0 opacity setting) to completely opaque (100 opacity setting).

Once you have set a positive opacity, you can then leave the fill at one color or a smoothly varying color, called a gradient. **Gradient mode** gives you control over how the color changes from the top of your dataset lines down to the following dataset's lines:

- **Opacity**: This varies the opacity, from the set fill opacity to **0** opacity
- **Hue**: This varies the color from the line color to more saturated color
- **Scheme**: This uses the color scheme set in the **Standard options** section

### Connect null values

How to set **Connect Null values** really depends on the specific nature of your data and how you want to display empty data points, referred to as *nulls*. Setting it to **Never** leaves gaps in your lines where the nulls exist. **Always** forces Grafana to interpolate between known values, essentially *ignoring* the nulls.

The **Threshold** setting will force the **Always** setting if the timespan between valid data points is below the threshold, and the **Never** setting is above it. **Threshold** is useful when you believe that below a certain sampling interval (the **Threshold** setting), the missing sample values would be close enough to the surrounding values to allow Grafana to simply interpolate the missing values.

### Stack series

Stacking displays multiple series, one on top of the other. Be mindful when stacking series such that all series are as follows:

- They should share the same measurement units
- They should comprise portions of a greater whole

If you deviate from one of those rules, you may increase the visibility of multiple series by stacking them onto the same graph, but you may also create a misleading association between the series, or even make it more difficult for someone looking at your graphs to discern the correct values.

If you can stack your series, you can also make a part-to-whole relationship even more explicit by setting **Stack series** to **100%**; otherwise, use **Normal**.

### Bars style

The **Bars** style setting has the same settings as the **Lines** style, with the only difference being a **Bar alignment** option rather than a **Line** interpolation setting. Bar alignment just sets where the bar should be drawn in relation to the data point – to the left, centered, or to the right. Typically, you want the setting to correspond to when the data point was sampled during the time interval represented by the bar.

### Points style

The **Points** style only has the **Stack styles** setting in common with the other styles. Its only other setting is **Point size**.

## The Standard options section

While we've been examining the various sections in the **Time Series** panel visualization, we can pause here for a short digression to discuss the **Standard options**. When Grafana Labs refined the implementation of the panel a few years ago, they grouped together a collection of settings common to all panels. We've seen a couple of these in the **Panel options** section – **Title** and **Description**. The **Standard options** section is where we'll find the rest of them:

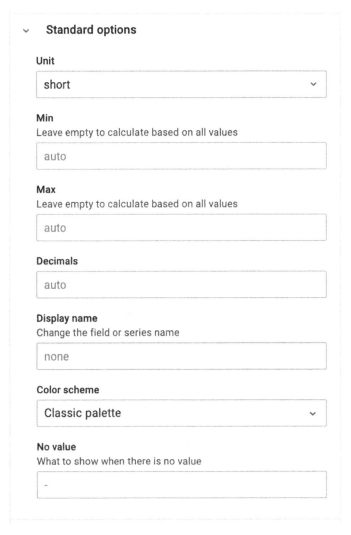

Figure 3.13 – The Standard options settings

The following settings will apply to any panel, regardless of the visualization:

- **Unit**: This sets the unit of measurement
- **Min**: This sets the minimum value for percentage calculation
- **Max**: This sets the maximum value for percentage calculation
- **Decimals**: This sets the maximum number of decimal places to display
- **Display name**: This sets the name of the dataset(s)
- **Color scheme**: This sets a palette of colors for the dataset(s)
- **No value**: This defines the value for `null` data points

While most of these settings are relatively straightforward, let's take a closer look at a few that tend to get more frequent use.

## Unit

Rarely do you have data that doesn't correspond to some unit of measurement. **Unit** is the field where you can set the measurement unit for the values in a dataset. While Grafana provides literally dozens of measurements, there may occasionally be a unit that just isn't on the list. Simply add the name of the unit to the box. You've now defined a custom unit for the dataset.

Besides a generic unit, you can specify custom units for counting, currency, SI units, and time. You can also set units with a custom prefix or a custom suffix. To set these values, just type in the name, followed by : and the unit:

- `count:<unit>`
- `currency:<unit>`
- `prefix:<unit>`
- `si:<base><unitchar>`
- `suffix:<unit>`
- `time:<timeformat>`

For example, if you wanted to set your own currency unit for the Canadian dollar to be `"$CAD"`, you would input the following:

```
currency:$CAD
```

If you wanted to use the SI velocity unit for millimeters/year, you would input the following:

```
si:mm/yr
```

Finally, if you wanted dates to look like December 25, 2025, you would input the following:

```
time:MMM DD, YYYY
```

You can find out all the various options Grafana uses for data formatting at `https://momentjs.com/docs/#/displaying`.

### Display name

**Display name** is where you can set the name of the dataset(s) in your panel. Simply type in the name of the dataset in the box, and the legend will reflect the value you set. Grafana will also let you use variables here so that you can tailor the name to a specific context or if you have multiple datasets in the panel.

### Color scheme

To set the colors for each dataset (or in any other situation where you need a palette of colors), use the **Color scheme** settings. If you want to use the original Grafana color mapping, which was a palette of several specific colors, use **Classic palette**. **Single color**, of course, allows you to specify a color. **From thresholds** uses the colors specified in the **Thresholds** section. The remaining color palettes are a variety of continuous color ramps, ranging from single colors that vary in brightness to the familiar triplets of color used in many visualizations.

### No value

What should you display when there is a missing value in your dataset? **No value** sets a default value, whether it is **0** or some other value. The default is the - character.

## The Data links section

Data links connect graph data points to external resources. They can be as simple as a single static URL or as complex as a system that leverages template variables, linking each data point in the graph with, for example, an external logging monitor. Metadata about each selected data point is available for you to construct a specific URL, corresponding to a log listing at the same point in time. To create a link from a point in this data series in another panel, use the **Data links** section.

Clicking + **Add link** launches a dialog box with three settings:

- **Title**: This sets descriptive link text
- **URL**: This links to an external URL
- **Open in new tab**: This opens a link in a new browser tab

Clicking on a graph data point will display up a popup, which will display the data links below **Add annotation**. We will explore techniques to link and annotate data and panels in *Chapter 10, Working with Advanced Dashboard Features and Elasticsearch*.

## The Value mappings section

Put simply, value mappings convert the quantitative into the qualitative. Setting a value mapping associates a text value and/or color with a specific data value. This is useful to tag specific values with text such as **Low** or **High**, or convert ranges into **High**, **Med**, and **Low**.

There are four kinds of value mappings:

- **Value**: This sets a mapping to a specific value
- **Range**: This sets a mapping to a range of values
- **Regex**: This sets a mapping to a regular expression match
- **Special**: This sets a mapping for NaN, null, true, false, or empty values

Let us see how to set a value mapping.

### Setting a value mapping

Let's set a value mapping for a range:

1. Click on + **Add threshold**. You will get a value mapping by default.
2. Click on + **Add a new mapping** and select **Range** from the pulldown.
3. Set **From** to a value that represents something in the middle of the dataset.
4. Set the **To** value to something above the **From** value.
5. Set **Display text** to medium.
6. Click **Update**.

In the case of the **Time series** visualization, you'll see every entry on the $y$ axis set to the display text. However, in other visualizations (such as the gauge), the text will be displayed rather than the numeric value.

## The Thresholds section

While Grafana has an extensive alerting system, which we will look at shortly, perhaps you only want to see when your data crosses specific boundaries but not necessarily get alerts. Perhaps you are preparing to establish alerts but first need to visualize what the typical boundary thresholds are. Thresholds graphically depict these boundaries as horizontal indicators set at specific numerical values.

Specifying a threshold is easy – simply click the + **Add threshold** button. Type in the value for the threshold, and then set the color for the threshold region. Depending upon the value you type, Grafana will auto-sort the thresholds by value. Clicking the trashcan icon deletes the threshold.

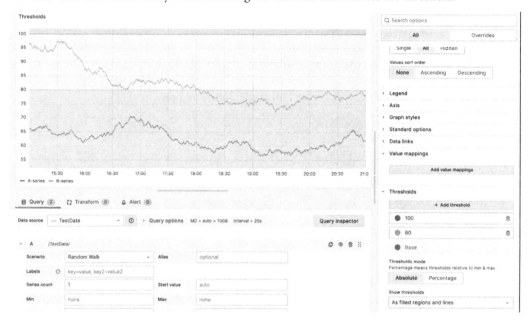

Figure 3.14 – Thresholds

Once you've specified a threshold, you can also determine how it is depicted on the graph, if at all. You have the choice to turn off the threshold display, display the thresholds as lines or filled regions, or both, as illustrated in the preceding example.

### Field overrides

Field overrides are a powerful tool for fine-grained control over some of the many settings Grafana typically provides by default, such as color, line, or point size, or stacking order, and it is based on matching the name of the data series to a collection of settings overrides. We will cover Field overrides in *Chapter 5, Extracting and Visualizing Data with InfluxDB and Grafana*.

## Monitoring with the Alert tab

In this section, we will take a peek at the **Alert** tab. We will take a much more in-depth look at alerting in *Chapter 12, Monitoring Data Streams with Grafana Alerts*, so at this point, I just want to show how alert creation, which we saw briefly in the last chapter, is tied to the panel visualization. Clicking on **Create an alert rule from this panel** will bring up an interface that can also be displayed by selecting **Alerting** | **Alert rules** | **Create alert rule** from the side menu.

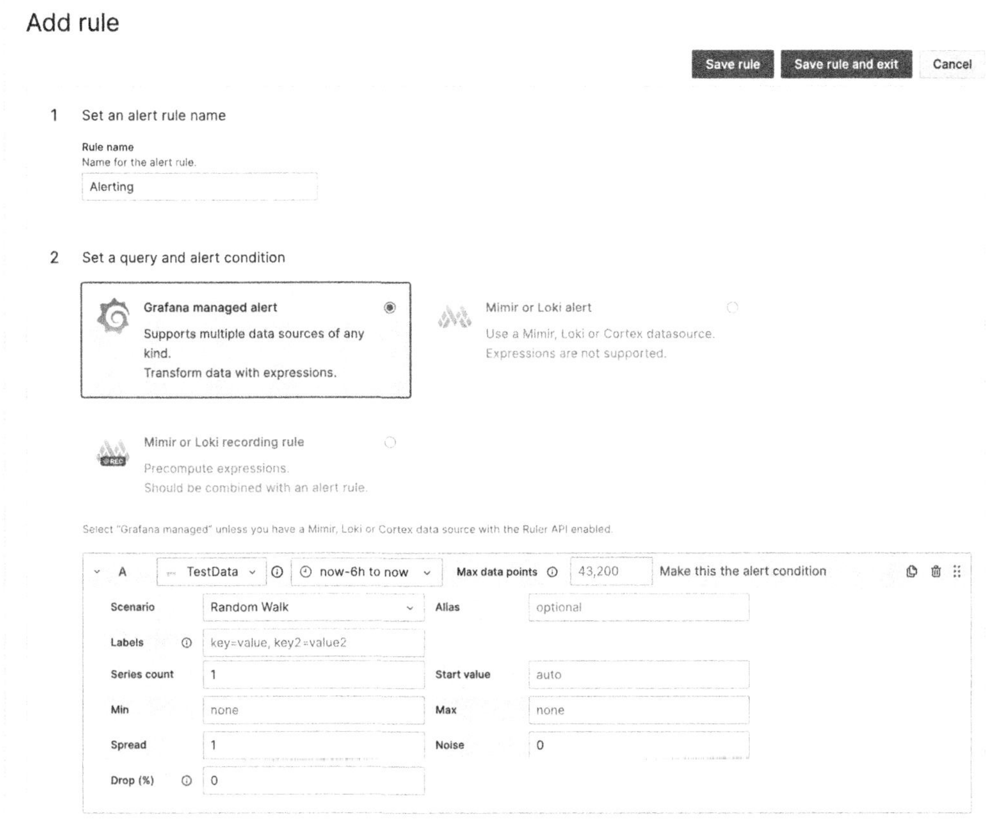

## Add rule

Save rule        Save rule and exit        Cancel

1    Set an alert rule name

**Rule name**
Name for the alert rule.

Alerting

2    Set a query and alert condition

Grafana managed alert
Supports multiple data sources of any kind.
Transform data with expressions.

Mimir or Loki alert
Use a Mimir, Loki or Cortex datasource.
Expressions are not supported.

Mimir or Loki recording rule
Precompute expressions.
Should be combined with an alert rule.

Select "Grafana managed" unless you have a Mimir, Loki or Cortex data source with the Ruler API enabled.

| ∨ A | — TestData ∨ | ⓘ | now-6h to now ∨ | Max data points ⓘ | 43,200 | Make this the alert condition | |
|---|---|---|---|---|---|---|---|
| **Scenario** | Random Walk ∨ | | **Alias** | optional | | | |
| **Labels** ⓘ | key=value, key2=value2 | | | | | | |
| **Series count** | 1 | | **Start value** | auto | | | |
| **Min** | none | | **Max** | none | | | |
| **Spread** | 1 | | **Noise** | 0 | | | |
| **Drop (%)** ⓘ | 0 | | | | | | |

Figure 3.15 – Alert rule creation

The interface will automatically select queries from the panel. It is from those queries that you select the one that will serve as the alert monitor. While we don't have the necessary knowledge to do so yet, ultimately you be looking to create a query or expression that will answer the question, "*During the evaluation time period, is there a condition that requires the triggering of an alert?*"

From that point, all that remains is the process of adding the components that identify an alert rule, including the rule name, folder, and group. Alert rules also need labels so that they can be associated with contact points for notifications. It's a bit beyond the scope of this chapter to go into detail, but we will fully walk through the process in *Chapter 12, Monitoring Data Streams with Grafana Alerts*.

# Further exploration

I invite you to play around with the various settings, especially those in the **Visualization** panel. Here are some simple exercises for you to try out:

1.  Create multiple data series in the **Query** tab. Try out the different scenarios to see how they create different kinds of data. Rearrange the order to see what effect it has on the graph.

2.  Play with different combinations of drawing objects in the **Display** section. Change the fill or size of points, lines, and bars.

3.  Turn on the legend and test out its many options. Try clicking on various elements in the legend itself – you might find some surprises!

It's always a good idea to try things out, break them, and then figure out how to fix them. That's how we learn – not just by following instructions in a book (although you wouldn't be here if wasn't also a good way to learn!)

# Summary

This chapter completes *Part 1, Getting Started with Grafana*. In this part, we installed the Grafana server, checked out the Grafana application interface, set up some simple dashboards, and graphed test data sources. In the next part, *Part 2, Real-World Grafana*, we'll start looking more deeply at these same features and learn how to use them in more realistic scenarios.

We'll start *Chapter 4, Connecting Grafana to a Prometheus Data Source*, by building a simple data pipeline with a Prometheus data source, which we'll query in Grafana Explore. The patterns established in the chapter will be the foundation for building even more complex pipelines in later chapters.

# Part 2 – Real-World Grafana

The goal of this section is to present a more detailed look at working with Grafana by leveraging realistic example data. In it, you will leverage Python and Docker Compose to ingest data into a variety of time series databases. You will use Grafana transformations to restructure query results. You will also examine several panel visualizations and discuss their potential use cases. Further, you will not only design and build dashboards using different panel visualizations but you will also gather real-time data, metrics, and logs for analysis and visualization, and explore observability features such as alerting.

This part comprises the following chapters.

4

# Connecting Grafana to a Prometheus Data Source

In previous chapters, we took a whirlwind tour of the Grafana UI. We looked at how graph panel visualizations query for datasets via data sources and how panels can be arranged to form dashboard pages.

In this chapter, we will begin to apply our newly gained skills to more practical considerations. We will use real data where possible, to try to analyze data with a focus on solving real-world scenarios and create the kind of comprehensive dashboards you would expect to see in a production environment.

Our first step in this journey begins (as always) with data. Here, we will configure a live database serving actual web service data (generated first by Prometheus, then by Grafana itself!). We'll pull that data into Grafana as a data source, then we'll use the **Explore** tool to get a feel for what kinds of metrics are available. We'll also look at visualizing the data through a variety of queries. Finally, we'll learn how data is analyzed in the context of data aggregation.

The following topics will be covered in this chapter:

- Installing the Prometheus server
- Exploring Prometheus
- Querying the Prometheus data source
- Detecting trends with aggregations
- Uncovering data source limitations

## Technical requirements

Tutorial code, dashboards, and other helpful files for this chapter can be found in this book's GitHub repo at `https://github.com/PacktPublishing/Learn-Grafana-10/tree/main/Chapter04`.

# Installing the Prometheus server

Our first task is to get a Prometheus server up and running so that we can start serving real data. **Prometheus** is a powerful open source time-series database and monitoring system originally developed by SoundCloud. It followed Kubernetes to become the second **Cloud Native Computing Foundation** graduating incubation project. Grafana, having partnered with the maintainers of Prometheus, includes the Prometheus data source as a first-class data source plugin. In this section, we will learn how to install Prometheus in a Docker container and then move on to configuring it.

## Installing Prometheus from Docker

We're going to start up Prometheus from Docker Compose and point it to a local configuration file. First, let's create the following configuration file and save it to our local ch4/prometheus directory as prometheus.yml:

```
global:
    scrape_interval:        15s # By default, scrape targets every 15
seconds.

    # Attach these labels to any time series or alerts when
communicating with
    # external systems (federation, remote storage, Alertmanager).
    external_labels:
        monitor: 'codelab-monitor'

# A scrape configuration containing exactly one endpoint to scrape:
# Here it's Prometheus itself.
scrape_configs:
    # The job name is added as a label `job=<job_name>` to any
timeseries scraped from this config.
    - job_name: 'prometheus'

    # Override the global default and scrape targets from this job
every 5 seconds.
    scrape_interval: 5s

    static_configs:
        - targets: ['localhost:9090']
```

> **Note**
>
> If you aren't already familiar with YAML, maintaining proper indentation is *very important*. I would recommend that you use an **interactive development environment** (**IDE**) such as Visual Studio Code that can give you visual cues to help you maintain proper YAML. If you're ever in doubt, these files are available in the book's GitHub repo for your reference.

It is beyond the scope of this book to give fully detailed information on the Prometheus configuration file format; you can go to `https://prometheus.io/docs/prometheus/latest/configuration/configuration` to find out more. This is a relatively simple configuration file designed to do a couple of things:

1.  Establish a default scrape interval. This determines how often Prometheus will *scrape* or *pull* data from the metric's endpoint—in this case, every 15 seconds.

2.  Set up the configuration for a job called `prometheus` that will scrape itself every five seconds. The target server is located at `http://localhost:9090`.

3.  Next, create a `docker-compose.yml` file (this file can also be downloaded from this book's GitHub repo):

```
services:
    grafana:
        image: grafana/grafana:latest
    ports:
        - "3000:3000"
    prometheus:
        image: prom/prometheus:latest
    ports:
        - "9090:9090"
    volumes:
        -$PWD/prometheus:/etc/prometheus
```

The preceding Docker Compose file does the following:

I.    Starts up a Grafana container and exposes its default port at `3000`.

II.   Starts up a Prometheus container and exposes its default port at `9090`.

III.  Maps the `$PWD/prometheus` local directory to `/etc/prometheus` in the `prometheus` container. This is so that we can manage the Prometheus configuration file from outside the container. `$PWD` is a shell variable describing the working directory.

Start up both containers with the following command:

```
% docker-compose up -d -pull-missing
```

The `docker-compose` command will pull down any necessary images and start up both containers in their own network so that the Grafana and Prometheus containers can contact each other. If you are successful, you should see something similar to the following output lines:

```
Starting ch4_prometheus_1 ... done
Starting ch4_grafana_1 ... done
```

To confirm Prometheus is running correctly, open a web browser page and enter `http://localhost:9090/targets`. You will see a screen similar to the following:

Figure 4.1 – Prometheus server interface

Now that we have the Grafana and Prometheus servers running, let's move on to creating a Prometheus data source so we can query it within Grafana.

## Configuring the Prometheus data source

From our `docker-compose.yml` file, we know that the Prometheus server host inside the Docker Compose network is called `prometheus` and the port is `9090` and we know from our `prometheus.yml` file that we set the scrape interval to five seconds. So, let's configure a new Prometheus data source:

1.  From the main menu, go to **Connections** | **Add new connection**.

2.  Type `prometheus` into the search bar and click on the Prometheus icon to add a new Prometheus connection.

3.  Set the following information, leaving the others at their defaults:

    *   **Name**: `Prometheus`

    *   **HTTP** | **Prometheus server URL**: `http://prometheus:9090`

    *   **Additional settings** | **Interval behaviour** | **Scrape interval**: `5s`

4.  At the bottom, click on **Save & Test**.

If everything worked correctly, you should now have a new data source, as shown in the following screenshot:

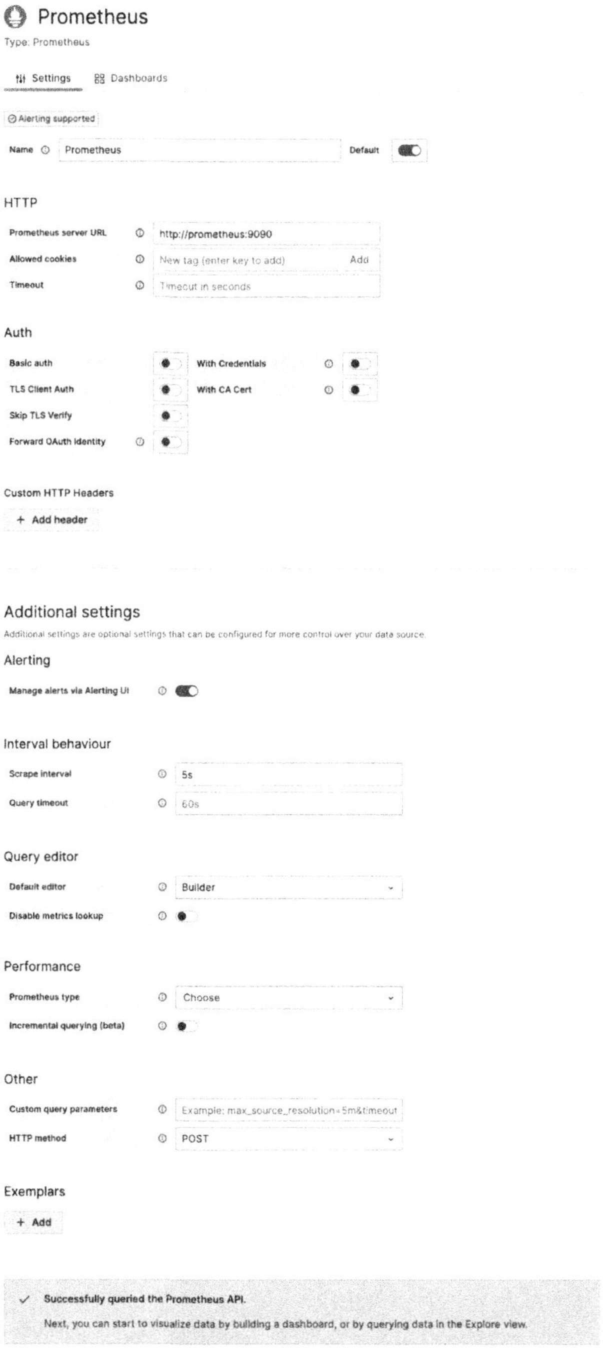

Figure 4.2 – Prometheus data source

Now that we have a working data source, let's look at the data we're capturing in Prometheus.

# Exploring Prometheus

Once we have the Prometheus data source properly configured, you might be wondering what kind of data we're likely to see. Turns out, since we configured Prometheus to scrape itself, we'll get a bunch of juicy internal server metrics delivered to the scraped endpoint and stored in the Prometheus database. So, let's dive in and get an idea of what's there.

## Using Explore for investigation

Clicking **Explore** in the Prometheus data source configuration, or selecting **Explore** from the main side menu, activates the **Explore** tool. Basically, **Explore** includes both graph and table visualizations, both looking at the same data source query. Make sure your Prometheus data source is selected from the data source dropdown, and select a metric data series from the **Metric** box menu. You'll see dozens of available metrics, but for now, select the **Up** metric.

> Tip
> You can type up in the **Metric** box to reduce the number of possible metrics to choose from.

This is probably the simplest metric available: it shows 1 if the server is up and 0 otherwise. Set the time range to **Last 30 minutes** so we can see relatively recent data, and click the **Run query** button. You'll see, as in the following screenshot, that the up metric indicates our Prometheus server is up and running:

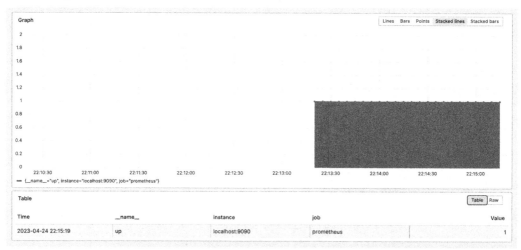

Figure 4.3 – Up metric in Explore

The graph shows a single series with a value of 1, and after clicking on the **Table** option at the bottom, it shows 1 in the **Value** column on the far right. You should also take note of the _name_ series. In this case, it refers to the up metric, tagged with localhost:9090 for the instance value and prometheus for the job value. Going back to our prometheus.yml configuration file, we can see where the job label comes from:

```
# The job name is added as a label `job=<job_name>` to any
timeseries scraped from this config.
  - job_name: 'prometheus'
```

But where does the metric itself come from, and how does Grafana know about all those metrics in the **Metrics** drop-down menu?

Every five seconds, Prometheus itself sends an HTTP request to a specific metrics endpoint at http://localhost:9090/metrics. Go ahead and try it; you can open the URL in a browser tab. You should see a page filled with metrics data. Here are the first few lines:

```
# HELP go_gc_duration_seconds A summary of the GC invocation
durations.
# TYPE go_gc_duration_seconds summary
go_gc_duration_seconds{quantile="0"} 7.057e-06
go_gc_duration_seconds{quantile="0.25"} 1.2362e-05
go_gc_duration_seconds{quantile="0.5"} 2.7312e-05
go_gc_duration_seconds{quantile="0.75"} 0.000259168
go_gc_duration_seconds{quantile="1"} 0.001061091
go_gc_duration_seconds_sum 0.006119489
go_gc_duration_seconds_count 36
# HELP go_goroutines Number of goroutines that currently exist.
# TYPE go_goroutines gauge
go_goroutines 39
# HELP go_info Information about the Go environment.
# TYPE go_info gauge
go_info{version="go1.13.1"} 1
.
```

As you can see, a lot of the metrics are simply a *metric name* and a *value* and are sometimes a duplicated metric name followed by a key-value pairing in braces, called a **label**. In other applications, the label might also be called a **tag**, but it performs the same function, which is to attach a piece of metadata to the metric to distinguish between similar metrics or add information about the metric itself.

Every few seconds, this page of data is queried, parsed, timestamped, and stored in the Prometheus database. When you launch the **Explore** tool in Grafana, the Prometheus data source plugin makes a service discovery query to find out what metrics are available, and based on the response, it builds a convenient metrics menu for you.

Let's now look at how a different metric, `go_gc_duration_seconds`, is depicted in **Explore**. Type `go` in the **Metric** box (`go`, in this case, refers to the initial portion of the metric name, called the metric's **namespace**). From the list, select `go_gc_duration_seconds` and then click **Run Query** to see the metric graph:

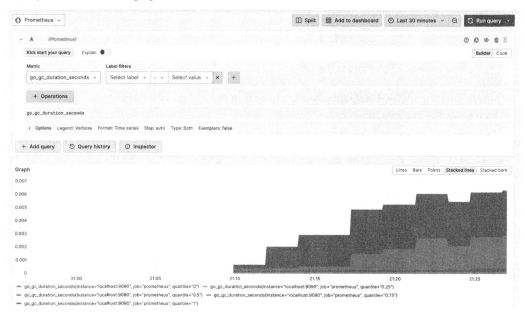

Figure 4.4 – go_gc_duration_seconds metric

Now, we can see from the legend that this particular metric includes a number of series, each one including a `quantile` value along with `instance` and `job` labels. Further down in the table, we can see the `quantile` value is treated as a field, much like in a typical database or spreadsheet. This is all well and good, but are we limited to Prometheus metrics? Not at all!

## Configuring Grafana metrics

Now that we have a handle on some of the rich metrics available in Prometheus, can we get similar metrics in Grafana? Indeed, we can, but in order to do so with the Docker versions of both Prometheus and Grafana, Prometheus will need to be able to connect to Grafana over the same network. That's why we brought them up as a dual-container app in Docker Compose. All containers in a Docker Compose app share a common network, complete with **Domain Name Service** (**DNS**) entries for each service, which by default is just the name of the service itself.

Let's go ahead and update our Prometheus configuration with a new job that will scrape the Grafana server. Add these additional lines to `scrape_configs` in the `prometheus.yml` file (also available as `prometheus-grafana.yml` from this book's GitHub repository):

```
scrape_configs:
    # The job name is added as a label `job=<job_name>` to any
timeseries scraped from this config.
    - job_name: 'prometheus'
    # Override the global default and scrape targets from this job
every 5 seconds.
    scrape_interval: 5s
    static_configs:
        - targets: ['localhost:9090']
- job_name: 'grafana'
    # Override the global default and scrape targets from this job
every 5 seconds.
    scrape_interval: 5s
    static_configs:
        - targets: ['grafana:3000']
```

Forcing a restart of the Prometheus container process should cause it to re-read the configuration file. Run the following command:

```
% docker-compose restart prometheus
```

Go back to the **Prometheus** page and check the targets at `http://localhost:9090/targets` to confirm that Grafana is now included as a target:

Figure 4.5 – Grafana and Prometheus servers

Let's go back to **Explore** and see what Grafana goodies Prometheus scraped for us.

## Querying the Prometheus data source

Now that we have a whole ton of Prometheus and Grafana logging metrics, let's play around with some more queries. I won't be able to give you a full rundown of every aspect of PromQL—the Prometheus query language—but I can give you enough of a taste to be able to examine many of the server metrics that can be accessed via the Prometheus data source.

To get a better understanding of how queries work in time-series databases such as Prometheus, let's first start with a more traditional database, such as MySQL. Typically, the structure of a query looks something like this:

```
SELECT some fields
    FROM some table
    WHERE fields match some criteria
```

You get back from the query some rows, each one containing the contents of `some fields`. In the case of time-series databases, things work a little differently. The query has a form that is more like the following:

```
SELECT metric
    FROM some data store
    WHERE metric tags match some criteria
        AND within some time range
```

In the case of a time-series database, you get back some number of data series, each containing metric data from the time range in question and matching any specified criteria. In general, you can think of a series as a collection of points, usually containing at least three types of information:

- A timestamp
- A metric value
- A set of key-value pairs for characterizing the data

The details differ from one time-series database to another. Some represent the value as a particular type that has a specific meaning to the database to optimize storage, searching, or aggregation. Others may store richer metadata. In any case, these three pieces of information are commonly found in some form or another across many of the current time-series databases.

## Typing in a metrics query

Previously, we used up to determine whether Prometheus was running or not. Let's look at what it looks like when we run it now:

Figure 4.6 – up metrics for Grafana and Prometheus

We can see that now, there are two series, one of which appears to be for Grafana and the other for Prometheus. Let's go ahead and alter the query to only select the series for Grafana:

1.  Switch modes from **Builder** to **Code**. This will allow us to type in the raw query text.

> **Note**
>
> You can switch back and forth between **Builder** and **Code** and your query will remain the same, allowing you to use either technique to craft a query.

2.  Immediately following the word up, type the { character into the **Metrics browser** text field. You will see the completed brace and a pop-up menu for selecting a label key. The data source plugin is smart enough to understand the syntax of PromQL and is guiding you toward making a valid query:

Figure 4.7 – Explore code mode query completion

3.  Since grafana is the name of the job we want (as seen in the data series legend), select **job** from the menu.

4.  Immediately, you should see another menu for selecting one of two possible job values: grafana or prometheus. If you lose the menu, just delete the = and type it in again to get the popup.

5.  Pick **grafana** from the menu:

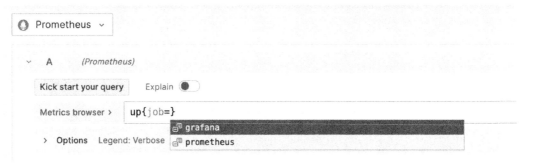

Figure 4.8 – Select grafana

If you have trouble with the command completions, just type in the query directly:

```
up{job="grafana"}
```

6.  Click **Run query**.

You now have just the single data series corresponding to the Grafana up metric:

Figure 4.9 – Grafana up metric

> **Tip**
> You can retrieve any of your past queries from **Query history**. Simply click on **Query history** and select a query from the **Query history** tab. Click on **Query history** again to close the tab.

There are dozens of metrics available in Prometheus; let's try to query for a few more of them.

## Querying for process metrics

Moving up the application stack, let's make a couple of queries to the Grafana process. First, let's query for the number of goroutines. While it isn't as descriptive as the Linux uptime command, it is readily available and can give a rough indication of server load.

Before I show you the query, try to guess what the metric should be. You might need to refresh your memory by examining the metrics web endpoint at http://localhost:3000/metrics. Also, remember that we only want to see the metrics for Grafana, not both Grafana and Prometheus:

1.    Click on the **Metrics browser**.

2.    In the step 1 box, type go, and from the list, select go_goroutines:

Figure 4.10 – Search for go metrics

3.  Under the step 2 box, you should now see two possibilities, each followed by the number of possible values. Click **job** to indicate we wish to choose one of two jobs:

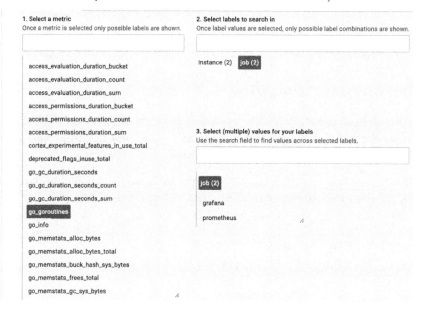

Figure 4.11 – Select job

4.  Under step 3, we should see the two possible jobs: **grafana** or **prometheus**. Select **grafana** to indicate we wish to query for the `grafana` label.

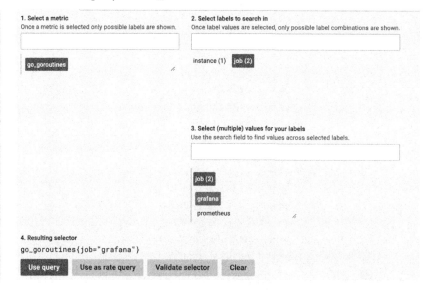

Figure 4.12 – Select grafana

5.  Click **Use query** to see the results:

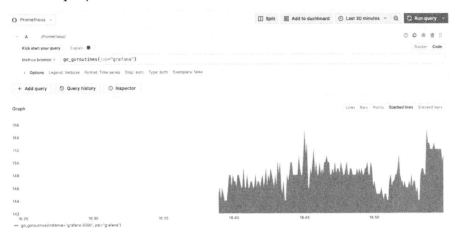

Figure 4.13 – Query results

From the graph, we can see the number of goroutines executing in Grafana at any given moment. We can see that the number of goroutines is often quite stable, punctuated by invocations of a single additional goroutine. This should give you a sense of how quickly we can query the Prometheus data source for a desired application metric, provided Prometheus is scraping the application.

## Querying for memory metrics

Let's also look at memory consumption, another indicator of how well the Grafana server process is performing. Running out of memory can seriously degrade performance, so you might need to build a panel with an alert for when the amount of free memory falls below a certain level. Again, try to determine what query would produce a data series for the memory consumed:

1.  Begin by typing `process` in the box next to **Metrics**.

    If you guessed `process_resident_memory_bytes`, congratulations!

2.  Use either technique we've discussed to set the filter to a Grafana job:

Figure 4.14 – Memory metrics query

Next, we're going to look at how to transform our data series in new ways by incorporating the concept of aggregation into our queries.

## Detecting trends with aggregations

As we continue up the stack, let's now examine some server performance metrics. How about an obvious web server metric? Enter `prometheus_http_requests_total` to get an idea of how many requests have been served so far:

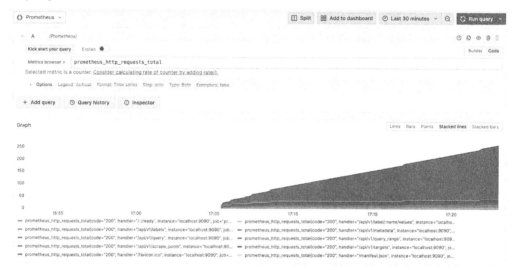

Figure 4.15 – Prometheus HTTP requests

Well, this is a bit of a mess. You can't see all 22 of the time series—they're all stacked on top of each other—and there's the ominous warning **Selected metric is a counter**. As we saw in the previous section, it's no problem to apply filters—say, to filter the 200 codes—but then we'd still have a stack of nearly 20 individual series.

## Applying aggregations to our query data

If only there were some way to combine all the individual data series into one. It turns out there is, and it's called an **aggregation**. We can tell Prometheus to apply an aggregation function (in this case, sum) after we specify what series we'd like to see.

While the actual query syntax differs from database application to database application, in the case of PromQL, you simply wrap parentheses around your existing query and add the word sum in front of it:

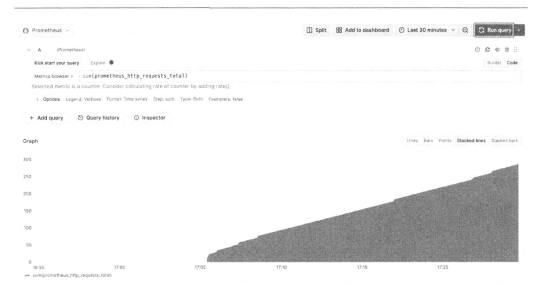

Figure 4.16 – HTTP requests sum aggregation

That's a rather clumsy way to describe it, however. In PromQL, sum is actually a function call that takes the metric query as an argument. The result of the query is passed to sum(), so on the Prometheus server, a new series is created by summing up the values of the data points in each series and is returned to the Grafana data source client. The power of PromQL as a query language is that you can chain these aggregations together and even combine them with the results of other queries.

But what about that **Selected metric is a counter** warning? First, let's clear up something that we glossed over earlier. Recall how we initially looked at the go_goroutines metric; you may have noticed a TYPE metadata string that preceded the metric on the endpoint page. You may have also noticed that the go_goroutines metric name was followed by the word gauge:

```
# HELP go_goroutines Number of goroutines that currently exist.
# TYPE go_goroutines gauge
    go_goroutines 33
```

However, checking the same metadata for prometheus_http_requests_total reveals the word counter:

```
# HELP prometheus_http_requests_total Counter of HTTP requests.
# TYPE prometheus_http_requests_total counter
    ...
```

While not every time-series database distinguishes between numerical metrics, Prometheus does, and it's important to appreciate the distinct difference between gauge and counter.

A gauge metric type is typically a point-in-time measurement that can fluctuate in either direction—for example, think of a thermometer or a car speedometer reading. Gauges in software are often registered with the internal metrics system as a dump of the contents of a variable at the point that the metrics page was requested.

On the other hand, a `counter` metric type is a cumulative measure that always increases, more like a rainfall gauge or a car odometer. Counters are registered in software as an increment to a running total value. Since the value is always incrementally increasing by a positive amount (monotonically), the data source plugin is warning us that unless we really care to know how much memory has been consumed to date, we might want to track the *rate* of increase instead.

Incidentally, Prometheus has two other metric types—`histogram` and `summary`.

So, why don't we check out the rate? Unfortunately, if you try to treat the rate as a function call that you can just drop the query into, you will run into issues because it requires an aggregation. We're going to discuss issues with aggregation in the next section. For now, we'll just select a single data series and run a rate:

1. For **Metric**, select `prometheus_http_requests_total` and **Run query**.

2. In the table, click on the **handler** column cell containing `/api/v1/query_range` and choose the + magnifying glass icon (which means include in filter).

3. In the table, click on the **code** column cell containing `200`.

4. Click on the + button to add an additional query.

5. Switch to **Code**.

6. Type the following into the second query:

```
irate(prometheus_http_requests_total{handler="/api/v1/query_
range", code="200"}[5m])
```

This is what your graph might look like:

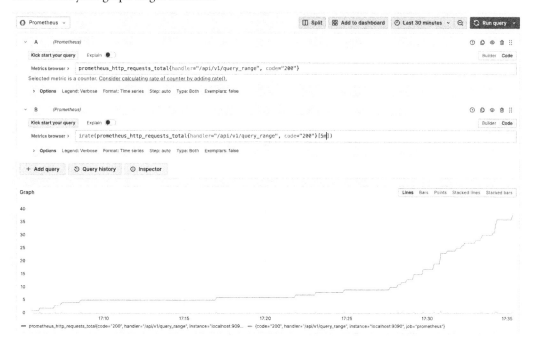

Figure 4.17 – HTTP requests rate

What we did was ask Prometheus to calculate the rate that `prometheus_http_requests_total` changed over a five-minute period. Since it changed very quickly, we used `irate` (instant rate) instead of `rate`, but they both work in similar ways. If you look very closely, you can see the rate increased momentarily as the request total increased.

This is just a taste of some of the aggregations and functions available in PromQL. Here's a list of some aggregations and functions derived from the Prometheus documentation:

- `sum`: Calculates the sum over dimensions
- `min`: Selects the minimum over dimensions
- `max`: Selects the maximum over dimensions
- `avg`: Calculates the average over dimensions
- `stddev`: Calculates the population standard deviation over dimensions
- `stdvar`: Calculates the population standard variance over dimensions

- `count`: Counts the number of elements in the vector

- `count_values`: Counts the number of elements with the same value

- `bottomk`: The smallest $k$ elements by sample value

- `topk`: The largest $k$ elements by sample value

- `quantile`: Calculates the $\varphi$ quantile $(0 \leq \varphi \leq 1)$ over dimensions

The list of functions is even longer, so be sure to consult the Prometheus documentation or the documentation for your specific data source.

# Understanding the data source limitations

After seeing how powerful even relatively simple PromQL queries can be, it is tempting to think you can query and graph virtually any metric in your data source. Unfortunately, there are limitations to certain kinds of calculations, either imposed by the nature of the data or by the data source application.

It is important to remember that when you create a graph, you are entering into a trust relationship between you and your audience (which might even be you). When you place a pixel on a graph that isn't explicitly represented by a corresponding data point, you are asking your audience to accept that what you are doing is, in essence, reconstructing a signal from the underlying data.

Therefore, you have an obligation to respect the integrity of the data and not abuse that trust by manipulating the data to say things that aren't true or lead the viewer to draw erroneous conclusions.

Throughout this book, we'll come back to this theme because I believe it is necessary to not only describe the wonderful possibilities that this application provides but also to make you aware of some of its limitations. In this section, I'll highlight the judicious use of aggregation in both the time domain and the value domain.

## Querying limits for series aggregations

The first thing to consider when querying for a new metric that we are considering for aggregation is whether the data can be aggregated at all. For example, examining the Grafana metrics endpoint page reveals an interesting metric:

```
# HELP go_gc_duration_seconds A summary of the GC invocation
durations.
# TYPE go_gc_duration_seconds summary
go_gc_duration_seconds{quantile="0"} 9.174e-06
go_gc_duration_seconds{quantile="0.25"} 1.3627e-05
go_gc_duration_seconds{quantile="0.5"} 2.2022e-05
go_gc_duration_seconds{quantile="0.75"} 9.0476e-05
go_gc_duration_seconds{quantile="1"} 0.000340337
```

```
go_gc_duration_seconds_sum 0.001069315
go_gc_duration_seconds_count 13
```

The `go_gc_duration_seconds` metric is a Prometheus metric type called a summary. A summary is a built-in pre-aggregated metric that can be graphed directly. It contains a histogram with five quantiles (0%, 25%, 50%, 75%, and 100%), the sum, and the count. Typically, you cannot calculate some other aggregation of the quantiles because they only describe the distribution of the data at any point in time, so any attempt to aggregate them over time yields meaningless results.

> **Note**
>
> If you wish to determine the aggregated value of a particular quantile over time, Prometheus recommends you first do the aggregation, followed by a quantile calculation.

When you are looking at raw (unaggregated) data, you again must be aware of the limitations of the data source. For example, in the case of Prometheus, it is safe to calculate a `rate` aggregation on a `counter` metric because, by definition, it is monotonically increasing. However, you can also get away with aggregations on a gauge, but only if the aggregation is monotonically (always) increasing. The `rate` calculation can be adjusted for value resets (set to `0`), but not negative (decreasing) values.

In general, you should consult the documentation for your data source if you find yourself attempting to compose multiple aggregations as there may be limits to what you can do.

Finally, and perhaps most obviously, you should try to understand what you're measuring and whether the aggregation is appropriate to the metric. You might justifiably want to work out the average over time of a gauge metric, such as `go_memstats_mcache_inuse_bytes`; however, taking the sum over time is probably nonsensical.

## Querying limits for time aggregations

As with the limits to series aggregations, you will need to exercise care in dealing with time aggregations. Unless you are combining multiple series into a single series, many of your aggregations will be calculated over an interval of time. It is outside the scope of the book to cover the nuances of how a data source such as Prometheus identifies certain data points within a time interval when making sophisticated aggregation calculations.

However, we can discuss some general concepts that hold when dealing with time-based aggregations. Primarily, the key to successfully working with time aggregation is to properly choose the size of the aggregation interval. This is the time period where all the values within an interval are aggregated (say with `sum`, `mean`, or `max`) and the result is displayed as representative of the interval.

Too big an interval and your data could become too smooth as all the variations get averaged out; too small and missed sample points might generate anomalous values or even return an error.

Along the same lines is Grafana's display aggregation. There are only so many pixels on the screen, and if there are more points to display than pixels, Grafana will throw some of them away. Setting a fixed aggregation interval risks the interval size issue if the interval is quite small relative to the time frame—say, a five-minute interval for a six-month dataset. Aggregating a lot of points that are essentially invisible will impact performance, so it's important to avoid this where possible.

In order to keep the display efficient, Grafana maintains an automatically adjusted time interval variable that you can insert in place of a fixed interval value. We'll be talking more about variables in later chapters, but for now, simply inserting the `$__interval` variable in place of a fixed time measurement is sufficient. For example, before, we had the following query:

```
irate(http_request_total{handler="/search/",method="get"}[
    5m])
```

The new query using the interval variable would look like this:

```
irate(http_request_total{handler="/search/",method="get"}[
    $__interval])
```

For more details on how Grafana manages its data display over varying time ranges, consult the Grafana documentation.

## Exploring data source dashboards

We've come to the end of our introduction to data sources and how to create queries for them. As a treat, go to **Configuration | Data sources** and edit your Prometheus data source configuration. You'll notice a second tab called **Dashboards**. Under that tab is a set of dashboards curated to work with a Prometheus data source.

If you import the **Grafana metrics** dashboard, you'll now have a full dashboard with several **Time series** and **Stat** visualization panels. Some of the queries we tried out in this chapter were inspired by those dashboard panels.

Open them up and edit them to get a look at the queries, see how they were constructed, and note the techniques that were used to extract information from the data series for use in the legend.

One of the best ways to get a better understanding of how to use Grafana is to simply import and open dashboard panels from different data sources and thereby glean knowledge from the work of others.

One of the more pleasant aspects of Grafana is that dashboards are not driven by a hidden API or some other trickery that makes it difficult, or even impossible, to replicate a panel. Rather, Grafana is an open application with easily accessible dashboards, so feel free to borrow from interesting examples you find from the community.

# Summary

In this chapter, we stood up both a Grafana and a Prometheus server and used Prometheus to scrape metrics data from both servers. We use the ad hoc analysis functionality of **Explore** to identify interesting metrics, possibly with an eye toward monitoring them. We looked at how to aggregate certain metrics to capture how they change over time. We examined how there can be limitations to our data that we must respect for the sake of accuracy and integrity.

Essentially, we've established the foundations for building observability workflows by first capturing metrics from services and then identifying important performance metrics. Finally, if necessary, we aggregated or otherwise transformed the metrics. Once we had the metrics we were interested in, we monitored them in real time, then we discussed how to associate alerts when our metrics deviate from normal.

In the next chapter, we'll take some of the concepts we've picked up through playing around with **Explore** to do something a little more realistic. We're going to capture real weather data, store it in InfluxDB, and display it as graph visualizations. Yes, we're going to make a little weather station, Grafana style!

# 5

# Extracting and Visualizing Data with InfluxDB and Grafana

In the previous chapter, we concentrated our efforts on understanding how a data source is primary to the Grafana visualization workflow. We launched a Prometheus Docker container along with a Grafana server, scraped data from both applications, and then configured a Grafana data source to connect to the Prometheus server. Finally, we used the **Explore** module to get a feel for how to make various queries to the data source and get immediate feedback in the graph display.

While **Explore** is a powerful mechanism for browsing a data source, it is somewhat limited in functionality compared to the time series visualization This is not surprising as it's mostly intended to support ad hoc, transient queries with more permanent graphs living on a dashboard. Those graphs have the advantage of providing several significant features that benefit presentation and alerting.

With that in mind, we're going to take what we've learned about working with data sources to the next step. We'll shift our emphasis from simply using **Explore** on a data source to actively crafting time series visualization queries and styling the panel's display elements to serve our needs – to communicate a message via the visual presentation of our data. You will be taking the first steps toward learning how to acquire a dataset, storing it in a data source, and working through the challenges inherent in working with real-world data.

In our case, we're going to capture weather data from the **National Weather Service** (**NWS**) and store it in an InfluxDB time series database. Some Python scripting will be involved, but the code has been written to use the InfluxDB HTTP API, so there's nothing particularly esoteric to it. If you have any programming experience, this should be completely straightforward. The goal of this chapter isn't to burden you with a coding challenge but to continue working with live data, which I hope you will find rewarding and fun.

Along the way, we'll tackle some obstacles – we'll need to write a little code to import our data and we're going to dive into the tricky concepts underlying displaying data at different time scales. By the end of this chapter, you will be able to build a nice little weather dashboard. Let's get started!

The following topics will be covered in this chapter:

- Making advanced queries
- Understanding the time series data display
- Setting vertical axes
- Working with legends

# Technical requirements

In this chapter, we'll be setting up InfluxDB and Grafana containers, so make sure you have installed Docker and Docker Compose.

> **Information**
>
> The tutorial code, dashboards, and other helpful files for this chapter can be found in this book's GitHub repository at `https://github.com/PacktPublishing/Learn-Grafana-10/tree/main/Chapter05`.

# Making advanced queries

Before we can start playing with our pretty data, we'll need to put together a simple data pipeline. Patience! This is likely to be one of the rare opportunities where you will have significant control of the data that goes into your data source. Even if you don't ever plan to involve yourself in data acquisition, it helps to know some of the techniques and issues surrounding it, if only to appreciate the work that often goes into tailoring and cleaning data so that it can be analyzed or visualized.

Our plan of attack for this part of our tutorial is quite straightforward:

1. Spin up both an InfluxDB and a Grafana server.
2. Code-review a simple **extract, transform, load** (**ETL**) script to gather weather data.
3. Execute the script to populate an InfluxDB database.
4. Configure an InfluxDB data source.

Let's get started!

## Launching server Docker containers

The first step is to run a `docker-compose` script that will download the Grafana and InfluxDB containers and then launch them. The `docker-compose.yml` file is available in the `Chapter05` directory of this book's GitHub repository.

If you haven't done so already, shut down any services you might have left running from the other chapters by executing the following command (first, change to the chapter folder where you started up the service):

```
% docker-compose down
```

Here's the short `docker-compose.yml` file:

```
version: "3"
services:
    influxdb:
        image: influxdb:latest
        ports:
            - "8086:8086"
        volumes:
            - $PWD/influxdb:/var/lib/influxdb
    grafana:
        image: grafana/grafana:latest
        ports:
            - "3000:3000"
        volumes:
            - $PWD/grafana:/var/lib/grafana
```

As you can see, this is quite simple. It does the following:

- References images for InfluxDB and Grafana

- Opens up standard application ports for both services

- Maps the current directory to a volume in the container to persistently store our data

The network connecting the pair of containers is controlled by Docker Compose so that each container can connect to the other container by using the service name.

Let's start up the containers:

```
% docker-compose up -d --pull missing
[+] Running 3/3
    Network chapter05_default       Created
                                                    0.1s
    Container chapter05-grafana-1    Started
                                                    1.1s
    Container chapter05-influxdb-1   Started
                                                    1.1s
```

You should be able to reach the Grafana application at the usual URL of `http://localhost:3000`. We'll access InfluxDB either via our Python script or Grafana data source. You can confirm it is running by using a simple `curl` command:

```
% curl -i http://localhost:8086/ping
HTTP/1.1 204 No Content
X-Influxdb-Build: OSS
X-Influxdb-Build: oss2
X-Influxdb-Version: 2.1.1
X-Influxdb-Version: 2.1.1
Date: Tue, 08 Nov 2022 05:06:51 GMT
```

Now that we have our applications running, let's start gathering some data.

## Writing the ETL script

I selected the NWS weather observation data for a few reasons:

- Everybody intuitively understands the weather; rain or shine, we experience it daily

- Most of the observational data is straightforward measurements that are typically referred to in a daily forecast, such as temperature, relative humidity, and wind speed

- The NWS API is open and simple to understand, especially for our limited use case

The Python script is available in this book's GitHub repository in the `Chapter05/weather.py` folder if you want to follow along. If you want to make code changes (feel free!), you'll need to rebuild the container using the provided Docker file as well. Let's get started.

The first line of our `main()` function sets up the logging level:

```
def main():
    logging.basicConfig(level=logging.INFO)
```

Next, we must parse the command-line options:

```
args = process_cli()
```

The `process_cli()` function specifies the command-line options:

```
    parser.add_argument(
        "--host", dest="host", default="localhost", help="database
host"
    )
    parser.add_argument(
        "--port", dest="port", type=int, default=8086, help="database
port"
```

```
    )
    parser.add_argument(
        "--db", dest="database", help="name of database to store data
in"
    )
    parser.add_argument(
        "--stations",
        dest="stations",
        help="list of stations to gather weather data from",
    )
    parser.add_argument("--token", dest="token", help="InfluxDB API
token")
    group.add_argument(
        "--input", dest="input_file", type=argparse.FileType("r"),
help="input file"
    )
    group.add_argument(
        "--output", dest="output_file", type=argparse.FileType("w"),
help="output file"
    )
```

Some of these command-line options are needed for connecting to a database such as our InfluxDB server, but some are specific to our little application, so let's go through them one by one:

- The `--host` option refers to the InfluxDB server, which is `localhost` by default.

- The `--port` option refers to the InfluxDB server port, which is exposed by Docker at port `8086`.

- The `--db` option refers to the database in InfluxDB. As in more traditional **relational database management systems (RDBMSs)**, data is efficiently stored in a database InfluxDB v2 refers to as a *bucket*. Since we will be making `REST` calls via v1 compatibility, we will instead refer to it as a database; for this exercise, we'll only be working in a single database.

- The `--input` option defines a file for outputting the data we gather from the NWS.

- The `--output` option is for loading that file into our InfluxDB database. I could have combined the operation into a single one, but it's sometimes handy to see the data before loading it. Grouping the `--input` and `--output` options prevents them from being used at the same time.

- The `--stations` option is for specifying a comma-separated list of NWS weather stations. They're typically located in major airports and bear names resembling radio stations, such as KSFO or KLGA.

With the niceties out of the way, we can process our command-line options.

Let's start with main():

```
if args.output_file:
    dump_wx_data(args.stations, args.output_file)
```

Here, we're going to handle the --output option. You'll want to run weather.py with this option first to download data from the NWS. Here's the code:

```
def dump_wx_data(stations, output):
    for s in stations.split(","):
        station_info = get_station_info(s)
        tags = [
]
f'station={escape_string(station_info["station_id"])}',
f'name={escape_string(",".join(station_info["station_name"]))}',
f'cwa={escape_string(station_info["cwa"][0])}',
f'county={escape_string(station_info["county"])}',
f'state={escape_string(station_info["state"])}',
f'tz={escape_string(station_info["timezone"][0])}'
```

The dump_wx_data() function takes two arguments: a stations list and the output file path. The function iterates on each station in the stations list. We call the get_station_info() function to get a dictionary of interesting data about the station. This information is compiled into a list of tags, represented as key-value pairs. Escape_string() is just a utility function that places an escape character (\) ahead of certain characters required by InfluxDB to be escaped.

Let's look at get_station_info():

```
def get_station_info(station):
    info = {}
    url = f"https://api.weather.gov/stations/{station}"
    response = requests.get(url)
    logging.info(response.url)
    if response.status_code != requests.codes.ok:
        raise Exception(f'get_station_info:
{response.status_code}:{response.reason}')
        station_properties = response.json()['properties']
        info['station_name'] = station_properties[
            'name'].split(',')
        info['station_id'] = station_properties[
            'stationIdentifier']
```

The first pass of the NWS API endpoint is done to gather information about the station itself, namely `name` and `stationIdentifier` (which should be the same as the station variable). As the station's name is a string containing the station city and station location separated by a comma, we split it into a list just in case we want to use only part of the name. We'll store the interesting information in the `info` dictionary.

The pattern for accessing the API is straightforward:

1. Construct the URL.
2. Submit a GET or POST request via the Python Requests library and save the response.
3. Examine the response status code; if it's not ok, raise an exception.
4. Finally, the response is decoded from the original JSON object into a Python object using the response object's `json()` method.

Next, we must use the station's `county` field to get another API endpoint, which will allow us to get county information:

```
url = station_properties['county']
response = requests.get(url)
logging.info(response.url)
if response.status_code != requests.codes.ok:
    raise Exception(f'get_station_info:
{response.status_code}:{response.reason}')
county_properties = response.json()['properties']
info['county'] = county_properties['name']
info['state'] = county_properties['state']
info['cwa'] = county_properties['cwa']
info['timezone'] = county_properties['timeZone']
```

Use the `station_properties` county field as a new URL. Copy interesting county information into the `info` dictionary. The cwa field is useful if we want to access forecast information, which is delivered by **County Warning Area** or **CWA** for short.

Now that we have a bunch of information about the station for our tags, let's get back to `dump_wx_data()`:

```
wx_data = get_station_obs(s)
```

Here's where we get the station's observations:

```
def get_station_obs(station):
    url = f"https://api.weather.gov/stations/{station}/observations"
    response = requests.get(url)
    logging.info(response.url)
```

```
        if response.status_code != requests.codes.no_content:
            raise Exception(f"get_station_obs:
{response.status_code}:{response.reason}")
        data = response.json()['features']
        return data
```

In this case, we'll just request the data from the endpoint and return most of the response data, namely the `features` field.

Now that we have all the observation data, let's extract the observations we're interested in, along with the timestamp for the observation itself:

```
for feature in wx_data:
    for measure, observation in feature[
        'properties'].items():
            if not isinstance(observation,
            dict) or measure in ['elevation']:
                continue
            value = observation['value']
            if value is None:
                continue
            unit = observation['unitCode']
            timestamp = iso_to_timestamp(
                feature['properties']['timestamp'])
```

We have a couple of loops here – one that goes through a list of observations, and within that loop, another loop that picks out the actual observation data that we're interested in. The steps are as follows:

1.  The observations are a list of dictionaries, so we'll skip over any dictionary fields that don't map to dictionaries, as well as the elevation field, which we're not interested in as a metric.

2.  Grab the field name as our InfluxDB *measurement* name. InfluxDB treats measurements much like a traditional RDBMS table does – a collection of metric data points.

3.  The value is the actual metric we're storing for each data point. InfluxDB lets you store more than one metric per measurement data point, but we want the metric to carry an observation unit, and gathering all the metrics with the same unit would unnecessarily complicate the code, so we keep it simple – one metric per data point. Since each observation shares a timestamp, they'll line up nicely.

4.  Convert `timestamp` from the ISO 8601 format string into a seconds-since-the-epoch InfluxDB timestamp.

We use the `dateutil` library to do the conversion for us. We do this with the `iso_to_timestamp` utility function, which wraps the `isoparse()` function:

```
def iso_to_timestamp(ts):
    return int(isoparse(ts).timestamp())
```

`Isoparse()` returns a Python `datetime` object, so we convert that using the `timestamp()` method.

Finally, we'll assemble the measurement, the comma-separated tags, the unit tag, the metric, and the timestamp into a single data point and write it to a file:

```
data = f'{measure},{",".join(tags)},
    unit={unit} value={value}
{timestamp}\n'
output.write(data)
```

Finally, in `main()`, we handle the `--input` option in `load_wx_data()`:

```
if args.input_file:
    load_wx_data(db_host=args.host, db_port=args.port,
db_name=args.database, input_file=args.input_file)
```

`Load_wx_data()` performs two pretty simple tasks – it creates an InfluxDB database and then loads it with data from a file using an HTTP POST request. The code is as follows:

```
def load_wx_data(db_host, db_port, db_name, token, input_file):
    if not db_name:
        raise Exception(f"load_wx_data:
            no database specified")

    url = f"http://{db_host}:{db_port}/write"
    headers = {"Authorization": f"Token {token}"}
    data = input_file.read()
    response = requests.post(
        url, params=dict(db=db_name, precision="s"),
            headers=headers, data=data
    )
    logging.info(response.url)
    if response.status_code != requests.codes.no_content:
        raise Exception(f"load_wx_data:
            {response.status_code}:{response.reason}")
```

As arguments, it takes the connection parameters for InfluxDB, the name of the database, and the input file:

1.  Check for a database name and exit if one isn't specified.

2.  Assemble the URL, query parameters, and header for the HTTP payload.

3.  Send a POST request to write the input file to the database and capture the response.

4.  The expected response should be 204 (No Content), so immediately raise an exception if any other response is received.

And that's pretty much all there is to it. Now, let's go capture some data!

## Running the script

Now that we've got a script ready, let's dump the data we gathered from a few stations. I've created a simple Python Dockerfile. This is what it looks like:

```
FROM python:3
WORKDIR /usr/src/app

COPY requirements.txt ./
COPY weather.py ./

RUN pip install --no-cache-dir -r requirements.txt

ENTRYPOINT [ "python" ]
```

It just creates a WORKDIR directory called /usr/src/app, copies the requirements.txt file and weather.py script, pip-installs the libraries from requirements.txt, and runs Python as ENDPOINT.

The requirements.txt file is so that you can build and run the script from a container. You won't need to concern yourself with downloading the appropriate Python libraries (there are only a couple anyway). In a directory that you've cloned from this book's GitHub repository, build the Docker image:

```
% docker build --pull --tag python/ch5 .
```

To see if you were successful, use the Docker container to run the script with the --help option:

```
% docker run python/ch5 weather.py --help
usage: weather.py [-h] [--host HOST] [--port PORT] [--db DATABASE]
    [--stations STATIONS] [--token TOKEN]
    [--input INPUT_FILE | --output OUTPUT_FILE]

read forecast data from NWS into Influxdb
```

```
options:
    -h, --help                  show this help message and exit
    --host HOST                   database host
    --port PORT                   database port
    --db DATABASE             name of database to store data in
    --stations STATIONS    list of stations to gather weather data from
    --token TOKEN               InfluxDB API token
    --input INPUT_FILE      input file
    --output OUTPUT_FILE   output file
```

Now that we've confirmed the script works, let's download some data. We'll output our data in a file called wx.txt (but you can name it whatever you like). We'll pick the station for San Francisco, which happens to be at the airport called KSFO. We'll map the local directory as a volume in the container so that we can access the file the container script creates:

```
% docker run --rm -v "$(PWD):/usr/src/app" \
    python/ch5 weatherweather.py \
    --output wx.txt \
    --stations KSFO
INFO:root:https://api.weather.gov/stations/KSFO
INFO:root:https://api.weather.gov/zones/county/CAC081
INFO:root:https://api.weather.gov/stations/KSFO/observations
```

To see if all went well, you can check the first few lines of data with the head shell command:

```
% head wx.txt
temperature,station=KSFO,name=San\ Francisco\,\ San\ Francisco\
International\ Airport,cwa=MTR,county=San\ Mateo,state=CA,tz=America/
Los_Angeles,unit=wmoUnit:degC value=11.7 1667883360
dewpoint,station=KSFO,name=San\ Francisco\,\ San\ Francisco\
International\ Airport,cwa=MTR,county=San\ Mateo,state=CA,tz=America/
Los_Angeles,unit=wmoUnit:degC value=7.2 1667883360
barometricPressure,station=KSFO,name=San\ Francisco\,\ San\ Francisco\
International\ Airport,cwa=MTR,county=San\ Mateo,state=CA,tz=America/
Los_Angeles,unit=wmoUnit:Pa value=100980 1667883360
seaLevelPressure,station=KSFO,name=San\ Francisco\,\ San\ Francisco\
International\ Airport,cwa=MTR,county=San\ Mateo,state=CA,tz=America/
Los_Angeles,unit=wmoUnit:Pa value=100960 1667883360
visibility,station=KSFO,name=San\ Francisco\,\ San\ Francisco\
International\ Airport,cwa=MTR,county=San\ Mateo,state=CA,tz=America/
Los_Angeles,unit=wmoUnit:m value=16090 1667883360
relativeHumidity,station=KSFO,name=San\ Francisco\,\ San\ Francisco\
International\ Airport,cwa=MTR,county=San\ Mateo,state=CA,tz=America/
Los_Angeles,unit=wmoUnit:percent value=73.905075949333 1667883360
```

These lines will contain the rows of time series data we will input into InfluxDB.

## Setting up an InfluxDB database

Now that we have our nicely formatted data, we'll send it to the InfluxDB server. We'll use the InfluxDB REST API to bulk upload the data in a single HTTP call. This is much more efficient than sending each row separately. While InfluxDB v2 features a powerful query language called **Flux**, it is beyond the scope of this book to cover Flux sufficiently for not only the queries to add data to InfluxDB but also the queries from Grafana to graph the data. Luckily, the older v1 query language, **InfluxQL**, is still supported in a special v1 compatibility API, so we will use that here and in our Grafana data source.

But first, to make sure that our InfluxDB will successfully accept the data from our Python script, we will need to perform two minor tasks:

1. Set up our InfluxDB instance by creating a new user and password, an organization, and a data bucket.
2. Generate an API token to give our script permission to access the InfluxDB REST API.

Let's get started.

### Setting up the InfluxDB server

Log into the InfluxDB UI at `http://localhost:8086`. If you haven't already set up the instance, you'll see a prompt to perform the initialization:

1. Set the username to whatever you like.
2. Add a password (8 characters minimum).
3. Choose an organization name; for example, `LearnGrafana`.
4. Create a bucket; for example, `Chapter05`.

### Generating an API token

Generating an API key is a straightforward process. You'll need this token to access the InfluxDB server from our script:

1. Go to **Load Data | API Tokens**.
2. Click **+ Generate New Token**.
3. Select **All Access API Token** from the pulldown.
4. Fill in a description such as `Chapter05 API Token` and click **Save**.
5. Copy the API token string to the clipboard.
6. Save the API token in a safe place as you won't be able to see it again without going through the process of creating a new one.

Let's go ahead and load it into the InfluxDB `chapter05` bucket with the `--input` option. We'll need to use `host` mode in the network for our Python application container to communicate with our InfluxDB server container at `localhost`. We also need to map the current directory into the `Dockerfile WORKDIR` area of `/usr/src/app` so that the container can find our `weather.py` script:

```
% docker run --rm --network host \
    -v "$(PWD):/usr/src/app" \
    python/ch5 weather.py \
    --input wx.txt \
    --db chapter05 \
    --token <API_TOKEN>
INFO:root:http://localhost:8086/write?db=chapter05&precision=s
```

Now, let's have a look at our data!

## Configuring the InfluxDB data source

Open your browser to the Grafana app and from the main menu, under **Connections**, select **Add new connection**. Search for and select the **InfluxDB** data source and click **Add new data source**. Fill out the following form fields:

- **Name**: `InfluxDB`
- **Query Language**: **InfluxQL**
- **HTTP | URL**: `http://influxdb:8086`
- **Custom HTTP Headers | Header**: `Authorization`
- **Custom HTTP Headers | Value**: `Token <API Token>`
- **InfluxDB Details | Database**: `chapter05`

> Note
> Make sure there is a space between `Token` and `API Token`.

Your data source configuration should look like this:

Figure 5.1 – InfluxDB data source

Click **Save and Test**. If everything is correct, you should see a message that reads as follows:

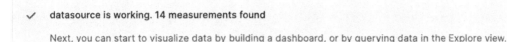

Figure 5.2 – Data source success

Now that we have a data source, click **Explore data** to check out our data and confirm we can query it.

There's a good chance that when you go into **Explore**, you won't see any data. That's okay because we need to generate a query first. Many of the typical parameters in an InfluxDB query are already filled out, so it's just a matter of making a couple of menu selections.

Set the time range to **Last 24 hours**. This will give us a nice spread of data and should guarantee a time range that contains at least some data.

Let's work through the query details step by step, starting with the **FROM** clause.

If you are already familiar with SQL database queries, the **FROM** clause will seem similar. You can leave the first segment set to **default**. This refers to the *retention policy* for the database. Consult the InfluxDB documentation for more information about retention policies.

The next segment in our **FROM** clause is **measurement**. For this tutorial, we stored each observation type in its own measurement. This may not always be the case as you can certainly store multiple fields of data in a single measurement. Select a **measurement** option from the dropdown. If you see a list of measurements, that is a good sign. It means our measurements were correctly stored in the database and **Explore** has helpfully queried the data source to acquire them. If you don't see any graph data, try clicking **Run query** to force a refresh. For **measurement**, I picked **temperature**; my **Explore** display looks like this:

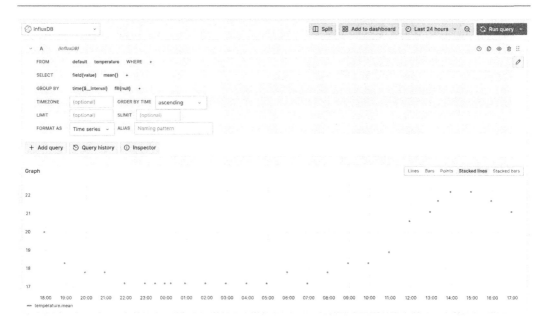

Figure 5.3 – The Explore data graph

One thing that stands out is that the data is not captured at strictly regular intervals. This isn't necessarily a bad thing, nor does it render the data unusable. Rather, it means we need to take some special care when we work with it – work that we might not ordinarily need to do if the data was more regular. That's a good thing since it forces us to grapple with some of the nuances regarding how to display time series data. In the meantime, since we have validated our pipeline, let's go big and gather some more data.

Let's delete our bucket so that we can load it with fresh data. Ordinarily, this isn't required as InfluxDB treats a data point with the same measurement, tags, field keys, and timestamp as the same point and overwrites the field values, but we want each additional data series to cover the same period, so we'll go ahead and delete the bucket.

If you ever want to start over with a clean bucket, you can use the InfluxDB UI to delete an existing bucket, and then create a new one:

1.  In the UI, select **Load Data | Buckets**.
2.  Click the small trashcan symbol in the top right corner of the bucket you wish to delete.
3.  Click **+ Create Bucket** to create a new bucket.
4.  Name the bucket with the previous name – that is, chapter05.
5.  Leave **Delete Data** set to **Never**.

Next, we'll add data from a few more stations, namely Denver, CO (KDEN), St. Louis, MO (KSTL), and New York, NY (KJFK):

```
% docker run --rm \
    python/ch5 weather.py \
    --output wx.txt \
    --stations KSFO,KDEN,KSTL,KJFK     INFO:root:https://api.weather.
gov/stations/KSFO
    INFO:root:https://api.weather.gov/zones/county/CAC081
    INFO:root:https://api.weather.gov/stations/KSFO/observations
    INFO:root:https://api.weather.gov/stations/KDEN
    INFO:root:https://api.weather.gov/zones/county/COC031
    INFO:root:https://api.weather.gov/stations/KDEN/observations
    INFO:root:https://api.weather.gov/stations/KSTL
    INFO:root:https://api.weather.gov/zones/county/MOC189
    INFO:root:https://api.weather.gov/stations/KSTL/observations
    INFO:root:https://api.weather.gov/stations/KJFK
    INFO:root:https://api.weather.gov/zones/county/NYC081
    INFO:root:https://api.weather.gov/stations/KJFK/observations
```

Load the data. Depending on the speed of your computer, it should take a couple of seconds to load about 10,000 data points into InfluxDB:

```
% docker run --rm --network=host \
    -v "$(PWD):/usr/src/app" \
    python/ch5 weather.py \
    --input wx.txt \
    --db chapter05 --token <API_TOKEN>
INFO:root:http://localhost:8086/query?q=CREATE+DATABASE+weatherdb
```

You should now have four data series, covering almost 10 days of observations that include temperature, wind, and rainfall. In the next section, we'll be looking very closely at this data to gain an understanding of how Grafana draws data. We'll even try out different drawing styles to better highlight various aspects of the data display. Later, we'll work with the *y axes* and the legend.

## Understanding the time series data visualization

In this section, we are going to cover some important concepts surrounding time aggregation. For us to do that, we're going to craft a time series visualization panel that illustrates those concepts. Along the way, we'll be covering some of the more advanced drawing features of the time series visualization.

The concepts are a bit technical, but understanding them is essential to mastering the depiction of time-based data in Grafana and other time series visualization tools:

1.  Start by creating a new dashboard and then click + **Add visualization**.
2.  Select the default **InfluxDB** data source.

3. Set the time range to **Last 24 hours**.

4. In the **Query** tab, click on the copy (two pages) icon to make a copy of the current query.

5. Click the visibility (eye) icon for the **B** query to disable it. We'll set it in a moment.

We are going to modify the **A** query so that it concentrates on a single data series – the one corresponding to the KSFO station. We're also going to remove all aggregation so that we can see the raw data points in the series. The steps are as follows:

1. Make sure the **Open** options pane is open by clicking the < symbol, if necessary.

2. Under the **Graph styles** section, select the **Lines** style.

3. In the **Query** tab, for the **A** query, click **select measurement** and select the **temperature** measurement.

4. Select the plus sign (+) next to **WHERE**.

5. Select **station::tag**.

6. Click **select tag value**, then select **KSFO**. Note that the display shows points scattered across the time range.

7. Next to **GROUP BY**, select **time**, and from the dropdown, click **remove**. This removes the `time()` GROUP BY statement and the default `mean` aggregation in the `SELECT` statement.

This should shift the display from points to line-connected points, as you might expect:

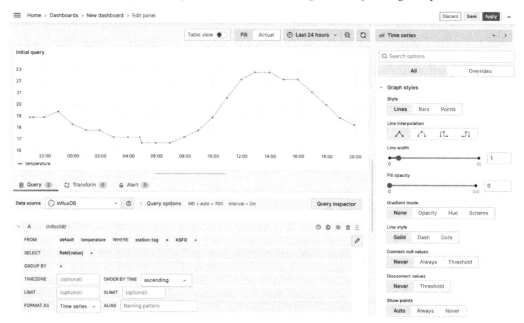

Figure 5.4 – Line-connected points graph display

But did the graph change from scattered points to lines? We are going to delve into that in a moment. Note that **Style** under **Graph styles** in the **Options** pane does appear to be set to **Lines**. Whew, that's reassuring! You might be thinking something along the lines of, hmm… the display of points despite me having selected **Lines** must be some sort of bug, and I do want to display lines, so I just need to delete `time() GROUP BY`.

Before you do that, consider what else might be going on. After all, we did delete a whole `GROUP BY` component of our query. Might that be a clue as to what happened? For now, let's keep that in mind while we examine the current display. We can see a set of relatively evenly spaced points joined by line segments.

If you enable the **Table view** switch at the top of the graph, you'll see a spreadsheet-like table of timestamps and corresponding temperature values. What we're seeing is a literal, point-by-point list of each data point in the dataset. Disabling **Table view** returns us to a similar point-by-point graph of our dataset.

A concept that you want to become familiar with early on is that what you're seeing is only a *representation* of your data, not the actual data. In reality, your data is nothing more than a collection of samples of some observed phenomenon. A graph is just a symbolic representation mapping those data points onto a simple *X/Y* coordinate grid with the timestamp on the *x axis* and the value of the data point on the *y axis*.

From here on out, your interactions with Grafana (or any data visualization tool for that matter) are essentially negotiations between you and the application as to what and how to display your data in a way that is meaningful to you and/or your audience. Sometimes, you will see things that make sense; other times, they won't.

This is because while Grafana is a sophisticated piece of software written by engineers who have accumulated the wisdom of thousands of end users to make working with it disarmingly easy, it can't always guess what you intend to do. Rather, you should always be aware of Grafana's strengths and limitations.

Let's take a closer look at the graph to see why this might be the case. While it's perfectly reasonable to work with the graph as-is, imagine a different scenario. Imagine a dataset not with a hundred points spanning a week, but one with millions of points spanning an entire month.

To give you a feel for that scenario, perform the following steps:

1. Make sure the **Open** options pane is open by clicking the < symbol.
2. In the **Graph styles** section, set **Style** to **Points**.
3. Zoom out the time range to **Last 90 days** or even **Last 1 year**.

Notice in the following screenshot how the points all appear to be bunched up into indistinguishable blobs, instead of the easily discernable string of points across the timeline:

Figure 5.5 – Data points compressed into a wide time scale

Here's the issue: if you keep zooming out, Grafana will find it increasingly hard to display all the points it's being asked for. Remember, while we're currently looking at a few days of data herded onto one side of the graph, we could just as easily be seeing those points spanning the entire timespan. Grafana is facing two challenging issues:

- Grafana tries to render each data point in the appropriate pixel(s), thus making it hard to distinguish between data points as they all tend to land on the same pixels.

- Rendering so many points taxes the rendering engine, which paints all those data points into pixels, making the interface less responsive.

Here is a schematic representation of how Grafana maps data into the pixels you see on the screen. The circles are sampled data, while the squares are the rendered pixels in the graph:

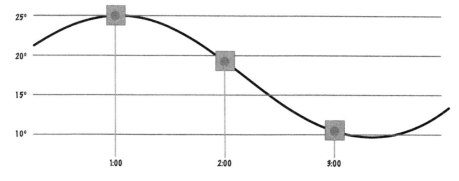

Figure 5.6 – Mapping points to pixels

Here is that same schematic showing, albeit exaggerated, what happened when we zoomed out in the time range:

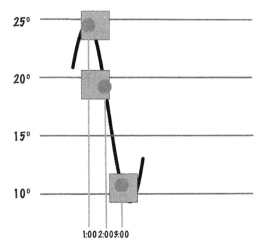

Figure 5.7 – The points display pixels in a wide time scale

Zoom out far enough, and given enough points, you'll end up with all the data landing on a handful of vertical pixels.

There is a solution, which is to somehow filter the points so that Grafana can display fewer points, but still do it in a way that makes it *seem* as representative as if all the data points were displayed. To do that, Grafana counts on a characteristic of the data that is often true, namely that the dataset represents a continuous function such that points closely spaced in time are also close enough in value that you could estimate the values between them, had they been sampled at a higher rate.

Selecting a point halfway between two existing points, colloquially called *splitting the difference*, is a form of *interpolation*, the action of estimating data points between other data points.

In this illustration, the intermediate points are determined to be at some position midway between an imaginary line connecting the known sample points. They don't line up on the actual function, but the rendered pixels are close enough that if you connect those points with line segments, you'll have a pretty good approximation.

We are talking about finding a way to reduce the points that are displayed, but not in such a way as to lose the overall character of the graph. To do that, we must use *aggregation* – that is, we must take a collection of points at regular intervals and perform a mathematical summary operation to replace the collection with a single point.

A typical method to calculate a single value that represents the contributions of a collection of values is to average them or find their *mean*. However, before you can average a set of values, you need to determine what those values are.

In the case of a time series visualization, we group them at regular intervals, calculate the aggregation of all the values that fall into the interval, and display the calculated value at some point in time that represents the interval. In the following figure, we've reduced the number of potentially rendered points from six to three by dividing the time into three intervals, each aligned on each regular timestamp:

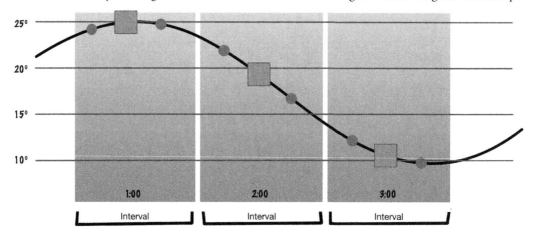

Figure 5.8 – Data points aggregated into display pixels

With this in mind, have another look at the **B** query. In the SELECT section, you can see the aggregation: mean(). But how is the interval specified? That is in the next section – GROUP BY. Here, the interval is specified as time($__interval). What does that mean?

In InfluxDB, the width of GROUP BY is specified by the time() function. However, the function requires a value. You could attempt to specify that value yourself, based on the current timespan on the graph, but you would have to keep adjusting the interval every time you change the scale of the timespan.

Happily, Grafana can do that for you, because it knows just how many pixels are covered by a given timespan. So, Grafana provides that value in a special variable called $__interval. Plug that variable into the time() function, and at any period, you will see the results of the aggregation at different GROUP BY intervals of time.

> **Tip**
> It's always useful to go back to the dashboard display to examine how your graph looks in that context. It's too easy to tailor a graph in the wide-open spaces of **Explore** or edit mode, only to find out your beautiful graph is a mush of lines and points on the dashboard.

## Displaying time-aggregated data

To see how that might work, let's try to aggregate those points in time over a set interval. Looking at the space occupied by the graph, it seems like the points cover a few days, so maybe aggregating over a day is a good choice. Return to the **Queries** tab and perform the following steps:

1. Next to the **A** query's GROUP BY, select (or type the first few characters) **time($interval)**.

2. Click on **$interval** and type in 1d.

Wait a minute! What happened to the data?

This is why we do things in a controlled scenario and not under the pressures of a production deadline. Understanding how things work will save you the nightmare of randomly clicking on various display options in the hope of getting the graph to work, but then making a potentially costly mistake.

## Debugging queries with Query inspector

When you run into a situation like this, you do have some debugging tools at your disposal. Clicking the **Query inspector** button in the top left of the **Query** tab opens a text box that shows the actual InfluxDB query and its results. Normally, it's just a big JSON blob of data points, but when you don't see any data, there's a good chance you've just confused InfluxDB with your query and it's quietly complaining. Click **Refresh** to get the results of the query, as shown in the following screenshot:

Figure 5.9 – Query inspector

**Query inspector** shows you both the request and the response objects, and in this case, we want to know what came back from the query. Open all the disclosure triangles below the response to see what happened:

```
response: Object
    results:Array[1]
        0:Object
        statement_id:0
            error:"GROUP BY requires at least one aggregate
function"
```

Here, we asked InfluxDB to do a GROUP BY time, but we didn't tell it how to aggregate the grouped points into a single value. Let's go with mean. If you noticed that we're working our way toward the **B** query, good for you! That's pretty much what we're doing.

The SELECT section is where the points are selected for display. Right now, you've asked Grafana to display all the grouped field(value) values, but we need to aggregate them. Click + and select (or type) **Aggregations | mean**. Yay – we got our data points back! Go ahead and set **Graph styles | Style** back to **Lines** as well:

Figure 5.10 – Effect of aggregations on displayed points

Now, zoom back into **Last 24 hours**. Yikes, what happened? Recall that we aggregated the data across 1 day. That means a single point now represents 24 hours, so the data is still there – the last 24 hours have just been replaced by that one point. If you don't see any points, try zooming out to **Last 2 days**.

So, now, every time we substantially change the time range, we'll also need to adjust the interval in the GROUP BY time, right? Thankfully, no. Remember, Grafana can automatically calculate the time interval that covers at least the width of a single pixel, so we just need to use it in the GROUP BY interval. This variable is called $__interval and is what Grafana refers to as a *template variable*. Template variables provide a powerful means for us to add responsiveness to our graphs, and we'll be talking about them in more detail in later chapters. For now, let's just refer to the **B** query, which already has the GROUP BY time with $__interval as the parameter.

Earlier, I said you can solve the problem of data point illegibility by simply using an aggregation with a GROUP BY time. Unfortunately, while that simplifies the data, technically, it represents a loss of fidelity to the original data and will have the effect of changing the appearance of data at different time range scales. This is not necessarily a bad thing, so long as you don't try to draw conclusions about the underlying data based solely on its aggregation. However, the change in appearance can be jarring if you don't know what causes it.

To give you an idea of this, let's modify the graph to highlight the effects of the aggregation:

1. In the **A** query, remove **GROUP BY time()** to return to the original points.

2. Enable the **B** query by clicking the eye icon.

3. Set the measurement for the **B** query to **temperature** and **station::tag** to **KSFO** so that it matches query **A**.

4. Leave **SELECT** set to **mean**.

5. Set the time range to **Last 24 hours**.

6. Go to the **Tooltip** section of the options pane and select **All** for **Tooltip mode**.

The following screenshot shows what you will get as output if you hover over one of the data points:

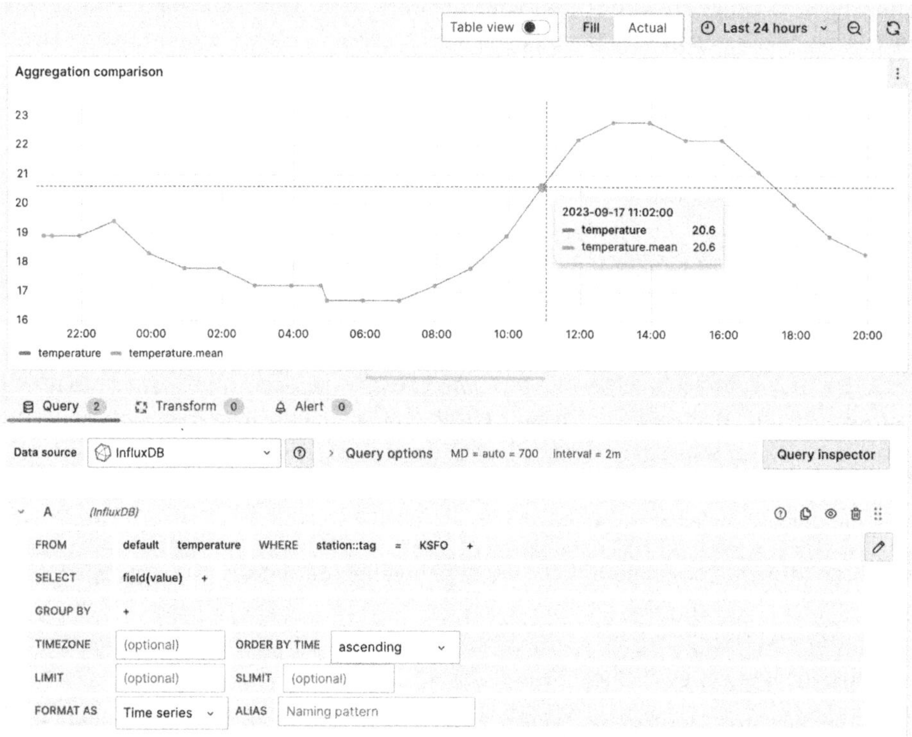

Figure 5.11 – Dual query display

You should see a bunch of **A** query points in the same positions as the **B** query points. You can confirm this by hovering over the data point and noting that `temperature` and `temperature.mean` are identical. Now, we want to observe the changing value of `$__interval`, so while we could look at the request in **Query inspector**, there's an easier way of doing things: using the **ALIAS** field.

## Observing time interval effects

**ALIAS** is the field that's used by Grafana to annotate the data series in the legend. If nothing is in the field, Grafana will default to constructing a series name based on the measurement and the aggregation. We're going to override that with our own series name using **ALIAS**. Type the following into each **ALIAS** text field:

```
$measurement.$col
```

The legend now reads out the **measurement** value with the **SELECT** value. Now, check out the **interval** value in the **Query options** box. If you are in the 24-hour time range, at my panel width, **Interval** equals **1m**, or 1 minute. Hovering over the points shows that they are identical. This makes sense when you examine the timestamps for the data points. Even the closest points are separated by more than 2 minutes, so each interval only contains one point to aggregate.

Despite the fact we can individually examine each data point, we'd like to visually emphasize whether the mean value is centered over the raw data point. Go to the **Graph styles** section in the **Options** pane and set **Point size** to **5**. Now, the green points are larger, but the yellow point obscures the green point below it. Every change we make to the style of one data series is reflected in the others as well. This is a common problem, and Grafana has a clever solution – field overrides. A field override allows you to specify the drawing style of one or more by matching an override rule with a selector on the field like a name or a regular expression.

Let's create one for the mean temperature:

1. At the bottom of the options pane, click the **+ Add field override** section.
2. Choose **Fields with name matching regex** from the menu.
3. Fill the text box with `/temperature\.mean/`. This is just a **regular expression** (**regex**) that matches any alias value containing the `temperature.mean` string.
4. Click **+ Add override property**, then **Graph styles | Point Size**, and set the **Points Size** slider to **5**.

Start progressively zooming out to **Last 90 days**. You should start to see that the aggregated points start to drift further and further away from the raw data as more and more points (within the increasing interval width) contribute to the mean. Here's what they look like at 7 days:

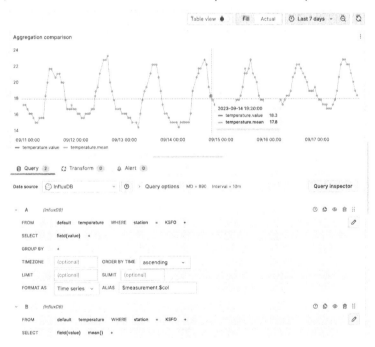

Figure 5.12 – Raw and aggregated data points display

By the time you reach 90 days, you should notice two things:

- The mean points are significantly different than the raw data around them

- They tend to span a narrower range (sometimes referred to as *regression to the mean*)

This is where some analysts might experience a certain amount of anxiety as the graph begins to flatten when they zoom out to wider and wider time ranges. To see how dramatic this can be, click on the **temperature.value** label in the legend. Repeatedly clicking on the label will alternately hide and display the points corresponding to the aggregate mean points, thus giving you a better view of their relative values.

It is here that you will want to make some decisions about what kind of aggregation to display. Don't assume that mean() is the only choice. If you want to emphasize the central tendency, use mean() or median(), while if you want to highlight extremes, try min or max.

## Setting the minimum interval

Going in the opposite direction, we need to explore a couple more aspects of the interval. Remember that we previously noticed the mysterious switch from points to lines when we deleted GROUP BY and its associated aggregation? We're now going to solve this mystery. To get set up, do the following:

1. Set the time range to **Last 90 days**.

2. Click the visibility (eye) icon to hide the raw data query **A**.

3. Make sure the **Lines** style is set in the **Graph** styles section, and set **Show points** to **Always**.

We're doing this as we want to see how the display is affected by the interval. You should note the points are connected by lines. Now, use the time range pulldown to zoom into progressively narrower time ranges. At even the **Last 30 days** time range, you should see many lines disappear. Where did they go? Note that the **Interval** reading in **Query options** is now (in my panel size) **10m**:

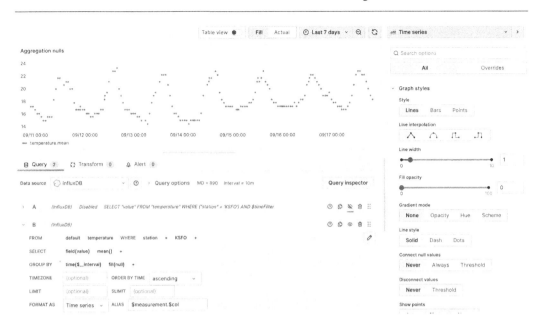

Figure 5.13 – Data aggregation gaps

Grafana has calculated an interval that roughly covers a pixel (the smallest display element) and that interval is 10 minutes. So, to aggregate the values, it divides the time into a series of intervals of 10 minutes each, groups (remember GROUP BY) every data point within each time, and calculates the mean of their value. If there are no points in the interval, no mean can be calculated and so no point is displayed.

Now, when Grafana wants to connect those points, it expects to find a point in each interval (per the definition of a line segment). This is where the additional term in GROUP BY comes into play. Fill(null) is responsible for setting any missing points to null. Checking the **Connect null values** setting, we see that **Never** means Grafana won't even try to connect other points, hence, no line is generated. The points in our dataset are so sparse that as we keep narrowing our time, the interval gets smaller and the likelihood of finding any points that fall into the interval also gets smaller and smaller.

To make matters even worse, though you may not notice it, Grafana is working harder and harder for little gain. When you have a single data point in a 1-hour time range, with an interval of 5 seconds, Grafana is trying to calculate a mean 60*12=720 times to only to generate a single displayed data point. To prove that is what is happening, drag a roughly 1-hour range around a single data point. Now, change fill() in the **B** query from **fill(null)** to **fill(0)**. You should now see hundreds of points (connected by lines) filling the graph end to end:

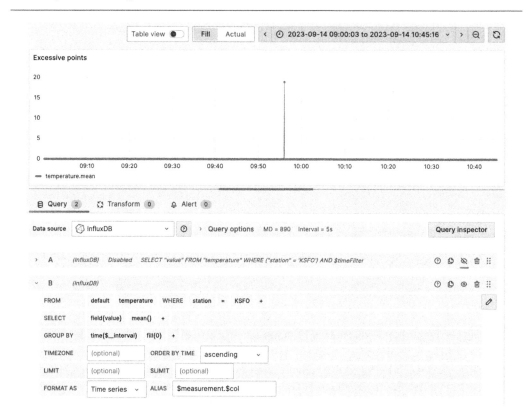

Figure 5.14 – Excessive fill() points

That is why we set a minimum interval to halt that calculation when it becomes pointless. Typically, if your data is regularly sampled, you'd set the minimum interval to your sample interval because you wouldn't have samples falling into a narrower interval. In the case of the NWS observation data, we don't have regular samples, so we'll rely on the precision of the data to guide us. We know the data doesn't appear to bear a timestamp with a second value, so we can infer the data is separated by no less than 1 minute. Click **Query options** to expose the query options and set **Min interval** to **1m**. You should immediately see that the number of points is reduced substantially.

Now, we need to fix this because we're still generating needless points. We can tell InfluxDB that we need it to fill in missing interval points with no point at all. Set **GROUP BY** to **fill(none)**. Now, when Grafana ignores missing points, and if the time range contains two or more points, it knows to connect each one to the next available point, and voilà! – you have proper lines connecting your data. That's why you might have to zoom out to **Last 6 hours** or even further to start seeing lines because at that range, you are likely to see multiple points:

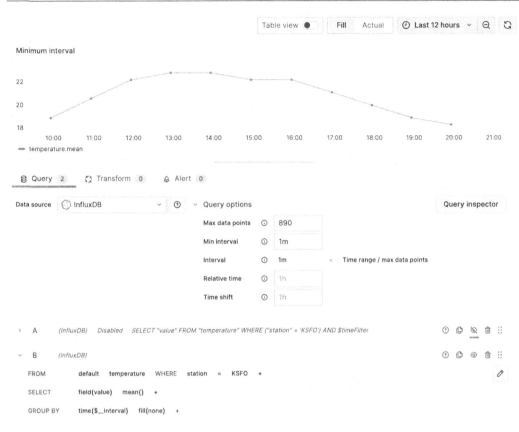

Figure 5.15 – Connected points

I hope this section clarifies things. It's a lot to take in, but it's fundamental if you wish to successfully manage the inevitable constraints that arise when you're faced with less-than-perfect data.

We'll now move on to adding panel-style details, including axes, measurement units, and legends.

## Setting the axis

Now that we've broken down how data points are graphed horizontally in time, let's look at how they are graphed vertically on the *y axis*. I'm sure whole books have been devoted to documenting how the *y axis* has been used and abused, from using a logarithmic scale instead of linear or vice versa to improper scale to truncation, but space doesn't permit going into all these issues.

Like any tool, we can abuse the flexibility of Grafana's *y axis* display. In this section, we're going to point out the opportunities for leveraging the *y axis* display to hopefully clarify or illuminate our data. We'll be creating a series of panels depicting various weather observations and then concentrating on different ways to adjust the *y axis*, including scaling, units, and even the use of multiple *y axes* on a single graph.

## Setting axis units

Let's start by creating a new dashboard panel by clicking the **Add | Visualization** drop-down menu at the top right of the dashboard. Make sure **Time series** is the visualization type, and set up the query as follows:

- Time range: **Last 24 hours**

- **FROM**: **temperature**

- **GROUP BY** (use the plus icon (+) to add): **time($__interval)**, **tag(station::tag)**, **fill(none)**

- Query options minimum interval: **1m**

It is always good practice to assign your units as early as possible. If you don't, you could end up forgetting a crucial piece of information. For instance, failure to properly account for units has caused the loss of millions of dollars worth of space hardware. If you don't want to be responsible for losing the next Mars probe, remember the units!

How do we know the units for the temperature readings? Since they are in the low teens, it's easy to assume they are in Celsius. You could also assume the NWS uses SI units. A better approach would be to check the data tags as we deliberately included them for just such an occasion.

Click **Apply** to save the panel. Click on the three-dot panel menu and select **Explore**. Confirm the following settings:

- Time range: **Last 3 hours**

- **FROM**: **default temperature**

- **SELECT**: **field(value) | mean()**

- **GROUP BY**: **time($__interval) | tag(unit::tag) | fill(null)**

- **FORMAT AS**: **Table**

This is what your **Explore** pane should look like:

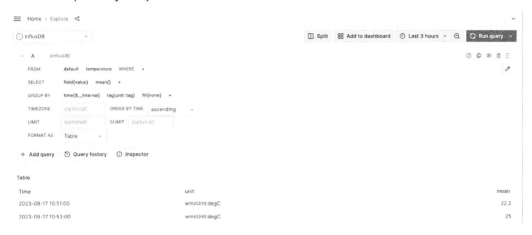

Figure 5.16 – Determining data set units

As you can see, the unit is degC or degrees Celsius. Let's go back to our graph panel and set the units:

1.  In the **Options** pane, scroll to the **Standard options** section.

2.  Under **Unit**, set **Temperature | Celsius (°C)**.

3.  In the **Graph styles** section, enable **Lines**, set **Show Points** to **Always**, and set **Point Size** to **5**. Your graph should look something like this:

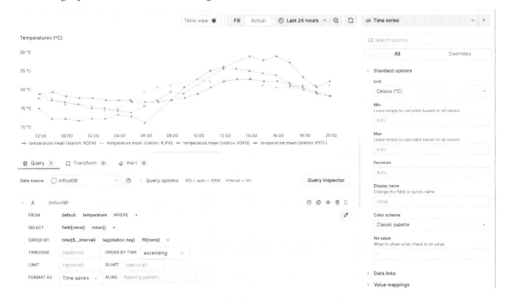

Figure 5.17 – Multiple temperature readings

## Converting temperature into Fahrenheit

Now, suppose you live in the United States, and you simply must display the data in Fahrenheit. If you were momentarily tempted to just change the units to °F and call it a day, I'll forgive you. Before you do that, however, you'll need to first convert the data values.

We're not going to open our weather script and start editing Python code, because there is a simpler way – simply modify our InfluxDB query to do the conversion. Since the query is executed on the database server rather than in your browser, it will be quite performant. Nonetheless, if you do need to convert all your temperature data into Fahrenheit, you might want to consider modifying the script to do the conversion before importing instead.

In the **Queries** tab next to **SELECT**, add a new operator by selecting **Math | math**. This will append a math calculation to the aggregated value. Delete the text in the operator and type the following into the field:

```
* 9/5 + 32
```

You should see the numbers change to substantially larger values. We've now converted the Celsius values into Fahrenheit. If you're curious, open **Query inspector** to examine the actual query. Now, go back to the **Standard options** section and set **Unit** to **Temperature | Fahrenheit (°F)** before you forget.

## Autoscaling the Y axis

One of the things you may have noticed when you click on a single data series in the legend is that the *y axis* scales automatically to accommodate the values for that series, then scales back when you display all the series. You may also have panels on your dashboard that have slightly different *y axes*:

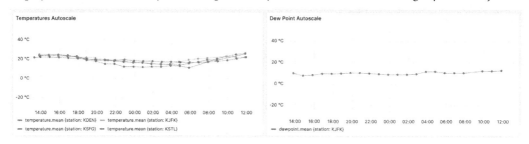

Figure 5.18 – Autoscaling the Y axes

This is less than ideal for a couple of reasons:

- The scale becomes inconsistent from one data series to the next
- It can be visually confusing if you choose to place different series in adjacent panels, each with its own scale

Let's disable that functionality (called *autoscaling*) by anchoring our minimum and maximum *y* values in the axis. Go to the **Standard options** section and set the following:

- **Min**: -30 (°F or °C)
- **Max**: 130 (°F) or 55 (°C)

As with all such things, you should be cautious about your choice of min and max. Too wide a range and your data will get squashed into a flat line. Too narrow, and Grafana will truncate the graph and leave some of your data running off the graph. You can either work empirically by determining the min and max of the data or use your best guess and start with something a bit too wide but narrow it later.

Alternatively, you can use the **Soft min** and **Soft max** settings in the **Axis** section. Setting **Min** and **Max** in the **Standard options** section will clamp the min and max values of the *y axis* to those values, regardless of the actual datapoint values; any value falling outside the range will not be displayed.

Setting **Soft min** and **Soft max** will also clamp the min and max values of the graph, but if a data point falls outside the range, the graph will adjust to make sure the value will still display.

It is tempting to scale each temperature graph with min and max values that seem appropriate to that dataset, but you risk confusing your viewers if the temperature distribution in one graph significantly differs from the distribution in the graph of another one.

Imagine one set of mostly extreme temperatures on a graph that is scaled so that they appear to be clustered in the middle of the graph. Now, take another set of mostly moderate temperatures that are on a graph that is also scaled so that they also appear to be clustered in the middle. A cursory glance might lead you to think the temperatures are the same in both graphs.

The lesson is to take the context of your data into account and establish a consistent scaling configuration for all graphs that display similar measurement types. If there is no similarity across your graphs or you can display the datasets inside the same graph, feel free to let the scale float.

## Dual y axis display

Another common scenario is one in which you need to display data with different units in the same graph. Often, the point is to show how data is correlated or related by visualizing the linear relationship between one or more data series to the correlated one. The rise or fall of values seems to match the rise and fall (or vice versa, if there is a negative correlation) of other values. We are going to create two graphs that demonstrate this property: one for relative humidity and another for wind chill.

### *Graphing relative humidity*

Create a new graph with the following queries:

- **A**: **measurement**: **relativeHumidity**
- **A**: **WHERE | station::tag = KSFO**

- **A**: GROUP BY | time($__interval) | fill(none)
- **B**: Same as **A**, but **measurement** set to **temperature**
- **C**: Same as **A**, but **measurement** set to **dew point**

Clean up the display by opening the **Graph styles** section and setting the following:

- **Style**: **Lines**
- **Show points**: **Always**

Now, you might (depending on the weather) see the relationship between dew point and temperature and the resulting relative humidity. It might not be that obvious because the temperature values range over 0-25, but the relative humidity value can be nearly 100. So, we're going to leave the *y axis* for relative humidity on the left axis and move the temperatures to the right axis. It won't change the data; instead, it will vertically rescale the temperature data independent of how the left axis data is scaled.

The easiest way to move a data series to the other axis is to select **Auto** by going to the **Placement** option under **Axis**. The first dataset axis will be on the left, and the rest will be on the right:

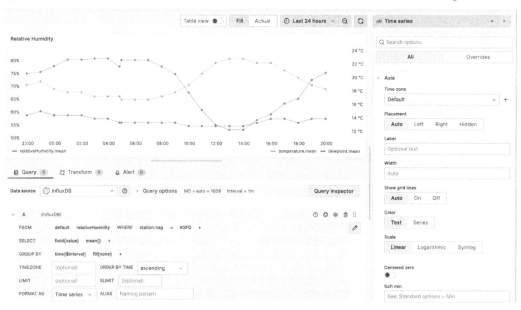

Figure 5.19 – Multiple Y axes in a single graph

If the axes don't behave at first, try switching back and forth between **Auto** and one of the other settings. You should now observe that since the temperature and dew point are close to the same values, the relative humidity moves closer to 100% and vice versa. Science!

## *Graphing wind chill*

The exercise for wind chill is similar. We'll create three queries:

- **A**: **measurement**: **windChill**
- **A**: **WHERE | station::tag = KDEN**
- **A**: **GROUP BY | time($__interval) | fill(none)**
- **B**: Same as **A**, but **measurement** set to **temperature**
- **C**: Same as **A**, but **measurement** set to **windSpeed**

Scroll to the **Graph styles** section and set the following:

- **Style**: **Lines**
- **Points**: **Always**

In the **Standard options** section, set the following option:

- **Unit**: **Temperature / Celsius (°C)**

In the **Axis** section, set the following option:

- **Placement**: **Left**

In this case, the derived value, windChill, is the same unit as temperature, so we'll move windSpeed over to the right *Y axis*:

1. Click + **Add field override**.
2. Select **Fields with name**.
3. Select windSpeed.mean.
4. Click + **Add override property**.
5. Select **Axis | Placement | Right**.
6. Select + **Add override property**.
7. Select **Standard options | Unit | Velocity / meter/second (m/s)**.

The following screenshot is what you will get as output:

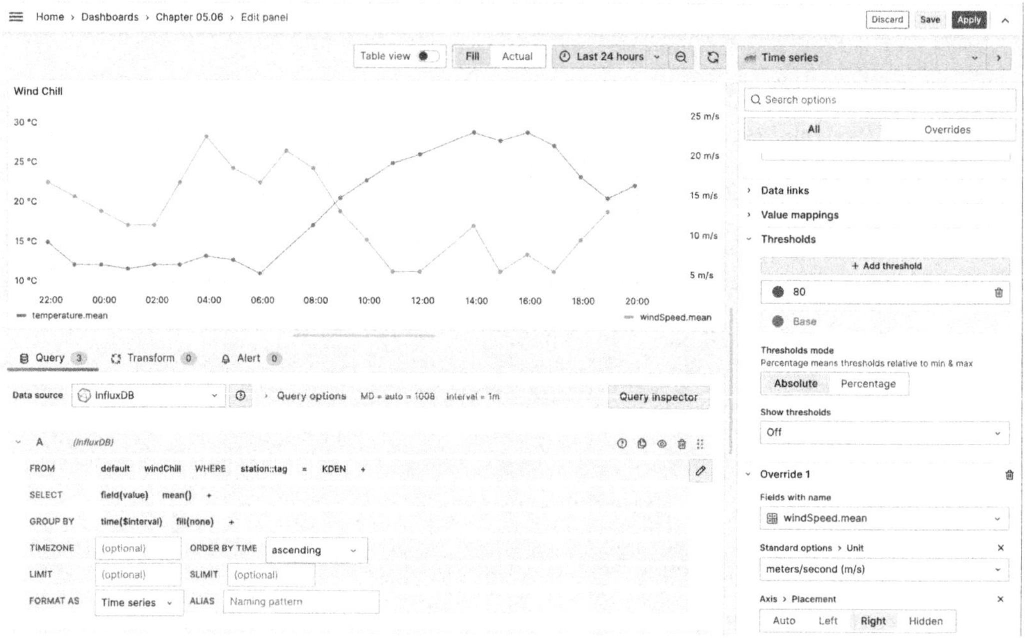

Figure 5.20 – Wind chill and temperature data

How I determined the units is left as an exercise for you! *Hint*: m_s-1 should be read as meter-seconds-1 or meters/second.

With this feature, you can pack a lot more information onto a single graph panel. Bear the following points in mind:

- The two axes will be scaled to fit the panel unless you explicitly set the $y$ minimums and maximums
- It should be natural to assume associations between the two sets of data

In the case of wind chill and relative humidity, we do want to associate the values because they are physically correlated. However, that may not always be the case.

## Working with legends

In the previous sections, we spent some time learning how to manage the horizontal and vertical display of our graph data. Now, we'll look at a key piece of graph display that is often overlooked: the legend. On many graphs, the legend seems like an afterthought, often floating in some non-specific whitespace where there's a convenient lack of data.

Grafana is somewhat more restrained about the legend. It can live below the graph (or to its right) and can take on a list or a table format; that's it. However, as we've seen, the label content of the graph can be set by the **Alias** field, and that field can be matched in field overrides. It's that functionality that we can leverage when interacting with the legend interface.

## Setting legend contents

Let's start with another graph, again for temperature. Use the following query settings:

- **FROM**: **temperature**
- **SELECT**: **field(value)** | **mean()**
- **GROUP BY**: **time($_interval)** | **tag(station::tag)** | **fill(none)**
- **Query options** | **Min time interval**: 1m

Scroll to the **Graph styles** section and set the following:

- **Style**: **Lines**
- **Points**: **Always**

In the **Standard options** section, set the following:

- **Unit**: **Celsius (°C)**

So, now, we have a nice graph of temperatures from four different stations, but we can't read the legend as it's down at the bottom of the graph:

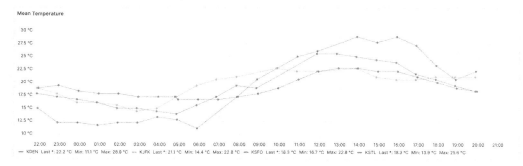

Figure 5.21 – Legend before table mode and right placement

Let's move it over to the right and format it. Open the **Legend** section and set **Mode** to **Table** and **Placement** to **Right**.

The legend now looks better, but it's now taking up a lot of space in the graph. Let's go ahead and remove some redundant information:

1.  Go to the **Panel options** section and enter Mean Temperature in the **Title** field.

2.  Go to the **Queries** tab and set **ALIAS** to $tag_station.

Now, the title carries the description of the metrics, and the legend just displays the station where the data was observed:

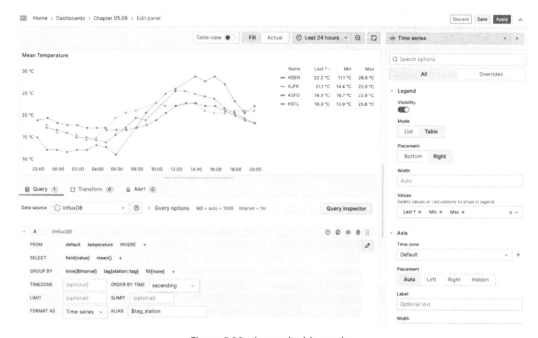

Figure 5.22 – Legend table mode

Nonetheless, you should only consider using this legend arrangement when you have the screen real estate to stretch out your graph and the legend, or the legend labels are relatively short.

## Enabling legend aggregations

You've probably seen TV weather forecasters note high and low temperatures as they run down a summary of the day's weather. We can produce similar information with the graph legend. In the **Legend** section, set the following values:

*   **Values**: **Last**, **Min**, **Max**

Next, we want the temperature time range to span only today, which is the time from midnight to now:

1.  Open the **Time range** menu dropdown.

2.  On the **Absolute time range** side, click inside the **From** text box or the adjacent calendar widget icon.

3.  From the calendar widget, click on today's date to set a starting date and time.

4.  Enter now in the **To** field to set the end date and time.

5.  Alternatively, you can select **Today so far** from the pulldown.

Here's what setting **Absolute time range** looks like:

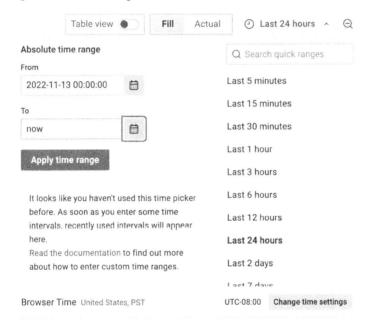

Figure 5.23 – Absolute time range

This sets the time range from midnight to now, the period during which the high and low temperatures are determined for a given day. Now, you have a little weather station!

If you want to sort the values based on a column value, simply click on the column header. Multiple clicks change the sort order and return it to the primary sort order (determined by the results of the query).

Of course, if you go back to the dashboard, you'll see how much real estate a legend takes up, especially if there are two dashboards on each row. You'll want to carefully consider whether you wish to set a table legend on the right. If so, you might want to significantly expand the width of the panel. As an alternative, you could leave the legend formatted as a table and set **Placement** to **Bottom**. Now, you can leave the panel width the same and drag the panel's height down until it is tall enough to display the full table.

## Summary

We've covered a lot of ground in this chapter. We wrote a simple Python ETL script to scrape data from a web-based API and import that dataset into InfluxDB. We also learned about key concepts behind time and field value aggregations. Then, we tried out different drawing styles and learned how to instruct Grafana on how to connect the dots when there is missing data.

We also set axis units, converted our data from one unit of measure into another, and displayed multiple series with different units on the same graph. Finally, we worked with the legend display to make it more space-efficient and aesthetically pleasing.

In the next chapter, we'll be diversifying our display panels so that they include panels that are more specialized in functionality. While these panels are somewhat more limited, they still complement the graph panel by characterizing data in truly unique ways.

# 6

# Shaping Data with Grafana Transformations

Now that you understand how to connect data source queries to visualizations, we're going to take a step back and look at one of the key features in Grafana's visualization pipeline: the **DataFrame**. A DataFrame is an object that contains data received from a data source query and provides the source data for visualization.

In this chapter, we will learn more about DataFrames, their role in how Grafana visualizes data, and how to manipulate them using Grafana's transformation operators. We will cover the following topics:

- About Grafana DataFrames and transformations
- Exploring the various transformation functions
- Expanding analysis with a transformation
- Chaining transformations into a visualization pipeline

First, we will answer the question of what a Grafana DataFrame is, its role, and how transformation operators affect it. Next, we will look at the most useful of the transformation operators and give some examples of how we might use them to modify a DataFrame. Finally, we will discuss some of the caveats around using transformation operators.

We will continue to use the code and data examples from *Chapter 5, Extracting and Visualizing Data with InfluxDB and Grafana*, so feel free to copy them over to a new chapter directory or use the code from this book's GitHub repository at `https://github.com/PacktPublishing/Learn-Grafana-10/tree/main/Chapter06`.

## About Grafana DataFrames and transformations

While it is easy to imagine that Grafana simply takes the results of one or more data source queries, and somehow feeds them to the panel visualization of your choice, the reality is a bit more complex than that.

Every query result from the **Query** tab is managed separately as an independent data series by Grafana. That way, you have full control over each series and how it may be displayed in a panel visualization.

Next, each of those datasets is packaged into a single object Grafana referred to as a DataFrame. If you are at all familiar with Excel or Google spreadsheets from the financial world, or pandas or Spark from the data science world, you already have experience with the concept.

A Grafana DataFrame is, like similar objects, a rows and columns (technically an array of arrays) data structure, with each row a combination of one or more columnar fields. Because the DataFrame is a consistent data structure, it can easily be abstracted for use by several different potential visualizations built to expect such a data structure.

When Grafana first introduced the DataFrame several years ago, the change was so significant that only a few visualizations were capable of taking advantage of it. That reality changes with each new release of Grafana as old visualizations are ported to DataFrames, and new ones are introduced.

Now that we've introduced this new data object that bridges to gap between queries and their visualization, let's introduce the mechanism by which we can manipulate the DataFrame itself, thereby altering what is visualized: **transformation functions**.

A transformation function is a simple operation that we perform on the contents of the DataFrame. Transformation functions have a variety of capabilities:

- Altering the structure of the entire DataFrame by adding or subtracting multiple rows or columns or by combining multiple DataFrames

- Modifying the contents or type of rows or columns

- Reducing multiple rows to a single value

- Sorting the order of rows or columns

- Converting rows into columns

- Forming a chain of transformations that pass data from one function to the next

As you can see, transformations provide many options for reconfiguring data before it's visualized. However, the ability to make significant changes to the structure of your DataFrame elevates the risk of also rendering it unusable if the resulting data structure doesn't correctly map into something that can be properly visualized.

# Exploring the various transformation functions

Now that we've looked at some of the capabilities of the transformation functions, let's take a closer look at some of the more commonly used transformations. Before we do that, however, let's identify the UI for the **Transform** tab to familiarize ourselves with the controls. This is one of the typical transformations in action:

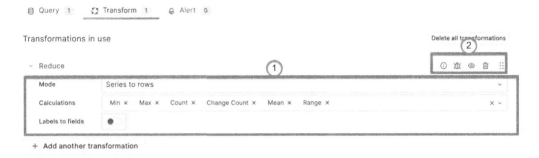

Figure 6.1 – Transformation UI

Besides the + **Add transformation** button, the **Transform** tab's interface bears some similarities to the **Query** tab's interface. Let's explore the UI, which is shown in the preceding screenshot with its main areas numbered for reference:

1.   The UI for setting the transformation parameters, which will vary from one to the next.

2.   Various controls for managing the transformation (from left to right):

   • Shows/hides help information about the transformation

   • Opens a debug window showing the data objects before and after the transformation

   • Disables/enables the transformation

   • Deletes the transformation

   • Draggable control for changing the order of transformations

At this point, I want to highlight a couple of important control aspects. First, the debug window can be very useful when you're troubleshooting various problems regarding how the transformation modifies data. At some point, you will run into a situation where the data just isn't what you expect, and it's helpful to see what is happening *under the hood*.

Second, the enable/disable control can be very helpful when you're trying to troubleshoot problems with the pipeline of transformations. Selectively disabling and enabling transformations can clarify where problems might arise, especially when there are several transformations chained together.

> **Note**
> If the visualization doesn't seem to be showing the correct data after you've added a transformation, the first step should be to click the **Refresh dashboard** button;  occasionally, the panel doesn't realize that it needs to update.

Now that we've got the preliminaries out of the way, let's proceed to our transformations. Next, we'll look at individual transformations to understand their function. After this, we'll see how data flowing through several transformations can be radically altered from what first comes out of a query.

## Installing the TestData data source

To follow along with the examples, you'll want to install the **Grafana TestData** data source. While transformations can handle a wide variety of potential DataFrames, especially ones that might arise from unique circumstances or are non-trivial to replicate for illustrative purposes, the **TestData** data source is simple and flexible enough for quickly conjuring up queries for our purposes.

To install the **TestData** data source, simply select **Connections | Add new connection** from the main menu, search for **TestData**, and click **Add new data source**. Here's what it looks like:

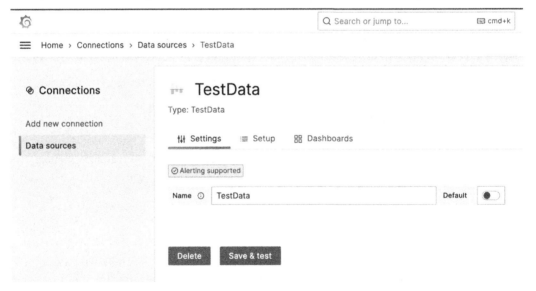

Figure 6.2 – The TestData data source

Now that we've set up a simple data source with test data, we can create some simple illustrations of how various transformations work.

## Selecting transformations

Determining the most appropriate transformation can be tricky – it's not always easy to visualize how transformations can modify your query data. Fortunately, the transformation selector displays handy symbolic representations of data manipulations performed by each transformation, as depicted here:

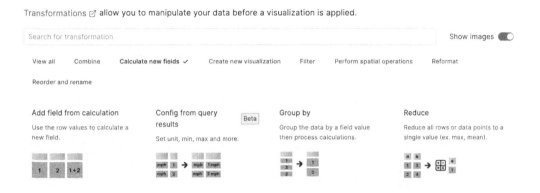

Figure 6.3 – Transformation images

While working with various transformations, the best way to analyze the results of transformations is to enable **Table view** from **Time series visualization** or switch to the **Table** visualization as not all the functions produce data that can be visualized with **Time series visualization**, and it will be easier to see the effects of transformations when using the more spreadsheet-like table.

## Adding fields

First, we'll look at a  transformation that adds new fields to a table of data.

### Adding a field from a calculation

This transformation can produce a new field by either mathematically combining two terms (two fields or a field and number) or performing a mathematical reduction operation on a single field.

For example, let's create a new query from **TestData**, select the **CSV File** scenario, and then choose the population_by_state.csv file. Here, we should see a table of states and their populations from 1980 to 2020.

This is what the query should look like:

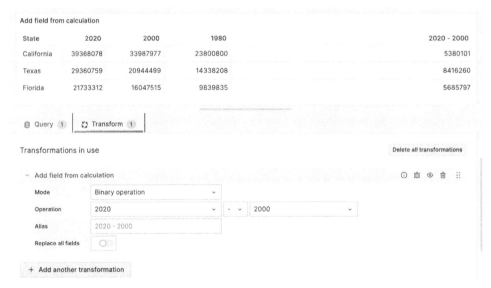

Figure 6.4 – Adding a field from the Query tab

To find out how much the populations grew from one 20-year period to the next, click on the **Transform** tab and select the **Add field from calculation** transformation from the list. Next, set the following transformation options:

- **Mode**: **Binary operation**

- **Operation**: **2020 - 2000**

Here, we just selected the **Binary operation** mode and then set each of the two fields and the minus (-) operator between them. We'll talk about the **Reduce** mode a little later, but for now, this is what should result from the transformation – a new field that's called 2020 – 2000 by default:

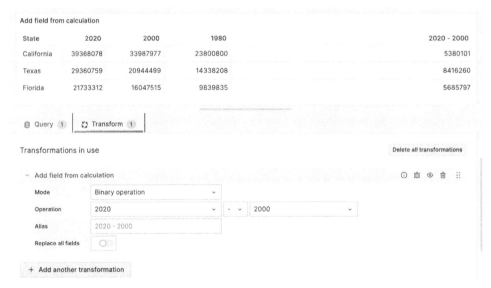

Figure 6.5 – Add field from calculation

You can fill in your field name in the **Alias** text field. If you want to replace all the fields with the one you just created, enable **Replace all fields**. You'll see this option a lot but use it with care as it will make your other fields unavailable to further transformations and visualizations.

Next, we will look at some of the transformations that can alter existing fields.

## Modifying fields

Field modification is used to alter a table's columns structure. With these transformations, you can change field types, rearrange field ordering, rename fields, or extract new fields by parsing them from the data.

### Converting field types

We need to convert field types when the data arriving from the query needs to be transformed so that it can be used by the visualization. Typically, this is useful when text time data isn't the correct type to be used in a time-series visualization, or the value of a field needs to indicate a Boolean value.

Let's look at a simple example of how this works.

Create a new query with the **TestData** data source. Select the **CSV Content** scenario. Now, add two CSV lines:

```
Time, Value
2022-04-05, 1000
```

You should have a small table with a single row containing **Time** and **Value**:

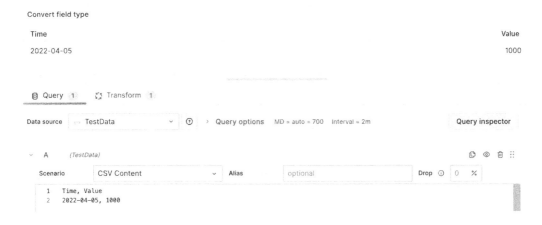

Figure 6.6 – The Convert field type query's results

Now, go to the **Transform** tab and add the **Convert field type** transformation function. For the first field, set **Field to Time, as type Time,** and leave the input format as-is (**YYYY-MM-DD**). For the second field, set **Field to Value as type Boolean**. If you are in the **Table** view or using **Table Visualization**, you should now see the Time field with an additional time of 00:00:00, indicating a properly parsed timestamp conversion. You should also see that Value is now true, confirming that the non-zero Value is now considered a Boolean true:

Figure 6.7 – The Convert field type transformation

## Organizing fields

When using the **Organize fields** transformation, field visibility can be turned on and off, the ordering of each field can be changed, and fields can be renamed. This is self-explanatory, but feel free to load up a query and experiment with the different possibilities.

## Extracting fields

Extracting from field data allows us to parse existing data and create new fields from the parsed data. Typically, the data is encoded in some way (JSON, for example) so that the new field name and associated data can be parsed out. This is useful when you're working with embedded JSON blobs that contain data that you wish to expose as field data. It's also useful for extracting key-value pairs embedded in text fields.

For this transformation, we'll use the same scenario as in the **Convert field type** example: **CSV Content**. This time, enter the following:

```
Text, Value
Time='2022-10-11 12:00:00' metric=3241.11, 323
```

You should see something similar to a two-field row with a text blob and a value:

Figure 6.8 – The Extract fields query's results

Next, create an **Extract fields** transformation. Set **Source** to **Text** and leave the rest as-is:

Figure 6.9 – The Extract fields transformation

Now, should see two new fields – one named `Time` and the other named `metric`. The transformation detected `key=value` patterns in the text and converted them into fields and values. Unfortunately, the type of the new `Time` field is `text` (as it is in the text blob), as is `metric`. We'll need to add another transformation to correct it; you know a transformation that could fix them, right?

## Labels to fields

Converting labels into fields takes data with embedded labels as key-value pairs and adds a new field with the name coming from the key and value of the field. This is a useful way of breaking embedded key-value labels out of a field and into their own field.

To set this one up, we will use the **USA generated data** scenario and **values-labeled-as-fields** mode. Add at least one field, such as **foo**, and one or more states. Your dataset should look like a row of data with US state abbreviations as fields:

Figure 6.10 – The Labels To fields query's results

Next, create a **Labels to fields** transformation. Set the fields to the following values:

- **Mode**: **Columns**
- **Labels**: **state**
- **Value field name**: **state**

It should look pretty much the same. We identified the labels for each field as **state** and then assigned the labels corresponding to **state** to be the field name for each value:

Labels to fields

| | AL | CA | GA |
|---|---|---|---|
| | 0.0865 | -0.998 | -0.700 |

⊟ Query  1     ⟨⟩ Transform  1

Transformations in use                                                    Delete all transformations

∨  Labels to fields                                              ⓘ  ☼  ◉  🗑  ⠿

Mode                    Columns    Rows

Labels                  state ✓

Value field name   ⓘ   state                        × ∨

Figure 6.11 – The Labels To fields transformation

Did anything happen? Well, yes it did, but it's a bit subtle. This is a good opportunity to examine what transformations do in detail, and not rely solely on what a visualization might show. To grasp what happened before and after the transformation, click on **Debug** to take a closer look at the data.

Use the disclosure triangle to open 0: Object in each fields: Array. On the left, open labels Object. By doing this, you can get a better look at the data:

Figure 6.12 – Labels to fields debugging

As shown on the left-hand side, each field contains `labels Object`, but no `name` attribute, so Grafana is happily using the label to describe the field. On the post-transformation side on the right, `labels Object` is now undefined, but `name` has now been defined, which the UI will use instead. It looks like nothing has happened, but a dramatic change has occurred.

It's worth noting that **Extract fields** and **Labels to fields** may seem like they do the same thing, but there is a subtle difference between the two. **Extract fields** detects key/value pairs in any field containing a text string with `key:value` or `key=value` patterns. In contrast, **Labels to fields** creates fields from labels already identified as such in the `labels` objects returned from the query.

## Filtering results

Filtering transformations take some criteria, such as a regular expression, and use it to remove results that match the pattern. You can filter by column names, row values, or panel queries.

### Filtering data by name

Filtering by name removes columns in tables, either by regular expression or direct selection. Using a regex is handy when you're facing a significant number of columns that need to be removed, and they all happen to have a string of characters in common (such as a common prefix or suffix).

Let's look at a quick example.

Open a new **TestData** data source query and select the **CSV File** scenario and the `flight_info_by_state.csv` file. You should have a pretty straightforward state-by-state dataset:

Figure 6.13 – The Filter data by name query's results

Now, go to the **Transform** tab and add a **Filter by name** transformation. Maybe you don't want to include the `Lat` and `Lng` fields because you won't be mapping them. In this case, you can simply uncheck them to remove the fields from the visualization:

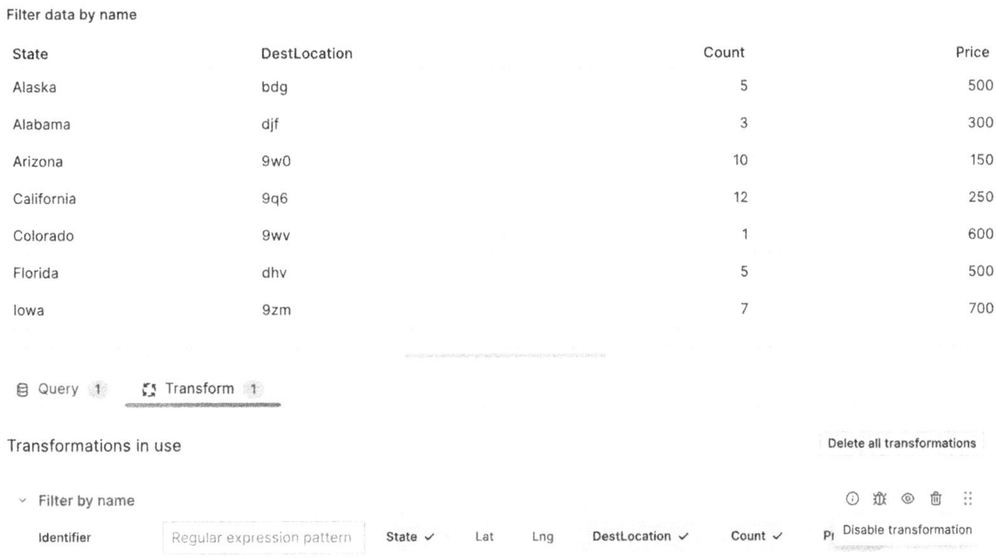

Filter data by name

| State | DestLocation | Count | Price |
|-------|--------------|-------|-------|
| Alaska | bdg | 5 | 500 |
| Alabama | djf | 3 | 300 |
| Arizona | 9w0 | 10 | 150 |
| California | 9q6 | 12 | 250 |
| Colorado | 9wv | 1 | 600 |
| Florida | dhv | 5 | 500 |
| Iowa | 9zm | 7 | 700 |

🗄 Query  1      ⌁ Transform  1

Transformations in use                                                        Delete all transformations

⌄  Filter by name                                                    ⓘ  🜏  ◎  🗑  ⠿

   Identifier    [ Regular expression pattern ]    State ✓    Lat    Lng    DestLocation ✓    Count ✓    Pᵣ  Disable transformation

Figure 6.14 – The Filter data by name transformation

Alternatively, suppose you wanted to keep *only* the `Lat` and `Lng` fields. You could add a regex such as `L.+` that would only match those fields (which would also become the only checked fields). Remember to use the *Tab* key to activate the field.

> **Tip**
> When using this transformation with time series data, remember to include the **Time** column by using the | (OR) symbol in your regex.

## Filtering data by values

Orthogonal to filter by name, filter by values removes rows from the table based on one or more specified conditions. Conditions are set to be either inclusive or exclusive and are set to work under all conditions or any condition.

For this example, we will work with the same `flight_info_by_state.csv` file as we did in the previous example, so you can either create a new query or work with the previous one.

For the transformation, use **Filter data by values**. Since we're looking at pricing data, let's only examine prices over $600. Set **Filter type** to **Include** and **Conditions** to either **Match any** (logical OR) or **Match all** (logical AND). Now, click **+ Add condition** to add a new filter condition. Set **Field** to **Price**, **Match** to **is greater or equal**, and **Value** to 600. You should now see only five or so rows of data. Play around with this one by adding additional conditions and see how switching **Filter type** and **Conditions** alter which rows match:

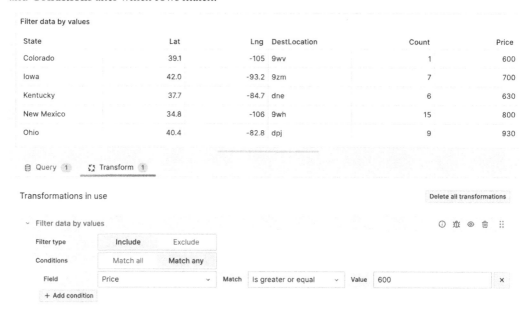

Figure 6.15 – The Filter data by values transformation

### Filtering data by query

If you wish to remove an entire query from the visualization, you can use the **Filter by query** transformation. It will present you with the names or refIDs of the data source queries, which can be turned on or off.

This is helpful when you don't have full control over the queries referenced by the panel or don't want to disable them for others referencing the panel's queries in their dashboard panels.

## Reducing rows

In the process of transforming your data, you may need to reduce the returned rows in the data series. Among the supported transformations are **Limit** and **Reduce**. Limit simply reduces the data series to a fixed number of rows, while Reduce works by aggregating or pivoting the data.

## Limit

Limit is handy if you only need a subset of rows for your visualization. You can often limit the results of any query by simply including a **LIMIT** option, but sometimes, it is more desirable to limit the results of all queries, perhaps because you are debugging and you don't want to see so many results.

## Reduce

Reduce performs an aggregation of each field on the rows of a query. It operates with two modes: **Reduce fields**, which simply replaces each field with the corresponding aggregations, and **Series to rows**, which pivots the results to rows of field names and aggregation values.

For example, let's look at the cryptocurrency CSV **open-high-low-close** (**OHLC**) chart for Dogecoin called `ohlc_dogecoin.csv`. Create a new **TestData** query and select the **CSV File** scenario and the `ohlc_dogecoin.csv` file:

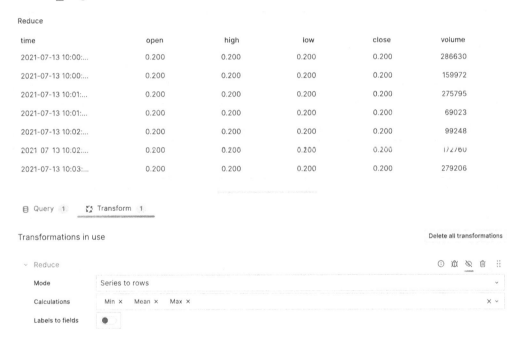

Figure 6.16 – The Reduce query's results

Next, create a **Reduce** transformation. Set **Mode** to **Reduce fields** and add **Min**, **Mean**, and **Max** to **Calculations** via the pulldown menu. Leave **Include Time** unchecked as the aggregation of timestamps has no meaning.

You should now see several fields, one for each calculation for each OHLC. Let's make it more readable by switching the mode to **Series to rows**. Now, there is one row per OHLC field, and one field for each calculation, which is much easier to process visually:

Figure 6.17 – The Reduce transformation

Now, let's move on from rows and columns to whole tables.

## Combining tables

Each query in the **Query** tab produces a single dataset, and consequently a single DataFrame. By using the panel's **Table view** option, you can see each data table corresponding to a data series by using the pulldown menu at the bottom of the table. However, you may want to join these series into a single dataset. To do that, you can use **Concatenate fields, Series to rows, Join by field**, or **Merge transformations**.

**Concatenate fields** is the simplest transformation and joins all the tables into a single one. **Series to rows** converts structured data into a traditional row-and-column format table. **Join by field** and **Merge transformations** are more sophisticated transformations that perform JOIN-like table combinations.

## Concatenating fields

Concatenating fields simply takes the fields in one table and adds them to the fields in another table to produce a single table. This is equivalent to taking the contents of one spreadsheet and copying it to the first available column alongside an existing one.

You have three ways to rename the fields:

- Copy the frame name to the field name

- Add a label with the frame name

- Ignore the frame name

## Series to rows

**Series to rows** takes tables of metrics and combines them into a single table with a `Metric` field containing the metric name and a `Value` field for the metric's value. You can see this in action by looking at the **USA generated data** scenario and the **timeseries** mode. Add the **foo** and **bar** fields, and at least one state:

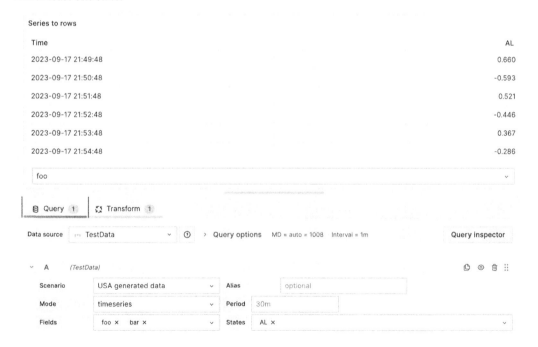

Figure 6.18 – The Series to rows query

Add the **Series to rows** transformation function. You'll see that the `foo` and `bar` metrics are now in the `Metric` field, and the `AL` value has been moved to the `Value` field:

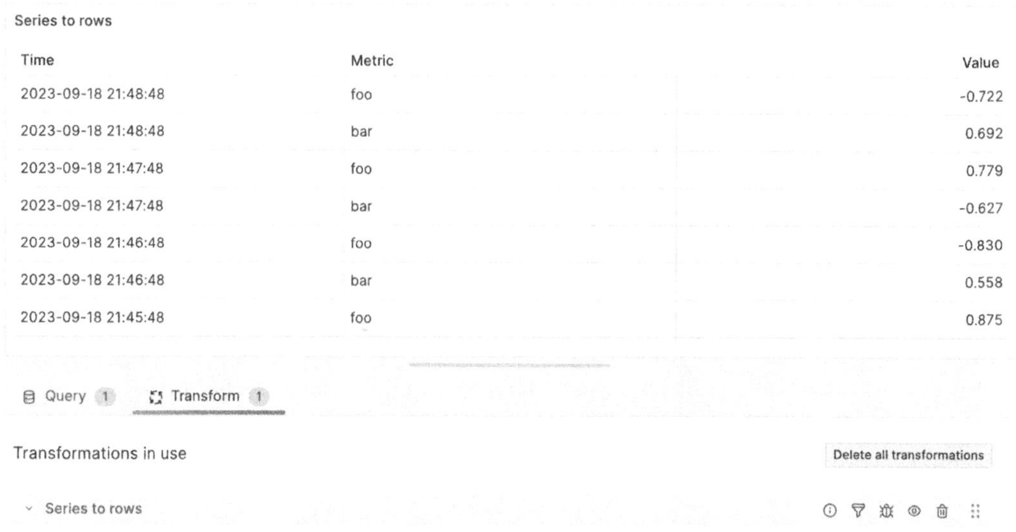

Series to rows

| Time | Metric | Value |
|---|---|---|
| 2023-09-18 21:48:48 | foo | -0.722 |
| 2023-09-18 21:48:48 | bar | 0.692 |
| 2023-09-18 21:47:48 | foo | 0.779 |
| 2023-09-18 21:47:48 | bar | -0.627 |
| 2023-09-18 21:46:48 | foo | -0.830 |
| 2023-09-18 21:46:48 | bar | 0.558 |
| 2023-09-18 21:45:48 | foo | 0.875 |

🗄 Query  1        ⟨⟩ Transform  1

Transformations in use                                          Delete all transformations

⌄  Series to rows                                    ⓘ ▽ ⚙ ◉ 🗑 ⠿

Figure 6.19 – The Series to rows transformation

This can help convert multiple metrics into a single table that you can then filter on the metric's name.

### Joining by field

Joining two tables by field is structurally similar to `JOIN` in SQL. It matches the data row by row with a common join field and then produces a single table with the combined fields. The key here is that the fields have to have the same name. Selecting **INNER** produces a table that only includes fields from the rows where the join field matches between the tables, while **OUTER** includes fields from the matching rows in both tables, but leaves the contents of any non-matching fields empty.

### Merging

Merging is a special kind of joining by field that combines all the attempts to join two tables by finding all fields that match between the tables then merges all the rows that match across those shared fields into a single row. While **Join by field** leaves the matching rows intact in the resulting set, **Merge** collapses matching rows into a single one. It sounds a little complicated, but it's straightforward.

We'll start by setting up two queries:

- **A Query Scenario**: CSV File

- **File**: population_by_state.csv

- **B Query Scenario**: CSV File

- **File**: flight_info_by_state.csv

You should now have two datasets, which you can view by flipping back and forth using the pulldown menu just below the table display:

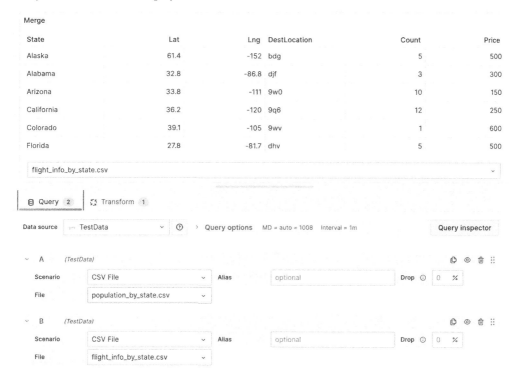

Figure 6.20 – The Merge query's results

Now, set up a **Merge** transformation. **Merge** is so powerful that it doesn't even bother to give you any controls! It checks both tables for matching field names, and when it merges the rows from both tables, including all fields from both tables, it identifies any rows that have the same values in the matching fields and combines them into a single row. Effectively, it's performing a **Join by field** transformation with **OUTER JOIN**.

In this case, the matching field in both tables is `State`, and the common values for the `State` field are `California`, `Texas`, and `Florida`, so their field data from both tables is merged. The rows for other states only get their fields from the one `flight_info_by_state.csv` table, thus the empty population fields:

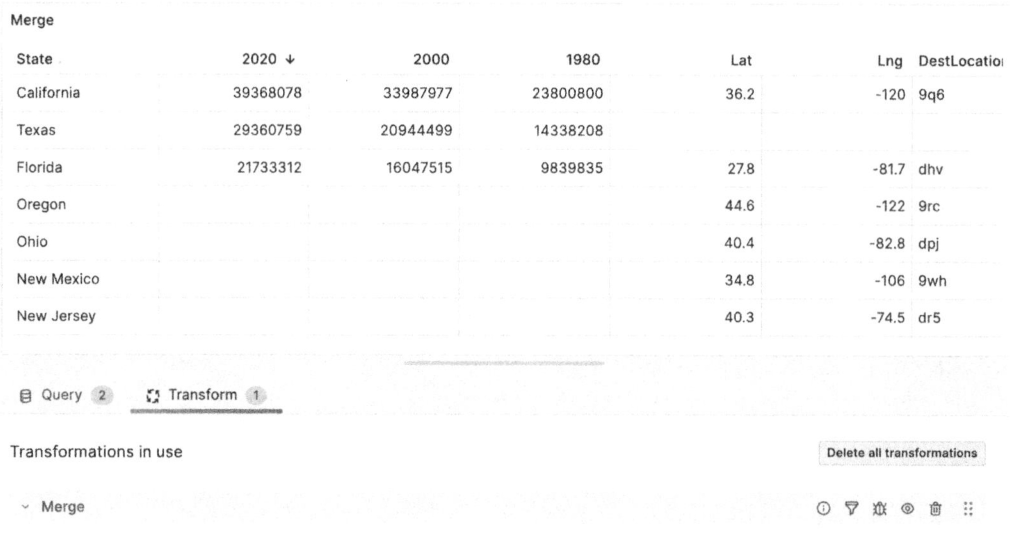

Merge

| State | 2020 ↓ | 2000 | 1980 | Lat | Lng | DestLocatio |
|---|---|---|---|---|---|---|
| California | 39368078 | 33987977 | 23800800 | 36.2 | -120 | 9q6 |
| Texas | 29360759 | 20944499 | 14338208 | | | |
| Florida | 21733312 | 16047515 | 9839835 | 27.8 | -81.7 | dhv |
| Oregon | | | | 44.6 | -122 | 9rc |
| Ohio | | | | 40.4 | -82.8 | dpj |
| New Mexico | | | | 34.8 | -106 | 9wh |
| New Jersey | | | | 40.3 | -74.5 | dr5 |

目 Query  2      ⟨⟩ Transform  1

Transformations in use                                                    Delete all transformations

  ˅  Merge                                                    ⓘ  ▽  ⚙  ◉  🗑  ⸬

Figure 6.21 – The Merge transformation

That wraps up our look at the transformation functions. We'll now apply some of these transformations to our real-world data to see their effects. First, we'll use just a single transformation to provide some simple insights into our data. Following that example, we will try a more complicated case where we'll build a chain of transformations to emulate a query.

# Expanding analysis with a transformation

Let's look at a relatively simple example of how we might use the transformation functions we've looked at to aid in analysis. We'll add a few queries, each representing a different metric, and then we'll use the **Reduce** transformation to create some aggregations of the data from each query, all in a tabular format.

The data we'll be using is derived from the ETL we created in *Chapter 5, Extracting and Visualizing Data with InfluxDB and Grafana*. Feel free to copy over the code from the `Chapter05` directory or use the `Chapter06` directory; both contain the same code.

The process is virtually identical to what we covered in *Chapter 5, Extracting and Visualizing Data with InfluxDB and Grafana,* so we won't go into the details. Here is the process in schematic format, so refer to *Chapter 5,* for the details:

1.  Run the Python `weather.py` script to download the NOAA weather data from a series of weather stations around the country.

2.  Create a new bucket in InfluxDB and name it `chapter06`.

3.  Generate an InfluxDB API key to access the InfluxDB from our script.

4.  Run the Python `weather.py` script with the API key from *step 3* to upload the weather data to the InfluxDB `chapter06` bucket.

5.  Set up an InfluxDB data source, using the API key for authentication and the `chapter06` bucket for the database.

6.  Set the time range to **Last 24 hours**.

At this point, you should have a database with weather measurements covering four different stations. Now, create a series of queries with the following setup:

*   **Query options minimum interval: 1m**

*   **FROM: default barometricPressure WHERE station::tag = KSFO**

*   **SELECT: field(value) | mean()**

*   **GROUP BY: time($interval) | fill(null)**

Now, repeat the same query but for the following measurements:

*   **temperature**

*   **dewpoint**

*   **relativeHumidity**

*   **windSpeed**

Feel free to try out a different station and a different collection of measurements. The following screenshot should give you an idea of what the query and data will look like:

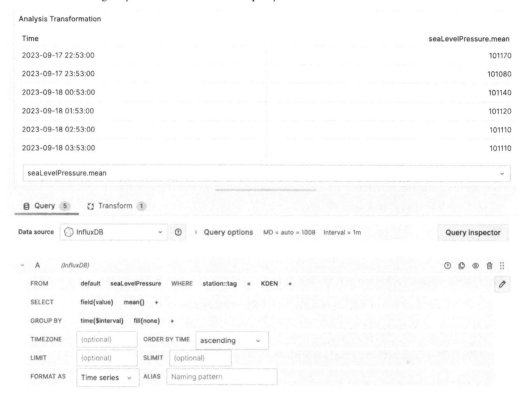

Figure 6.22 – InfluxDB query results

Next, create a **Reduce** transformation. Use these settings:

- **Mode**: **Series to rows**

- **Calculations**: **Min Max Mean Range Count Change Count**

- **Labels to fields**: **disable**

What we have now is a nice table of columns, each representing aggregations of our datasets, with each dataset now represented as a single row. Most of these aggregation calculations should be familiar but **Change Count** and **Range** might be new. **Change Count** is just the number of times the measurement changes during the time range, while **Range** is the span between the extremes.

Here's what mine looks like, but your values will undoubtedly be different:

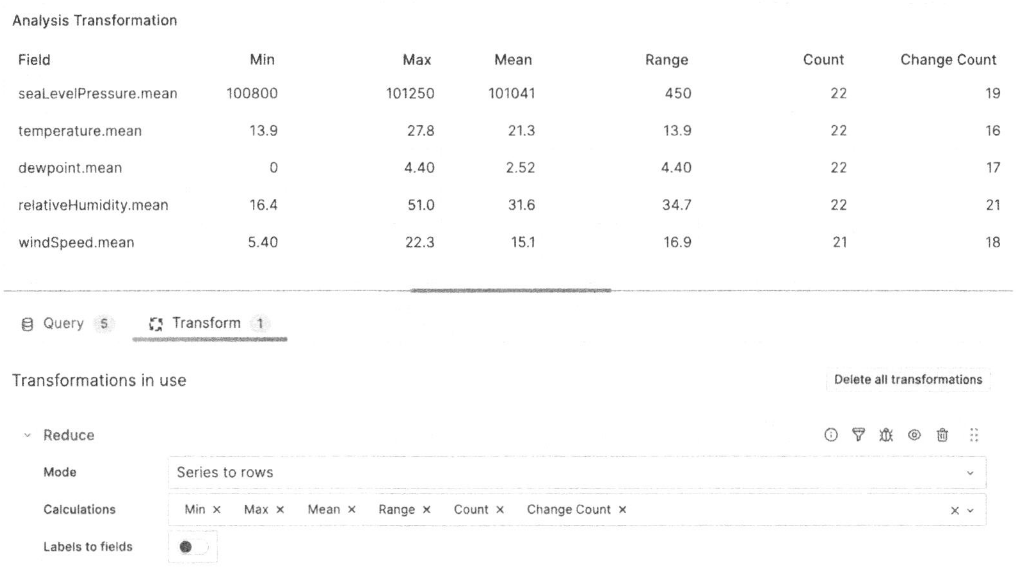

Analysis Transformation

| Field | Min | Max | Mean | Range | Count | Change Count |
|---|---|---|---|---|---|---|
| seaLevelPressure.mean | 100800 | 101250 | 101041 | 450 | 22 | 19 |
| temperature.mean | 13.9 | 27.8 | 21.3 | 13.9 | 22 | 16 |
| dewpoint.mean | 0 | 4.40 | 2.52 | 4.40 | 22 | 17 |
| relativeHumidity.mean | 16.4 | 51.0 | 31.6 | 34.7 | 22 | 21 |
| windSpeed.mean | 5.40 | 22.3 | 15.1 | 16.9 | 21 | 18 |

🗄 Query  5     ⟨⟩ Transform  1

Transformations in use                                        Delete all transformations

ⴠ Reduce                                            ⓘ ▽ ⚖ ◉ 🗑 ⠿

Mode            Series to rows                                          ⌄

Calculations    Min ×  Max ×  Mean ×  Range ×  Count ×  Change Count ×       × ⌄

Labels to fields    ●

Figure 6.23 – InfluxDB query with the Reduce transformation

Play around with this example – add more measurements to the query or add more calculations to the transformation.

Let's move on and try something a little more complex: multiple transformations.

# Chaining transformations into a visualization pipeline

Now that we've worked out how to add a single transformation to a set of query data frames, let's take it one step further and chain together a series of transformations to create a *visualization pipeline*. This example might seem a bit trivial, but it illustrates how to work through the process of manipulating tables via transformations to produce a result that facilitates a specific visualization.

In this case, we are going to take some of our weather data and make transformations to the query result, a use case that resembles a situation where you might not have the data in the format you want.

From there, we will do some transformations that will produce a dataset suitable for the time series visualization. The results will be along the lines of what we accomplished in the previous chapter, but the idea here is to get the results by transformation rather than by modifying the query. Remember, there may be occasions where you won't have control over the query, or the data returned by the query just won't be in the proper form.

We'll be working with a different set of queries, so open a new dashboard panel, if you haven't done so already. In the **Query** tab, create a single query and click on the pencil icon to open **Query Editor**. Type in this query:

```
SELECT mean("value") FROM "temperature" WHERE $timeFilter GROUP BY
time($__interval), "name"::tag, "cwa"::tag, "cwa"::tag, "county"::tag,
"station"::tag fill(none)
```

This is not a particularly complex query. It simply queries the temperature measurement along with time interval and groups by a set of labels so that we can include the labels as part of our data series:

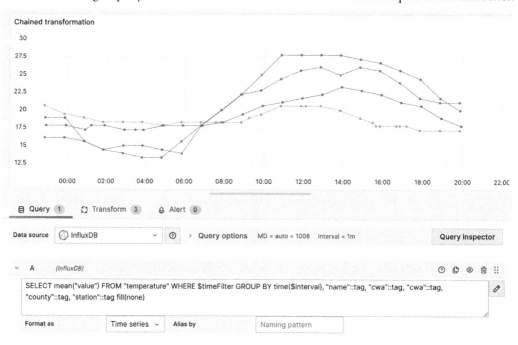

Figure 6.24 – InfluxDB Query Editor

You should see four data series; switching to **Table view** should make each accessible from the pulldown menu at the bottom of the graph, as well as a set of labels from each one. Remember that a *row* in InfluxDB is a combination of a metric measurement, a timestamp, and a combination of tag labels. Since the set of labels is identical for each station, the multiple GROUP BYs are still just grouping on each station – there's no hierarchy beyond the stations themselves.

Once you have switched over to the **Transform** tab, we'll start by switching to **Table view** so that we can see what effect our transformations have on the data. Our goal is to coerce our multiple datasets, one for each station into a single dataset with each station represented as a field, which we can then use to filter.

First, we will add a transformation to convert our labels (the GROUP BY in the query) into fields. Add a **Labels to fields** transformation:

- **Mode: Columns**
- **Labels**: **county cws name station**
- **Value field name: name**

The transformation should produce a table with several columns and our measurement column renamed to the name of the station. This has the effect of converting the labels in each data series into fields (**column** mode), enabling the county, cwa, name, and status fields, and assigning each station's name field to represent the temperature value field.

Next, we'll need to merge the four datasets, which should produce a single table with the same fields, so add a **Merge** transformation. This part has no options, but you should see the effect it has by the disappearance of the data series pulldown menu. Remember, you can always disable/enable the action of a transformation by clicking on the *eye* icon at the top right of the transformation.

Finally, we'll filter the table to only give us the data from a single station. Add the **Filter data by values** transformation and use these settings:

- **Filter type: Include**
- **Conditions: Match all**

Now, add a condition:

- **Field**: **station** | **Match**: **is equal** | **Value**: **KSFO**

Disable **Table view**. You should now see only a single data series graph. Go ahead and add a legend so that you can properly identify the data by name. Note that while you are only visualizing the single series corresponding to the station in the filter, the legend is mapping data returned by **Query**, which includes the four series created by GROUP BY:

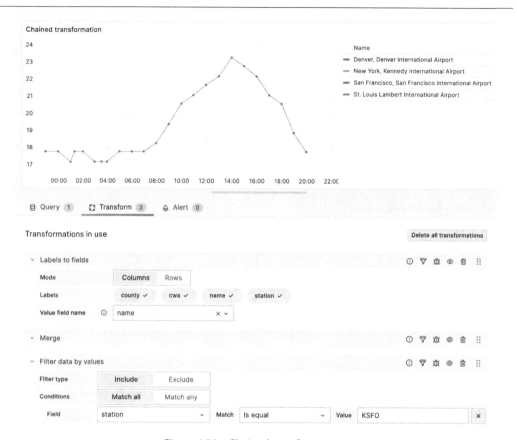

Figure 6.25 – Chained transformation

Clicking on **San Francisco, San Francisco International Airport** in the legend isolates it from the other data series, which are not visible due to the filter. To hide the other series in the legend, go down to the **Series Override** option, which was created by clicking on the series name in the legend, and turn off the **Legend visibility** option as well in the **Series | Hide in area** override:

Figure 6.26 – Series visibility

Again, this is a bit of a contrived example considering we have full control of the data structure from ETL ingress. However, this might not always be the case; you may be faced with a data source where you are only allowed access to a single massive DataFrame, and you will need to make some clever transformations to fit with your visualizations.

On the other hand, you may never need to open the **Transform** tab, but it's a good idea to keep up with the ever-changing population of transformations anyway – you never know what the future holds! As powerful as transformations are, there are a few things to watch out for. Next, we'll talk about some of their limitations.

## Limitations of transformations

There are some things to keep in mind while working with transformations. The Grafana documentation on transformations is a bit sparse, so you may find that some trial-and-error is required, and remembering these concepts may save you some difficulties.

### The visualization pipeline only runs in one direction

Data in the transformation pipeline originates in queries, is processed through transformations, and finally lands in your visualizations. While the results of a query can be accessed as a data source from a dashboard panel, if you enable the transformation in the query, you will indeed get the transformed data.

Unfortunately, that data cannot then be queried as if it were a true data source. If you wish to perform a query on transformed data, you will need to go back and modify the original query or add subsequent transformations, such as **Filter data by values**.

### Visualizations ultimately "see" the results of the last enabled transformation

When you create a transformation pipeline, all data flows downward from the top function to the bottom in the **Transform** tab. If your pipeline includes any transformations that would reduce the overall structure of the data (number of rows or columns, for example), it will be reflected in your visualization, provided the structure of the data is compatible with the visualization you select.

For example, don't add transformations that remove Time columns when using the time series visualization. If you don't wish certain transformations to be active, use the **Disable/Enable visualization** option on the transformation itself.

### Unless directly specified, transformations are applied to all query data series

The architecture of the Grafana visualization requires that all DataFrames pass through the transformations. If you wish to exclude certain queries from your transformations, you'll need to create them and their specific transformations on separate dashboard panels and then import them as **Dashboard** panel data sources. Alternatively, you can use **Filter data by query** as your first transformation and select only the data series you wish to further transform.

# Summary

We covered a lot in this chapter! We learned about the three components of the visualization pipeline – query, transformation, and visualization – and how the DataFrame is the key data structure that's processed by the pipeline. We explored the purpose of transformations and the many capabilities of transformation functions. We explored several common transformation functions with example use cases. We also tried out real-world transformations both singly and multiply in transformation chains. Finally, we examined some limitations of transformations.

In the next two chapters, we'll continue down the visualization pipeline and look at some of the more commonly used visualizations: the stat, gauge, and bar chart visualizations in *Chapter 7, Surveying Key Grafana Visualizations*; followed by the geomap and heatmap, and revisiting the table visualization in *Chapter 8, Surveying Additional Grafana Visualizations*. This will open up the possibility of creating more expressive dashboards than with just time series or table visualizations alone.

# 7

# Surveying Key Grafana Visualizations

In the previous chapter, we looked at transformation, the second stage of what I like to call the **visualization pipeline**. Before this, we looked at the initial stage of this pipeline, the data source query, and the final stage of the pipeline, visualization, specifically the time series panel visualization. In this and the following chapter, we'll concentrate almost exclusively on the visualization stage of the pipeline.

By now, Grafana has built an impressive number of panel visualizations, encompassing all manner of data and information presentation. Indeed, at the time of writing, there are nearly 25 visualizations in various stages of release, not including third-party add-on visualizations, which bring the total to over 100.

Up until now, we've been using the time series visualization in our panels, and not without reason; it's a powerful tool and has existed in some form since Grafana was initially released. While the time series panel is indeed powerful and versatile, it isn't the only way to display data in Grafana. Sometimes, you need a different way to present your data, and other times you may just want to break up a visually monotonous grid of graphs. For these reasons, Grafana provides other panel visualizations that can depict data in other ways. We'll examine a few of them in this chapter.

Rather than using mostly test data as we did in the previous chapter, we'll be leveraging the same real-world weather data we started ingesting back in *Chapter 5, Extracting and Visualizing Data with InfluxDB and Grafana*. In *Chapter 9, Creating Insightful Dashboards*, we'll take this *toolkit* of data and visualizations and build useful and attractive weather-based dashboards!

In this chapter, we'll first review the **table visualization** and how to use transformation functions to coerce our data into a useful form for our visualizations. We'll also look at the use of field overrides to help craft our visualizations, even when they encompass diverse data.

Then, we'll move on to the **stat visualization**, a useful panel visualization for condensing a data series into a single value. We'll also introduce value mapping, a technique for mapping numerical data into text.

Along with the stat visualization, which is useful for displaying a single value, we'll also look at the **gauge** and **bar gauge** panels, which, like stat, are useful for single values; but rather than just displaying a value, they also incorporate a physical gauge.

The following topics will be covered in this chapter:

- Launching server Docker containers
- Setting up the InfluxDB database
- Reviewing the table visualization
- Introducing the stat visualization
- Adding visual interest with a gauge
- Going linear with a bar gauge

## Technical requirements

Before we get started with our visualizations for this chapter, we'll need to set up InfluxDB and Grafana servers, install a Python Docker container to run our scripts, and ingest some data into an InfluxDB bucket. These steps are like those we used when we introduced this data ingestion pipeline back in *Chapter 5, Extracting and Visualizing Data with InfluxDB and Grafana*.

> **Note**
>
> Tutorial code, dashboards, and other helpful files for this chapter can be found in this book's GitHub repository at `https://github.com/PacktPublishing/Learn-Grafana-10/tree/main/Chapter07`.

## Launching server Docker containers

We'll go through the same steps as in the previous chapters:

1. If you haven't done so already, shut down any services you might have left running from other chapters by executing the following (in the other chapter directories):

   ```
   % docker-compose down
   ```

2. Run the `docker-compose` script that will download the Grafana and InfluxDB containers and then launch them. The `docker-compose.yml` file is available in the `Chapter07` directory of the GitHub repository for this book:

   ```
   % docker-compose up -d --pull missing
   [+] Running 3/3
     Network chapter07_default    Created       0.0s
   ```

```
Container chapter07-grafana-1   Started     0.5s
Container chapter07-influxdb-1  Started     0.5s
```

# Setting up the InfluxDB database

Here, we'll log in to our InfluxDB server, set up an initial account and bucket, and generate an API key so we can connect to it from our Python script and the Grafana data source.

## Initializing the InfluxDB server

Log in to the InfluxDB UI at `http://localhost:8086`. If you haven't already set up the instance, you'll see a prompt to perform the initialization:

1.  Set the username to whatever you like.

2.  Add a password (a minimum of eight characters minimum).

3.  Choose an organization name, in our case, `LearnGrafana`.

4.  Create a bucket, in our case, `Chapter07`.

## Generating an API token

Generating an API key is a very straightforward process. You'll need this token in order to access the InfluxDB server from your script:

1.  Click on **Load Data | API Tokens**.

2.  Click the gear icon on the right side of the user you created previously and select **Clone**.

3.  Click on **Copy to clipboard** to save the API token string.

4.  Save the API token in a safe place as you won't be able to see it again without going through the process to create a new one.

## Configuring the InfluxDB data source

Now that we have our InfluxDB server ready to accept data, let's get Grafana ready to communicate with it:

1.  Open your browser to the Grafana app and select **Connections | Add new connection** from the main menu.

2.  Search for **InfluxDB** and click on it.

3.   Click on **Add a new data source**. Fill out the following form fields:

- **Name**: InfluxDB

- **Query Language**: **InfluxQL**

- **HTTP | URL**: http://influxdb:8086

- **Custom HTTP Headers | Header**: Authorization

- **Custom HTTP Headers | Value**: Token <API Token>

- **Database**: Chapter07

---

**Note**

Make sure there is a space between Token and the API token.

---

Your data source configuration should look like this:

Figure 7.1 – InfluxDB data source

Click on **Save and Test** to confirm you can successfully connect to the InfluxDB server.

## Building the Python Docker container

We'll use the same process we used in *Chapter 5, Extracting and Visualizing Data with InfluxDB and Grafana*, to build and run our Python scripts:

1.  Before we build our Docker container, let's make a couple of small tweaks. We are going to make our Dockerfile more agnostic to the script it runs, and not install the script in the container. We now only need to copy one thing into the container, and that's the `pip` installation requirements file `requirements.txt`. Our new Dockerfile should look like this:

    ```
    FROM python:3

    WORKDIR /usr/src/app

    COPY requirements.txt ./

    RUN pip install --no-cache-dir -r requirements.txt

    ENTRYPOINT [ "python" ]
    ```

2.  To build it, type the `docker build` command:

    ```
    % docker build --pull --tag python/ch7 .
    ```

3.  Now, we want to tidy things up, so we're going to put our `weather.py` file in an `app` directory; we also need to map that directory into the container. Finally, it's a good practice to name (with `--name`) the container so we don't confuse them. Confirm the Docker container can properly execute the `weather.py` script by running it with the `--help` option:

    ```
    % docker run --rm \
        -v "$(PWD)/app:/usr/src/app" \
        --name python_ch7 python/ch7 \
        /usr/src/app/weather.py --help
    ```

You should see a nice help message.

## Loading the data

From here, we just need to pull down our data from the **National Weather Service** (**NWS**) and then load it into our InfluxDB server bucket:

1.  To keep things tidy, we want to put our data in its own `data` directory. That means another volume map. Execute the script to download data from four weather stations:

```
% docker run --rm \
    -v "$(PWD)/app:/usr/src/app" \
    -v "$(PWD)/data:/data" \
    --name python_ch7 python/ch7 \
    /usr/src/app/weather.py \
    --output /data/wx.txt \
    --stations KSFO,KDEN,KSTL,KJFK
```

2.  Execute the script to upload the data file to InfluxDB:

```
% docker run --rm --network=host \
    -v "$(PWD)/app:/usr/src/app" \
    -v "$(PWD)/data:/data" \
    --name python_ch7 python/ch7 \
    /usr/src/app/weather.py \
     --input /data/wx.txt \
    --db Chapter07 --token <API_TOKEN>
```

That should get us started with a dataset in our InfluxDB server, and a Grafana data source to query it. Let's move on to the visualizations, starting with a review of the table visualization, which you may have already seen back in the previous chapter.

# Reviewing the table visualization

Our first visualization is one of the least graphically interesting of the visualizations you will encounter in Grafana. We introduced it in the previous chapter, mostly to expedite the visualization of raw data. However, there is more to the table visualization, so let's see how it is not simply a tool for displaying raw data (although it does do that too).

As you may know, the table visualization provides a spreadsheet-like data grid that is useful if you want to see the rows of actual data, along with any aggregations. When rolling up your data series into an aggregation or troubleshooting transformation functions, the table visualization can be more useful than the table view.

## Comparing aggregations

To give you an idea of how the table visualization compares to the time series visualization legend table, let's create a panel and have it display a set of common aggregations. Create a new panel and select **Table** from the visualization pull-down menu. Pick **Today so far** as the time range. Enter these parameters for the **Query** tab by using the raw query editor (pencil icon):

- `SELECT mean("value") FROM "temperature" WHERE $timeFilter GROUP BY time($__interval), "station"::tag, "name" fill(none)`
- **Format As**: **Time series**

- **Query options | Min interval**: 1m

Once you've added a query, you should see our raw data:

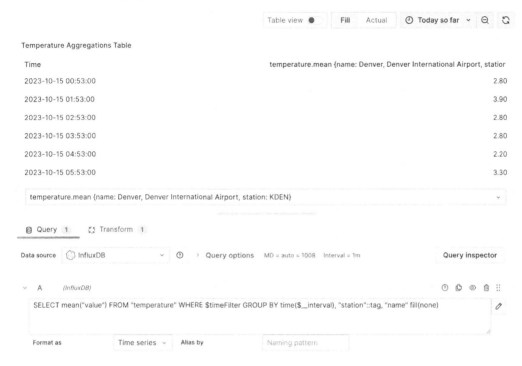

Figure 7.2 – Table visualization query

The table panel's interface works much like a standard spreadsheet application:

1.  Sort the rows by clicking on a column.

2.  Adjust the column widths by dragging the column divider.

3.  Select a different series with the drop-down menu at the bottom of the panel.

When working with the table visualization, it's often best to start with the raw data and work it into the form you wish to display in the table. In this case, we'd like to display a set of aggregations over the time period, so we will go to the **Transform** tab and add a function to reduce each time series to an aggregation:

1.  On the **Transform** tab, click on **Reduce**.

2.  Set **Mode** to **Series to rows**.

3.  In the **Calculations** text field, delete the **Max** value already in the field, then click and select **Mean** from the dropdown.

After adding the transformation function, it should look like this:

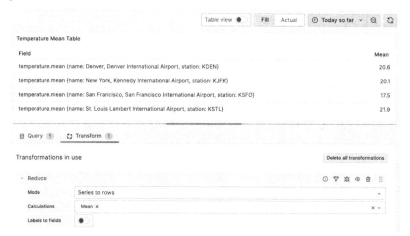

Figure 7.3 – Query with reduce transformation

You should now see that our rows of time series data have been replaced with a single row for each data series, and all the associated values are aggregated by **Mean**. Go ahead and use the dropdown next to the **Calculations** setting to add the **Min**, **Max**, and **Last\*** columns.

If you were to duplicate this panel, disable the `Transform` function, convert the visualization into a time series, and set the legend values to **Min**, **Max**, **Avg**, and **Last\***, you would see matching entries:

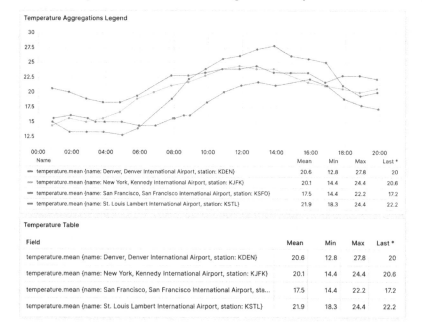

Figure 7.4 – Comparing time series legend and table aggregations

Let's go ahead and set the **Unit** under **Standard options** to **Celsius (ºC)** for our table values. Now, the **Standard options** setting applies to all the column fields in the table, so if we happen to have fields with different units, we are going to need some way to set some fields with one unit and others with a different unit.

If you recall from *Chapter 5*, *Extracting and Visualizing Data with InfluxDB and Grafana*, the look of a specific data series in the time series visualization can be set by a **field override**. We'll use the same technique to override those settings for specific fields.

## Overriding field settings

In the case of the table visualization, field overrides are intended to provide a generalized mechanism for formatting virtually any cell or group of cells in the table. Here's the simple, yet powerful, process:

1. Add an override.

2. Set a matcher for one or more field names.

3. Set one or more of the override properties found under the **Field** tab.

Let's walk through an example to illustrate how to use the column styles to format multiple cells at once. We want to display a barometer reading for several stations, as well as the temperature. We also want to set the cell to display a certain color depending on the barometric pressure, and we want to set a color for the text of the temperature cells.

First, we'll set up a query to pull in the data. Create a new panel and set the time range to **Today so far**. Set up an **A** query:

- `SELECT mean("value") /1000 FROM "barometricPressure" WHERE $timeFilter GROUP BY time(1h), "station"::tag fill(none)`

- **Format as**: Time series

- **Query options | Min interval**: 1m

Next, set up a **B** query:

- `SELECT mean("value") FROM "temperature" WHERE $timeFilter GROUP BY time(1h), "station"::tag fill(none)`

- **Format as**: Time series

- **Query options | Min interval**: 1m

In the **Standard options** section, set the color scheme:

- **Standard options | Color scheme: From thresholds (by value)**

Just a few things to note – we're pulling in two data series, one for the barometer reading and the other for the temperature reading:

- When the tags and timestamps are the same for the data point in different queries, Grafana will line them up in the same row of the table.

- Unfortunately, the timestamps are all over the place, and since we only care about hourly reading, we'll roll them up in GROUP BY into hour-long intervals.

- For the **A** query, we want to convert the value from pascals to kilopascals, so we'll divide the returned value by 1,000 using a math() operator.

- We also need to pivot the table so that each column represents a series. We'll use the **Join by field** transformation function on the **Transform** tab. Set **Mode** to **INNER** and set **Field** to **Time**, or leave it set to the default. This combines the fields of all rows with a matching **Time** field into a single row. **INNER** mode means any rows not matching are left out. Your table should now look like this:

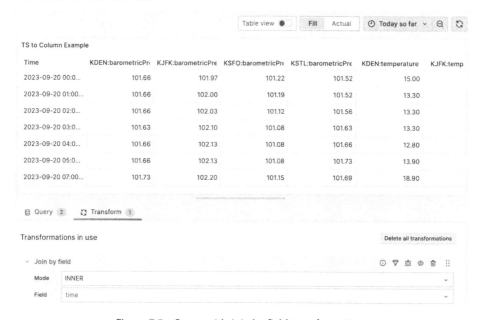

Figure 7.5 – Query with Join by field transformation

Now, at this point, we could set various options for units, name, color, and so on. But since we have two different measurements (pressure and temperature), anything we set at the panel level will apply to all columns, which wouldn't be appropriate. We want to change a few things for each column field:

- The units for the temperature and barometric pressure

- The names of the fields so that the columns look more readable

- The thresholds for the cell color
- Whether the cell background or text is colored
- The number of decimals for the temperature values

To accomplish this for all the columns, we'll need to make liberal use of field overrides. We just need to go through and match the column to a field override step by step, then for each override, configure a series of one or more override properties.

Our first field override will match the KDEN station `temperature.mean`:

1. Click + **Add field override**.
2. Click on **Fields with name** to add a new field name-based override.
3. Choose the field name from the scrolling menu – in this case, **temperature.mean {station:KDEN}**.

Then, we start adding our overrides beginning with the unit:

1. Click on + **Add override property** to add the field property to be overridden.
2. Click on **Standard options | Unit** from the scrolling menu.
3. Set the units in the fields to **Temperature | Celsius (°C)**.

Next up, we'll go ahead and change the field's name:

1. Click on ı **Add override property** to add the field property to be overridden.
2. Click on **Standard options | Display name** from the scrolling menu.
3. Change the field display name to KDEN temperature.

We set up some thresholds to modify the displayed color based on the temperature. We've already set the color scheme to be controlled by thresholds:

1. Click on + **Add override property** to add the field property to be overridden.
2. Click on **Thresholds | Thresholds** from the scrolling menu and add thresholds by clicking on + **Add threshold**:

   - **Blue**: Base
   - **Yellow**: 5
   - **Red**: 10

We next set the override for cell display mode:

1. Click on the + **Add override** property to add the field property to be overridden.
2. Select **Cell type** mode from the scrolling menu.

3.  Set the mode to **Colored text**.

The last thing for this column is to set the number of decimals to 1:

1.  Click **+ Add override property** to add the field property to be overridden.

2.  Select **Standard options | Decimals** from the scrolling menu and set the value to 1.

Now, we'll do something similar for one of the barometric pressure columns. I won't go through this step by step; you just need to know the basic override settings:

- **+ Add field override | Fields with name: barometricPressure.mean {station:KSFO}**

- **Override Property | Standard options | Unit: Pressure / Kilopascals (kPa)**

- **Override Property | Standard options | Display name:** `KSFO barometer`

- **Override Property | Thresholds:**

  - **Red: Base**

  - **Orange:** `100.8`

  - **Green:** `101.8`

- **Override Property | Cell type: Colored Background**

## Setting a display name

As you go through the process of setting the **Standard options | Display name** override you do have some control over how to set the text, especially if you don't want to explicitly specify the name in a field override. While you can type any arbitrary text into the **Display name** field, if you wish to customize it with text specific to the data series, you should use these special Grafana variables described in the Grafana documentation. Let's assume we have a series that measures `windSpeed` and is grouped by the `station` tag:

- `${__field.displayName}`: The name of the field along with any labels. Can be overridden by the **Alias By** field:

  - `${__field.displayName}|windSpeed {station: KSFO}`

- `${__field.name}`: The name of the field column from the SELECT query. Same as `${__field.displayName}` but without the labels:

  - `${__field.name}|windSpeed`

- `${__field.labels}`: The labels on the field column. Same as `displayName` without the name:

    - `${__field.labels}` | `{station: KSFO}`
- `${__field.labels.X}`: `X` indicates the key for a specific label:
    - `${__field.labels.station}` | `KSFO`
- `${__field.labels.__values}`: An array list of the values of the labels:
    - `${__field.labels.__values} | KSFO, KDEN...`

As you can see, these variables give you many options for pulling meta-information from the query, so you don't always need to be explicit when you need to configure a descriptive text field such as **Display name**. This pattern will repeat itself as we learn more about Grafana. The notion of embedding variables in text fields becomes a powerful way to create abstract information in panel configurations, thus making them generalized for different queries, panels, and even dashboards.

Armed with this information, and as an additional exercise, go ahead and do the same for the other columns. You can simply replicate the settings for each column. Can you pull it off with just two field overrides? When you're done, you should see a table that looks something like the following:

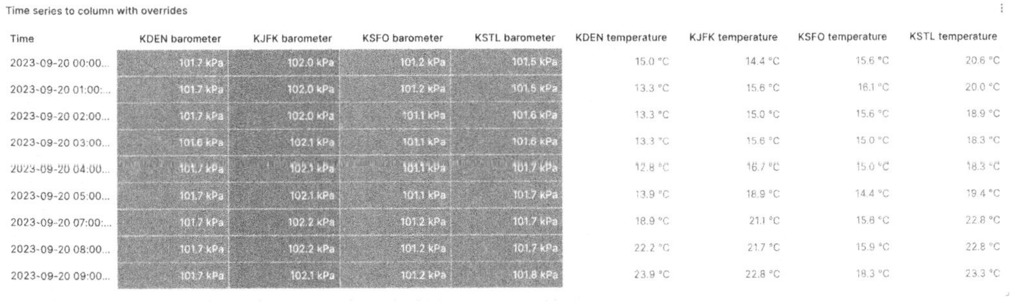
Time series to column with overrides

| Time | KDEN barometer | KJFK barometer | KSFO barometer | KSTL barometer | KDEN temperature | KJFK temperature | KSFO temperature | KSTL temperature |
|---|---|---|---|---|---|---|---|---|
| 2023-09-20 00:00... | 101.7 kPa | 102.0 kPa | 101.2 kPa | 101.5 kPa | 15.0 °C | 14.4 °C | 15.6 °C | 20.6 °C |
| 2023-09-20 01:00:... | 101.7 kPa | 102.0 kPa | 101.2 kPa | 101.5 kPa | 13.3 °C | 15.6 °C | 16.1 °C | 20.0 °C |
| 2023-09-20 02:00... | 101.7 kPa | 102.0 kPa | 101.1 kPa | 101.6 kPa | 13.3 °C | 15.0 °C | 15.6 °C | 18.9 °C |
| 2023-09-20 03:00... | 101.6 kPa | 102.1 kPa | 101.1 kPa | 101.6 kPa | 13.3 °C | 15.6 °C | 15.0 °C | 18.3 °C |
| 2023-09-20 04:00... | 101.7 kPa | 102.1 kPa | 101.1 kPa | 101.7 kPa | 12.8 °C | 16.7 °C | 15.0 °C | 18.3 °C |
| 2023-09-20 05:00... | 101.7 kPa | 102.1 kPa | 101.1 kPa | 101.7 kPa | 13.9 °C | 18.9 °C | 14.4 °C | 19.4 °C |
| 2023-09-20 07:00:... | 101.7 kPa | 102.2 kPa | 101.2 kPa | 101.7 kPa | 18.9 °C | 21.1 °C | 15.6 °C | 22.8 °C |
| 2023-09-20 08:00... | 101.7 kPa | 102.2 kPa | 101.2 kPa | 101.7 kPa | 22.2 °C | 21.7 °C | 15.9 °C | 22.8 °C |
| 2023-09-20 09:00... | 101.7 kPa | 102.1 kPa | 101.2 kPa | 101.8 kPa | 23.9 °C | 22.8 °C | 18.3 °C | 23.3 °C |

Figure 7.6 – Table with field overrides

Here's a couple of hints:

1. Use a **Fields with name matching regex** matcher so you only need to set one field override for all the columns from the same query.
2. Leverage variables in **Display name** to set the column using labels.

The answers can be found in the **Time series to column with overrides** panel on the **Chapter 07.02 Table Visualization** dashboard found in the `Chapter07/Dashboards` folder of the GitHub repo. That's it for the table visualization. This visualization, when coupled with transforms, has the potential to enable very sophisticated analysis.

# Introducing the stat visualization

After the time series visualization, the stat visualization may well be the next most used panel for several reasons:

- It makes it extremely easy to see the value at a distance
- It boils down a large dataset into a single value
- It can feature several visually important cues

## Creating a stat visualization panel

Let's get started with a simple panel using the stat visualization:

1. From a new or existing dashboard, create a new panel with the following query:

```
SELECT "value" FROM "temperature"
WHERE ("station"::tag = 'KSFO') AND $timeFilter
```

2. Set **Format** to **Time series**.

3. Now, go to the **Panel options** tab and select the **Stat** visualization. Next, we'll format the panel to represent the current temperature.

   Here's a look at the results of our query so far:

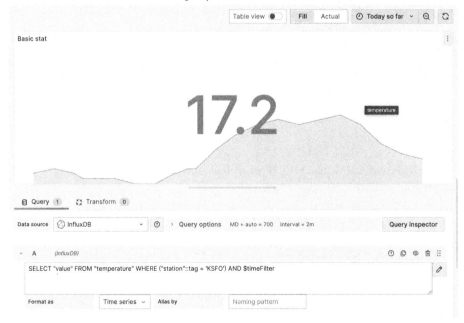

Figure 7.7 – Stat visualization query

4.  In the **Value options** section, set **Calculation** to **Last** *.

Let's see what our **Value options** and **Stat styles** settings look like so far:

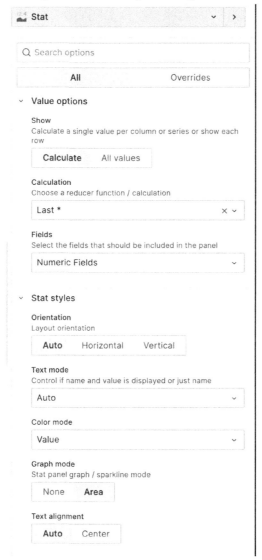

Figure 7.8 – Value options and Stat styles settings

5.  Under the **Standard options** section, we'll set the units and the number of decimals:

    *   **Standard options | Unit: Temperature | Celsius (°C)**
    *   **Standard options | Decimals**: 1

6.    Change **Color scheme** to **Single Color** and pick a color from the picker to the right.

Now, let's see what the panel settings should look like:

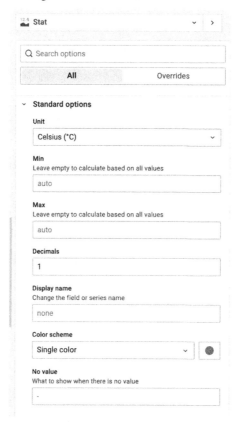

Figure 7.9 – Stat standard options settings

When you return to the dashboard, your panel should look something like this:

Figure 7.10 – Stat with area graph

To get a better idea of how the value of the stat panel relates to your data, I recommend you duplicate the panel and convert the copy into a time series panel. To duplicate it, click on the drop-down menu on the panel title and select **More...** | **Duplicate**. Select **Time series** to change the panel visualization. Now, when you configure the stat visualization, you can compare the value you see with the corresponding value in the time series visualization panel, as long as the two panels have the same query.

Here is where we come across a realization – the value of the stat panel is the representation of the entire data series in a single value. It may be an aggregation such as **Mean** or **Total**, or it may be a selection such as **First** or **Last**. Previously, in our time series panels, we worked with aggregations as well, such as mean(), but those only pertained to data groupings by time. In the case of the stat visualization, we can certainly use a calculation such as an aggregation for our query, but how do we derive its ultimate value?

Well, we aggregate again in the panel itself, so the stat calculation can be thought of as an aggregation on an aggregation! Now, as long as you don't try to create a meaningless calculation (such as a total of the temperatures), you should have no trouble working with the stat visualization; but be careful.

Along with the common settings found in many of the visualizations, the stat visualization has one specific to the visualization itself:

- **Stat styles**: Sets the graphical representation of the visualization

Let's take a closer look at the **Stat styles** settings.

## Setting stat styles

While the **Value** options are responsible for configuring the numerical display of the stat visualization, the **Stat styles** options configure the graphical aspects of the visualization, most notably the color and whether a graph is displayed on the panel. Bear in mind that there are typically two text objects to be displayed: the name of the numerical value (sometimes referred to as the title) and the value itself. Here are those options summarized:

- **Orientation**: Sets the stacking orientation of multiple values to either **Vertical** or **Horizontal**, or auto-sets it based on the shape of the panel.

- **Text mode**: Determines whether the name, value, name and value, or none are displayed. **Auto** displays them if space permits.

- **Color mode**: Sets either the **Background** color or the color of the displayed value.

- **Graph mode**: **None** hides, or **Area** displays, a sparkline graph at the bottom of the panel. The **Min** and **Max** settings under **Standard options** determine the extents of the values plotted on the graph, truncating the graph if necessary.

- **Text alignment**: **Auto** sets the name and value text to span the sides of the panel and **Center** places both at the center.

The last set of options specific to the stat visualization controls the size of the two objects, the text and the value:

- **Title**: Sets the size of the title text, if displayed

- **Value**: Sets the size of the value text, if displayed

## Defining value mappings in a stat visualization

Frequently, you will want to make a translation from quantitative information to qualitative information. The way Grafana accomplishes this is through **value mapping**. Put simply, value mapping converts numbers into text. A mapping identifies a text string with a value or a range of values. To create a value mapping, click **Add value mappings** in the **Value mapping** section.

To see how value mapping works, we're going to map a series of temperature ranges to familiar terms such as Hot and Cold. Duplicate your existing stat panel and add the following mappings in the **Value mapping** section:

- **Condition | Range | From**: 20, **To**: 30

  - **Display Text** | Hot

- **Condition | Range | From**: 10, **To**: 20

  - **Display Text** | Warm

- **Condition | Range | From**: 0, **To**: 10

  - **Display Text** | Cool

- **Condition | Range | Range | From**: -10, **To**: 0

  - **Display Text** | Cold

Your **Value mappings** section should look something like this:

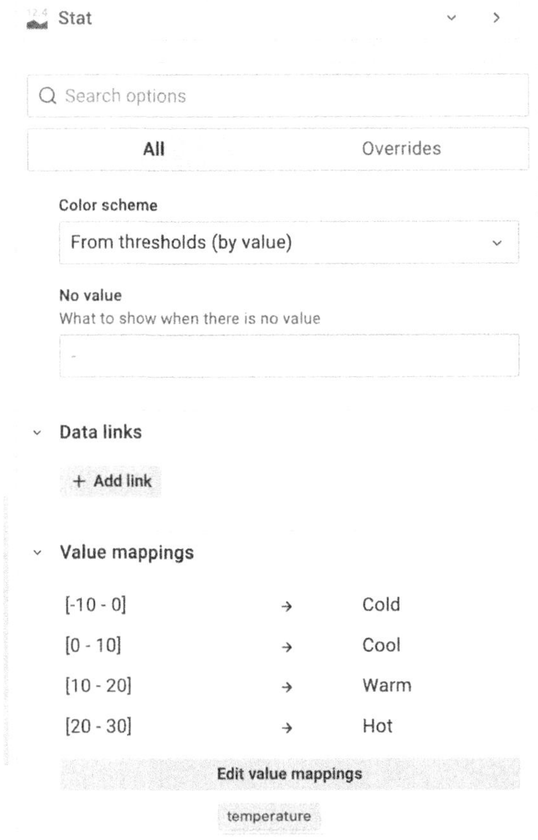

Stat

Q Search options

| All | Overrides |

Color scheme

From thresholds (by value)

No value
What to show when there is no value

-

˅ Data links

+ Add link

˅ Value mappings

| [-10 - 0] | → | Cold |
| [0 - 10] | → | Cool |
| [10 - 20] | → | Warm |
| [20 - 30] | → | Hot |

Edit value mappings

temperature

Figure 7.11 – Stat thresholds

Now, instead of a mysterious number for the temperature, you can display a more user-friendly textual description:

Stat with mapping

Figure 7.12 – Stat with value mapping

Now, let's build a fully tricked-out stat panel, with thresholds, background colors, and a graph – the works! Follow these steps:

1. Create a new panel and set up the following query:

```
SELECT mean("value") FROM "temperature"
WHERE $timeFilter
GROUP BY time($__interval), "station" fill(none)
```

2. Set **Format as** to **Time series**.

3. Set **Alias by** to `$col $measurement $tag_station`.

4. Set **Query options | Min interval**: `1m`.

5. Set the title in the **Panel options** section:

   • **Panel title**: `Station temperatures`

6. Configure **Value options**:

   • **Value options | Show: Calculate**

   • **Value options | Calculation: Last** *

7. Configure **Stat styles**:

   • **Stat styles | Orientation: Auto**

   • **Stat styles | Color mode: Background Solid**

   • **Stat styles | Graph mode: Area**

   • **Stat styles | Text alignment: Center**

8. Set **Standard options** on the **Field** tab:

   • **Standard options | Unit: Celsius (ºC)**

   • **Standard options | Decimals**: `1`

   • **Standard options | Display name**: `${__series.name}`

   • **Standard options | Color schema: From thresholds (by value)**

9. Next, we'll establish some thresholds:

   • **Blue: Base**

   • **Yellow**: `0`

   • **Red**: `10`

This is how my panel turned out:

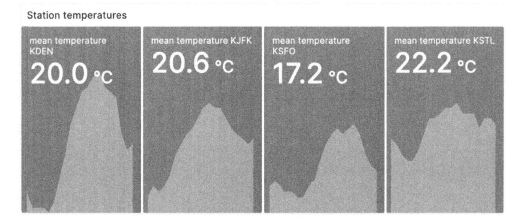

Figure 7.13 – Stat with multiple series

Now, try these exercises:

1. With a custom time range starting from midnight of the current day (**Today so far**), create a stat panel with a high temperature for the day.

2. With the same time range, create a stat panel to display the low temperature for the day.

You may find that when you compare an aggregated stat value with the same value in a time series visualization legend, they may not agree when querying across large time ranges. Why is that? Hint – use **Query Inspector** to examine the query sent to InfluxDB.

Here's why they may not agree: the $__interval variable, determined automatically by Grafana, is set on a per-panel basis. Consequently, if you compare the interval in the query for different panel visualizations (time series and stat), you'll find that they may calculate different intervals at large time ranges. This means that they may also end up aggregating different sets of points and thus display different aggregation values. This is something to be aware of. In the next chapter, we'll see how sharing queries between different panels can be a workaround for this problem.

## Adding visual interest with a gauge

The **gauge** visualization is intended to emulate the look of a semicircular analog graph, and it comes with a comprehensive set of controls for text and color. To get a feel for using this gauge, let's set up a set of wind-speed gauges, one for each station.

First, let's set up a query for the wind speed for all the stations. We'll use the `math()` operator to convert the value from the native meters per second setting to kilometers per hour:

*   `SELECT "value"  / 1000 * 3600 FROM "windSpeed" WHERE $timeFilter GROUP BY "station"::tag`

*   **Format as**: **Time series**

*   **Query options | Min interval**: `1m`

Now that we have a query, let's start by configuring the look of our visualization. We begin with **Value options**:

*   **Value options | Show**: **Calculate**

*   **Value options | Calculate: Last \***

We'll set up the gauge settings, but let's go over them first.

## Exploring the gauge options

The **Display** settings section determines the nature of what is displayed in the gauge. As with the stat panel, the following controls are available:

*   **Orientation**: Sets the stacking orientation of multiple values to either **Vertical** or **Horizontal** or auto-sets it based on the shape of the panel.

*   **Show threshold labels**: Displays the threshold labels on the gauge perimeter.

*   **Show threshold markers**: Displays the threshold colors on the gauge perimeter.

*   **Neutral**: Sets the neutral or base point on the graph where the fill begins. By default, it starts at the **Min** point.

Here are the gauge settings we want to set:

*   **Gauge | Show threshold labels**: On

*   **Show threshold markers**: On

Go ahead and set these **Standard options** settings next:

*   **Standard options | Unit: kilometers/hour (km/h)**

*   **Standard options | Min**: 0

*   **Standard options | Max**: 125

*   **Standard options | Decimal**: 1

*   **Standard options | Display name**: `${__field.labels.station}`

- **Standard options | Color scheme**: From thresholds (by value)

> **Note**
>
> You should take care to calibrate your gauge so that the **Min** and **Max** spread covers the general range of possible values. Setting **Min** too high or **Max** too low could result in an empty or full gauge, respectively. Setting **Min** too low or **Max** too high leaves too much of an empty gauge, making it useless.

We do want our gauges to give us some idea of how strongly the wind is blowing, so we're going to need visual cues as the wind speed rises. We can provide those cues with thresholds.

## Setting the threshold values and colors

Let's set up some thresholds for our wind gauge; just to keep things interesting, we'll map the Beaufort scale (`https://en.wikipedia.org/wiki/Beaufort_scale`) to a series of thresholds. The **Beaufort scale** is a measure of wind speed based on its observed effects on the environment, so we set up a threshold at each level of the scale to map the current wind speed to its corresponding level on the scale.

Starting from the bottom and working upward, we set the following thresholds, using the color names to guide our color picker selections:

- **White**: Base
- **Light blue**: 2
- **Medium blue**: 5
- **Blue**: 11
- **Light green**: 19
- **Medium green**: 28
- **Green**: 38
- **Medium yellow**: 49
- **Dark yellow**: 61
- **Light orange**: 74
- **Medium orange**: 88
- **Dark orange**: 102
- **Red**: 117

This is what your **Thresholds** panel should look like when you're done:

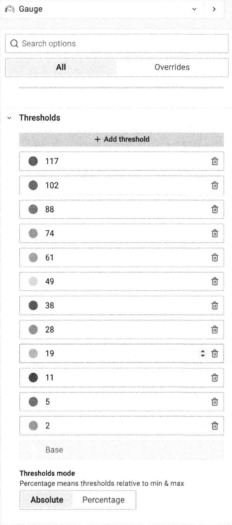

Figure 7.14 – Gauge with thresholds

**Note**

If you're reading a physical copy of this book, it might be a bit difficult to discern the gradations in color from a grayscale image. Rest assured; you can download the images in glorious full color from this book's website. Details can be found in the *Preface* section of this book.

Once we have the thresholds in place, this is what our final panel looks like:

Figure 7.15 – Gauge with multiple series

As an exercise, try creating value mappings for each level of the scale to the corresponding Beaufort scale values. Let's move on from the gauge panel to its close cousin – the bar gauge panel.

# Going linear with a bar gauge

The bar gauge panel has similar functionality to the gauge panel but produces its data in a substantially different form. It's designed to produce either vertical or horizontal bars, whose full extent represents a maximum quantity, and the length of the rendered bar represents what proportion of the extent is covered by the value. Think of the fuel gauge in a car that maps some value between *full* and *empty*.

## Exploring the bar gauge settings

Working with the bar gauge is not terribly different than working with the gauge or even the stat visualization. There are just three or four settings listed under the **Bar gauge** section:

- **Orientation**: Sets the **Vertical** or **Horizontal** orientation. **Auto** switches between the two depending on the size of the panel.

- **Display mode**: Sets the visual display, from a smooth **Gradient** to a segmented **Retro LCD** to a **Basic** colored bar.

- **Show unfilled area**: The **Basic** and **Gradient Display** modes also enable an option to fill the empty space with a gray color.

- **Min height/width**: Sets a minimum height or width for the bars.

## Building a bar gauge

We're now going to make a bar gauge to display relative humidity. This should be simple to grasp as relative humidity is measured as a percentage from 0 to 100:

1.  First, we set up our query in the editor:

    ```
    SELECT "value" FROM "relativeHumidity"
    WHERE $timeFilter GROUP BY "station", "name"
    ```

    - **Format as: Time series**
    - **Query options | Min interval**: 1m

2.  We next establish the value to be displayed:

    - **Value options | Show: Calculate**
    - **Value options | Calculation Value: Last** *

3.  We set the style of the bar gauge:

    - **Bar gauge | Orientation: Horizontal**
    - **Bar gauge | Display mode: Retro LCD**

4.  Next up is **Standard options**:

    - **Standard options | Unit: Percent (0-100)**
    - **Standard options | Min**: 0
    - **Standard options | Max**: 100
    - **Standard options | Decimals**: 1
    - **Standard options | Display name**: ${__field.labels.station}

5.  Finally, the thresholds:

    - **Blue: Base**
    - **Yellow**: 25
    - **Orange**: 50
    - **Red**: 75

**Thresholds** and **Standard options** should look like this:

Figure 7.16 – Bar gauge settings

This is what the resulting bar gauge visualization should look like:

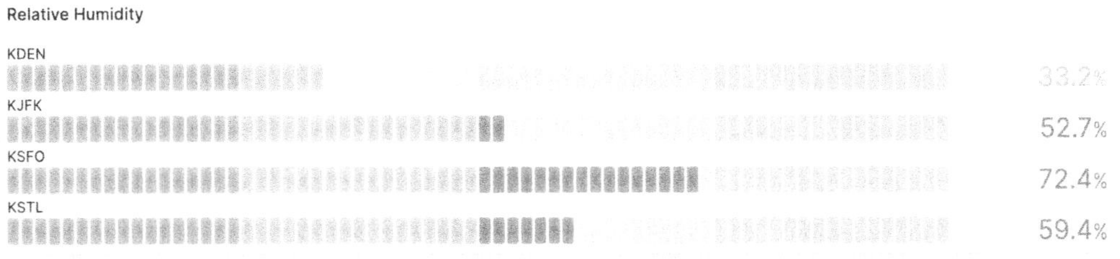

Relative Humidity

KDEN
33.2%

KJFK
52.7%

KSFO
72.4%

KSTL
59.4%

Figure 7.17 – Bar gauge

Have fun with the gauge and bar gauge panels! They can prove useful not only to provide visual excitement but also to complement your other panels, especially the stat visualization. From a distance, the large fonts, saturated colors, and dynamic graphics serve to draw the viewer's attention. Adding a time series panel then invites the viewer to take a deeper dive into the data.

## Summary

This concludes the survey of some of the most versatile panel visualizations Grafana offers. We reviewed the table visualization and introduced the stat, gauge, and bar gauge visualizations. Along the way, we learned more about field overrides, value mappings, and thresholds, all of which we will return to again and again over the course of this book.

In the next chapter, we will take a look at more panel visualizations, this time some of the newer visualizations, such as geomap, histogram, bar chart, and heatmap. This should prove to be interesting!

# 8
# Surveying Additional Grafana Visualizations

In the last chapter, we looked at several venerable panel visualizations. From the **table** to the **stat** and **gauge** visualizations, each is a key component in your visualization toolkit—the panel visualizations that you will combine on the canvas of the dashboard to highlight your data and tell its story.

In this chapter, we will be looking at a few of the newer visualizations, mostly concerned with the display of data in more qualitative ways, from the use of spatial mapping with the **geomap** visualization to categorical data in the **bar chart** and **heatmap** visualizations.

We'll also be working with a new dataset from our friends at the **United States Geological Survey** (**USGS**), a real-time catalog of earthquakes around the globe.

We'll first drop the data on a map, locating each earthquake in its spatial location with the geomap visualization. Next, we'll look at how to display earthquake category data with the bar chart visualization. Along the way, we'll create and display our own quantitative categories by using the **histogram** transformation and visualization. We'll display the histogram data using the bar chart visualization Finally, we'll visualize histogram data over time with the heatmap.

In this chapter, we will be launching both Grafana and InfluxDB servers via Docker Compose. We'll be running a modification of the **extract, transform, and load** (ETL) ingestion script used in previous chapters to gather weather data. The script will be run by Python installed in a Docker container.

Here's the list of topics that we will cover in this chapter:

- Launching server Docker containers
- Setting up the InfluxDB database
- Configuring the InfluxDB data source
- Exploring spatial data with geomap visualization
- Displaying category data with a bar chart visualization

- Displaying histogram data with the bar chart visualization
- Visualizing histogram data over time with the heatmap

So let's get started!

# Technical requirements

Before we create our visualization panels, we'll need to set up InfluxDB and Grafana servers, install a Python Docker container to run our script, and then ingest data into an InfluxDB bucket. These steps should recall those we used when we introduced this data ingestion pipeline back in *Chapter 5, Extracting and Visualizing Data with InfluxDB and Grafana.*

> **Information**
> Tutorial code, dashboards, and other helpful files for this chapter can be found in this book's Github repository at `https://github.com/PacktPublishing/Learn-Grafana-10/tree/main/Chapter08`.

Let's start!

# Launching server Docker containers

We'll go through the same steps as in the previous chapters:

1. If you haven't done so already, shut down any services you might have left running from the other chapters by executing the following:

   ```
   % docker-compose down
   ```

2. Run the Docker Compose script that will download the Grafana and InfluxDB containers and then launch them. The `docker-compose.yml` file is available in the `Chapter08` directory of the GitHub repository for this book:

   ```
   % docker-compose up -d --pull missing
   [+] Running 3/3
     Network chapter08_default       Created      0.1s
     Container chapter08-influxdb-1  Started      0.5s
     Container chapter08-grafana-1   Started      0.5s
   ```

This will start up our Grafana and InfluxDB services. Next, we'll need to configure our InfluxDB database server.

# Setting up the InfluxDB database

Here, we'll log in to our InfluxDB server, set it up with an initial account and bucket, and generate an API key so we can connect to it from our Python script and the Grafana data source.

## Initializing the InfluxDB server

Log in to the InfluxDB UI at `http://localhost:8086`. If you haven't already set up the instance, you'll see a prompt to perform the initialization:

1.  Set the username to whatever you like.

2.  Add a password (8 characters minimum).

3.  Choose an organization name: `LearnGrafana`.

4.  Create a bucket: `Chapter08`.

## Generating an API token

You'll need to generate a new token in order to access the InfluxDB server from our script:

1.  Click on **Load Data | API Tokens**.

2.  Click the gear icon on the right side of the user you created previously and select **Clone**.

3.  Click on **Copy to clipboard** to copy the API token string.

4.  Save the API token in a safe place as you won't be able to see it again without going through the process to create a new one.

# Configuring the InfluxDB data source

Now that we have our InfluxDB server ready to accept data, let's get Grafana ready to communicate with it:

1.  Open your browser to the Grafana app and select **Connections | Add new connection** from the main menu.

2.  Search for the InfluxDB data source and select it.

3.  Click on **Add a new data source**. Fill out the following form fields:

    *   **Name**: `InfluxDB`

    *   **Query Language**: `InfluxQL`

    *   **HTTP | URL**: `http://influxdb:8086`

    *   **Custom HTTP Headers | Header**: `Authorization`

- **Custom HTTP Headers | Value**: Token <API Token>

- **Database**: Chapter08

> **Note**
> Make sure there is a space between Token and <API Token>.

Your data source configuration should look like this:

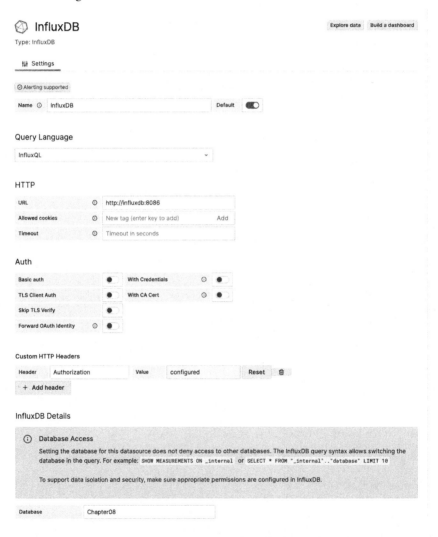

Figure 8.1 – InfluxDB data source

Click on **Save and Test** to confirm you can successfully connect to the InfluxDB server.

## Building the Python Docker container

Use the `requirements.txt` file in the `Chapter08` repository to create a Docker container with a Python build and the appropriate libraries:

1. From the repository directory, type the following:

   ```
   % docker build --pull --tag python/ch8 .
   ```

2. Confirm the script runs by executing it with the `--help` option:

   ```
   % docker run --rm \
       -v "$(PWD)/app:/usr/src/app" \
       --name python_ch8 python/ch8 \
       /usr/src/app/earthquake.py --help
   ```

# Exploring spatial data with the Geomap visualization

You should be all set up at this point to start downloading our data and then storing it in our InfluxDB bucket.

## Ingesting a new earthquake dataset

The USGS maintains a comprehensive earthquake catalog and it is freely available via a simple REST interface at `https://earthquake.usgs.gov/earthquakes/feed/v1.0/geojson.php`. The USGS provides continually updated catalogs of earthquakes, which are filtered by size over a variety of time periods ranging from one hour to one month.

To load the earthquake data, we only need to create a new Python script that is similar in structure to `weather.py` from *Chapters 5*, *6*, and *7*. We'll call this new script `earthquake.py`, and you can find it in the `Chapter08/app` folder of the repository. Let's take a quick peek at the changes we made from `weather.py` to `earthquake.py`.

### *Updating process_cli()*

The first big change occurs in `process_cli()`. First, we change the parser description:

```
def process_cli():
    parser = argparse.ArgumentParser(description="read earthquake
data from
    USGS into Influxdb")
```

Next, we replace the --station option to add two new options—one to select the minimum size of the earthquake and another to indicate the width of the time period covered by the catalog. Together, we'll use the values to construct our REST URL:

```
parser.add_argument("--size", dest="size",
    choices=['significant','4.5','2.5','1.0','all'],
    default='significant', help="earthquake size")
parser.add_argument("--window", dest="window",
    choices=['hour', 'day', 'week', 'month'],
        default='hour', help="earthquake time window")
```

## Updating main()

In main(), we'll need to create a new data dump subroutine called dump_eq_data(). It takes the command-line arguments for the size, window, and output file as parameters:

```
if args.output_file:
    dump_eq_data(args.size, args.window,
        args.output_file)
```

## Adding dump_eq_data()

The code for dump_eq_data() is very simple. First, we construct a request URL from the size and window parameters and get the response:

```
def dump_eq_data(size, window, output):
    url =
f"https://earthquake.usgs.gov/earthquakes/feed/v1.0/summary/
{size}_{window}
.geojson"
    response = requests.get(url)
    logging.info(response.url)
    if response.status_code != requests.codes.ok:
        raise Exception(f"dump_eq_data:
{response.status_code}:{response.reason}")
```

Next, we iterate through each feature in the response and extract the magnitude and depth for the metrics, as well as the latitude, longitude, and place names as tags. Here's the list of variables that we are interested in:

- lat: Earthquake epicenter latitude

- lon: Earthquake epicenter longitude

- place: The place name for the location of the earthquake epicenter

- alert: Earthquake alert level: None, Green, Yellow, or Red

- `mag`: Earthquake magnitude

- `cdi`: Earthquake **Community for Data Integration** (CDI) intensity from **Did You Feel It** (**DYFI**) responses

- `mmi`: **Modified Mercalli Intensity** measure

- `felt`: Number of people who felt the earthquake, based upon DYFI responses

- `sig`: USGS significance rating, from 0 to 1000

- `dep`: Earthquake depth

- `time`: Earthquake event time

Some of these variables are interesting but we won't necessarily reference them in our tutorials. However, you are welcome to try them out in your exercises to see what they look like and how they are distributed.

Here's the loop code:

```
for feature in response.json()['features']:
    measure = "event"

    properties, geometry = feature["properties"],
        feature["geometry"]

    timestamp = properties['time']
    lon, lat, dep = geometry['coordinates']

    mag = properties['mag']
    if mag is None:
        logging.error(f"bad event: {feature}")
            continue
```

Assemble the `tags`, `fields`, and `timestamp` components of our output line:

```
tags = [
    f"tag_latitude={lat}",
    f"tag_longitude={lon}",
    f"tag_place={escape_string(properties['place'])}",
    f"tag_alert={properties['alert']}",
]

fields = [
    f"magnitude={properties['mag']}",
    f"cdi={properties['cdi'] if properties['cdi'] else 0.0}",
    f"mmi={properties['mmi'] if properties['mmi'] else 0.0}",
```

```
                f"felt={properties['felt'] if properties['felt'] else
    0}",

                f"sig={properties['sig']}",
                f"depth={dep}",
        ]
            timestamp = properties['time']
```

Output each event as a line in our output file:

```
            data = f"{measure},{','.join(tags)} {','.join(fields)}
    {timestamp}\n"
            logging.debug(data)
            output.write(data)
```

That's pretty much all there is to it. Let's load up some data.

### Loading the data

From here, we just need to pull down our data from the USGS, and then load it into our InfluxDB server bucket:

1.  Execute the script to download earthquake data for a week:

    ```
    % docker run --rm \
        -v "$(PWD)/app:/usr/src/app" \
        -v "$(PWD)/data:/data" \
        --name python_ch8 python/ch8 \
        /usr/src/app/earthquake.py \
        --size all \
        --window week \
        --output /data/eq.txt
    ```

2.  Execute the script to upload the data file to InfluxDB. I've left out the API token as you will need to provide your own. Note that we pass in the millisecond precision per the USGS API documentation:

    ```
    % docker run --rm --network=host \
        -v "$(PWD)/app:/usr/src/app" \
        -v "$(PWD)/data:/data" \
        --name python_ch8 python/ch8 \
        /usr/src/app/earthquake.py \
        --input /data/eq.txt \
        --precision ms \
        --db Chapter08 \
        --token=<API_TOKEN>
    INFO:root:http://localhost:8086/write?db=Chapter08&precision=ms
    ```

Now that you have a new InfluxDB data source populated with a week's worth of earthquake data, let's see what this looks like when plotted around the world, shall we?

## Mapping earthquake data with the Geomap visualization

We'll begin as we usually do by creating a new panel on a new dashboard. Once you've created the panel, switch to the Geomap visualization. Add the following query:

```
SELECT "magnitude", "cdi" FROM "event"
WHERE ("magnitude" > 0) AND $timeFilter
GROUP BY "tag_latitude", "tag_longitude", "tag_place"
```

In **Format as**, select **Table**.

This sets up a query on earthquake magnitude and the CDI value for intensity, and GROUP BY makes the tags for latitude, longitude, and place available for use in mapping our data. There are quite a few options sections specific to the Geomap, and it can seem overwhelming. We can boil down the process of mapping geo data into four phases:

1.  Setting up an appropriate basemap – the map onto which our data will layer be layered. The basemap settings can be found in the **Basemap layer** section.

2.  Mapping the data points onto the base map. Typically, different kinds of information are drawn onto the base map in a series of layers. We'll be representing our data points as a series of "markers," but the **Map layers** section can handle many kinds of data.

3.  Styling the data point markers. Here, we can set various styling attributes to reflect different aspects of our data, from the shape of the marker to the size and even the color. These attributes are also found in the **Map layers** section.

4.  Setting global map controls. The **Map controls** section contains the majority of the global settings for our map. There are a few other settings that can be found in other sections as well.

Let us look into these four phases.

### Setting the basemap

The first order of business will be to determine the basemap. We don't want to just map our data point onto a blank background, do we? In the **Basemap layer** section, we can find several available basemaps. Currently, beyond the default map layer, there are also layers available from Open Street Map, the CARTO basemap, ArcGIS MapServer, or a tiled web map. Information about the use of tiled web maps can be found in the Grafana documentation and in the Wikipedia entry here: `https://en.wikipedia.org/wiki/Tiled_web_map`. We will be selecting **ArcGIS MapServer** with the **Topographic** server instance as it shows a lightly shaded relief map. Here's a look at the **Basemap layer** section:

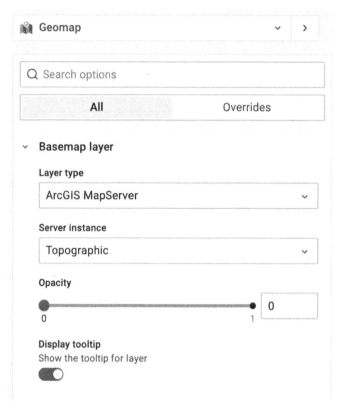

Figure 8.2 – Geomap basemap layer settings

## Mapping the data

Now that we have a basemap, we'll need to start overlaying map layers. In our case, we only plan on creating a single layer, but Geomap supports a number of different layer types from markers, heatmaps, and GeoJSON data (from which our earthquake data is derived), as well as the basemaps described previously. To add a layer of marker data, click on + **Add layer** and select **Markers**. A new layer is created, and **Layer type** is set to **Markers**.

From here, we need to indicate which series contains our geo data, and how to indicate where on the map to place the points. Select **Query A** under the **Data** option, if isn't already selected. If the latitude and longitude data were named as such, we could use the auto selection under **Location Mode**. However, we can use the **Coords** selection to give it a hint. Set the latitude field to **tag_latitude** and the longitude field to **tag_longitude**, and you should start seeing data points appear on the map display.

The **Map layers** section should look like this:

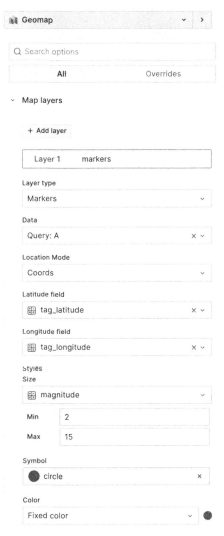

Figure 8.3 – Geomap Map layers settings

## Styling the data markers

Once we have our data points on the map, we can continue to use the settings under the **Map layers** section to style the data points. It is traditional for the USGS to scale the size of mapped data points to the magnitude of the earthquake, so we'll do the same, by setting the **Size** option under **Styles** to **magnitude**. We'll set **Min** and **Max** to 2 and 15, respectively, so small earthquakes aren't invisible and large ones don't overwhelm the map.

The traditional symbol on the USGS earthquake map is a circle, so we'll leave **Symbol** set to **circle**. Feel free to try out the other shapes (plane or star, for example) for fun. Feel free to choose a color that stands out. We'll also set **Fill opacity** to 0.6 as there can often be several earthquakes in roughly the same location, so we don't want to obscure them when we're zoomed out.

I want to set the color of each circle to be based on the CDI value. I'll set up a threshold for CDI intensity level IV, which is consistent with a moderate earthquake. We set up **Thresholds**, **Color scheme**, and **Color**:

- **Thresholds | Green: Base**
- **Thresholds | Red**: 4.0
- **Standard options | Color scheme: From thresholds (by value)**
- **Map layers | Styles | Color: cdi**

The value in the cdi field is checked against **Thresholds** (according to **Color scheme**) and the circle is colored based on where the value falls in **Thresholds**.

Finally, let's go ahead and set **Text label** for our data points. We want them to display the magnitude of the earthquake along with the circle. Here are some reasonable settings:

- **Text label | Source: Field**
- **Text label | Field: magnitude**
- **Text label | Font size**: 14
- **Text label | Y offset**: 12
- **Text label | Align: Center**
- **Text label | Baseline: Top**

Here's the **Styles** section of the **Map layers** section:

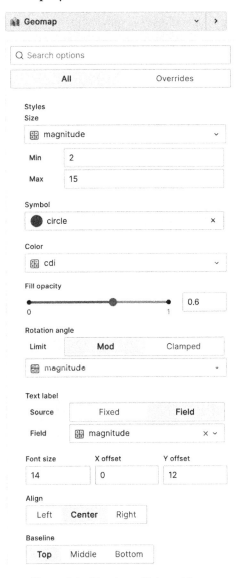

Figure 8.4 – Map layer Styles settings

That should give us nicely sized text offset just below the circle to make the text labels legible. You may have to zoom in a bit to get them to resolve properly. We've already got a nice-looking map with a lot of useful information. Let's add some finishing touches by setting our controls, the tooltip, and an initial location for the map.

## Finishing our map

We just need to tidy things up a bit and turn on some of the map controls. First, we name our layer by clicking on the layer label and edit the name to something descriptive, such as Earthquakes. Next, we enable the **Show legend** option to show the name of the layer.

Scrolling down to **Map controls**, let's turn on the following controls: **Show zoom control**, **Mouse wheel zoom**, **Show attribution**. Set **Tooltip** to **Details** so that when we hover over an earthquake, we'll be able to see important information. This is what **Map controls** should look like:

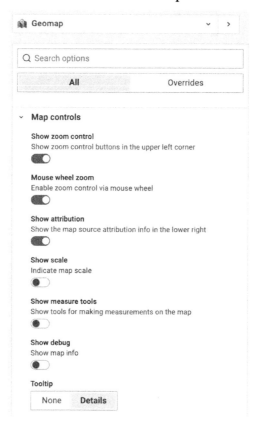

Figure 8.5 – Geomap Map controls

There is one last thing we should do: set the initial state of the map. It's a bit cumbersome to launch the dashboard and have the Geomap visualization show us the entire globe, which forces us to scroll around and zoom into the part of the world we are interested in. We can set an initial zoom point, so the map always starts at an interesting point.

To do this, simply zoom and pan the map to the point you find interesting (I picked out the state of California) and click **Use current map settings**. You can certainly enter specific **Longitude**, **Latitude**, and **Zoom** values but if you don't know those values, this will be easier. This is a look at the final results for the panel:

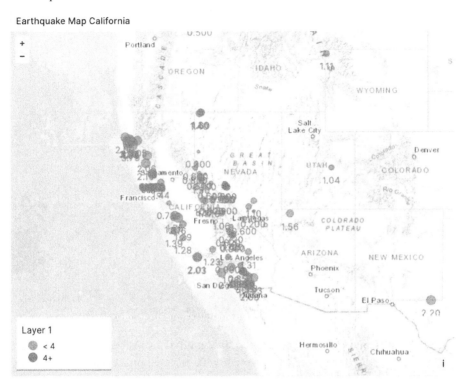

Figure 8.6 – Geomap with mapped earthquakes

That takes care of our Geomap visualization. Play around with the different settings in the Geomap. Think about the weather data from our previous chapter. Is there a way to map weather data with a Geomap visualization? Check out the API documentation from the **National Weather Service** (**NWS**) to see whether latitude and longitude are available for weather stations.

We're not done with earthquakes, however! Next up, we're going to look at earthquakes from a more analytical perspective with our next visualization, the bar chart.

## Displaying category data with a bar chart visualization

We will now move on to talk about the bar chart visualization. This visualization is designed to display a simple bar chart reflecting the relationship between a set of categories and their associated values.

Basically, it works much like you would expect a Microsoft Excel spreadsheet graph to work by taking a series of text value pairs and graphing their relative sizes.

An example from the Grafana documentation using the `TestData` data source should make things clear. Here, we select the **CSV file** scenario and the `browser_marketshare.csv` file option. By setting the visualization to **Bar chart**, you should see a graph of various web browsers and their relative market share depicted as a bar chart.

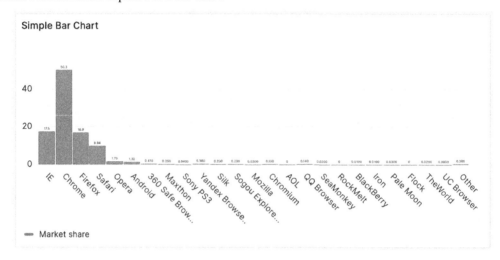

Figure 8.7 – Browser market share bar chart

Switching to **Table view** shows the dataset is nothing more than a series of browser/market share category/value pairs. Can we do something similar with our earthquake data? That is what we will explore in this section.

Unfortunately, the data we received from the USGS isn't available to us as a series of category/value rows. First, the data is formatted as a series of timestamped rows of earthquake metrics and associated tagging. Second, our metrics are only tagged with a single low-cardinality (fewer unique values) field: `tag_alert`. This makes it a bit of a challenge to identify a data case that lends itself to a bar chart visualization.

Nevertheless, let's give it a try by looking at the `alert` field data in context. Open a new panel and create an InfluxDB query:

- **Query** (raw query mode): `SELECT "magnitude" FROM "event" WHERE ("magnitude" > 0) AND $timeFilter GROUP BY "tag_alert"`

- **Format as**: **Time series**

Switch to **Table view** to see the data. You should see a series of rows with a `Time` field and the associated event magnitude. These rows will be in one or more data series, each corresponding to a different `tag_alert` value. They should be from a set that includes `None`, `Green`, `Yellow`, and `Red`. We know this because our query explicitly grouped the data by the `tag_alert` tag value.

What we need to do is find a way to aggregate the count of rows in each data series, and then associate that with the tag value. It just so happens that we spent a chapter working on how to transform data returned from a query. Could we use the **Transform** tab to perhaps create a series of transformations that ultimately produce the data in the form we're looking for?

Why yes, we could! There are several ways to accomplish the task, but the simplest is to use a **Reduce** transform:

1. Open the **Transform** tab, and switch to **Table view** so you can see the data in raw form.
2. Select the **Reduce** transformation and set **Mode** to **Series to rows**.
3. Remove the **Max** calculation and replace it with `Count`. You should be able to bring it up in the drop-down menu by typing the initial characters.
4. Switch on **Labels to fields** so our `tag_alert` labels become a new field containing its values. You should end up with a few rows with three fields: `Field`, `tag_alert`, and `Count`.

Switch off the table view so we can configure our bar chart to display the results of our handiwork.

At this point, all we need to do is tell the bar chart what to display as the **X-axis** categories. The bar chart will then look for a single numerical field to calculate the size of the bars. In the **Bar chart | X-axis** drop-down menu, select **tag_alert**. That's it! You should see a nice bar chart with a big value for None, and hopefully other bars, depending on characteristics of the earthquakes that occurred during the time range:

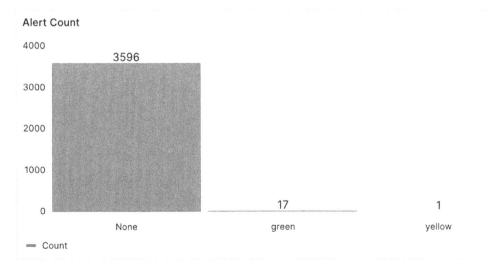

Figure 8.8 – Alert level bar chart

The bar chart has a handful of configuration values for tailoring the display. Let's review them; you should try them out on your panel to see what effect they have:

- **X-axis**: This option identifies the field containing the categories. If there is only one such field of text values, it will be used by default.

- **Orientation**: Sets up whether **X-axis** should be **Horizontal** or **Vertical**. The **Auto** option will select the orientation based on the height of the panel.

- **Rotate bar labels**: In the **Vertical** orientation, this sets the rotation of the **X-axis** labels to improve readability when they are tightly packed.

- **Bar label max length**: Sets the maximum length of the **X-axis** labels.

- **Bar labels minimum spacing**: Sets the spacing between **X-axis** labels.

- **Show values**: Determines whether to display the value above the bar. **Auto** disables the value when there is no room.

- **Stacking**: Setting **Normal** places additional numerical fields on top of each other. **100%** displays them proportional by percentage. Use this only if the values represent parts of a whole.

- **Color by field**: Use the values in the selected field to determine the bar color. The colors can then be set in the **Color scheme** option in the **Standard options** section – for example, by a standard color palette or from **Thresholds**.

- **Line width**: Sets the width of the bar's outline.

- **Fill opacity**: Sets the opacity of the bar's fill.

- **Gradient mode**: Sets the color gradient.

The remainder of the settings are consistent with their counterparts in other visualizations as you've previously seen in, for example, the time series.

## Understanding histograms

Let's take this a step further. Can we create something with the bar chart that handles the other earthquake data fields, especially the non-text ones? What can we do if we want to answer the question, *Are there more or less high-magnitude earthquakes compared to low-magnitude ones?*

There is a way to divide up all the possible values of a field into coherent groups, perform some aggregation (such as `Count`), and then graph the results. Believe it or not, we've been working with a similar concept this whole time. Recall the `$__interval` variable that governs the width of the `Group By` option, `time`. In that case, we are grouping all the data points within a consistent time interval and performing an aggregation before graphing the result as representing the entire interval. This gives Grafana the ability to consistently display data at a variety of timescales.

What we are describing is similar to the idea behind a histogram. A histogram is a division of a dataset into even groupings called **bins** or **buckets**, which are then represented by an aggregation of all the values, usually by `count`. In the time series visualization, the bins are set by `$__interval` and are represented by the aggregation in the query. In the **Histogram** visualization, the bins are by value and are represented by `count`.

To get a feel for the histogram, open a new panel and create a `TestData` query from the **CSV** file scenario (you may need to add a `TestData` data source connection). Use the `gdp_per_capita.csv` file. Switch to the **Histogram** visualization. You should see a series of bars representing the number of countries with **Gross Domestic Products** (**GDPs**) falling into each bin.

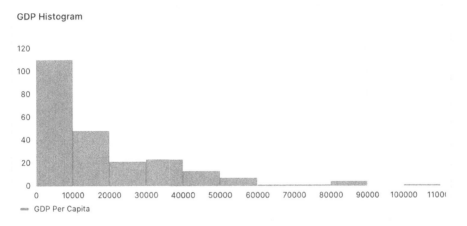

Figure 8.9 – GDP Histogram

As you might expect, the number of countries with low GDP is quite high, and the number of high-GDP countries is quite low. This is a common distribution, sometimes called a **power-law distribution**. Do earthquake magnitudes also follow a similar distribution? Let's find out!

## Producing histograms with transformations

The first thing we want to do is to get data into a shape that will work with the histogram visualization. The visualization requires not much more than a series of rows, each with a numerical value that will be used for binning, the process of determining the size of each bin, and the determination of which bin a row falls into. The histogram picks the first numerical field, so we must be careful to structure our data accordingly.

To do this, we'll again rely on our transformations. Let's start by creating a new panel with a histogram visualization. Set the following:

- **Query** (raw query mode): SELECT "magnitude" FROM "event" WHERE magnitude >= 1.0 GROUP BY "tag_place"

- **Format as**: **Table**

We add the GROUP BY option tag_place in case we might want to filter our data on place name. We're selecting all the earthquakes greater than the first magnitude to eliminate some of the noise of small earthquakes that almost no one feels anyway.

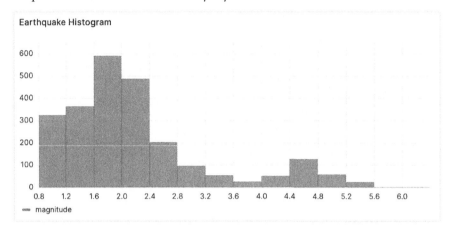

Figure 8.10 – Earthquake Histogram

You should quickly see a histogram with a similar distribution to the GDP Histogram, with many small earthquakes and few large ones. Can we leverage the greater functionality of our bar chart? And by the way, what if we want to limit our set of earthquakes to a specific place?

## Displaying histogram data with the bar chart visualization

It turns out the answer to the first question is yes. Again, we can leverage transformations to shape our data in a way that makes it compatible with the bar chart. At this point, we're going to break away from the pattern we've followed in this chapter in order to demonstrate a better workflow practice than simply creating the bare minimum to illustrate a concept.

The goal is to set up a visualization pipeline, both the **Query** and the **Transform**, to maximize our flexibility as we perform analysis. This way, if we want to produce multiple panels with different slices of data or different metrics, we don't have to create entirely new panels each time. Follow these steps:

1. Create a new bar chart visualization panel.
2. Add the following query (raw editor): SELECT "magnitude", "cdi", "mmi", "sig", "depth" FROM "event" WHERE $timeFilter GROUP BY "tag_place"::tag, "tag_latitude"::tag, "tag_longitude", "tag_alert"::tag. The $timeFilter template variable gives us the ability to constrain our analysis by time. GROUP BY allows us to access all the tagging in case we want to filter on those values.

3.  Set **Format as** to **Table**.

4.  Switch to the **Transform** tab and add **Filter data by values**.

5.  We want to filter on place first, and we only want to look at earthquakes in California. Around the time of this writing, Northern California experienced a moderate earthquake, which generated many smaller aftershocks, so let's concentrate on California. We can filter on the place name. It is a bit crude because the state experiences earthquakes in many different locations, but it does illustrate the concept:

    *   **Filter type**: **Include**

    *   **Conditions**: **Match any**

6.  Next, click + **Add condition** and add the following conditions:

    *   **Field**: **tag_place** | **Match**: **regex** | **Value**: `California`

    *   **Field**: **tag_place** | **Match**: **regex** | **Value**: `, \sCA`

7.  Next, we also want to filter on magnitude, so click + **Add another transformation** and add another **Filter data by values** transformation. We could try to add to our existing filter, but it makes things too complicated. This way, we can also disable it if necessary:

    *   **Filter type**: **Include**

    *   **Conditions**: **Match all**

8.  Click + **Add condition** and set the following:

    *   **Field**: **magnitude** | **Match**: **is greater or equal** | **Value**: `1.0`

9.  Add the **Organize fields** transformation.

10. Disable, by clicking the "eye" icon, all the fields except **tag_place** (we want to filter on **tag_place**) and **magnitude** (the value we plan to histogram).

11. Add a **Histogram** transform. The transform will create a series of rows, each representing a range from `BucketMin` to `BucketMax` and a count in the `magnitude` field.

> **Note**
> There are some data sources that support producing histogram data directly from the query; in fact, InfluxDB queries using the Flux query language will generate histogram results.

12. Neaten up the bucket by setting the **Histogram Bucket** size to `0.5`.

13. Add a **Convert field type** transform. We need to convert the histogram-created xMin and xMax to text fields for the bar chart:

- **Field**: **xMin** | **as**: **String**
- **Field**: **xMax** | **as**: **String**

14. Finally, over in **Bar chart** | **X-axis**, set to either **xMin** or **xMax**, depending upon whether you want to display the lower bound or the upper bound on the histogram bin.

This is what my results look like. The shape of yours should be similar, even if the numbers are different:

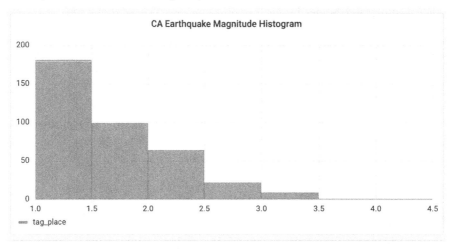

Figure 8.11 – California earthquake magnitude histogram

As an exercise, go back to the **Histogram** panel and try to get it to match our bar chart. Will you use the **Query** or **Transform** to filter on **magnitude**? What about the bucket sizing?

As we can see, the transform is now quite complex, and the query is somewhat complex as well. Now, however, we have the ability to work with additional fields for analysis, say the mmi field, which represents the **Modified Mercalli Intensity** (**MMI**), a subjective measure of earthquake intensity. Try out a histogram bar chart for mmi, cdi, or sig, all of which correspond to measures of earthquake magnitude.

## Visualizing histogram data over time with the heatmap

Armed with the tools to produce histograms and corresponding bar chart visualizations for our earthquake data, we now turn to an additional dimension: time. What if you could see how histogram data changes over time? Enter the heatmap, a visualization capable of mapping histogram bins with the *x* axis representing time, the *y* axis representing the bin, and the bin count by color.

In order to leverage the heatmap, we only need to make a small change to our existing panel, so let's make a copy first. To duplicate a panel, click on the title of the panel on the dashboard and select **More... | Duplicate**. Now, open the new panel for editing.

Disable the **Histogram** and **Convert field type** transformation functions. They are not relevant for this visualization.

When you switch the panel over to use the **Heatmap** visualization, you may either see something that looks like a bunch of colored rectangles or you may get an error. The first thing you should do is make sure none of the tag fields are enabled in the **Organize fields** transformation but do make sure the **Magnitude** and **Time** fields are.

Next, add an additional transformation called **Sort by**. Set **Field** to **Time**. This will ensure that no matter how the rows are organized by the query's GROUP BY, all rows are correctly ordered by their timestamp.

Over in the **Heatmap** section, set **Calculate from data** to **Yes**. If you were working with actual histogram data, you'd leave that set to **No**. Leave **X Bucket** set to **Size**. **Y Bucket** is for magnitudes (think of the **X-axis** buckets from the bar chart), so you can set its **Size** and enter 0.5 or leave it empty.

If all goes well, you now have a beautiful heatmap showing how earthquake magnitudes distribute over several days. Think of each vertical slice as a single bar chart per time bucket, only viewed from the top. The height of each bucket is coded by color rather than height and/or a count. By hovering over a bucket cell, the tooltip will show you the time period, the bucket of magnitude, and the count (corresponding to the color code). It might be a little hard to get your head wrapped around it but give it time.

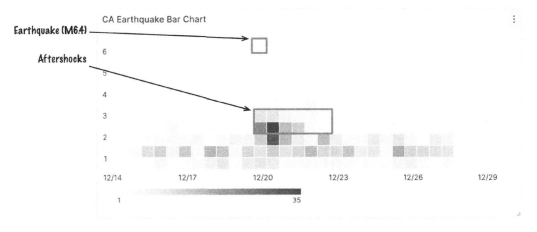

Figure 8.12 – California earthquake heatmap

From this analysis, I can see from the tooltip that a magnitude 6 earthquake occurred in California between 12/19/2022 22:00 and 12/20/2022 04:00. The actual time was 12/20/2022 02:34. Looking later in time (to the right), the number of smaller earthquakes in the state (looking down) went up (brighter colors) in the immediate period after the initial earthquake. So now we can see the distribution of smaller earthquakes compared to large ones, especially those in the same region, but we can also see how they distribute over time.

> **Note**
>
> If you wish to replicate these exercises with the same earthquake data, you will find it in the repository under `Chapter08/data` in `eq_20221214.txt`. The time period spans from 2022/12/14 to 2022/12/27.

These kinds of analyses have broad applications where singular events can trigger numerous follow-on events. For example, tracking logs by severity may show an initial high-severity event, but later follow-on logs will show many lower-severity events triggered by the initial event.

## Summary

I hope this was an interesting (and informative) exploration into some of the science behind one of the more destructive forces on Earth. In this chapter, we learned about several new visualizations including geomap, bar chart, histogram, and heatmap. We have also become familiar with the transformation functions and how they can help shape data to facilitate analysis. We even learned a little about the power-law distribution (`https://en.wikipedia.org/wiki/Power_law`) and how it governs many of the common processes in nature.

In our next chapter, we bring together much of what we've learned in the past few chapters. We'll apply these skills toward a concrete result: assembling panels into engaging and informative dashboards.

# 9

# Creating Insightful Dashboards

In the previous chapters, we've mostly concentrated on panels and how to use and configure them. We did this pretty much exclusively on the dashboard, which is the canvas that we display our panels on. In the next few chapters, we will zoom out from the panel level to the dashboard level. We'll continue to learn more about various panels, but this will mostly be in the context of making our dashboard layouts and queries more efficient.

In this chapter, we're going to take on the task of designing a couple of dashboards – one packed with information suitable for viewing on a workstation or laptop, and another containing only key pieces of information suitable for being viewed at a glance or from a distance.

In both cases, we'll pick up some workflow techniques that can help speed up the often laborious task of creating, configuring, and laying out panels. We'll also look at ways to take our numerical data and convert it into a textual format, thereby increasing the richness of our dashboard content.

Here's what we'll cover in this chapter:

- Designing a dashboard
- Creating a high-information display dashboard for weather data
- Creating a high-information visibility dashboard for earthquake data

Let's get started!

> **Note**
> Grafana may have changed since this book went to press, so there might be subtle changes in the interface that may cause my instructions to drift slightly. If you ever find the results not quite matching the text, reference dashboards are located in the GitHub repository, which you can import and examine for comparison.

# Technical requirements

Before we create our visualization panels, we'll need to set up InfluxDB and Grafana servers, install a Python Docker container to run scripts, ingest the data into InfluxDB buckets, and finally, set up Grafana data sources. These steps should remind you of those we used when we introduced this data ingestion pipeline back in *Chapter 05, Visualizing InfluxDB Data with Grafana Panels*.

For this chapter, we will be working with both the `weather.py` and `earthquake.py` scripts, so we'll go ahead and put them into a `bin` directory to keep our repository directory tidy. We'll also need to manually create two InfluxDB buckets, one for each dataset. Finally, we will need to create two separate data sources, each connecting to one of the two buckets.

> **Info**
>
> Tutorial code, dashboards, and other helpful files for this chapter can be found in this book's GitHub repository at `https://github.com/PacktPublishing/Learn-Grafana-10/tree/main/Chapter09`.

## Launching server Docker containers

Initially, we'll go through similar steps as in the previous chapters:

1. If you haven't done so already, shut down any services you might have left running from the other chapters by executing the following:

   ```
   % docker-compose down
   ```

2. Run the `docker-compose` script, which will download the Grafana and InfluxDB containers and then launch them. The `docker-compose.yml` file is available in the `Chapter09` directory of the GitHub repository for this book:

   ```
   docker-compose up --pull missing -d grafana influxdb
   [+] Running 3/3
     Network chapter09_default        Created      0.0s
     Container chapter09-influxdb-1   Started      0.5s
     Container chapter09-grafana-1    Started      0.4s
   ```

## Setting up the InfluxDB database

Here, we'll log in to our InfluxDB server, set it up with an initial account and bucket, and generate an API key so we can connect to it from our Python script and the Grafana data source.

## Initializing the InfluxDB server

Log in to the InfluxDB UI at `http://localhost:8086`. If you haven't already set up the instance, you'll see a prompt to perform the initialization:

1.  Set the username to whatever you like.

2.  Add a password (8 characters minimum).

3.  Choose an organization name: `LearnGrafana`.

4.  Create a bucket: `Chapter09`. This is just *pro forma* as we'll be creating specific buckets for our data later.

## Generating an API token

You'll need to generate a new token in order to access the InfluxDB server from a script or the command line:

1.  Click on **Load Data | API Tokens**.

2.  Click the gear icon on the right side of the user you created previously and select **Clone**.

3.  Click on **Copy to clipboard** to capture the API token string.

4.  Save the API token in a safe place as you won't be able to see it again without going through the process to create a new one.

## Building the Python Docker container

Use the `requirements.txt` file in the `Chapter09` repository to create a Docker container with a Python build and the appropriate libraries:

1.  From the repository directory, type the following:

    ```
    % docker build --pull --tag python/ch9 .
    ```

2.  Be sure to put the `weather.py` script in the app directory. Confirm the script runs by executing it with the `--help` option:

    ```
    % docker run --rm \
        -v "$(PWD)/app:/usr/src/app" \
        --name python_ch9 python/ch9 \
        /usr/src/app/weather.py --help
    ```

That's all we need to do to prepare for our tutorial. In the next section, we'll create a bucket, run our ETL scripts, and set up the Grafana data source.

# Designing a dashboard

Before we get started and work on a new dashboard, it's best to have a plan of action. Ask yourself a few questions:

- What information do I want to convey?
- What is the visual context for the dashboard?
- What is most important and what is least important?

Let's take a look at these questions in more detail.

## Conveying information

In the case of our dashboard, we will be building a dashboard that can be used to produce a display of the current weather. For this purpose, we will need to describe the following conditions:

- Current temperature and dew point
- Barometer reading and trend – rising, falling, or steady
- Wind direction and speed
- Visibility

We also want to know the current temperature as that will help us decide what to wear, for example. The dew point is an indication of humidity (and relative comfort, depending on the temperature) as well as providing an indication of how low the temperature is likely to drop. We want to know the current barometer reading and trend as that could give a forecaster an indication of an approaching low-pressure system and possibly inclement weather. The wind direction and speed can indicate the passage of weather fronts.

## Determining the visual context

What is the likely context for how the dashboard is to be viewed? Will it be a computer screen on a desk or a massive display in an operations center?

In our case, we'd like the weather report to be available to a hypothetical weather forecaster and viewed on a relatively small screen such as a laptop or a tablet. In this case, we will be more concerned with providing high information density as it is likely to be viewed over a moderate period of time. Were the display to be on a large screen and viewed by non-practitioners, we may want to emphasize lower information density instead.

## Prioritizing elements of importance

Importance works hand in hand with the visual context. If the viewer can control the display, importance dictates that the most important information appears at the top, while less important information appears lower or even below the viewable window. If the viewer doesn't have control of this, as in a kiosk display, the highest priority information might be located at the top left and lower priority information below and/or to the right, depending on how a typical view scans for reading purposes.

Let's take these concepts and apply them to our dashboard designs. First off, we will create a dashboard designed to convey as much information as possible in a relatively small area, such as a workstation monitor. Following that, we'll design a dashboard for a large-scale kiosk-type display.

# Creating a high information-density dashboard

In our first example, we'll be constructing a fairly detailed dashboard of graph panels. This dashboard is similar to one you might find accompanying a metrics-driven server application. It's intended to provide a number of metric graphs that might also serve as the top layer for further drill-down exploration. In our example, we'll be assembling a series of graphs to cover the weather metrics we've scraped from the **National Weather Service** (**NWS**) using the application we developed in *Chapter 5, Extracting and Visualizing Data with InfluxDB and Grafana*.

If you've been following my instructions in the previous chapters, you're probably well aware of how much work goes into getting a panel just so, and you could be forgiven for being a little anxious about the idea of creating a lot of panels for a dashboard. It's a valid concern, and for these examples, I'm going to take you step by step, as well as offering some effort-saving tips where I can, so that when you have to build your own dashboards, you'll be equipped with a toolbox of techniques to streamline the process.

In the next chapter, we'll be looking at even more powerful techniques for making dashboard creation even more efficient. But before we can run, we need to walk, so let's get started!

## Ingesting the weather data

Before we get too far into our dashboard designs, we should set up our weather data pipeline. We've already installed Grafana and InfluxDB, and a Python container, so now we just need to create a bucket in InfluxDB, download and ingest the data to the bucket, and add a Grafana data source so we can query it.

### Creating an InfluxDB bucket

In previous chapters, we've ingested data into buckets we created at the time we first logged into the InfluxDB server. Now, since we're going to handle two datasets, we'll need to create two buckets, so even if we used the one we've already created, we'd still need to create a second one. Happily, InfluxDB provides a **command-line interface** (**CLI**) that will allow us to not only create buckets for our data but also delete them if we so choose.

The InfluxDB CLI is installed automatically along with the server; in order to run them, we would need to somehow get inside the server container and then run the commands from a shell. Docker Compose provides an easy subcommand to run commands from inside a container, called `exec`. The command we'll run is `influx bucket create`. Here's how to run it:

```
% docker-compose exec -T \
    influxdb influx bucket create  \
    --org LearnGrafana \
    --token=<API_TOKEN \
    --name weatherdb
ID      Name     Retention  Shard group duration  Organization
ID    Schema Type  c89cf9270  weatherdb  infinite  168h0m0s
8b0bea56cc2e149a  implicit
```

Let's break down what I did here. The `docker-compose exec -T influxdb` command is the Docker Compose command to execute whatever follows it in the container itself. The `-T` option disables the creation of a pseudo-TTY (command shell interface), which we don't need as we're not interacting with the shell command.

The InfluxDB CLI command begins with `influx bucket create`. We need to pass in an `--org` option to indicate the organization (which we specified during the initial login, remember?). Next is the API token with the `--token` option, so we authenticate without needing to log in. Finally, the name of the bucket itself is specified with the `--name` option. The output from the command indicates the successful creation of our bucket with an infinite retention policy, and an implicit schema, that is, derived from the data we pass into it.

If you'd like to delete the bucket – say, because you want to delete its contents – you run a very similar command:

```
% docker-compose exec -T influxdb \
    influx bucket delete  \
    --org LearnGrafana \
    --token=<API_TOKEN> \
    --name weatherdb


ID      Name     Retention  Shard group duration  Organization
ID    Schema Type  Deleted
5e1ee84c89cf9270  weatherdb  infinite  168h0m0s
8b0bea56cc2e149a  implicit  true
```

I've removed the API token; you'll provide your own when you run the command. As you can see from the `Deleted` column, the bucket has been deleted; we will need to recreate our original bucket if we wish to load our data.

## Configuring the InfluxDB data source

We just need to configure a Grafana data source to point at our bucket and we'll be ready to start setting up panels:

1. Open your browser to the Grafana app and select **Connections** | **Add new connection** from the main menu.

2. Search for the InfluxDB data source and select it.

3. Click on **Add a new data source**. Fill out the following form fields:

   - **Name**: InfluxDB Weather
   - **Default**: **off**
   - **Query Language**: **InfluxQL**
   - **HTTP | URL**: http://influxdb:8086
   - **Custom HTTP Headers | Header**: Authorization
   - **Custom HTTP Headers | Value**: Token <API Token>
   - **Database**: weatherdb

> **Note**
> Make sure there is a space between Token and <API Token>.

Your data source configuration should look like this:

Figure 9.1 – InfluxDB data source for weatherdb

Click on **Save and Test** to confirm you can successfully connect to the InfluxDB server.

## Designing the dashboard

It's often a good strategy to make a little sketch or note about what you want to do before digging in and creating a full dashboard. If you have a list of dashboards and an idea of how you'd like to lay them out, it may not seem very challenging to build up a dashboard containing 10 or even 20 panels.

For our dashboard, we have something like this in mind:

- First row:
  - A **Title** panel for identifying the station
  - A **Current conditions** panel
- Second row:
  - A panel for temperature-related measurements
  - A panel for moisture-related measurements
- Third row:
  - A pair of panels for barometer pressure and the trend
- Fourth row:
  - A set of panels for wind speed
- Fifth row:
  - A panel for visibility

Let's get started by creating a new dashboard and setting the time range to **Today so far**. Don't forget to save it! Next, we'll start creating and laying out our panels, starting with our first panel, which will display the station's name.

## Adding the first row

From our specification, we want to set up the first row of our dashboard to include two panels: a title panel to display the name of the weather station and a panel to indicate the current conditions in text format. Let's go step by step to lay those out on our dashboard.

## Building a station text panel

In order to display the title information for our dashboard, we'll need to introduce a new panel visualization: the **Text** visualization. This visualization is for displaying formatted text, either Markdown or HTML. In our case, we want a little bit more control over formatting, so we'll fill in the content in HTML format.

Create a new panel and change **Visualization** to **Text**. For these examples, we are going to use the KSFO station for our dashboards, but feel free to use a different station if you prefer. In the **Text** section, set the following values:

- **Mode**: **html**
- **Text**: `<h1><center>San Francisco CA (KSFO)</center></h1>`

In the **Panel Options** section, set **Title** to `Station`.

If you're familiar with HTML, you'll probably recognize the HTML markup that centers some H1 text. If you didn't want to center the text, you could switch to Markdown mode. It's beyond the scope of this book to cover either HTML or Markdown, but the panel help provides a link to get you started with easy-to-learn Markdown text.

Here's the **Panel** tab in action:

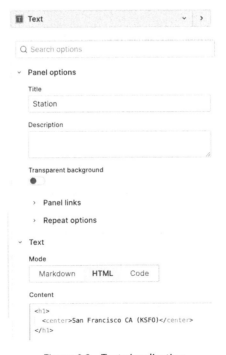

Figure 9.2 – Text visualization

Now that you have an initial panel, you'll want to start thinking about the layout. Each panel you create will end up in the top-left corner of your dashboard, so you'll then want to resize it and drag it to its ultimate position. For the layout of this dashboard, you'll be working with essentially a two-column layout, so your task will be to simply size the panel to fit half the width of the page and drag it into position in either the left or the right column.

The layout process is relatively simple. In Grafana, panel geometry is defined by two pairs of numbers: the $x$ and $y$ coordinates (in grid units) of the panel's top-left corner and the panel's width and height. To adjust the panel's position, simply hover over the top of a panel until its header turns gray and the pointer becomes a cross-arrow, then click and drag it. To adjust its size, simply hover over the lower-right corner of the panel until the pointer becomes an arrow pointing downward-right, then click and drag.

The dashboard is defined by an invisible grid that your panel will snap to in both position and size, so you only need to drag the panel to the appropriate position and adjust the sizing with the control at the bottom right of the panel. The grid points are fairly widely spaced, so you don't need to worry about precision – just drag the panel or the resize control until an outline appears and then release. You can use the border cue to get an idea of where a move or resize will land, as shown in the following screenshot:

Figure 9.3 – Border cue

The dashboard layout manager can only tile panels, so resizing or positioning a panel so that it overlaps another panel will cause the other panel to move down to get out of the way. I've found that if you want panels to stay on the same row, it's best to resize them down first, arrange them, and then resize them up to fill in any empty space. It can be a little tricky to get things to look just right, but with a little practice, you'll find it almost becomes second nature to drag panels around into the layout you desire.

### Modifying the weather.py script

Our next panel is our new friend, the **Stat** panel. However, we'll be using it to display text describing the current conditions. We'll need to make a couple of modifications to our script in order to add the data field, but it's only a few lines. Let's look at the changes we'll make to our weather.py script.

We want to add a string as a metric value, so we'll need to capture the textDescription field from the retrieved object. But when using a string as a field value, we need to quote it first. We need to add a little routine to quote the string:

```python
def quote_string(string):
    return f'"{string}"'
```

Next, we need to make a slight modification to the `dump_wx_data` routine to capture the `textDescription` field:

```
wx_data = get_station_obs(s)
for feature in wx_data:
    for measure, observation in feature['properties'].items():
        if measure in ['elevation']:
            continue
        if measure in ['textDescription']:
            value = quote_string(observation)
            unit = None
        elif isinstance(observation, dict):
            value = observation['value']
            unit = observation['unitCode']
        else:
continue
```

Here, we did the following:

- We checked to see whether the observation is an elevation and if so, skipped it

- Otherwise, we captured the `textDescription` value as our value (with `textDescription` as the field key, but no associated `unit` tag)

- We grabbed any observations represented by a dictionary

- We skipped over everything else

That's all there is to it! Let's get some data for our new dashboard.

### *Ingesting weather data*

First, we download our data. Feel free to pick any NWS stations you might be interested in. Make sure to create a `data` directory to store your data files:

```
% mkdir data
% docker run --rm \
    -v "$(PWD)/app:/usr/src/app" \
    -v "$(PWD)/data:/data" \
    --name python_ch9 python/ch9 \
    /usr/src/app/weather.py \
    --output /data/wx.txt \
    --stations KSFO,KDEN,KSTL,KJFK INFO:root:https://api.weather.gov/
stations/KSFO
INFO:root:https://api.weather.gov/zones/county/CAC081
INFO:root:https://api.weather.gov/stations/KSFO/observations
INFO:root:https://api.weather.gov/stations/KDEN
```

```
INFO:root:https://api.weather.gov/zones/county/COC031
INFO:root:https://api.weather.gov/stations/KDEN/observations
INFO:root:https://api.weather.gov/stations/KSTL
INFO:root:https://api.weather.gov/zones/county/MOC189
INFO:root:https://api.weather.gov/stations/KSTL/observations
INFO:root:https://api.weather.gov/stations/KJFK
INFO:root:https://api.weather.gov/zones/county/NYC081
INFO:root:https://api.weather.gov/stations/KJFK/observations
```

Next, we ingest the data we just downloaded:

```
% docker run --rm --network=host \
    -v "$(PWD)/app:/usr/src/app" \
    -v "$(PWD)/data:/data" \
    --name python_ch9 python/ch9 \
    /usr/src/app/weather.py \
    --input /data/wx.txt \
    --db weatherdb \
    --token=<API_TOKEN>
INFO:root:http://localhost:8086/write?db=weatherdb&precision=s
```

Note how we passed in the bucket name in the --db option.

### Building the current conditions panel

Space doesn't permit me to enumerate all the panel configuration settings, so I'm concentrating on the ones that change from their defaults. However, Grafana may have changed since this book went to press, so there might be subtle changes in the interface that may cause my instructions to drift slightly. If you ever find the results not quite matching the text, reference dashboards are available from this book's GitHub repository, which you can import and examine for comparison.

Once we've reloaded our data with the new field values, we can set up a **Stat** panel to display it. Add a new panel. In the **Query** tab, set up the following query:

- **Data source**: **InfluxDB Weather**

- **Query**: SELECT "value" FROM "textDescription" WHERE ("station"::tag = 'KSFO') AND $timeFilter

Set the visualization to **Stat**. In the **Panel options** section, set up the following:

- **Title**: Current Conditions

In the **Value options** section, set up the following:

- **Value**: **Last** \*
- **Fields**: **textDescription**

In the **Stat** styles section, set the following:

- **Graph Mode**: **None**

In the **Field** tab, under the **Thresholds** section, set the following:

- Delete any existing thresholds (trash can icon)
- **Base** | **Color**: **Custom** | `gray/rgb(128,128,128)`

To get the custom gray color, do the following:

1. Click the color circle.
2. Select the **Custom** tab.
3. Type `grey` or `gray` in the text field.

You can now lay out the two panels in an appropriate two-column style. Resize them so that they take up approximately half the page width. Give them the smallest height that will display all the content in the panel. Drag the **Station** panel to the left-hand side and the **Current Conditions** panel to the right. You might have to do a little jockeying to get both to sit next to each other with no space between them, but once you get the hang of it, you will have fairly mastered layout, so take your time and play around with the controls.

You should end up with a row that looks like this:

Figure 9.4 – First row

We're off to a good start. Let's make this dashboard useful and put some temperatures on there!

## Adding the second row

On to the next row! Here, we're going back to time series visualization. As you're well aware, configuring time series visualization can be an elaborate process involving many settings, so it will take some additional diligence to keep the panels looking and functioning consistently. I recommend that you create a general base panel with some common settings so that when you need to create a new panel, you can simply replicate your base panel and customize it.

## Creating a base panel

Here's an example of a base panel that has many settings already preset. Create a **Time series** visualization panel, go to the **Query** tab, and set up the following:

- **Data source**: **InfluxDB Weather**
- **Query**: `SELECT mean("value") FROM "measurement" WHERE $timeFilter GROUP BY time($__interval) fill(none)`
- **Query options/Min interval**: 15m

In the **Panel** tab, set the following:

- **Visualization**: **Time series**
- **Legend | Visibility**: On
- **Legend | Mode**: **Table**
- **Graph styles | Style**: **Lines**
- **Graph styles | Line Interpolation**: **1st option**
- **Graph styles | Line width**: **1**
- **Graph styles | Fill opacity**: **0**
- **Graph styles | Gradient Mode**: **None**
- **Graph styles | Line style**: **Solid**
- **Graph styles | Connect null values**: **Never**
- **Graph styles | Show points**: **Auto**
- **Graph styles | Point size**: **5**
- **Graph styles | Stack series**: Off

To replicate this panel, you have two options. If you click on the panel title, you'll get a drop-down menu with several options. You're already familiar with the **Edit** option. Clicking on **More...** yields a submenu with the **Duplicate** option. Clicking it will give you a new identical panel. The other option is to use the **Copy** option instead. Now, you can create a new panel, but you will have a new option called **Paste Copied Panel**. If you click it, you will convert the panel into an identical copy.

There is no inherent advantage to one or the other when working with panels on the same dashboard. The **Copy** option becomes much more useful when you need to copy a panel from one dashboard to another.

## Building the temperature panel

Now, let's create our **Temperature** panel. Here, we want to track up to three different data series – one for the actual temperature and two for *perceived* temperature, that is, wind chill and the heat index. The wind chill is heavily dependent on the wind and cold temperatures, whereas the heat index is heavily dependent on humidity and high temperatures. If the temperatures are not extreme enough or there are light winds or little humidity, there won't be any readings for those series (we deliberately don't include null readings when we import the observation data).

Just in case, we'll go ahead and include queries for all three:

- **Data source: InfluxDB Weather**

- **A Query**: `SELECT mean("value") FROM "heatIndex" WHERE $timeFilter GROUP BY time($__interval) fill(none)`

- **Alias By**: `$col $measurement`

Now, make two copies of the **A** query and change the `FROM` measurement in each as follows:

- **B Query**: `SELECT mean("value") FROM "temperature" WHERE $timeFilter GROUP BY time($__interval) fill(none)`

- **C Query**: `SELECT mean("value") FROM "windChill" WHERE $timeFilter GROUP BY time($__interval) fill(none)`

We have the series from our queries, but depending on the weather conditions, it's likely you will only see the temperature. Let's assume we will see the others if we choose a different station in the future when we set up the visualization. If you've copied this panel from a base panel, as we discussed earlier, you might not have to change much:

- **Graph styles | Style: Lines**

- **Graph styles | Line Interpolation: 1st option**

- **Graph styles | Line width: 1**

- **Graph styles | Fill opacity: 0**

- **Graph styles | Show points: Auto**

- **Graph styles | Point size: 5**

- **Legend | Visibility**: On

- **Legend | Mode: Table**

- **Legend | Values**: Last \*, Min, Max

- **Standard options | Unit: Temperature / Celsius (°C)**

You would be fine sticking with the default color scheme for the three data series, but it would be consistent for all your panels, and that can get visually monotonous. We can alter the colors of the series by clicking on the series' color line in the legend. Since we probably can't do that with all three series, we'll do it with **Field Override** instead.

We'll use the color as a bit of visual cueing, with *blue* representing *cold* for our `windChill` series, *red* representing *hot* for our `heatIndex` series, and *orange* representing *warm* for our `temperature` series. Bear in mind that these are only suggestions and that there is no right or wrong decision regarding how to represent the data visually. For your dashboards, you may find yourself choosing different colors, or you may get feedback from viewers requesting different colors. Choose the colors and styles that help you connect the story you want to tell your audience.

Create three field overrides, one for each series:

- **Fields with name matching regex**: `/temperature/`

  - **Standard options > Color scheme: Single color**
  - **Color: Orange**

- **Fields with name matching regex**: `/windChill/`

  - **Standard options > Color scheme: Single color**
  - **Color: Blue**

- **Fields with name matching regex**: `/heatIndex/`

  - **Standard options > Color scheme: Single color**
  - **Color: Red**

We chose a regex for the data series name just in case we want to create aliases that include the column text (`temperature.mean`, for example). In this case, we only need to match the series measurement and not the entire alias.

Name the panel title `Temperature` in **Panel options** and click on **Apply**.

### Building the moisture panel

For the **Moisture** panel, we'll be querying for three interrelated data series: the temperature, the dew point, and the relative humidity. The easiest thing would be to simply duplicate the **Temperature** panel and modify the copy. To make a duplicate, click on the panel's title bar and select **More... | Duplicate**.

After making the duplicate, go to the **Query** area and set the following queries:

- **Query A**: `SELECT mean("value") FROM "dewpoint" WHERE $timeFilter GROUP BY time($__interval) fill(none)`

- **Query B**: `SELECT mean("value") FROM "relativeHumidity" WHERE $timeFilter GROUP BY time($__interval) fill(none)`

- **Query C**: `SELECT mean("value") FROM "temperature" WHERE $timeFilter GROUP BY time($__interval) fill(none)`

To set the colors, go ahead and update the three field overrides with new regexes and colors:

- **Fields with name matching regex**: `/relativeHumidity/`

  - **Standard options | Color scheme: Single color**

  - **Color:  Yellow**

- **Fields with name matching regex**: `/dewpoint/`

  - **Standard options | Color scheme: Single color**

  - **Color: Blue**

- **Fields with name matching regex**: `/temperature/`

  - **Standard options | Color scheme: Single color**

  - **Color: Red**

Since the relative humidity is a completely different scale than the temperature and dew point, we'll set it up to use the right *y* axis. Add these additional override properties to the **Field** override corresponding to `relativeHumidity`:

- **Axis | Placement: Right**
- **Standard options | Unit: Misc | Percent (0-100)**
- **Standard options | Min**: `0`
- **Standard options | Max**: `100`

We want to lock the minimum and maximum to 0 and 100, respectively, so that the graph doesn't scale up and down depending on the range of values in the displayed time frame. When these values are set in this way, the graph is vertically scaled to fit the entire panel.

Since **Percent** is a quantity, we can go ahead and add a color fill to help reinforce that. Add another override property to the `relativeHumidity` field override. Set the **Graph styles | Fill opacity** override to **10**.

After adding several property overrides to the single field override for `relativeHumidity`, you might be wondering whether it might be better to have set the panel's axis for `relativeHumidity` and Axis overrides for the other two temperatures. That certainly is an option; either approach is valid. Choose whichever approach works best for you.

Go to the **Panel options** section and set **Title** to `Moisture`. With that, you've completed another row! The two rows should look similar to the following output:

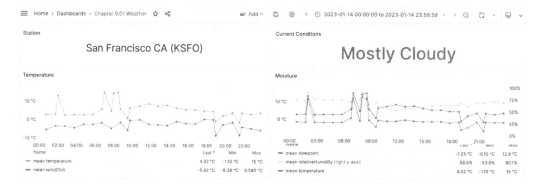

Figure 9.5 – Second row

Next up, we'll work on the panels displaying barometric pressure readings.

## Adding the third row

On this row, we're going to build two panels with slightly different views of the same data, namely the barometric pressure. To do this, we're going to create a single panel with both queries, but only one enabled. Then, in a copy of the same panel, we're going to swap the enabled queries. Just like copying the panel and tweaking the queries, this is another technique you can use to produce several similar panels.

### Building the barometric pressure panel

Copy your base panel (or create a new panel) and set the following two queries:

- **Data source: InfluxDB Weather**
- **Query A**: `SELECT mean("value")  / 1000 FROM "barometricPressure" WHERE ("station"::tag = 'KSFO') AND $timeFilter GROUP BY time($__interval) fill(none)`
- **Query A/Alias by**: `$col $measurement`
- **Query B**: `SELECT derivative(mean("value"), 1h)  / 1000 FROM "barometricPressure" WHERE ("station"::tag = 'KSFO') AND $timeFilter GROUP BY time($__interval) fill(none)`
- **Query B/Alias by**: `$col $measurement`
- **Query options/Min Interval**: `15m`

In the A query's SELECT statement, we're querying for the barometric pressure. Since the NWS is sending the data in **Pascals (Pa)**, we'll divide them by 1,000 to convert this into **kilopascals (kPa)**. In the B query's SELECT statement, we want to calculate the rate of change in barometric pressure. The derivative will analyze the aggregated mean of barometric pressure over an interval – in this case, 1 hour – and determine the rate at which it's changing. In calculus terms, we're asking InfluxDB to get the slope of the tangent to a curve that represents the pressure readings for a single hour.

Since this panel is only intended to show the actual barometric pressure, for now, disable the B query by disabling its visibility (clicking the eye icon).

Next, we'll style the graph. The style will be consistent with the temperature graphs:

- **Graph styles | Style**: **Lines**
- **Graph styles | Line Interpolation**: **1st option**
- **Graph styles | Line width**: **1**
- **Graph styles | Fill opacity**: **0**
- **Graph styles | Show points**: **Auto**
- **Graph styles | Point size**: **5**
- **Legend | Visibility**: **on**
- **Legend | Mode**: **Table**
- **Legend | Values**: **Last \*, Min, Max**
- **Standard options | Unit**: **Pressure | Kilopascals**

Set **Title** in **Panel options** to Barometer Reading.

### Building the barometric pressure trend panel

For the next panel, we'll simply copy the **Barometer Reading** panel and duplicate it. In the **Query** area, disable the **A** query and enable the **B** query.

We'll need to make some adjustments to the axis to reflect a different measurement. Since the derivative we calculate is over a period of 1 hour, the true unit is kilopascals per hour. Unfortunately, Grafana doesn't provide such a unit, but we can easily create a custom unit by typing it into the **Unit** text box:

- **Standard options | Unit**: suffix: kPa/hr

Set the **Panel** options **Title** as follows: Barometer Trend.

That was pretty easy! The **Barometer Trend** panel is used to depict the barometer reading trend. If the derivative value is positive, that means the slope at the point is positive, so the barometer reading is rising, which is usually a sign of building high pressure and better weather. On the other hand, if the derivative value is negative, we know the pressure is dropping, which can signal an approaching low-pressure system and possible inclement weather. In the next section, we'll leverage the same derivative but convert it into a rising/falling readout.

Our dashboard rows now look like this:

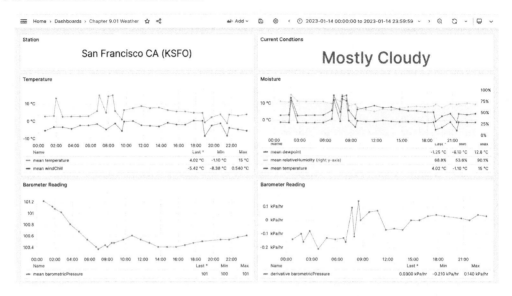

Figure 9.6 – Third row

The next row of panels will cover our wind panels.

## Adding the fourth row

On our third row, we'll use a third technique to streamline our panel creation. In this case, we want to create two panels – one for wind speeds and another for wind direction. As we did previously, we'll create a single panel with all the necessary queries, but this time, we'll keep them enabled and use series overrides to hide the series we're not interested in.

### Building the wind speed graph panel

For the **Wind Speed** panel, we'll start by creating our panel with three queries. First, we'll set up the **A** query for wind speed:

- **Data source: InfluxDB Weather**

- **Query A**: SELECT mean("value")  FROM "windSpeed" WHERE ("station"::tag = 'KSFO') AND $timeFilter GROUP BY time($__interval) fill(none)

- **Query A | Alias By**: $col $measurement

Next, we'll set up the **B** query for wind gust speed:

- **Query B**: `SELECT mean("value")  FROM "windGust" WHERE ("station"::tag = 'KSFO') AND $timeFilter GROUP BY time($__interval) fill(none)`
- **Query B | Alias By**: `$col $measurement`

Finally, we'll set up the **C** query for the wind direction:

- **Query C**: `SELECT distinct("value")  FROM "windDirection" WHERE ("station"::tag = 'KSFO') AND $timeFilter GROUP BY time($__interval) fill(none)`
- **Query C | Alias By**: `$col $measurement`
- **Query options | Min interval**: `15m`

Don't worry if you don't see any data points for the `windGust` measurement. If the wind is fairly steady, there really just may not be any data. For the case of the **C** query `SELECT` statements, calculating an aggregation value for a compass direction would be essentially meaningless, so we use `distinct`, with the understanding that wind direction is relatively consistent in the intervening time periods between samples.

Depicting wind speed in the graph is a bit tricky. I'm opting to use points to emphasize these are spot averages; adding a line would imply the change in speed is continuous between samples, which is not necessarily the case:

- **Panel options | Title**: `Wind Speed`
- **Legend | Visibility**: **on**
- **Legend | Mode**: **Table**
- **Legend | Values**: **Last \*, Max**
- **Graph styles | Style**: **Points**
- **Graph styles | Point size**: **5**
- **Standard options | Unit**: **kilometers/hour (km/h)**

We're not that interested in minimum wind speeds as they are normally 0 anyway.

Since we may not have a `windGust` data series, it would be prudent to color the series using series overrides. We'll color the `windSpeed` series in a light purple and the `windGust` series in a dark purple to help it stand out. We'll also hide the `windDirection` series by setting a series override to hide it and remove it from the legend, as follows:

- **Fields with name matching regex**: `/windSpeed/`

- **Standard options | Color scheme: Single Color | light purple**
- **Fields with name matching regex**: `/windSpeed/`
- **Standard options | Color scheme: Single Color | dark purple**
- **Fields with name matching regex**: `/windDirection/`
- **Series | Hide in area**: Tooltip off, Viz off, Legend off

### Building the wind direction stat panel

Now that we have a panel containing all our wind-based queries, we can leverage it to set up a wind panel for the direction. Instead of copying the **Wind Speed** panel, we just need to create a new panel or copy our base panel.

For the query, we're going to use a built-in dashboard data source to reference the existing query from another panel on our dashboard. This plugin improves the efficiency of your dashboard by leveraging the cached data retrieved from the query in another panel. It also improves maintenance as you are changing multiple panels whenever you need to make a change to a single query they may have in common.

A dashboard data source is available from the **Query** dropdown in the **Queries** tab. When you select -- **Dashboard** -- you'll then need to identify the query set from one of the dashboard's panels by selecting a panel from the **Source** menu. Since the selections in that menu are derived from panel titles, I recommend that you uniquely identify any panels you plan to share in this way; it will make your life easier. As we discussed previously, reference the panel results:

- **Source/Use the same results as panel**: `Wind Speed`

You can set the color of the data series using either the color bar in the legend or a series override. We need to set up the styles, as follows:

- **Graph styles | Style: Lines**
- **Graph styles | Line Interpolation: 1st option**
- **Graph styles | Line width: 1**
- **Graph styles | Fill opacity: 0**
- **Graph styles | Gradient mode: Opacity**
- **Graph styles | Show points: Auto**
- **Graph styles | Point size: 5**
- **Legend | Visibility**: on
- **Legend | Mode: Table**

- **Legend | Values**: Last *
- **Standard options | Unit**: Angle/Degrees (°)

I opted for turning on both the lines and points as I think it helps to make any discontinuities in wind direction stand out. Significant and sustained wind direction changes can be a sign of a frontal boundary passage. However, max and min values are inherently meaningless, so we left them off in the legend. We'll also add our series overrides, as follows:

- **Fields with name matching regex**: `/windSpeed/`
- **Series > Hide in area**: Tooltip off, Viz off, Legend off
- **Fields with name matching regex**: `/windGust/`
- **Series > Hide in area**: Tooltip off, Viz off, Legend off
- **Fields with name matching regex**: `/windDirection/`
- **Series > Hide in area**: Tooltip on, Viz on, Legend on

Scrolling down a bit, this is what the bottom rows now look like:

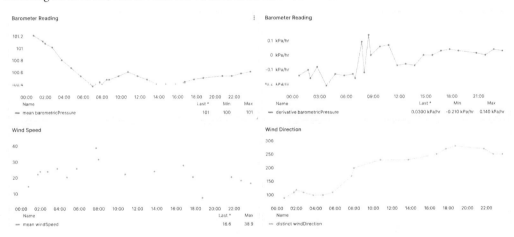

Figure 9.7 – Fourth row

There's only one more panel to go and we're done!

## Adding the fifth row

We're down to our last row, and there's only one panel we'll build. The other space is left up to you.

## Building the visibility panel

Our final panel is simply intended to depict visibility and it's straightforward to set up:

- **Query**: **InfluxDB Weather**
- **Query A**: `SELECT mean("value") /1000 FROM "visibility" WHERE ("station"::tag = 'KSFO') AND $timeFilter GROUP BY time($__interval) fill(none)`
- **Query A | Alias by**: `$col $measurement`
- **Query options | Min interval**: `15m`

The value is measured in meters, so we convert it into kilometers in the `SELECT` statement. Since the visibility has a fixed range (10 miles or 16.09 km is considered the maximum visibility), I'm opting for a more stylized graphical representation of the visibility graph:

- **Panel options | Title**: `Visibility`
- **Graph styles | Style: Lines**
- **Graph styles | Line Interpolation: 3rd option (Step before)**
- **Graph styles | Line width: 1**
- **Graph styles | Fill opacity: 100**
- **Graph styles | Show points: Auto**
- **Graph styles | Point size: 5**
- **Legend | Visibility**: on
- **Legend | Mode: Table**
- **Legend | Values: Last \*, Min, Max**
- **Standard Options | Unit: kilometer (km)**
- **Standard Options | Max**: `16.09`
- **Standard Options | Color scheme: Single Color | light blue**

We turned on the **Step before** option to help emphasize the discrete nature of the visibility observation. Adding the fill helps reinforce the notion that visibility extends from 0 to the observation value.

## Building the wind gust panel

As an exercise, try adding a **Wind Gust** panel in the last panel slot on the page. Here's my version (alas, there were no wind gusts at the time):

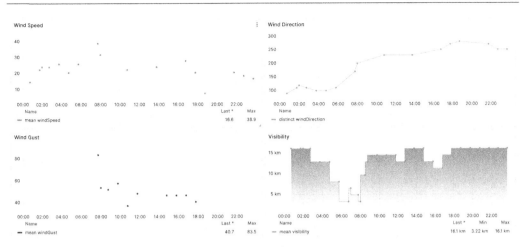

Figure 9.8 – Fifth row

To help you work through any issues, I've included this dashboard in the GitHub repository for this book. You'll find it in the `Chapter09/dashboards` directory.

# Creating a high-information visibility dashboard

In this second example, we'll create a dashboard intended to provide information at a much higher level of view; that is, a display intended to be scanned rapidly for us to get a *big-picture* viewpoint. Typically, you'd see this type of dashboard in a kiosk-type context, such as in an operations center or a public informational display.

We'll be making extensive use of the **Stat** visualization as opposed to the **Time series** visualization, as we did previously. The idea we're trying to convey is that the dashboard will be displayed in a context that makes details hard to read from a distance.

## Designing the dashboard

What we want to do is create and arrange a set of panels that will fit on a single page as we may not have the ability to scroll around or even interact with the page (kiosk mode). In keeping with the strategy we described previously, here's what we have in mind:

- First row:

  - Two **Stat** panels – one for the highest-magnitude earthquake, and one with the most recent earthquake.

- Second row:

  - Two **Table** panels, one for the top-N highest-magnitude earthquakes, and one with the top-N most recent earthquakes. We'll decide N when we lay out the dashboard.

- Third row:

  - Three **Geomap** panels, depicting earthquakes from three different regions.

In this example, we'll try to use some of what we've learned about efficient panel creation to quickly set up these panels. We'll also try to reuse some of what we built for the previous dashboard, with the idea being that since we've already determined the queries, we can reference them from other panels. Duplication of panels will speed up the process as well.

## Ingesting the earthquake data

Before we acquire our earthquake dataset, we'll need to make some simple changes to our pipeline. To correctly display time information in our **Stat** panels, we will need a text version of the earthquake timestamp. Since Grafana has no facility for formatting a timestamp (a numeric value) into a formatted string, we'll just accomplish it as part of the ETL script.

However, to properly translate the timestamp from UTC to the local time (which Grafana automatically does), we'll also need to set the local time zone in our Docker container. By default, Docker containers are set to UTC, not the local time zone. It's relatively simple to add an environment variable to the Docker container at build time, and we'll go ahead and use that facility in Docker Compose.

Whew! That was a bit long-winded as an explanation, but it will become clear shortly enough. In summary, we need to do the following:

- Update our Docker container with the local time zone to match Grafana

- Update the `earthquake.py` script to add a `Tag` field containing a string representation of the earthquake time, converted to our local time zone

- Load our earthquake data with the additional field

### Creating the InfluxDB bucket

As it will have a different schema from our weather data, we'll need to create a new InfluxDB instance to store our data and a new Grafana data source to access it. The command is virtually identical to the one we used to create our weather bucket:

```
% docker-compose exec -T \
    influxdb influx bucket create  \
    --org LearnGrafana \
    --token=<API_TOKEN> \
```

```
    --name earthquakedb
s
ID       Name      Retention   Shard group duration   Organization
ID     Schema Type
abc0fc2527da0949   earthquakedb   infinite   168h0m0s
8b0bea56cc2e149a   implicit
```

Once we've created the bucket, we'll need to add an InfluxDB data source to Grafana.

## Configuring an InfluxDB data source

We just need to configure a Grafana data source to point at our bucket, and we'll be ready to start ingesting data and building panels:

1. Open your browser to the Grafana app and select **Connections | Add new connection** from the main menu.

2. Search for the InfluxDB data source and select it.

3. Click on **Add a new data source**. Fill out the following form fields:

   - **Name**: InfluxDB Weather

   - **Default**: **off**

   - **Query Language**: **InfluxQL**

   - **HTTP | URL**: http://influxdb:8086

   - **Custom HTTP Headers | Header**: Authorization

   - **Custom HTTP Headers | Value**: Token <API Token>

   - **Database**: earthquakedb

> **Note**
>
> Make sure there is a space between Token and <API Token>.

Your data source configuration should look like this:

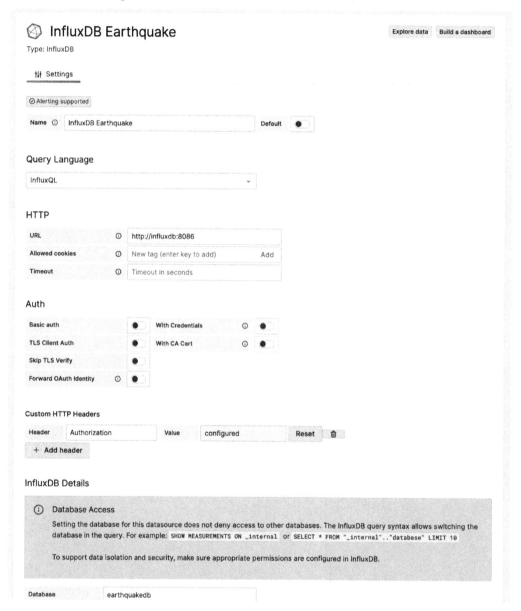

Figure 9.9 – InfluxDB data source for earthquakedb

Click on **Save and Test** to confirm you can successfully connect to the InfluxDB server.

### Updating docker-compose.yml

Open your `docker-compose.yml` file, and add the following lines:

```
python:
    build: .
image: python:ch9
    environment:
    TZ: "America/Los_Angeles"
volumes:
    - "${PWD-.}/app:/usr/src/app"
    - "${PWD-.}/data:/data"
```

This is basically just a Docker Compose representation of the earlier instructions on how to build and run our Python container:

- The `build` section indicates our `Dockerfile` lives in the same directory as the `docker-compose.yml` file.

- The `image` section is just the name of the Docker image that we'll build.

- The `environment` section adds a `TZ` environment variable to correspond to my local time zone. You should set this to your own time zone. A full list can be found in Wikipedia at `https://en.wikipedia.org/wiki/List_of_tz_database_time_zones`.

- The `volumes` section maps the app directory into `/usr/src/app` so the container can see our `earthquake.py` script. Make sure your `earthquake.py` script is in the app directory.

Next, run the Docker Compose `build` command to create a new image:

```
% docker-compose build python
[+] Building 0.8s (9/9) FINISHED
 => [internal] load build definition from Dockerfile      0.0s
 => => transferring dockerfile: 81B      0.0s
 => [internal] load .dockerignore            0.0s
 => => transferring context: 2B      0.0s
 => [internal] load metadata for docker.io/library/python:3.10   0.7s
 => [1/4] FROM docker.io/library/python:3.10@sha256:0e85513fb9bbdd1
a4fdf4a54b44844c5d60dc2f33f7584fec81d080d00213ede            0.0s
 => [internal] load build context            0.0s
 => => transferring context: 87B         0.0s
 => CACHED [2/4] WORKDIR /usr/src/app         0.0s
 => CACHED [3/4] COPY requirements.txt ./      0.0s
 => CACHED [4/4] RUN pip install --no-cache-dir -r requirements.
txt            0.0s
 => exporting to image         0.0s
 => => exporting layers          0.0s
```

```
=> => writing image sha256:0c65b706de094975ece5cee92fb6
2bc23a8bfd46d87d7eafcb5cbc3a9b856c68        0.0s
=> => naming to docker.io/library/python:ch9
```

Let's move on to take care of the script.

### Modifying the earthquake.py script

We just want to add a new tag field containing the formatted string representation of an earthquake timestamp. We add a new routine called `time_to_string`:

```python
def time_to_string(t):
    epoch_secs = int(t/1000)
    ltime = time.localtime(epoch_secs)
    ftime = time.strftime('%Y-%m-%d %H:%M:%S', ltime)
    return ftime
```

We just convert the timestamp argument from milliseconds to seconds, then create a `time` struct in the local time zone, and finally format the time into a string that matches the format in Grafana.

We'll insert the call to this routine along with the code that creates our list of tags:

```python
    f"tag_alert={properties['alert']}",
    f"tag_time={escape_string(time_to_string(properties[
        'time']))}"
]
```

We need to use `escape_string` for our time string because it will have spaces in it. We should be ready to download our data now.

### Loading earthquake data

We'll pull down about a week's worth of data, although we'll mostly concentrate on the current 24-hour period:

```
% docker-compose run python \
    /usr/src/app/earthquake.py \
    --size all \
    --window week \
    --output /data/eq.txt INFO:root:https://earthquake.usgs.gov/
earthquakes/feed/v1.0/summary/all_week.geojson
```

Note how much cleaner the command is compared to the Docker version. As an exercise, look into what options you might have to load a smaller set of data, possibly with a smaller set of large earthquakes and covering a smaller range of time.

Next, we load the data into our InfluxDB `earthquakedb` bucket. Now that we're contacting InfluxDB from within a Docker Compose network, we don't use `localhost` as the address; we need to use the network name defined by the InfluxDB service: `influxdb`.

```
% docker-compose run python \
    /usr/src/app/earthquake.py \
    --host=influxdb \
    --input /data/eq.txt \
    --precision ms \
    --db earthquakedb \
    --token=<API_TOKEN>
INFO:root:http://influxdb:8086/write?db=earthquakedb&precision=ms
```

That's it! We just need to create a new Grafana data source to query our data.

## Adding the first row

We begin the dashboard-building process by creating a new dashboard, taking care to save any previous dashboard we were working on. Again, space doesn't permit me to enumerate all the panel configuration settings, so I'm concentrating on the ones that change from their defaults.

We start off by querying our earthquake InfluxDB bucket:

- **Data source**: **InfluxDB Earthquake**
- **Query**: `SELECT "magnitude" FROM "event" WHERE $timeFilter AND "magnitude" >= 2.0 GROUP BY "tag_place"::tag, "tag_time"::tag`
- **Format as**: **Table**

Unlike the weather dashboard, queries will be fairly simple and consistent across this dashboard. We are pulling in the magnitude metric from each event and bringing in the place and newly created time tags. Convert the visualization to **Stat**.

### Building the highest-magnitude Stat panel

This first panel is going to show off the time, place, and magnitude of the highest-magnitude earthquake in the time range, so let's set the time range to **Last 24 hours**. Additionally, set **Title** in the **Panel** options to **Highest Magnitude**.

We need to first sort all the data by magnitude so the highest-magnitude earthquake is at the top of the list. We'll do this with **Sort Transform**. Set the **Sort by** field to **magnitude** from the drop-down menu.

Now, we display all the fields we want in this panel, but we want to set threshold colors based on magnitude, and since they can be set independently for each field, it will be hard to control that behavior if they're kept separate. We'll use another transform to collect them all into a single field using the **Rows to fields** transform. Set the fields as follows:

- **Time**: **Ignore**
- **Tag_place**: **Field label**
- **Tag_time**: **Field name**
- **Magnitude**: **Field value**

This will enable us to combine all the information we want into a single *composite* field, and we'll also be able to set a threshold based on the **Magnitude** field's value.

For the **Value** options, normally, we would use the **Last\*** option, but since we've combined all our data into a single row with many fields, that option is out. We'll go ahead and select **All values** and set **Limit** to 1. That should give us a panel with a single value. Set **Fields** to **All Fields** to finish up.

In the **Stat** styles, we just want to make sure the **Stat** visualization has a background and no sparkline graph. You should feel free to experiment with this to see what looks good to you; here are my settings:

- **Orientation**: **Auto**
- **Text mode**: **Value and name**
- **Color mode**: **Background**
- **Graph mode**: **None**
- **Text alignment**: **Auto**

For the **Text** size, we want to display our text with a smallish text label and a large magnitude label:

- **Title**: 60
- **Value**: 120

The convention for earthquake magnitudes is to refer to them with a single decimal, so set **Decimal** in the **Standard** options to 1. We want to control the background with thresholds, so set **Color scheme** to **From thresholds (by value)**.

Finally, we just need to set our thresholds and we're done. I created three thresholds (plus the default **Base** threshold) to give a sense that the higher the magnitude, the more serious the earthquake:

- **Color**: **red** | 7
- **Color**: **orange** | 5

- **Color: yellow** | 3
- **Base**: **green**

*Building the most recent Stat panel*

To make our other **Stat** panel, size the current one to about half the width of the row and high enough to accommodate the text. Then duplicate the panel. We want to change a couple of things:

1. Set **Title** in the **Panel** options to Most Recent.
2. In the **Query** tab, set **Data source** to -- **Dashboard** -- and **Source** to the **Highest Magnitude** panel.
3. In the **Transform** tab, set **Field** in the **Sort by Transformation** function to **Time** and enable the **Reverse** option.

That should complete our first row. Mine looks like this:

Figure 9.10 – First row

We'll be using a similar query and transform approach for the next row but using table visualizations instead.

## Adding the second row

It turns out the **Table** panels for our second row will be functionally similar to the **Stat** visualization panel, only we will be looking at several rows of data at a time. We'll build the first panel, then copy it and alter it to suit our needs.

Name a new panel 5 Highest Magnitude. We'll use almost the same query:

- **Data source: InfluxDB Earthquake**
- **Query**: SELECT "magnitude" FROM "event" WHERE ("magnitude" >= 2.0) AND $timeFilter GROUP BY "tag_place"::tag
- **Format as**: **Table**

Next, we use the **Sort by Transformation** function, followed by **Limit**, which we picked to fit on a single page of the table:

- **Sort by | Field: magnitude**
- **Limit | Limit**: 5

From here, we just need to keep most of the defaults, making sure to enable the **Show table header** option in the **Table** section. We'll add the same thresholds as before:

- **Standard options | Color scheme: From thresholds (by value)**
- **Color: red** | 7
- **Color: orange** | 5
- **Color: yellow** | 3
- **Base: green**

We'll add a bit of visual interest to the table by adding a basic gauge to the magnitude cells with a field override. Add a field override for **Fields with name** field and select **magnitude**. Next, add these override properties:

- **Cell display mode: Basic gauge**
- **Standard options | Min**: 0
- **Standard options | Max**: 10

Here's what the field override should look like:

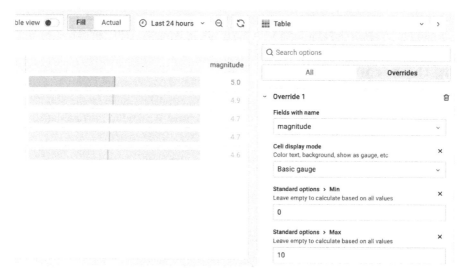

Figure 9.11 – Magnitude field override

Apply the panel settings and size it to roughly half the width and enough to show a little more than the 5 rows of data, then duplicate it. You'll change the following settings to display the five most recent earthquakes:

1.  Set **Title** in the **Panel** options to 5 Most Recent.

2.  In the **Query** tab, set **Data source** to -- **Dashboard** -- and **Source** to the **5 Highest Magnitude** panel.

3.  In the **Transform** tab, set **Field** in the **Sort by Transformation** function to **Time** and enable the **Reverse** option.

You've now completed the second row! Here's what my dashboard looks like so far:

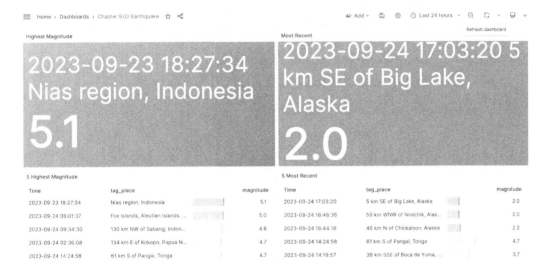

Figure 9.12 – Second row

Configuring the panels for the final row is the same process we followed in the previous chapter. We'll query for earthquakes, and then map them by size.

## Adding the third row

Create a new panel, set **Visualization** to **Geomap**, and add the following query:

- **Data source**: **InfluxDB Earthquake**

- **Query**: SELECT "magnitude" FROM "event" WHERE $timeFilter AND ("magnitude" >= 2.0) GROUP BY "tag_latitude"::tag, "tag_longitude"::tag

- **Format as**: **Table**

There is no need to transform the data, so we'll go right to mapping our earthquakes. Here are the settings:

- **Map layers | Layer 1 | Layer type: Markers**
- **Map layers | Layer 1 | Location mode: Coords**
- **Map layers | Layer 1 | Latitude field: tag_latitude**
- **Map layers | Layer 1 | Longitude field: tag_longitude**
- **Map layers | Layer 1 | Styles | Size: magnitude**
- **Map layers | Layer 1 | Styles | Min:** 2
- **Map layers | Layer 1 | Styles | Max:** 15
- **Map layers | Layer 1 | Styles | Symbol: circle.svg**
- **Map layers | Layer 1 | Styles | Color: Fixed color | green**
- **Map layers | Layer 1 | Styles | Fill opacity: 0.4**
- **Map layers | Layer 1 | Show legend: disabled**
- **Map layers | Layer 1 | Show tooltip: enabled**
- **Basemap layer | Layer type: ArcGIS MapServer**
- **Basemap layer | Server instance: World Physical**
- **Basemap layer | Opacity: 0.5**
- **Map Controls | Show zoom control: enabled**
- **Map Controls | Mouse wheel zoom: disabled**
- **Map Controls | Show attribution: disabled**
- **Map Controls | Tooltip: Details**

It's left as an exercise for you to find out how to set the thresholds for each marker. We will want to create three different panels, each looking from a different scale and/or region. The first one will look at California, so set the title and the map view:

- **Panel options | Title:** California
- **Map view | Initial view | View: Coordinates**
- **Map view | Initial view | Latitude:** 37.441912
- **Map view | Initial view | Longitude:** -120.53232
- **Map view | Initial view | Zoom: 5.5**

These are not intended to be exact, so feel free to center the display on whatever you'd like; these are just where the map will zoom when first launched. Resize the panel to roughly a square shape, measuring roughly a third of the width of the dashboard. You'll need to make two copies, with these settings for the second panel:

- **Panel options | Title**: North America
- **Query | Data source**: -- Dashboard --
- **Query | Source: California**
- **Map view | Initial view | View: Coordinates**
- **Map view | Initial view | Latitude**: 40
- **Map view | Initial view | Longitude**: -100
- **Map view | Initial view | Zoom: 4**

The third panel will have these settings:

- **Panel options | Title**: Oceania
- **Query | Data source**: -- Dashboard --
- **Query | Source: California**
- **Map view | Initial view | View: Coordinates**
- **Map view | Initial view | Latitude**: -10
- **Map view | Initial view | Longitude**: -140
- **Map view | Initial view | Zoom: 2**

When completed, the completed dashboard should look something like this:

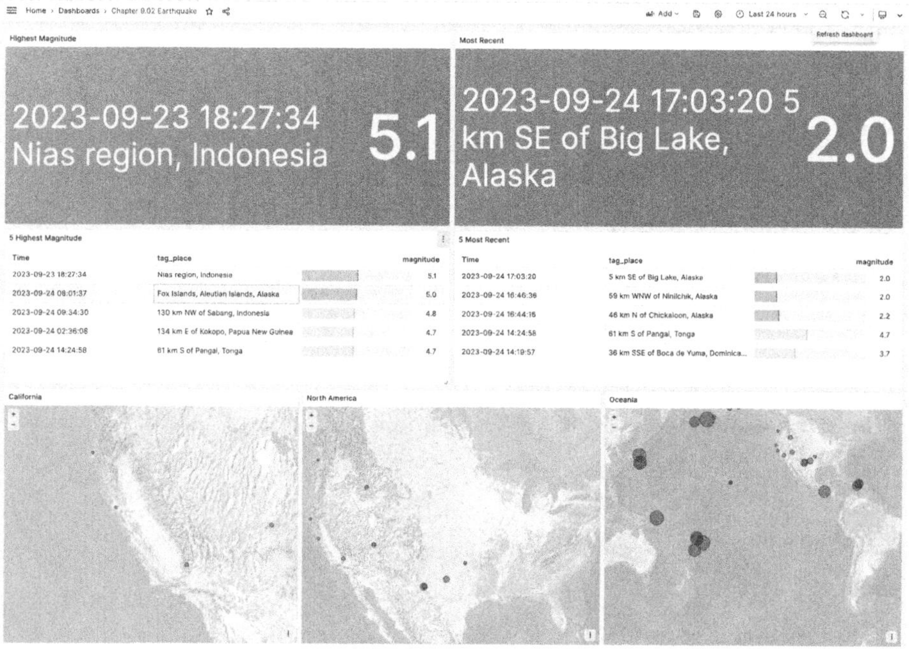

Figure 9.13 – Final dashboard

And that completes our efforts. Don't forget to save your dashboard! You now have two beautiful dashboards to play with, and hopefully some new techniques for efficiently creating new ones.

# Parting thoughts

Before we move on to the next chapter, there are a couple of things you should take away from this exploration of how to develop meaningful Grafana presentations. The first deals with visual display considerations and the second deals with automating the process of ingesting your data.

## Considering layout

Play with your dashboards' panel arrangements to see what various combinations look like. This is a good opportunity to get a better understanding of how to work with the Grafana layout manager. While you experiment with the ordering of the various panels, keep a few things in mind:

- Different cultural groups read from left to right, right to left, or from top to bottom. Know your audience and arrange your dashboard panels to reveal information in the order that your viewers typically scan.

- Use color, size, and visual contrast to draw the eye of the viewer toward the information you want to particularly highlight. Finally, depending on the context, you may want to avoid packing too much information onto a single dashboard. Too much visual information can be confusing for the viewer.

- While it is beyond the scope of this book, bear in mind the accessibility considerations when developing these dashboards and laying them out. Visually impaired viewers may have trouble discerning certain color combinations, they may have trouble discerning small text, or they may have difficulty with fine details such as lines and points.

## Automating ingestion

Also, you may have noticed that if you want to continuously keep your dashboards up to date, you must manually run the ETL scripts over and over again. That is certainly not my kind of fun, but what's the alternative? It's beyond the scope of this book to explore how to orchestrate ETL execution, but I would recommend some ideas.

One of the most simple and venerable tools for *nix operating systems is called **cron**. It is a system task that can be configured to run arbitrary scripts on a regular basis, from every few seconds to monthly. The computer you are working on most likely is using some form of `cron` as we speak.

At the other extreme is a full-production ETL orchestration system such as the open source Apache Airflow. It is a complex, powerful system that can schedule complex Python script assemblages called **Directed Acyclic Graphs** (**DAGs**) and even comes with a number of open source ETL plugins ready-made for connecting to various third-party applications such as Salesforce or MySQL.

## Summary

In this chapter, we first looked at how to break down the requirements for designing dashboards. We compared the challenges of maximizing content or maximizing visibility by examining two use cases. Finally, we mentioned the social need to consider audience perception and the technical need to continuously update data.

In the next chapter, we'll look at more ways to make panel creation more efficient and responsive. We'll also look at some more advanced dashboard features that can expand the scope of your dashboards by linking them together into a coherent, interactive whole.

# 10

# Working with Advanced Dashboard Features and Elasticsearch

By now, you're probably feeling comfortable with Grafana but have legitimate concerns about the effort involved. You may be thinking that the possibility of writing a lot of code to handle **extract, transform, and load** (**ETL**) tasks might eat into your time budget to build the dashboards. Perhaps the number of panels you will have to configure and organize on multiple dashboards seems potentially tedious, error-prone work.

In this chapter, we're going to look at how to reduce the ETL burden using off-the-shelf tools, as well as how to use templates to fill a dashboard with variants, using only a single panel. We'll also show you how annotations make it possible to **drill down** into aggregated data in order to examine individual data points. Then, we'll take our dashboards and link them together with simple UI elements. Finally, we'll look at strategies to share our dashboards with others.

The following topics will be covered in this chapter:

- Building the data server
- Templating dashboards
- Linking dashboards
- Annotating dashboards
- Sharing dashboards

Let's get started!

# Technical requirements

The tutorial code, dashboards, and other helpful files for this chapter can be found in this book's GitHub repository at `https://github.com/PacktPublishing/Learn-Grafana-10/tree/main/Chapter10`.

# Building the data server

Imagine for a moment that you are working for the public works department of a major city. Throughout the day, citizens use their phones and computers to report problems via the 311 service (`https://www.open311.org`). You've been tasked with accessing the 311 data, building dashboards, and presenting them to various stakeholders within the city government. They will want to see how many of the various types of calls are made to the system, as well as how they are distributed across the city in various council districts.

Before we can build our dashboards, we'll need to get some data. Luckily, many major cities make anonymized 311 data publicly accessible in many popular data formats, including JSON and CSV. For this exercise, we'll be working with 311 data from the city of San Francisco. This data is available via their extensive data portal at `https://data.sfgov.org/City-Infrastructure/Current-FY-Cases/iy63-pi3t`.

To get started with this exercise, open a Terminal shell window, change directory into the `Chapter10` folder in your clone of this book's GitHub repository, and download the dataset (in the CSV format) from the **DataSF** website (or grab a copy from this book's GitHub repository). After downloading the file, we'll set up an Elasticsearch server to serve our data. Elasticsearch is part of a powerful triad of software, including Logstash and Kibana, that comprises the Elasticsearch ELK stack. Rather than writing code to import the data into Elasticsearch, we'll use Logstash to read our file and send it to the server. Here's a quick look at the `docker-compose.yml` file:

```
services:
    elasticsearch:
        image: docker.elastic.co/elasticsearch/elasticsearch:8.10.2
        ports:
            - "9200:9200"
        environment:
            - discovery.type=single-node
            - xpack.security.enabled=false
            - ingest.geoip.downloader.enabled=false
        volumes:
            - "${PWD-.}/elasticsearch/data:/usr/share/elasticsearch/data"


    grafana:
        image: "grafana/grafana:${GRAF_TAG-latest}"
```

```
    ports:
        - "3000:3000"
    volumes:
        - "${PWD-.}/grafana:/var/lib/grafana"

    logstash:
        image: docker.elastic.co/logstash/logstash:${LS_TAG-8.6.1}
    volumes:
        - "${PWD-.}/logstash:/usr/share/logstash/pipeline"
        - "${PWD-.}/data:/data"
```

In this file, we first define an Elasticsearch service:

1.  Use the latest image (8.10.2 at the time of writing) of Elasticsearch.

2.  Expose the Elasticsearch port at `9200`.

3.  Disable the security settings and the `geoip` downloader, as they are not needed for this exercise; lock Elasticsearch to a single node cluster.

4.  Map the `/usr/share/elasticsearch/data` directory in the container to a local Elasticsearch directory.

5.  Set up a single worker node. Since you may be running Elasticsearch on a local platform such as a laptop, we've set up an insecure configuration.

> **Warning**
>
> Elasticsearch normally ships with all security features enabled. However, to keep this exercise as simple as possible, we have disabled those features. For safety, do not use this configuration in production or in a way that exposes your site to the internet.

For Grafana, do the following:

1.  Use the most current image.

2.  Expose port `3000`.

3.  Map `/var/lib/grafana` in the container to a local Grafana directory.

Finally, we need to specify the Logstash service:

1.  Use the latest image (8.6.1 at the time of writing) of Logstash.

2.  Map the `/usr/share/logstash/pipeline` directory in the container to a local Logstash directory.

We won't actually run Logstash as a persistent service; instead, we will just use this service specification in Docker Compose to give Logstash access to the network that our Elasticsearch and Grafana servers are running on.

Launch the services by running `docker-compose`:

```
% docker-compose up --pull missing -d elasticsearch
% docker-compose up --pull missing -d grafana
```

We specify each service individually because we don't want to spin up a Logstash service just yet. It won't hurt anything if you accidentally run all three services, but we want to control when Logstash processes the CSV file.

Before we can import our file with Logstash, we need to configure it. It is beyond the scope of this book to go into a lot of detail on the many features and capabilities of both Elasticsearch and Logstash (in fact, there are whole books available from Packt and other publishers). In short, Logstash is designed to deliver a log-processing pipeline in a single tool, configured through a single configuration file that specifies the actions of a sequence of plugins.

A Logstash configuration includes three components: **input**, **filters**, and **output**. Here's a simple schematic diagram and how it maps into the traditional ETL pattern:

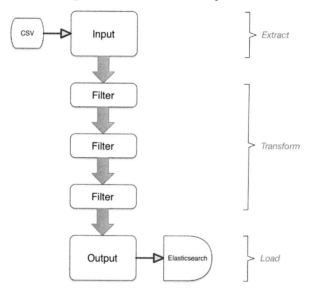

Figure 10.1 – The Logstash pipeline

In our case, the input will be a file read in from standard input (`stdin`). In order to properly clean and conform our file so that it can be imported into Elasticsearch, we will configure some filters so that they can process a CSV file. Finally, the output will be routed to standard output (`stdout`, for debugging purposes) and our Elasticsearch server.

Let's walk through the configuration file; first up is the `input` section:

```
input {
    stdin {}
}
```

It doesn't get any simpler than this. Typically, Logstash is configured as a service that periodically looks for changes in one or more files, and it then reads them in for processing. We only need to run Logstash once to input our CSV file, so we use the `stdin` plugin so that Logstash gracefully exits after the file processing is completed. Next up, we have the `filter` section:

```
filter {
    if "CaseID" in [message] {
        drop {}
    }
    csv {
        columns => ["CaseID","Opened","Closed",
        "ResponsibleAgency","Category","RequestType",
        "Address","Street",
        "SupervisorDistrict","Neighborhood",
        "PoliceDistrict","Latitude","Longitude","Source",
        "MediaURL"]
    convert => {
        "Latitude" => "float"
        "Longitude" => "float"
        }
    }
    date {
        match => ["Opened", "MM/dd/yyyy HH:mm:ss a"]
        target => "Opened"
    }
    date {
        match => ["Closed", "MM/dd/yyyy HH:mm:ss a"]
        target => "Closed"
    }
}
```

This is the section where the real work happens:

1. First, we check each line of the file (in Logstash, each line is treated as an event with the contents of the line stored in `message`) for the `CaseID` string, which should only be present in the header. If the line is indeed a header line, drop it from further processing.

2. Next, we configure the `csv` plugin to process each line, mapping each field in the parsed line to the corresponding element in the `columns` list (copied from the header).

3.  We convert the `latitude` and `longitude` into `float` values if we want to map them.

4.  By default, the `csv` plugin won't recognize the `Opened` and `Closed` fields as dates, so we will use the `date` plugin to convert them by matching the string contents of the two named date fields against the format string and storing the converted date objects back in their original fields.

Once we've parsed and processed the CSV file, we'll need to ship the results to Elasticsearch. This is handled in the `output` section:

```
output {
    elasticsearch {
        hosts => "elasticsearch:9200"
        index => "data-index"
    }
    stdout {}
}
```

We use two plugins to handle output – `elasticsearch` and `stdout`. The `elasticsearch` plugin is given two parameters, with `hosts` specifying the host and port for the connection to Elasticsearch and `index` specifying the destination index for the data. Think of an Elasticsearch index as analogous to a database table or an InfluxDB bucket. The `stdout` plugin line is optional and is included as it also prints out the same processed data it will transmit to the Elasticsearch server in the Terminal window. This output is often helpful to monitor progress and troubleshoot any problems that may arise when processing the data.

To load the data into Elasticsearch, run the following `docker-compose` command:

```
% docker-compose run logstash logstash < data/Current_FY_Cases.csv
```

This command runs `logstash` from the Logstash service and redirects its input from the CSV file. The file in question is pretty big (~815 MB), so depending on your computer's performance, it may take around 30–60 minutes to load all the rows into Elasticsearch, so take a break!

If you'd rather not work with the entire dataset, use a standard text editor or (if available on your OS) the `tail` command to extract the last few weeks. If you'd rather not wait to download or process the full dataset, I've added some smaller datasets to the repository for you to experiment with.

Because we are using the `stdout` plugin for output, you should be able to see the data rows printed to the screen as they are processed. It can often be helpful to leverage these kinds of tricks to help troubleshoot problems with data ingestion. If you don't see what you're expecting, you may have a problem!

Let's start working with that data by connecting Grafana to Elasticsearch!

## Connecting Grafana to Elasticsearch

Now that we have our data loaded into Elasticsearch, we'll need to create a data source connection in Grafana to read it. Connecting to Elasticsearch is not substantially different from the InfluxDB data sources we've been using. The authorization controls for our Elasticsearch container allow open access to the data source, so we won't need to use an API token to access it:

1. Open your browser to the Grafana app and select **Connections | Add new connection** from the main menu.

2. Search for the Elasticsearch data source and select it.

3. Click on **Add a new data source**. Fill out the following form fields:

    - **Name**: `Elasticsearch`

    - **HTTP | URL**: `http://elasticsearch:9200`

    - **Elasticsearch details | Index name**: `data-index`

    - **Elasticsearch details | pattern**: **No pattern**

    - **Elasticsearch details | Time field name**: `Opened`

    - **Elasticsearch details | Min time interval**: `5m`

The data source page should look something like this:

Figure 10.2 – Elasticsearch data source

Since we are using Docker Compose to manage networking for our services, namely Grafana and Elasticsearch, we need to configure the data source to access a URL with the service name from our docker-compose.yml file. If you are able to successfully connect your data source to Elasticsearch, you should see a green message near the bottom reading **Data source successfully connected**. This indicates that the data source can access the index and identify the Opened field as a proper date field, for use as a time field.

# Querying with Elasticsearch

Now that we have a functioning data source, let's build a regular time series visualization panel to get a feel for how we're going to present the data. Remember that we want to be able to look at the kinds of calls made to 311 across different neighborhoods, so let's first make a query just to get an idea of how many graffiti calls are made. You can do this in Explore, but we're going to build on our panel as we go, so you'll want to start with a dashboard and a new time series panel visualization.

Go to the panel's **Query** tab to access the Elasticsearch data source query. You'll notice its similarity to the InfluxDB **Query** tab from previous chapters. The terminology may be a little different between Elasticsearch and InfluxDB, but the concepts are very similar. Let's enter a query string into the **Query** field. Elasticsearch leverages a powerful Google-like search engine called Lucene to perform text queries, so simply type in the word `Graffiti`, and you should get a response back with all the matching data.

If you don't see anything change, make sure your query time frame is wide enough. If you downloaded the dataset recently from DataSF, set it to **Last 7 days**; if you are using data from this book's repository, the data goes back to February 6, 2023. If your query found the data (called *documents* in Elasticsearch terminology) in your Elasticsearch server and you have the approximate time range, you should see an output similar to the following:

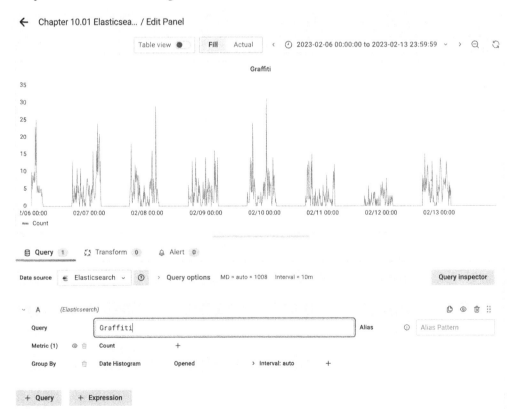

Figure 10.3 – An Elasticsearch query

The next field is called **Metric**, but it is easier to think of it as just an **aggregation** function. If you use **Date Histogram** for **Group By**, the specified metric – in this case, **Count** – is calculated for each time interval. For **Group By**, you can modify the time interval, but let's leave it set to **Interval: auto** for now. We will set the associated time field in the data to **Opened**, which we also configured as the Time field name when we first set up the data source.

Next, let's add another **Group by** option to give us a further grouping by supervisor district. Click the + icon to the right of the **Group by** field. This should give you another **Group by** option, but with **Terms**. **Terms** in the context of Elasticsearch, is much like an InfluxDB tag in that it represents a field of text values. Let's select **SupervisorDistrict.keyword** from the select field arrow dropdown. Since there are 11 supervisor districts in San Francisco, click on the dropdown to the right of **SupervisorDistrict. keyword**, and select **15** from the **Size** dropdown:

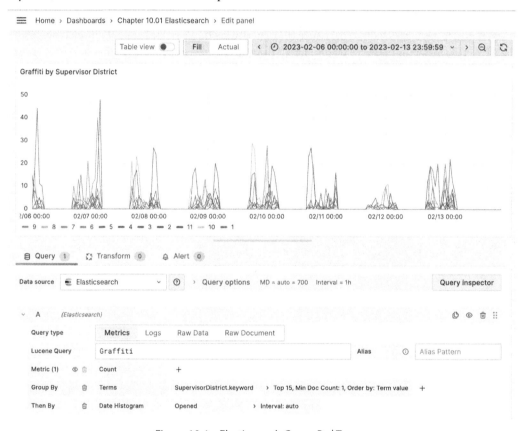

Figure 10.4 – Elasticsearch Group By | Terms

While we're at it, let's get more specific about our query. By placing `Graffiti` as the only entry in the **Query** box, we're asking Elasticsearch to find the `Graffiti` string across all of the text fields in our index. We only care about `Graffiti` as it pertains to a particular index field, namely the `Category` field. Since we are looking at the `Graffiti` category, we want to search for our value of the corresponding `Category.keyword` field. Let's modify our query by entering the following in the **Query** field (as shown in *Figure 10.5*):

- **Query**: `Category.keyword:Graffiti`
- **Query options** | **Min interval**: `1h`

The **auto** time interval setting uses the `$__interval` set by Grafana, so we set the **Min interval** option of `1h` to give us a simpler look at the data. Alternatively, we could have set the query time interval to **1h**, but this gives us a bit more flexibility if we want to change the time range.

> **Info**
>
> Let's pause for a moment to clarify something about text queries in Elasticsearch. Since we used Logstash to add our data to the Elasticsearch index without specifying the index mapping (an index configuration that works much like a database schema), Elasticsearch created one for us. For each field not otherwise specified, Elasticsearch creates and indexes two fields – a text field named for the field itself and a special `.keyword` version of the same field.
>
> The content in the text fields is automatically broken up (analyzed) into word-like objects called tokens and then indexed by those tokens. This is the way Elasticsearch matches a search on the words in a field. Keyword fields are unanalyzed, so to search for a keyword field, you will need to either exactly match the text or use wildcards.

Before we move on, let's go ahead and configure some panel settings. I'll point out the settings that we need to change, leaving the rest to the defaults:

- **Panel options** | **Title**: `Graffiti Calls by Supervisor District`
- **Legend** | **Visibility**: on
- **Graph styles** | **Style**: **Bars**
- **Graph styles** | **Fill opacity**: **100**
- **Graph styles** | **Stack series**: **Normal**

Here is what the term bars look like when they're stacked up:

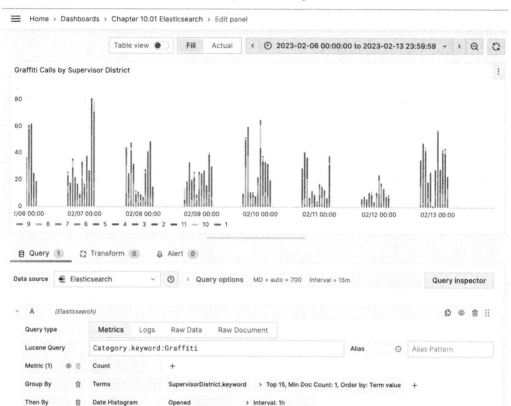

Figure 10.5 – Elasticsearch querying by category name

This is all well and good, but constantly having to change the query every time we want to look at a different category is going to be tedious. We're going to address this problem next.

## Creating a template variable

Now that we have an idea of what our panel might look like, we observe that if we were to create additional panels, one for each category of 311 call, we might need to create many panels, with each being a virtually identical panel, except for the value of the category in question. This seems tedious at best, and a potential maintenance nightmare at worst. What would happen if, say, you wanted to tailor the color scheme for the breakdowns or change the stacking options? You might end up clicking through dozens of panels, just to make a single change.

What if we could put a placeholder string in our query, and then set the value of that placeholder from a menu selection? You would then be creating a kind of *template* panel, with a placeholder standing in for the actual query value. In the panel query, you would fill a template panel variable. A *template variable* is a special string that represents a placeholder that Grafana will substitute from a selection of predefined values.

Template variables have three main characteristics:

- The variable definition, which determines its name and the set of possible values

- The variable embedding in various dashboard components, including panels and rows

- The evaluated variable, which, depending on the context, may be a defined constant, a user-specified selection via a drop-down menu, or even a value calculated from other dependent variables

So, the first step in working with a template variable is to define one. We'll start by defining a template variable to represent a 311 category, and let's call it 311Category.

Open **Dashboard Settings**, select **Variables**, and click **Add Variable**. Select the **Query** variable type and use these settings:

- **General** | **Name**: 311Category

- **General** | **Label**: 311 Category

- **Query Options** | **Data Source**: **Elasticsearch** (the Elasticsearch data source)

- **Query Options** | **Query**: {"find": "terms", "field": "Category.keyword"}

- **Query Options** | **Sort**: **Alphabetical (asc)**

- **Query Options** | **Refresh**: **On dashboard load**

- **Selection Options** | **Include All Option**: on

If you typed in the query correctly, and your time frame encompasses a reasonable cross-section of data (at least a day or two), you should see a list of possible values under **Preview of values**:

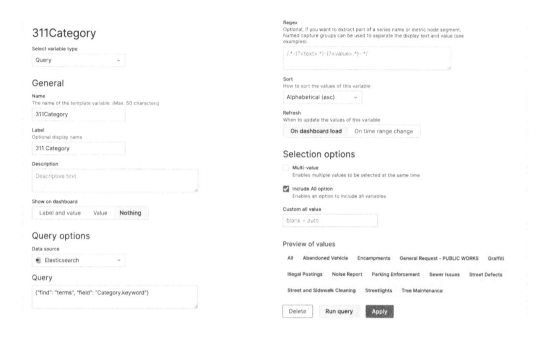

Figure 10.6 – Template variable creation

> **Tip**
>
> To check to see that your query correctly returns the values you need, click **Run query**. If you don't see results immediately after adding the data to Elasticsearch, you may want to give it a few minutes to index before trying again.

Now, let's go over these settings:

- **Select variable type** is one of several possible template variable types we'll explore. In this case, it is one that is derived via a data source query.

- **Name** is the actual name you will reference in the dashboard elements.

- **Label** is simply the label for the drop-down menu you will use to select the template variable's value.

- **Query** is a snippet of JSON that will go into an Elasticsearch query, which generates the values for the template variable.

The snippet we're using in the template variable's query indicates that it should find the unique values (terms) for the `Category.keyword` field. The default maximum number of terms returned is `500`, but if the cardinality (number of unique values) of a field is higher than a few dozen, you may want to consider setting a limit by adding a `size` key to the query. A high-cardinality field is likely to substantially slow down your UI. See the following example:

```
{"find": "terms", "field": "Category.keyword",
    "size": limit}
```

Moving on down with remaining settings:

- Set **Sort** to **asc** (ascending) in alphabetical order
- Enable **Include All Option** to give us the option to see all the categories

Don't forget to click **Apply** when you have finished editing the template variable. It's all too easy to click away to one of the other settings pages and, sadly, lose your changes. Don't forget to save your dashboard as well!

## Adding template variables to the graph panel

Now that we've added a template variable, we'll put it to use. First, we'll stop the query. In the **Query** field, change `Graffiti` to `$311Category`:

- **Query**: `Category.keyword:$311Category`

Let's also include the variable when we set **Panel title**:

- **Title**: `$311Category by Supervisor District`

As we can see, our variable works in other places besides the query! To reference a variable in a row or panel, either use $ followed by the variable name, or if the variable is part of a string, surround it with double brackets, `[[` and `]]`. Now that you've set up the panel, try out different values from the **311 Category** dropdown. Note how both the results and the title change in response to the variable's settings:

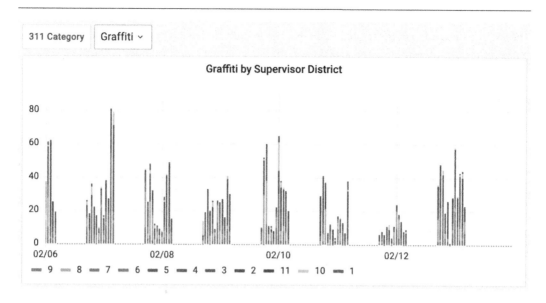

Figure 10.7 – A query with a template variable

Once you get a taste of the power of template variables, you'll begin to see all sorts of places where you can use them. When you do, your dashboards will become that much more flexible without a lot of extra effort.

## Templating additional variables

Why stop here? Perhaps we could template the interval? Let's create a new variable that we will use to set different **Date Histogram** intervals. That way, we can see what the call volume looks like when aggregated across periods of time. But how do we specify possible values for time intervals? Happily, Grafana provides the answer with the **Interval** variable type. Create a new variable and call it `HistInterval`:

- **Select variable type**: **Interval**
- **General | Name**: `HistInterval`
- **General | Label**: `Histogram Interval`

Feel free to modify the list of possible time intervals. There is an additional option you can activate called **Auto Option**. Turning this on will present a new interval, called **Auto**, that will automatically divide up the overall time range into **Step count** intervals, but never create an interval smaller than **Min interval**.

Once you've set up the variable, go to the **Query** tab in your panel, and next to **Then by Date Histogram**, open the **Interval** section and type in `$HistInterval`. The Elasticsearch data source detects the list of **Interval** values from the variable and makes them available in the dropdown.

Try out your new panel and experiment with different intervals. You may need to adjust your time range to accommodate some of the larger intervals. Likewise, you may get an error from Elasticsearch if you set the interval time too small. Don't be alarmed – this just means that you've asked Elasticsearch to break down the graph data into too many chunks of returned data (called buckets) than it has been configured to aggregate. In a production environment, you would tune your Elasticsearch configuration to handle higher bucket counts, if necessary, but for now, just scale down your time range width.

Here's what a one-day interval across a seven-day time range might look like:

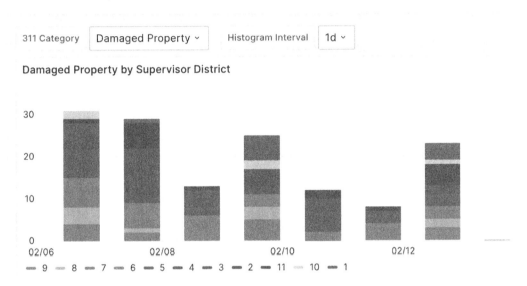

Figure 10.8 – Interval set by template variable

Why stop there? Behold the power of the template variable! Create a new **Query** variable called FieldName:

- **General | Name**: FieldName
- **General | Label**: Field Name
- **Query Options | Data Source**: **Elasticsearch**
- **Query Options | Query**: {"find": "fields", "type": "keyword"}
- **Query Options | Regex**: /(.*)\.keyword/
- **Query Options | Sort**: **Alphabetical (asc)**

We use **Regex** to trim off the .keyword portion of the string. Only the text that matches the regex within the parentheses is retained. Since we remove .keyword from the variable, you'll still need to append it when you reference the variable in your queries.

Next, we will create a new template variable that will take the result of the field name, creating a variable with the terms for that field on the fly:

- **Select variable type**: **Query**
- **General** | **Name**: `FieldTerms`
- **General** | **Label**: `Field Terms`
- **Query Options** | **Data Source**: **Elasticsearch**
- **Query Options** | **Query**: `{"find": "terms", "field": "$FieldName.keyword"}`
- **Query Options** | **Sort**: **Alphabetical (asc)**
- **Selection Options** | **Include All Options**: **on**

Don't worry if you don't see a proper preview – the variables editor doesn't know what the dependent `$FieldName` variable is set to, so it can't evaluate the full variable. If you want to get a sense of how and where these dependencies might affect your variables, use the **Show dependencies** tool in the **Dashboard settings** | **Variables** pane.

Now, update your panel query so that it uses both variables:

- **Query**: `$FieldName:$FieldTerms`

Also, update the title to `$FieldName:$FieldTerms calls by Supervisor District`.

Here's an example where I selected **Category** as the field name and **Abandoned Vehicle** from the listed field terms:

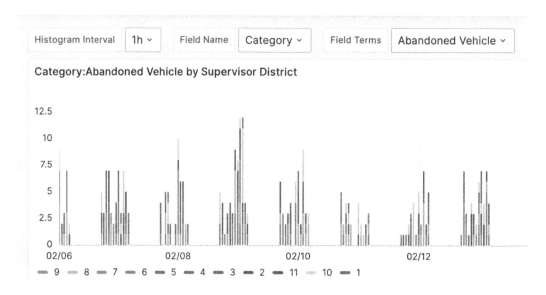

Figure 10.9 – Template variable substitution for the Query field and search term

Try out different combinations of settings for $FieldName and $FieldTerms, and see how they affect both the graph and the title. Also, note how the contents of the **Field Terms** dropdown change when you pick a different field name.

## Creating ad hoc filters

Grafana has developed a special template variable that functions in a similar fashion to our terms query. Called an **ad hoc filter**, it is designed to perform as a filter you would use to reduce a broad query to a more specific query. There is almost no setup involved in using ad hoc filters. You simply specify a name and the data source that corresponds to your panel queries. Once in place, it operates on all of the dashboard's panel queries. By clicking the + icon, you can continue to add **Field Name/ Field Terms** pairs to produce tighter filters.

Ad hoc filters can be very powerful to create quick queries on your data source without the need to open and edit each panel. However, you have no control over the number of possible fields and how many terms they produce, so they should be used with some caution. Here is an example that produces similar results to the preceding **Field Name/Field Terms** combination:

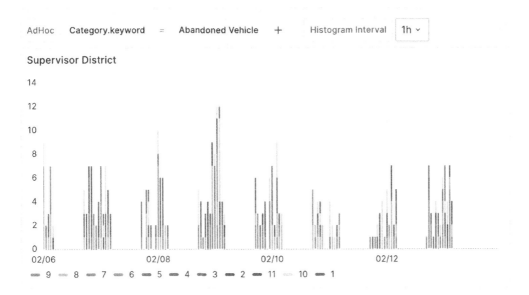

Figure 10.10 – An ad hoc filter

In this case, I selected Category.keyword when I selected + to initiate the filter. Grafana automatically adds the = comparison operator and the dropdown containing the possible Category. keyword terms.

## Repeating rows and panels with template variables

The dashboard layout is one of the more powerful uses for template variables. Instead of the grid layout system that we looked at previously, earlier versions of Grafana used a layout model centered around lining up panels on discrete rows. The panels could vary in size, but all the panels on a row would render within the confines of the row they belonged to. This mechanic for laying out dashboards wasn't very flexible, and it could be very tricky to use, but it did necessitate a powerful feature that still exists today – repeating rows and panels.

How does a repeating row or panel work? Simply put, when you designate the repeat template variable for a row or panel, Grafana will, for each value of the variable, generate a copy of that row or panel and set the panel's template variable(s) to the corresponding value(s). You can find the **Repeat options** setting in the **Panel options** section of each panel or row.

Let's try an example that should give you a good idea of how the **Repeat options** settings work, helping you to see how they react to different template variable settings. Start by creating a new dashboard, and on that dashboard, create a single panel on a single row.

You can create a new row by clicking the dashboard's **Add** dropdown and selecting **Row**. Open **Dashboard settings** | **Variables** and create a new variable:

- **Select variable type**: **Query**
- **General** | **Name**: `PanelRepeatField`
- **Query Options** | **Data source**: **Elasticsearch**
- **Query Options** | **Query**: `{"find": "fields", "type": "keyword"}`
- **Query Options** | **Regex**: `/(.*)\.keyword/`
- **Query Options** | **Sort**: **Alphabetical (asc)**
- **Other options**: **off**

Next, create another variable for the terms:

- **General** | **Type**: **Query**
- **General** | **Name**: `PanelRepeatTerms`
- **Query Options** | **Data source**: **Elasticsearch**
- **Query Options** | **Query**: `{"find": "terms", "field": "$PanelRepeatField.keyword"}`
- **Query Options** | **Regex**: `/(.*)\.keyword/`
- **Query Options** | **Sort**: **Alphabetical (asc)**
- **Selection Options** | **Multi-value**: **on**
- **Other options**: **off**

Now, create a second pair of these variables, but name them `RowRepeatField` and `RowRepeatTerms`, respectively. The query for the `RowRepeatTerms` variable should, of course, reference the `$RowRepeatField` variable. You'll use those to control what each row should display.

In the row, click the settings (gear symbol) icon; you will see the dialog shown in the following screenshot:

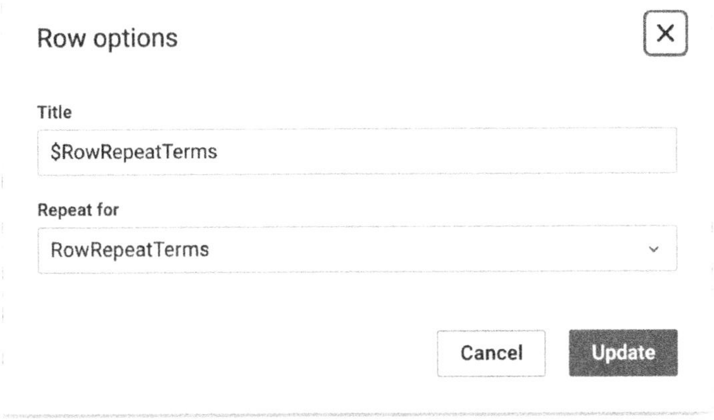

Figure 10.11 – Row options with the template variable

Here, set the following values:

- **Title**: `$RowRepeatTerms`
- **Repeat for**: **RowRepeatTerms**

This sets the repeat for the row. The row itself is what I will refer to as a *canonical* row. Now, go to the **Options** section in the (canonical) **Panel** tab. We're going to put in some Markdown to display the variables as they're set for the panel:

```
| Variable | Value |
|--- | --- |
| _RowRepeatField_ | $RowRepeatField |
| _RowRepeatTerms_ | $RowRepeatTerms |
| _PanelRepeatField_ | $PanelRepeatField |
| _PanelRepeatTerms_ | $PanelRepeatTerms |
```

Here are the rest of the settings you need:

- **Panel options | Title**: `$PanelRepeatTerms`
- **Panel options | Repeat options | Repeat by variable**: **PanelRepeatTerms**
- **Panel options | Repeat options | Repeat direction: Horizontal**
- **Panel options | Repeat options | Max per row**: 6

The first option I set was **PanelRepeatField**; this will generate **PanelRepeatTerms**, which we will use to set the title and generate panels. I then selected **Category**. Next, I selected **311 External Request**, **Abandoned Vehicle**, **Graffiti**, and **Muni Service Feedback**. For the rows, I'll set **RowRepeatField** as **RequestType**, which will generate the terms we'll select for our rows. I'll select **Abandoned Vehicle** and **Blocked_Sidewalk**.

Note how quickly we were able to generate an entire grid of panels with just a few variable definitions and the settings in a single row and panel. As you can see, any number of rows can repeat in the vertical direction, but you can only limit the number of panels in the horizontal direction:

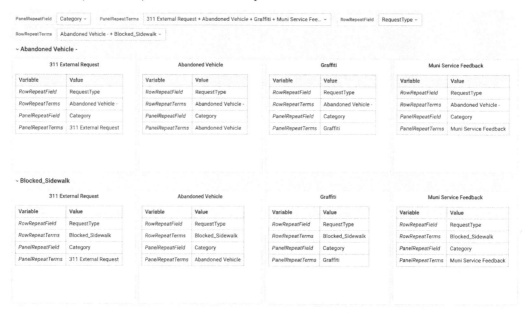

Figure 10.12 – Repeating rows and panels

Now, bear in mind, that you won't get any useful information from these variable selections; this is only going to be useful to illustrate the relationships between template variables and repeating rows and panels. Nonetheless, try out different combinations of variables and see how they affect the rows and panels.

Try out the new dashboard by selecting various repeat fields and their terms. Observe how the number of rows and panels increases and decreases. Also, note how the size of the panels adjusts as the number of panels increases. You may need to tweak the canonical panel to get a nice look for the table when the panels get smaller.

# Creating a new dashboard

Now, we have everything we need to begin building some dashboards with repeating rows and panels. Observe that the data fields group roughly into four major types:

- **Call type**: (`Category` and `RequestType`)
- **Responsibility**: (`PoliceDistrict`, `ResponsibleAgency`, and `SupervisorDistrict`)
- **Location**: (`Address`, `Neighborhood`, `Street`, `Latitude`, and `Longitude`)
- **Date**: (`Opened`, `Closed`, and `@timestamp`)

What we will do here is create a series of dashboards, each one dedicated to a `Responsibility` entity. Each dashboard will be split into two-column panels, one for each `Call` type. We will then allow the user to decide the **Group By** terms for the panel queries. We'll need to create several template variables to drive the dashboard, but once they're created, things should fall into place. Let's get started!

First, we will need to create a dashboard. On the dashboard, we'll create some template variables.

## Setting up the template variables

The first set variable will set the `Responsibility` entity for the dashboard. Since we can't query for it and it has only three possible values anyway, we'll create it as a custom variable. Custom variables are just a comma-separated list of possible values:

- **Select variable type**: **Custom**
- **General | Name**: `Entity`
- **Custom options | Values separated by comma**: `PoliceDistrict, ResponsibleAgency, SupervisorDistrict`

Here are the details for the custom variable:

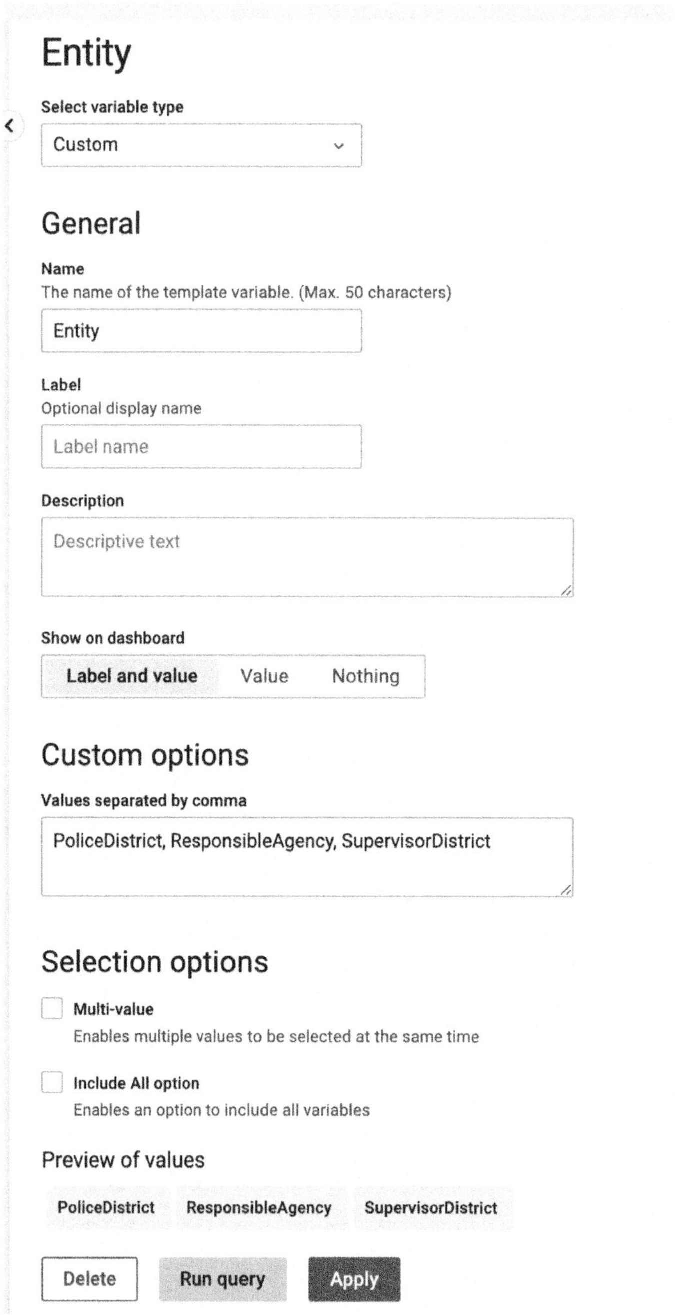

# Entity

**Select variable type**

Custom                                                 ⌄

# General

**Name**
The name of the template variable. (Max. 50 characters)

Entity

**Label**
Optional display name

Label name

**Description**

Descriptive text

**Show on dashboard**

| **Label and value** | Value | Nothing |

# Custom options

**Values separated by comma**

PoliceDistrict, ResponsibleAgency, SupervisorDistrict

# Selection options

☐ **Multi-value**
   Enables multiple values to be selected at the same time

☐ **Include All option**
   Enables an option to include all variables

**Preview of values**

PoliceDistrict     ResponsibleAgency     SupervisorDistrict

| Delete | **Run query** | Apply |

Figure 10.13 – The Custom variable type

We follow up the `Entity` variable with the corresponding term's variable, which we'll call `EntityAgency`. These will be the repeat variables for the dashboard rows:

- **Select variable type**: **Query**
- **General | Name**: `EntityAgency`
- **Query Options | Data source**: **Elasticsearch**
- **Query Options | Query**: `{"find": "terms", "field": "$Entity.keyword"}`
- **Query Options | Sort**: **Alphabetical (asc)**
- **Selection Options | Multi-value**: **on**

Next, we'll create the two pairs of variables that represent the two columnar panels, one pair for `Category` and the other for `RequestType`:

- **Select variable type**: **Query**
- **General | Name**: `Category`
- **Query Options | Data source**: **Elasticsearch**
- **Query Options | Query**: `{"find": "terms", "field": "Category.keyword"}`
- **Query Options | Sort**: **Alphabetical (asc)**
- **Selection Options | Multi-value**: **on**
- **Selection Options | Include All Option**: **on**

The **Group by Terms** variable needs to be set as follows:

- **Select variable type**: **Query**
- **General | Name**: `CategoryGrouping`
- **Query Options | Data source**: **Elasticsearch**
- **Query Options | Query**: `{"find": "fields", "type": "keyword"}`
- **Query Options | Regex**: `/(.*)\.keyword/`
- **Query Options | Sort**: **Alphabetical (asc)**

`RequestType` and `RequestTypeGrouping` are pretty much the same. Just duplicate `Category` and `CategoryGrouping` and modify the query for `RequestType` to match. The last variable is `AggregationInterval` for **Date Histogram**, which we created previously:

- **Select variable type**: **Interval**
- **General | Name**: `AggregationInterval`
- **Interval Options | Values**: `1m,10m,30m,1h,6h,12h,1d,7d,14d,30d`

Don't worry – if you ever get stuck or lose track of all the various option settings, these dashboards can be found in the GitHub repository for this book. Next up, we'll configure the panels.

## Configuring the panels

Each panel will be similar, with just a few differences between them, so once we've configured our first panel, we'll just copy it and make the necessary tweaks. We'll need to create a time series panel, and the first order is to set up the query, as follows:

- **Data source: Elasticsearch**
- **Query type: Metrics**
- **Query:** `$EntityAgency AND $Category`
- **Metric: Count**
- **Group By | Terms: $CategoryGrouping**
- **Group By | Terms | $CategoryGrouping | Order: Bottom**
- **Group By | Terms | $CategoryGrouping | Size: No limit**
- **Group By | Terms | $CategoryGrouping | Order By: Term value**
- **Then By | DateHistogram: Opened**
- **Then By | DateHistogram | Opened | Interval: $AggregationInterval**
- **Query options | Min interval:** 5m

Here, we first query for the values of the documents that match both the value of `$EntityAgency` and the value(s) of `$Category`. We group by `$CategoryGrouping`, which might normally be `Category.keyword`, but it could be some other grouping. We set the **Order** from the bottom up with a size of no limit so that we can see all the possible terms, and the `Term` value will appear in proper alphabetical order (from the lowest value up) in sort **Order By**. Finally, we set the interval to `$AggregationInterval`. For good measure, we set the minimum time interval to something reasonable, such as five minutes.

In the **Panel** tab, we'll turn on the bars and the legend; this is nothing too complicated:

- **Legend | Visibility: on**
- **Legend | Values: Mean**
- **Graph styles | Style: Bars**
- **Graph styles | Stack series: Normal**

Finally, we set the title in **Panel options** to `$Entity ($EntityAgency) $Category by $CategoryGrouping`.

That takes care of the **Category** panel. Now, let's move on to the second panel, which is much the same, but we will make a few tweaks. Duplicate the **Category** panel and make these changes to the query:

- **Query**: `$EntityAgency AND $RequestType`
- **Group by | Terms**: `$RequestTypeGrouping`

Then, make the following change to the title, and we're done:

- **Panel options | Title**: `$Entity ($EntityAgency) $RequestType by $RequestTypeGrouping`

Now, we need to set up the repeating at the row level. Create a row, and make sure both panels are positioned below the row header. Also, make sure to resize the panels if necessary so that they share the row evenly. Here are the row settings:

- **Row options | Title**: `$Entity $EntityAgency`
- **Row options | Repeat for**: **EntityAgency**

From the template variables, select the following:

- **Entity**: **Police District**
- **EntityAgency**: **BAYVIEW + RICHMOND**
- **Category**: **All**
- **CategoryGrouping**: **Category.keyword**
- **RequestType**: **All**
- **RequestTypeGrouping**: **RequestType.keyword**
- **AggregationInterval**: **1d**

Be sure to save your dashboard, and name it something relevant. When complete, the dashboard should look something like this:

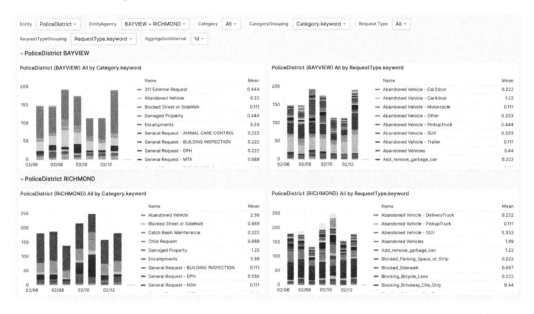

Figure 10.14 – Repeating panels driven by a single template variable

The neat thing about this is that you've effectively created three dashboards, each of which you can see by just changing that single **Entity** variable. From here, you have a few choices, depending on what works best. If you feel like your user would be happy switching between dashboards, then you could publish this as it stands. If, on the other hand, your client doesn't want to see the other dashboards, you could do one of two things:

- Make a special copy of the dashboard with the client's settings for `Entity`, and then hide the `Entity` variable (set **Show on dashboard** to **Nothing**) so that it can't be changed

- Make a special copy of the dashboard and convert the `Entity` variable into a constant type set to the value pre-selected by the client

Next, we're going to look at how to treat the dashboards as separate but still connected, via dashboard linking.

## Linking dashboards

Now that you have your dashboards set up, you may have noticed that navigating between dashboards can be a bit tedious. To go to a different dashboard, you click the dashboard's name, click the Grafana logo, or click the **Dashboards** sidebar menu, and then you look for your dashboard and click on it.

This isn't very efficient, and it makes it difficult to deploy your dashboards as a coherent site that doesn't force your users to go rummaging through a lot of dashboards that aren't relevant to them, in search of the ones that are.

Fortunately, you're in luck! Grafana provides a simple, dashboard-level linking system to facilitate the creation of navigable dashboards. Dashboard linking supports intra-dashboard links via tagging, or inter-dashboard via URL. Let's see how that works for our newly created dashboards.

## Adding dashboard tags

The first step is to make a copy of the dashboard you created in the previous section. Ultimately, we're going to make three different versions of this dashboard. You can copy a dashboard by going to **Dashboard settings** and clicking **Save As....** Then, rename the dashboard to something that references the Entity variable you will choose for this dashboard.

First off, we will need to tag the dashboard. Go to **Dashboard settings | General** and set the following option:

- **Tags**: 311 Calls

The following screenshot shows the **General** panel, showing the tag settings for the dashboard:

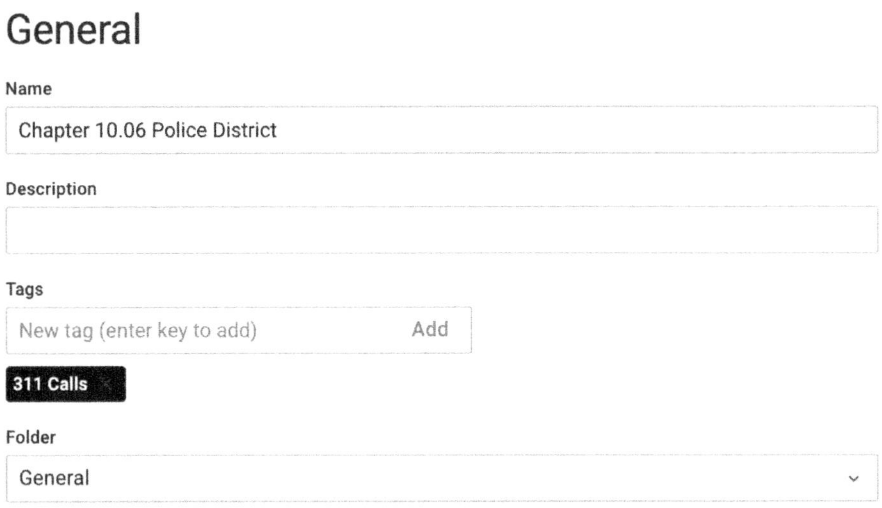

# General

Name

Chapter 10.06 Police District

Description

Tags

New tag (enter key to add)          Add

311 Calls ✕

Folder

General                                                              ⌄

Figure 10.15 – The dashboard tag

Once we've tagged our dashboards, we'll be able to easily create dashboard links based on the tag.

## Locking down a template variable

Next, we'll lock down the `Entity` variable. Go to **Dashboard settings | Variables**, and for the `Entity` variable, remove all but one of the values in **Values separated by comma**. Set **Show on dashboard** to **Nothing**. This step will go more smoothly if you pick the value that matches the `Entity` variable that was selected for the dashboard. Otherwise, you may have to do some selecting and reloading to make sure that all the variables reflect the correct one for the dashboard.

## Creating dashboard links

Open the **Dashboard settings | Links** menu and select **Add Dashboard Link**. Immediately, you will be presented with the option, via the dropdown, to create either a dashboard link or a URL link. Create the link with these settings:

- **Title**: 311 Calls

- **Type**: **dashboards**

- **With tags**: 311 Calls

- **Options | Show as dropdown**: **on**

- **Options | Include current time range**: **on**

- **Options | Include current template variable values**: **on**

Here's a closer look at the configuration for **Dashboard Links**:

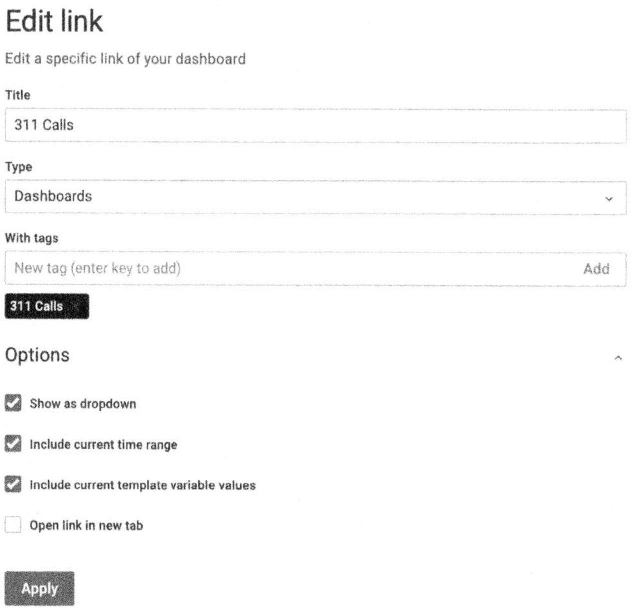

Figure 10.16 – Dashboard linking

This will give you a menu that appears on the header, below the template variables. The menu will navigate you to the other dashboards that share the same tags. The settings will preserve the time range and variable values so that you don't lose your settings if you need to switch back and forth between different dashboards.

As an exercise, try to make copies of the dashboards to cover the other two entities, and link them all together. When finished, you should be able to navigate between all three; each menu should have two entries for the other two dashboards, as shown in the following screenshot (on the right):

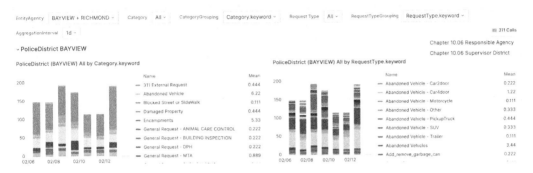

Figure 10.17 – The dashboard link menu

Next, we're going to move on to another advanced dashboard feature – the ability to create annotations of individual data points, both manually in the UI and automatically via an Elasticsearch query.

# Annotating dashboards

Annotations are a versatile mechanism to highlight individual events in a time series. By singling out a single data point at a particular time and marking it with metadata, you have the capability to mark up your dashboard panels with rich data, such as text and tagging. Grafana provides two annotation capabilities to choose from – native annotation queries are created interactively and stored with the dashboard on the Grafana server, while data source annotation queries are created as data source queries, with the query and annotation configuration stored with the dashboard.

## Annotating the graph panel

Since data source annotations can be resource-intensive, we'll demonstrate annotation with just a single-panel dashboard. Create a new dashboard and a single **Time series** panel with the following settings:

- **Data Source**: Elasticsearch
- **Query**: RequestType:Graffiti
- **Query options | Min interval**: 1h

- **Legend | Visibility**: on
- **Graph styles | Style**: **Bars**
- **Graph styles | Stack series**: **Normal**

It's not critical that you get the settings exactly right; the goal here is to just come up with a panel depicting some of our data. Once you have a working panel, manually adding annotations is quite simple:

1. Identify the appropriate moment in time.

2. On the graph, either *Option + click* and select **Add annotation**, or *Command + click* to bring up an annotation popup. If this doesn't work, try simply clicking on the data point to bring up the popup.

3. Fill in the text with descriptive text.

4. Add one or more tags (complete a tag by typing and then using the *Return* or *Tab* key).

An annotation is visually depicted on the time series panel as a vertical dashed line with a pointer triangle, just below the graph baseline, as shown here:

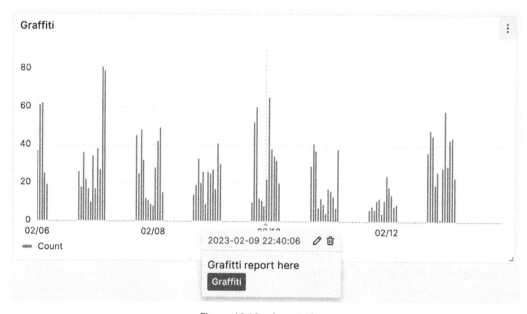

Figure 10.18 – Annotation

That's pretty much all there is to creating a native annotation! Next up, we'll look at how to query for our annotation data.

## Querying tagged annotations

Once you've created some annotations, you'll of course want to be able to see and potentially query for them. To provide visibility into any native annotations, Grafana provides a built-in query, which you'll find in **Dashboard settings | Annotations**. The query is referred to as **Annotations & alerts**, and among the configuration options are the following:

- Name
- Data source
- Enabled/disabled on every dashboard refresh
- A hidden annotation queries toggle
- Annotation marker color
- Query filtering by dashboard or tag
- Maximum number of annotations to display

So, if you toggle **Hidden** to **off**, you'll now see a visibility toggle control on the heading, which enables and disables the query for dashboard annotations. Now, let's add a new annotation query and see how that behaves. Earlier, I added an annotation for `Graffiti` with the following settings:

- **Description**: `Graffiti report here`
- **Tags**: `Graffiti`

Let's go to **Dashboard Settings**, open **Annotations**, and create a new annotation query:

- **Name**: `Graffiti`
- **Data source**: **--Grafana--**
- **Enabled**: **on**
- **Hidden**: **off**
- **Color**: **Red**
- **Filter by**: **Tags**
- **Tags**: `Graffiti`

When you return to your dashboard, you should see two toggle switches – one for **Annotations & Alerts** and the other for **Graffiti**. Now, toggle the **Annotations & Alerts** query off. You should now see a red annotation marker, corresponding to our original **Graffiti** annotation query. Hover over the triangle; you'll see our **Graffiti** annotation.

Now, swap the settings so that **Graffiti** is **off** and **Annotations & Alerts** is **on**. You should now see the same annotation in blue. Hovering over the annotation triangle shows the same annotation. This indicates that our annotation queries are, in fact, independent. The annotations are always there, stored in Grafana's internal database; the reason you can normally see annotations is that each dashboard contains one annotation query dashboard filter that is both enabled and hidden.

Let's move on to querying our Elasticsearch data source for annotation data.

## Creating Elasticsearch annotation queries

Along with native annotations, Grafana also allows us to leverage data sources to serve annotation queries. Unlike the native annotation queries, no actual annotation data is produced. Instead, the data source annotation query provides a view into the underlying data, which is then displayed by Grafana as annotations. Consequently, you wouldn't be able to produce a data source annotation query and then capture a native annotation query for any of the tags generated by the data source annotation query.

Since the annotations are generated from the results of a data source query, you must be very cautious of how many annotations your data source query might generate. Depending on the number of panels you have on the dashboard, and the number of annotations returned from the query, you can easily lock up your page as Grafana struggles to track the thousands of annotations.

You should use **Explore** to vet your query, especially as Elasticsearch can often return a significant number of hits from a query. Use the **Explore Inspector | Stats** options to calculate the number of documents returned from your query.

In this example, we'll create a query for a specific annotation that is a common issue in metropolitan areas – waste on the streets. We'll create a query to look for street waste (both human and animal) with associated photo URLs in a specific supervisor district, tag the annotations with the appropriate `RequestType`, and embed the link in the photos in the **Text** field. Ready?

Add a new annotation query in **Dashboard settings | Annotations**. Here are the settings:

- **Name**: `District 8 Waste`
- **Data source**: **Elasticsearch**
- **Enabled**: **on**
- **Hidden**: **off**
- **Color**: **Orange**
- **Query**: `RequestType.keyword:*Waste AND MediaURL.keyword:http* AND SupervisorDistrict.keyword:8`
- **Field mappings | Time**: **Opened**

- **Field mappings** | **Text**: `MediaURL`
- **Field mappings** | **Tags**: `RequestType`

This is what the Elasticsearch annotations query looks like:

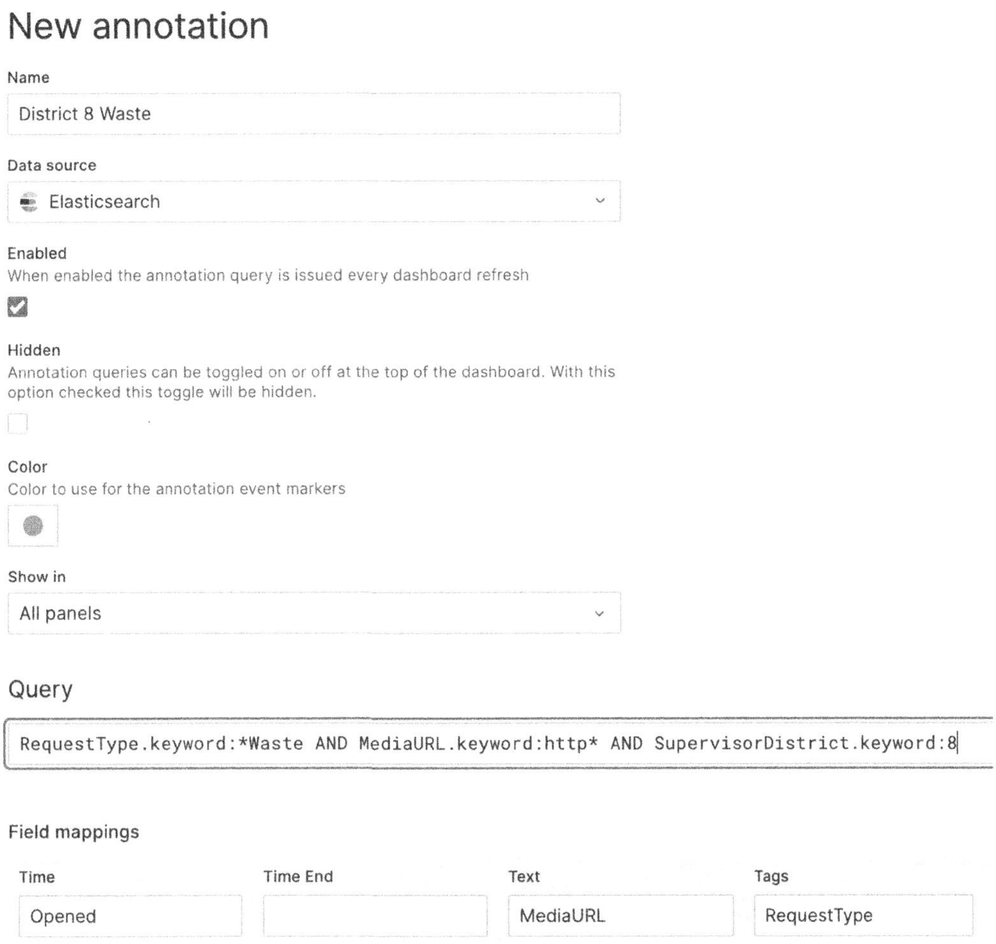

# New annotation

Name

District 8 Waste

Data source

Elasticsearch                                                      ˅

Enabled
When enabled the annotation query is issued every dashboard refresh

☑

Hidden
Annotation queries can be toggled on or off at the top of the dashboard. With this
option checked this toggle will be hidden.

☐

Color
Color to use for the annotation event markers

⬤

Show in

All panels                                                        ˅

Query

```
RequestType.keyword:*Waste AND MediaURL.keyword:http* AND SupervisorDistrict.keyword:8
```

Field mappings

| Time | Time End | Text | Tags |
|------|----------|------|------|
| Opened | | MediaURL | RequestType |

Figure 10.19 – An Elasticsearch annotation query

Here, the biggest difference between a native annotation query and this data source annotation query is the settings for the **Query** and **Field mappings**. The query looks for either *Human and Animal Waste* or *Medical Waste*, with the `*Waste` wildcard string in the **RequestType** field, the `http*` wildcard in the `MediaURL` indicating a URL to a photo, and a `SupervisorDistrict` value of 8. Then, we use the **Field mappings** option to use the **Opened** field to set the time for the annotation (useful for creating alerts), `MediaURL` in the **Text** field, and create a tag using the **RequestType** field.

Once you've set up the query, look at a day or two's worth of data:

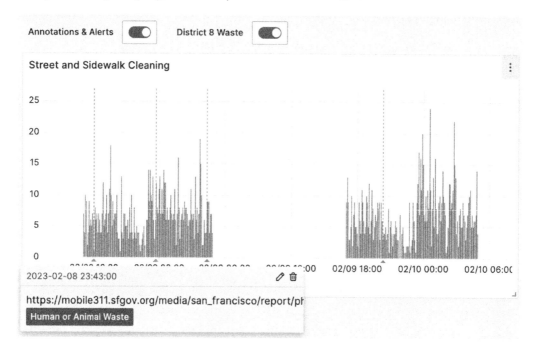

Figure 10.20 – Annotation hover

There should be a few annotations per day. Hovering over one of them reveals a URL in the **Text** field and the Request Type tag. Unfortunately, the URL isn't clickable, but it does illustrate the potential to embed rich data into an annotation.

## Sharing dashboards

Now that you've created these lovely dashboards, how do you share them with the world (or just your boss)? One of the first questions you must consider is the link between your dashboards and your data sources. For the sake of this exercise, we'll keep the data sources and the dashboards in proximity – that is, on the same host and the same network. If you wish to share your dashboards, they will need to access your machine and possibly your network. You'll want to give some serious thought to how best to share them. Here, we'll discuss a few strategies and their pros and cons.

## Sharing dashboard links

The most straightforward sharing mechanism is to simply give out a URL to your Grafana server that references the dashboard in question. Click the **Share dashboard** button (the three circle interface icon in the dashboard bar and use the **Link** tab to create a link. If you want the dashboard to preserve the current view, make sure you enable **Current time range** and **Template variables**. Grafana will generate a custom URL you can copy and mail out.

This technique will only work if the client has access to your server and you've configured it to serve other browsers on your network. If that's not the case, you might have some difficulties. This option is most suitable for production environments where the Grafana server has been configured for multiple clients. However, the Grafana setup for this book is only able to serve `localhost` at port `9200`, which is essentially the computer that you're running Grafana on.

## Sharing dashboards by exporting

The next best option is to export your dashboards if you know that your client also has access to the same data sources. You can then export to JSON and transfer the text file. Then, your clients just need to import the JSON file and make sure they've properly configured the data source(s). This is a good option if you are in an environment where you have centralized database servers and you want to transfer your dashboards for someone to review, modify, or install them on another server with the same data sources. This is how I shared the dashboards that were created for this book.

The process is quite simple – just click **Share dashboards** and use the **Export** tab to save the JSON to a file, or copy it to a dashboard so that you can paste it into an email. The **Export for sharing externally** toggle is used when you want to share your dashboard publicly (such as on `grafana.com`) but want to make sure there are no explicit data source names embedded in the file. Instead, they are templated so that the importer of the dashboard file will assign them to their own data sources, using a data source template variable.

## Sharing dashboard snapshots

The final option is the one that is the most isolated and is for scenarios where you may have nothing more than access to a local Grafana server. For example, you may be giving a demo and you have no **virtual private network** (**VPN**) connection to your data sources, or possibly no network access at all. The snapshot option is intended to export the dashboard and a sample dataset, either to a local file or to a Grafana sharing service such as `https://snapshots.raintank.io`:

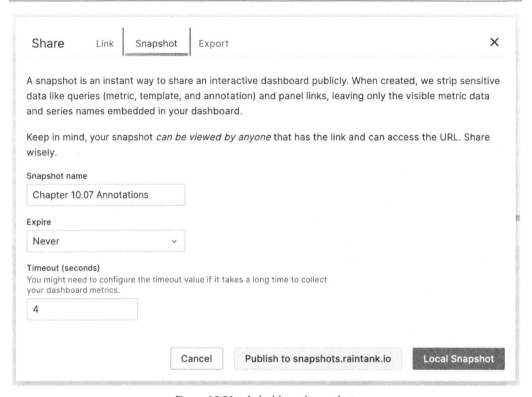

Figure 10.21 – A dashboard snapshot

The snapshot is limited to the current time frame, so choose one that you feel gives the best representation of the data. You will also be limited to some of the data you can show. The dashboard view is intended to be strictly read-only, so you will have no ability to edit the panels or even see the queries. The snapshot can be limited, but if you are looking to give a report on a specific timeslice of data and you don't mind having some functional limitations, the snapshot can be very useful.

## Summary

We've accomplished a lot in this chapter. Here, we created an Elasticsearch server, imported a realistic textual dataset with Logstash, and learned about several different types of template variables, as well as how to set them up to parameterize our dashboards. Then, we applied template variables to repeat rows and panels and discovered the native annotation feature, as well as how to create annotations from an Elasticsearch query. Finally, we explored different sharing options and their pros and cons.

At this point, you have been exposed to enough of Grafana to now go off and create dashboards built around your own data sources. We've looked at two of the more popular data sources, InfluxDB and Elasticsearch, but we've only scratched the surface of their capabilities, apart from being used with Grafana. I encourage you to explore them; the more you understand how data sources manage data, the better you will be able to tailor your datasets to get the most out of Grafana.

In the next chapters, we will be pivoting toward the exciting field of observability. Observability is one of the hottest areas for visualization, and Grafana is right up there. We will start in *Chapter 11, Streaming Real-Time IoT Data from Telegraf Agent to Grafana Live,* by looking into how to ship real-time metrics to Grafana with Grafana Live. In *Chapter 12, Monitoring Data Streams with Grafana Alerts,* we'll look at how to set up and communicate alerts when metrics exceed certain thresholds. In the final chapter of our observability trilogy, *Chapter 13, Exploring Log Data with Grafana's Loki,* we'll use Loki to examine logging data and metrics for potential patterns we can use to create alerts.

# 11

# Streaming Real-Time IoT Data from Telegraf Agent to Grafana Live

In this chapter, we're going to dip a toe into the exciting world of **observability**. While you've probably heard that observability is currently one of the hottest fields in IT, you may be wondering what it is, and how Grafana supports it. Here is a definition of observability from Wikipedia (https://en.wikipedia.org/wiki/Software_observability):

> *"In distributed systems, observability is the ability to collect data about program execution, internal states of modules, and communication between components."*

This is a little bit abstract, so let me offer my refinement:

*Observability is the practice of collecting metrics data from telemetered systems, scanning, detecting, and alerting on anomalous behavior, and distributing state metrics at an appropriate frequency for analysis.*

This divides observability into three core functions:

- Metrics collection

- Alerting

- Data distribution

In the next few chapters, we're going to be looking at these functions in more detail. In this chapter, we will concentrate on the collection of data – specifically, IoT data in real time or near real time. In *Chapter 12, Monitoring Data Streams with Grafana Alerts*, we will look at how to monitor for anomalous data and generate alerts. Finally, in *Chapter 13, Exploring Log Data with Grafana's Loki*, we will look at how to manage and analyze the sometimes overwhelming log data that our processes generate.

In this chapter, we will cover the following topics:

- Streaming real-time data from Telegraf to Grafana

- Sending IoT data to Telegraf with MQTT and Mosquitto

- Generating messages to an IoT pipeline

## Technical requirements

The tutorial code, dashboards, and other helpful files for this chapter can be found in this book's GitHub repository at `https://github.com/PacktPublishing/Learn-Grafana-10/tree/main/Chapter11`.

## Streaming real-time data from Telegraf to Grafana

In previous chapters, we typically sourced a collection of metrics from, say, a website or a data file, and after storing that data in a time-series database, we then used Grafana to query that data for analysis and visualization. This process of working a corpus of data as a single entity is sometimes referred to as **batch handling**. By contrast, in this chapter, we will be continuously moving time samples of data as they are generated, or **streaming** the data from source to destination.

This style of handling data is suitable for many applications where the data needs to be visualized or otherwise processed in real time for monitoring and alerting. It is also most useful in those cases where it would be difficult or impractical to wait for all the data to arrive before analyzing, or where sampled, non-transactional data is the norm.

To get an idea about how to distinguish between these two use cases, imagine the case where you need to process all sales receipts for a single day, month, or quarter. To close the books in keeping with regulations, you need to establish all the receipts for a fixed period of time, and missing a single receipt could have drastic consequences. This is a use case where batch processing of data is a requisite.

However, now imagine a refinery or a power plant where thousands of processes are continuously generating data every millisecond, second, or minute. If one of those metrics indicates a process or machine exceeding safe tolerances, a delay of seconds could mean the difference between life and death. Waiting for arbitrary time periods would be ill-advised, and thus streaming is the better choice.

In this chapter, we'll be generating several data streams and developing the pipelines to transfer them in real time for Grafana to display, beginning with the very systems that drive the computer you're working on. Later, we'll extend the pipeline to a data stream that simulates an IoT device such as a smart thermostat. This will involve our most complex pipeline so far, but rest assured, we'll go through it step by step.

## Setting up Grafana for streaming

We're going to work on this tutorial in a kind of reverse order. In the past exercises, we've started with the data collection and worked forward to Grafana dashboard panels. In this case, we're going to first set up Grafana to provide a destination for our data, then we'll set up a Telegraf metrics collector to route the data to Grafana.

Here's a schematic representation of the pipeline we will build:

Figure 11.1 – Telegraf to Grafana pipeline

The first order of business is to set up our processes, beginning with Grafana. We'll use our trusty `docker-compose.yml` file to establish a Grafana service:

```
services:
    grafana:
        image: "grafana/grafana:${GRAF_TAG-latest}"
    ports:
        - "3000.3000"
    volumes:
        - "${PWD-.}/grafana:/var/lib/Grafana
```

This is the standard Docker Compose pattern for setting up our Grafana container. Launch the service and connect to `http://localhost:3000`:

```
docker-compose up --pull missing -d grafana
[+] Running 1/1
   Container chapter11-grafana-1  Started
                                                        0.5s
```

Normally, this is the point where we'd create a Grafana data source that we'd query for our dashboard panels. This time, we'll be taking advantage of a built-in Grafana data source called Grafana Live, which will accept streaming data. We just need to generate some real-time data to stream. That's where Telegraf comes in.

## Installing the Telegraf agent

Telegraf is a data collection agent application developed by InfluxData and designed to transfer metrics data from almost any platform. It consists of a long-running *agent* process that can be configured to collect, process, and transmit data efficiently to a waiting process.

Installation is simply a matter of launching a Telegraf Docker container configured with the necessary plugins to acquire and transmit data to Grafana. In our case, we will be collecting stats from our local computer and transmitting them to the Grafana Live endpoint.

Configuring Telegraf is easy. All we need to do is define what metrics it must monitor, how to send the metrics to Grafana, and how often to sample and transmit. But before we do that, let's set up our `docker-compose.yml` file with the additional service:

```
telegraf:
    image: "telegraf:${TELE_TAG-latest}"
    volumes:
        - "${PWD-.}/telegraf/etc:/etc/telegraf
```

Here, we just create a new service by pulling down the latest version of Telegraf. We also specify a local directory for storing our `telegraf.conf` file. There is no need to create any other persistent storage as Telegraf is only acting as a conduit for sending data to Grafana. In fact, we won't be storing any data in this chapter.

## Configuring the Telegraf agent

Before we launch our service, let's configure it. In the `Chapter11` directory of your repository, create a `telegraf/etc` directory. In it, store a `telegraf.conf` file. We start by setting up the frequency of how often the service should poll and transmit metrics data:

```
[agent]
    interval = "1s"
    flush_interval = "1s"
```

Here, `interval` sets how often to poll for data, and `flush_interval` sets how often to transmit the data. You should set the two intervals to whatever you'd like; just don't set `flush_interval` to be less than `interval`.

### Setting the input plugins

Telegraf's metrics pipeline has a very simple model of four phases, not dissimilar to that of Elasticsearch's Logstash from *Chapter 10, Working with Advanced Dashboard Features and Elasticsearch,* **Input**, **Process**, **Aggregate**, and **Output**. Each phase is implemented as a Telegraf plugin. For many applications, it will be enough to configure a set of inputs and an output. Indeed, for our initial exercise, that is what we will do.

First up, we'll configure our inputs – that is, the metrics we want to track. The full catalog of Telegraf plugins numbers in the hundreds and can be found in the InfluxLabs Telegraf documentation at `https://www.influxdata.com/products/integrations`. The catalog also contains links to the configuration documentation for each plugin. Initially, we'll use the same metrics as documented in the official Grafana documentation tutorial: `input.cpus`. They make a good initial choice because they are supported across multiple platforms and they are easy to conceptualize.

The configuration is located in the `input.cpus` GitHub repository at `https://github.com/influxdata/telegraf/blob/master/plugins/inputs/cpu/README.md`. In it, we see that there is only a handful of configuration options, and the plugin produces several output metrics. The documented configuration options are defaults and don't need to be added to our `telegraf.conf` file unless we plan to override them. In our case, we don't want to overwhelm Grafana with too many metrics, so we'll override `percpu` and set it to `false`. This sets the metrics to represent the aggregation of however many CPUs exist on the computer, rather than breaking them out separately. Add the following to your `telegraf.conf` file:

```
[[inputs.cpu]]
    percpu = false
```

### Setting the outputs plugin

Now that we have our inputs, we move on to the outputs. It won't do us any good to have Telegraf collect our metrics if we don't also tell it where to send them! We'll use the outputs plugin to send our data to the Grafana Live facility inside the Grafana server. Grafana Live is a messaging service that continuously monitors various **channels** for events, and then passes along those events to subscribers in the Grafana frontend. In our case, we are passing along a Telegraf-captured data stream in InfluxDB format to Grafana Live, which will pass it along to an internal data source that we can then access from a **Dashboard** panel or Grafana **Explore**.

The data we capture will be broken out into several fields of data, which we can then access in Grafana just like a normal dataset. Grafana provides an API for sending data using the `/api/live/push/<:streamId>` endpoint, where `:streamId` is the name of our stream. We'll use the `outputs.http` section to send our data stream to the Grafana Live endpoint using HTTP REST. Have a look at the settings documentation at `https://github.com/influxdata/telegraf/tree/master/plugins/outputs/http`. There are quite a few of them, but let's zero in on the most important one: `url`. This sets the destination endpoint for our output, so let's set that first:

```
[[outputs.http]]
    url = http://grafana:3000/api/live/push/telegraf_id
```

Remember, our URL must point to the Grafana running in our container *as seen from the perspective of the Telegraf container*. That's why we use the network name `grafana`, not `localhost`. We also set our `:streamId` value to `telegraf_id`. For security, we also need to set up a way for Grafana to authenticate our Telegraf process. We'll issue a Grafana service account key and add it to the header of our HTTP REST calls.

## Generating a service account key

Before we go any further, we need to return to Grafana and generate a **service account key**. Formerly programmatic access was implemented in the form of **API keys**, Grafana replaced the API key with a token generated as part of a service account. Service accounts give finer control over the access granted to simple API keys, so they are more secure. Happily, a service account token can be used anywhere you need an API key, as in this case. Follow these steps:

1.   Go to **Administration** from the main menu and select **Service Accounts**.

2.   Click **Add service account** and name it `Telegraf`. Give it an **Admin** role. Your service account page should look something like the following screen capture:

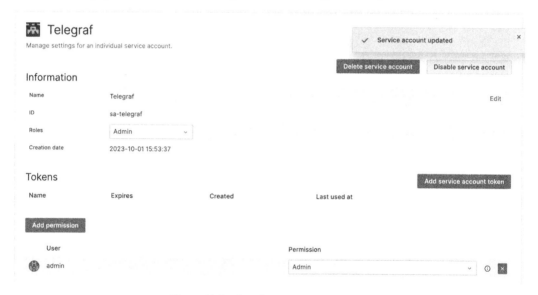

Figure 11.2 – Creating a service account

3.   Finally, click on the new Telegraf service account and then on **Add service account token**.

4.  Copy the token to the clipboard for later entry, as shown here:

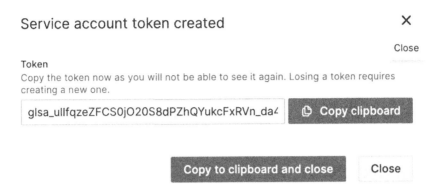

Figure 11.3 – Service account token

## Running Telegraf

In the `telegraf.conf` file, add the authentication configuration to the `outputs.http` configuration:

```
[outputs.http.headers]
    Authorization = "Bearer <your token here>"
```

This is basically the inverse of the authentication setting for the InfluxDB data source: instead of setting the authentication for Grafana to connect to the InfluxDB API as we did in previous chapters, now you're doing the opposite and authenticating from Telegraf to Grafana.

Now, launch the Telegraf agent:

```
% docker-compose up --pull missing -d telegraf
[+] Running 1/1
   Container chapter11-telegraf-1  Started
                                                              0.6s
```

You might need to check the logs for errors. The following is a somewhat abbreviated representation of the logging; in it, you should see mentions of your `telegraf.conf` configuration settings:

```
% docker-compose logs -f telegraf
chapter11-telegraf-1  | 2023-02-24T04:18:06Z I! [agent] Hang on,
flushing any cached metrics before shutdown
chapter11-telegraf-1  | 2023-02-24T04:18:06Z I! [agent] Stopping
running outputs
chapter11-telegraf-1  | 2023-02-24T04:18:06Z I! Using config file: /
etc/telegraf/telegraf.conf
```

```
chapter11-telegraf-1    | 2023-02-24T04:18:06Z I! Starting Telegraf
1.25.2
chapter11-telegraf-1    | 2023-02-24T04:18:06Z I! Available plugins:
227 inputs, 9 aggregators, 26 processors, 21 parsers, 57 outputs, 2
secret-stores
chapter11-telegraf-1    | 2023-02-24T04:18:06Z I! Loaded inputs: cpu
...
chapter11-telegraf-1    | 2023-02-24T04:18:06Z I! Loaded outputs: http
chapter11-telegraf-1    | 2023-02-24T04:18:06Z I! Tags enabled:
host=30a2a03d7a3d
chapter11-telegraf-1    | 2023-02-24T04:18:06Z I! [agent] Config:
Interval:1s, Quiet:false, Hostname:"30a2a03d7a3d", Flush Interval:1s
```

If you don't see any errors, head on over to Grafana and go to **Explore** to see our data.

From **Explore**, you need to set -- **Grafana** – as your data source. If you don't have any other data sources configured, it will be the only choice. Set **Query type** to **Live Measurements**.

Grafana identifies each channel as a triplet of *scope/namespace/path*. There should be only one channel available to you with the `stream` *scope*, the *namespace* corresponding to the `:streamId` value in our Telegraf configuration for the `outputs.http` URL, and the *path* corresponding to our `inputs` plugin: `stream/telegraf_id/cpu`. Here's what the **Explore** configuration should look like:

Figure 11.4 – Telegraf data streams in Explore

Once you have selected the correct channel, set the time range to **Last 15 minutes**, and click on **Run query**. If you get a query error, try refreshing the page. With any luck, you'll start seeing data flowing almost immediately. Click on the **Lines** display type to get a good view of the slight variations.

Over time, you should see something like the following as the data starts coming in:

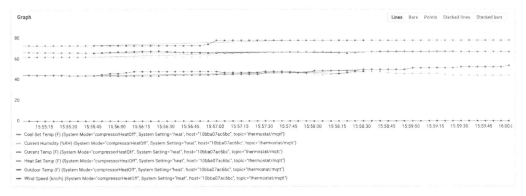

Figure 11.5 – Telegraf data stream graph in Explore

Refresh the time range or choose one to see the latest data. Click **Cancel** to stop the streaming display. Congratulations, you're streaming data into Grafana!

# Streaming IoT data with MQTT and Mosquitto

Now that we've established the basis for communicating real-time data with Telegraf and Grafana, we can move on to integrate that knowledge with the world of the **Internet of Things** (**IoT**). The IoT makes it possible for virtually any properly equipped device to transmit its telemetry data over the internet using lightweight messaging protocols. One of the most common of these protocols is called **MQTT**, an abbreviation for **Message Queuing Telemetry Transport**. MQTT, now on version 5, is simple, open, and requires only a small software footprint.

However, unlike REST calls over the HTTP protocol, which tend to connect directly from client to server and back, MQTT requires an intermediary broker to maintain the message queue and facilitate transport between message producers and message consumers. To simulate an IoT message producer, we will be developing a simple Python script to create messages, and we will rely on Telegraf to consume those messages and deliver the data to Grafana.

## Describing the pipeline architecture

Knowing what we do about MQTT, let's propose a pipeline architecture for simulating our IoT device. We will need something to simulate a device that generates metrics. For that, we will write a simple Python script that will read in some CSV test data as a basis for generating messages. Next, we will set up an MQTT broker that our script will send those messages to and will also relay those messages to Telegraf. For that function, we will use the open source Eclipse Mosquitto broker. From there, we will be using the combination of Telegraf and Grafana. A visual schematic of our pipeline is shown here:

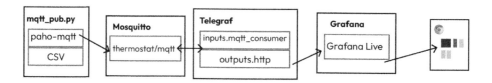

Figure 11.6 – MQTT streaming data pipeline

As we did in the previous section, we will be working *backward* from the destination of our messages (Grafana). Since we have already set up our connection between Telegraf and Grafana using the `http` output plugin, we next need to set up a connection between Telegraf and the Mosquitto broker. Telegraf comes with an MQTT consumer plugin, so we will configure it next.

## Configuring the Telegraf MQTT consumer

The Telegraf MQTT consumer plugin is an input plugin and can be found in the Telegraf repository at `https://github.com/influxdata/telegraf/blob/release-1.24/plugins/inputs/mqtt_consumer/README.md`. The list of configuration options is pretty long, but we won't need to address most of them. We'll be concerned with the address of our broker, the `servers` option, and the list of topics the agent should monitor.

In this case, the address of our server (we only have one, but it's possible to have many) is the name of the broker service as seen from the Telegraf service configured in our `docker-compose.yml` file: `mosquitto`. We don't have a name for our topic, so let's name it `thermostat/mqtt` now, keeping it in mind for when we produce our messages later. Add the following to your `telegraf.conf` file:

```
[[inputs.mqtt_consumer]]
    servers = ["tcp://mosquitto:1883"]
    topics = ["thermostat/mqtt"]
```

We'll be communicating with the broker over the common TCP port of `1883`, as described in the default configuration, so let's note that for our broker configuration.

## Installing the Mosquitto broker

The Mosquitto broker is available as a Docker container, so we'll add it to our `docker-compose.yml` file. Here is the service configuration:

```
mosquitto:
    image: "eclipse-mosquitto:${MOSQ_TAG-latest}"
    ports:
        - "1883:1883"
    volumes:
```

```
    - "${PWD-.}/mosquitto/config/mosquitto.conf:/mosquitto/
config/mosquitto.conf"
```

As we've done for other services, pull an image, set the ports, and map a volume for persisting a local file or directory. Let's go over the configuration:

1.  Bring in the latest Mosquitto Docker image.

2.  Map the internal port `1883` to the standard external port `1883`.

3.  Map the `mosquitto.conf` configuration file to a local file in the `mosquitto/config` directory.

4.  Next, we need to create that configuration file, so create a `mosquitto/config` subdirectory in your `Chapter11` repo directory. Edit a file in the `config` directory named `mosquitto.conf` with the following contents:

    ```
    listener 1883
    allow_anonymous true
    ```

This configuration performs two functions:

*   Allows connections on port `1883` from external hosts

*   Allows anonymous connections without needing to authenticate

To start up the service, run the following `docker-compose` command:

```
% docker-compose up --pull missing -d mosquitto
[+] Running 1/1
  Container chapter11-mosquitto-1  Started


                                          1.1s
```

You might want to review the Mosquitto logging for information. It should confirm the broker startup:

```
% docker-compose logs -f mosquitto
chapter11-mosquitto-1  | 1677732679: mosquitto version 2.0.15
terminating
chapter11-mosquitto-1  | 1677907267: mosquitto version 2.0.15
starting
chapter11-mosquitto-1  | 1677907267: Config loaded from /
mosquitto/config/mosquitto.conf.
chapter11-mosquitto-1  | 1677907267: Opening ipv4 listen socket
on port 1883.
chapter11-mosquitto-1  | 1677907267: Opening ipv6 listen socket
on port 1883.
chapter11-mosquitto-1  | 1677907267: mosquitto version 2.0.15
running
```

Now that we have our infrastructure in place, we need to generate our simulated IoT metrics data in the form of messages sent to the Mosquitto broker. To do that, we'll write a simple Python script to read a file of metrics data and transmit the data to the broker.

# Generating messages to an IoT data pipeline

Before we write any code, let's take a look at the schema of the metrics data we'll be sending to the broker.

## Examining the simulated metrics data

Our data is based on consumer metrics generated by a smart thermostat. While it isn't the raw data directly transmitted by the device to the thermostat company's servers, it can be considered representative of the kind of data typical of such a device. This is the list of fields from the header of `data/thermostat_events.csv`:

```
System Setting,System Mode,Calendar Event,Program Mode,Cool Set Temp
(F),Heat Set Temp (F),Current Temp (F),Current Humidity (%RH),Outdoor
Temp (F),Wind Speed (km/h),Cool Stage 1 (sec),Heat Stage 1 (sec),Aux
Heat 1 (sec),Fan (sec),DM Offset,Thermostat Temperature (F),Thermostat
Humidity (%RH),Thermostat Motion,Upstairs (F),Upstairs2
```

Most of the fields we're interested in are temperatures, denoted by `(F)`. We'll also add the `Current Humidity (%RH)` and `Wind Speed (km/h)` fields. In order to add some tagging information, we'll also include the `System Setting` and `System Mode` fields. When we write our script, we'll be sure to identify these fields as ones to extract from the CSV to include in our messages.

In the previous chapters, I've laid out any Python scripting without much of an explanation of how we got there. Now I'll take this opportunity to introduce a couple of *best practices*.

Our first best practice is to gather the requirements for our script, and then use them to drive our design. The next best practice will be to sketch out a few design principles that will serve our requirements. Once we have our design principles in place, our final best practice will be to use object-orientation features such as classes and objects in our implementation. After our code review, we'll need to spin up a Python Docker container to run it.

Before we can write any code, we should first determine the goals for our script and the requirements that will satisfy those goals. The goals for the script are straightforward:

1.   Load up a CSV file of test data.
2.   Convert the rows into messages.
3.   Send them to our MQTT broker.

Now that we've established our goals, let's break down the requirements that will get us to those goals:

1.  Accept various configuration options on the command line:

    A.  Input CSV file

    B.  Broker address

    C.  Broker port

    D.  Message topic

    E.  Message transmission interval

2.  Open a CSV file and parse it for message fields.

3.  Select some subsets of CSV fields for metrics as either InfluxDB tags or fields and use them to create a message conforming to the InfluxDB line protocol.

4.  Open a connection to the MQTT broker and send the message.

5.  Wait a fixed interval of time and repeat steps 3–5 for the next row of CSV.

6.  Also, since the data is dummy test data, there is no need to checkpoint the last sent message. There is no need to check whether the message was sent.

We'll handle some of these tasks using Python classes; for others, we'll just use regular functions. Let's reiterate the requirements, along with the functions and classes that we created to handle them:

1.  Accept various configuration options on the command line (`parse_cli`).

2.  Open the CSV file and parse it for message fields (`csvfile`).

3.  Select some subset of CSV fields for metrics as either InfluxDB tags or fields and use them to create a message conforming to the InfluxDB line protocol (`MQTTMetric`).

4.  Open a connection to the MQTT broker and send the message (`MQTTPublisher`).

We will continue with the model from previous scripts of using a `load_event_data` function to act as a *controller* for driving the various execution stages. Let's go over the code now.

## Reviewing the mqtt_pub.py script

Now that we have everything we need to fulfill our requirements, let's walk through the proposed Python script, called `mqtt_pub.py`.

## Parsing the command line

First up, we need to parse the command line for various options. This code is structurally similar to our previous scripts in that we create an `argparse.ArgumentParser` object, add arguments, and then parse the command line and return the results:

```python
def process_cli():
    parser = argparse.ArgumentParser(
        description="publish MQTT messages")
    parser.add_argument(
        "--broker", dest="broker", default="localhost",
            help="MQTT broker host"
    )
    parser.add_argument(
        "--port", dest="port", type=int, default=1883,
            help="MQTT broker port"
    )
    parser.add_argument("--topic", dest="topic",
        help="MQTT topic")
    parser.add_argument(
        "--interval",
        dest="interval",
        type=int,
        default="5",
        help="publish interval (secs)",
    )
    parser.add_argument(
        "--input", dest="input_file",
            type=argparse.FileType("r"), help="input file"
    )
    return parser.parse_args()
```

Since you've seen this pattern before, I'll only call attention to the `--input` option. The `argparse.FileType` type specification causes the parser to open the file path from the command line and store a file object in `input_file`, not the name of the file. This is helpful as we don't need to deal with the process of opening the file. Let's move on to the `load_events` function to get an idea of the control flow before going over the objects.

## Controlling the program flow

Like in our previous scripts, we use the `load_event_data` function as a general controller for driving the overall workflow. The code is very simple because we've delegated most of the work to objects:

```python
def load_event_data(config, broker, port, topic, csvfile, interval):
    reader = CSVReader(csvfile).reader
```

```
publisher = MQTTPublisher(broker, port)

for r in reader:
    metric = MQTTMetric(
        measurement="thermostat",
        data=r,
        tag_names=config["tags"],
        field_names=config["fields"],
    )

publisher.publish(topic, metric.message)
time.sleep(interval)
```

We'll take this step by step:

1.  Instantiate a new `CSVReader` object with the `csvfile` file object and get a `csv.DictReader` object.

2.  Instantiate an `MQTTPublisher` object with the broker address and port number.

3.  Iterate through each row in the `csv.DictReader` object.

4.  For each iteration, instantiate a new `MQTTMetric` object setting `thermostat` as the measurement, along with the row, and the configuration of which tags and fields to use.

5.  Publish the message to `topic`.

6.  Put the process to sleep for `interval` seconds.

That is the bulk of the control flow, but the actual work happens in the object methods.

### Loading and parsing the CSV

Our first object is `csvfile`, which is really just a bit of wrapper code around the `csv.DictReader` object:

```
class CSVReader:
    def __init__(self, csvfile):
        self._csvfile = csvfile
        self._dialect = csv.Sniffer().sniff(
            self._csvfile.read(1024))

    @property
    def csvfile(self):
        self._csvfile.seek(0)
        return self._csvfile

    @property
```

```
def dialect(self):
    return self._dialect

@property
def reader(self):
    reader = csv.DictReader(self.csvfile,
        dialect=self.dialect)
    return reader
```

We start off each class with the initialization:

1.  Initialize the object with the `csvfile` file object. Use `csv.Sniffer.sniff` to sample the first 1,024 characters of the file to discover the header fields and the dialect of the CSV file.

2.  Specify three accessor methods, decorated as properties so they can be called as *attributes* on the object.

3.  `csvfile` returns the file object after the `seek` pointer has been reset to the start of the file. The `csv.Sniffer.sniff` function leaves the `seek` pointer 1,025 characters into the file.

4.  `dialect` returns the dialect discovered by `csv.Sniffer.sniff`.

5.  `reader` returns an opened and parsed `csv.DictReader` object. The `csv.DictReader` object is an iterator that converts each line of the CSV into a dictionary so you can reference each field in the row by name.

The next object we encounter is `MQTTPublisher`, but since we don't use it until later, let's come back to it after we look at the `MQTTMetric` class.

### Building messages

The `MQTTMetric` class is responsible for picking through the fields in each CSV row and converting them to either an InfluxDB tag or field. It's the longest bit of code in the whole script, so we'll break it down into the initializer, the accessors, and the utility methods:

```
class MQTTMetric:
    def __init__(
        self, measurement: str, data: dict,
            tag_names: list, field_names: list
    ):
        self._measurement = measurement
        self._data = data
        self._tag_names = tag_names
        self._field_names = field_names
        self._tags = []
        self._fields = []
```

There isn't much to talk about here; it's mostly just the initialization of different object attributes. Let's move on to the accessor methods:

```
@property
def measurement(self):
    return self._measurement

@property
def timestamp(self):
    return int(time.time() * 1e9)

@property
def message(self):
    for k in self._tag_names:
        self.add_tag(k, self._data[k])
    for k in self._field_names:
        self.add_field(k, self._data[k])
    return f"{self.measurement}{self.tags_to_string} {
        self.fields_to_string} {self.timestamp}\n"
```

The key thing to note is that the `message` accessor is where we create the actual message. We use three Python class properties to construct the message components:

- `measurement` just accesses the internally stored measurement attribute

- `timestamp` creates a timestamp for the current time in nanoseconds

- `message` creates a single InfluxDB line protocol string, constructed from the measurement, any tags, the fields, and the timestamp

Next are the various utility methods mostly used to build the lists of tags and fields and convert those lists to proper strings for use in the message:

```
def add_field(self, key, value):
    self._fields.append(f"{self.escape_string(key)}={
        value}")

def add_tag(self, key, value):
    self._tags.append(f"{self.escape_string(key)}={
        self.escape_string(value)}")

def _fields_to_string(self):
    return ",".join(self._fields)

def _tags_to_string(self):
```

Streaming Real-Time IoT Data from Telegraf Agent to Grafana Live

```
        if self._tags:
            return f",{','.join(self._tags)}"
        else:
            return ""

    @staticmethod
    def escape_string(string):
        return string.translate(string.maketrans(
            {",": r"\,", " ": r"\ ", "=": r"\="}))

    @staticmethod
    def quote_string(string):
        return f'"{string}"'
```

Of note are the escape_string and quote_string static methods. I set those just in case they might be used in a library. By decorating them as staticmethod, they can be referenced from the library directly without the need to create an object instance. Here is the rundown of those utility methods:

- add_field adds a key-value pair to the fields list, with the field name properly quoted.

- add_tag adds a key-value pair to the tags list, with the tag name and value properly quoted.

- fields_to_string converts the fields list to a comma-separated string for use in the message.

- tags_to_string converts the tags list to a comma-separated string for use in the message.

- escape_string properly quotes any special characters, such as quote marks or spaces in the string, so they can be used in the message.

- quote_string wraps the entire string in quote marks. We would use this if we were including fields with string values. We won't in this case, but it's there for future use.

The only object left is MQTTPublisher, which we will return to now.

### Sending messages

To send our messages, we will rely on the open source Python library called paho-mqtt. We'll include all the extra libraries when we build our Python container. For now, let's look at our MQTTPublisher class:

```
class MQTTPublisher:
    def __init__(self, broker: str, port: int):
        self.broker = broker
        self.port = port

    def publish(self, topic, message):
```

```
publish.single(topic, payload=message,
    hostname=self.broker, port=self.port)
logging.info(f"Published `{message}` to topic `{
    topic}`")
```

It really doesn't get much simpler than this:

1.  Initialize the class with the broker address and the port number.

2.  Publish the message to the topic using the `publish.single` function. The function takes the topic, message, broker, and port as arguments, connects to the broker, and publishes the message. It takes a few other optional arguments, but these are the minimum necessary.

In this case, we are using the minimum amount of code to get a message published per our requirements. If you are interested, there are other functions available in the `paho-mqtt` library that can give a `return` status and even trigger callback functions on `publish` events.

That completes our code review. Let's get this script running!

## Running the mqtt_pub.py script

As we've done in previous chapters, we'll launch our script using a containerized Python interpreter executable. It's easy to spin one up with a simple Dockerfile and a `requirements.txt` file for adding any additional library dependencies. We can even configure our `docker-compose.yml` file to do most of the work for us.

### Building a Python container

First, we need a Dockerfile in order to build our container with the ability to add additional dependencies with `pip`. We've used this same file in previous chapters, so I include it here without modification:

```
FROM python:3
WORKDIR /usr/src/app
COPY requirements.txt ./
RUN pip install --no-cache-dir -r requirements.txt
ENTRYPOINT [ "python" ]
```

Before we build the container, we need to update our `requirements.txt` file to include a couple of extra library packages – namely, `paho-mqtt` for our MQTT publisher, and `pyyaml` to parse our snippet of YAML configuration. Here's the `requirements.txt` file:

```
paho-mqtt
pyyaml
```

If we add our Python container as a service to `docker-compose.yml`, we can use Docker Compose to help us build and run the container, so let's do that next:

```
python:
    build: .
        image: python:ch11
    environment:
        TZ: "America/Los_Angeles"
    volumes:
        - "${PWD-.}/app:/usr/src/app"
        - "${PWD-.}/data:/data"
```

Here, we just need to do the following:

1. Tag the image we'll build.

2. Set the internal time zone so timestamps generated by the container will be consistent in Grafana. Feel free to change it to your local time zone. The zone names are listed in Wikipedia: `https://en.wikipedia.org/wiki/List_of_tz_database_time_zones`.

3. Map the local `app` and `data` directories into a volume so the container can *see* our script to run it and our data to load it.

To build our container, simply use the Docker Compose `build` command:

```
% docker-compose build --pull python
```

### Running the script

To run the script, we can again use Docker Compose; however, we do need to invoke our script and the associated command-line options. Make sure your `mqtt_pub.py` script is in the `bin` directory and the `thermostat_events.csv` file is in `data`. Here is how I would run it, with a 5-second interval, and a topic named `thermostat/mqtt`:

```
% docker-compose run --rm \
    --name python python \
    /usr/src/app/mqtt_pub.py \
    --broker mosquitto \
    --topic "thermostat/mqtt" \
    --input "/data/thermostat_events.csv" \
    --interval 5
INFO:root:Published `thermostat,System\ Setting=heat,System\
Mode=compressorHeatOff Cool\ Set\ Temp\ (F)=73,Heat\ Set\ Temp\
(F)=62,Current\ Temp\ (F)=68.3,Outdoor\ Temp\ (F)=49.6,Current\
Humidity\ (%RH)=46,Wind\ Speed\ (km/h)=0 1677961726451509248
` to topic `thermostat/mqtt
```

It is critical that your topic name matches the topic Telegraf is monitoring as specified in the `telegraf.conf` file. If all goes well, you should see output similar to the preceding output appearing every 5 seconds.

It is a good practice to additionally check the Mosquitto logs and the Telegraf logs to verify the messages are reaching the broker:

```
% docker-compose logs -f mosquitto
chapter11-mosquitto-1   | 1677961801: New connection from
172.25.0.3:58891 on port 1883.
chapter11-mosquitto-1   | 1677961801: New client connected from
172.25.0.3:58891 as auto-05B8B76E-CBB7-A912-B59C-8B954C1EDE23 (p2, c1,
k60).
chapter11-mosquitto-1   | 1677961801: Client auto-05B8B76E-CBB7-A912-
B59C-8B954C1EDE23 disconnected.
```

Also, check that Telegraf is not having any issues connecting to either the broker or Grafana:

```
% docker-compose logs -f telegraf
```

## Exploring the IoT data

Let's return to Grafana and have a look at Explore. If it isn't already, configure **Explore** to use the -- **Grafana** -- data source, with the **Live Measurements** query type. Set **Channel** to **steam/telegraf_id/thermostat**. The channel should describe the number of messages received per minute. Your **Explore** configuration should look something like this:

Figure 11.7 – Thermostat data stream in Explore

Within a matter of moments, you should start seeing a flow of data on this channel. Refreshing the time range over time should result in the **Explore** graph looking something like the following:

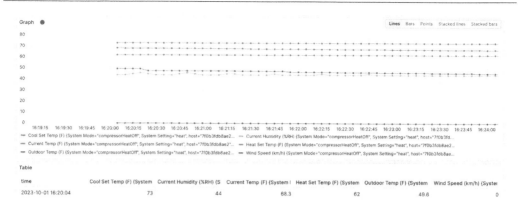

Figure 11.8 – Thermostat data stream graph in Explore

It's possible that since we're pulling data with different tags, the number of fields will change until all the possible tag/field combinations arrive. This is because InfluxDB determines a unique dataset by the combination of tags and fields. Simply click on any of the fields in the legend to isolate one, then click it again. That should refresh the display with the additional datasets.

Now would be a good time to look at the pipeline and see what else you can do to improve it:

- Add other inputs to the Telegraf agent configuration.

- Add status checks and callbacks to the `mqtt_pub.py` script when messages are published.

- Look at how we configure the fields with a YAML specification. Could the command-line options be defined similarly? Could this configuration be read in from an external file?

## Summary

There you have it! We've accomplished a lot in this chapter, probably without even realizing it. Of course, we learned about a new Grafana capability in Grafana Live, and we learned a little bit about streaming data with Telegraf. We also picked up a sampling from the world of message brokering in IoT.

But I also slipped in a couple of other aspects you may not have noticed. We learned about using requirements to drive software development. Our code was cleaner and easier to understand when we adopted object orientation and the principles of delegation and separation of responsibilities. Finally, we also developed our script as a **minimum viable product** (**MVP**) by implementing only those aspects deemed important at this stage.

In our next chapter, we'll look at how to monitor our real-time data for anomalous metrics and how we might not only detect them but also trigger warning alerts. We'll even learn how to leverage Grafana's alerting system to flexibly distribute alerts to multiple channels for better observability. Stay tuned!

# 12

# Monitoring Data Streams with Grafana Alerts

In our last chapter, we explored the world of real-time data streaming by combining Telegraf's input plugins to capture CPU metrics, and by simulating an IoT metrics pipeline with the addition of a Mosquitto broker and a simple Python script standing in for an IoT device.

As part of our three-chapter exploration of Grafana's observability features, we're going to move from simply streaming metrics to adding a key observability feature: the ability to trigger some form of an alert when certain conditions are met. Without the ability to monitor our systems and then alert when we detect anomalous behavior, we risk deterioration, instability, or even significant outages.

We'll start out by discussing aspects of monitoring and observability with an eye toward good strategies for identifying the alert conditions we want to watch for. Next, we'll talk about Grafana's alerting features, especially the key features of alert rules and contact points.

After we get through the brief overview of monitoring in general and Grafana alerting specifically, we'll set about to define typical alert rules. Initially, we'll be monitoring Docker Compose service containers for alert conditions, then we'll establish similar monitoring for an NGINX web server.

Next, we'll be integrating three different contact points with Grafana: email, Slack, and PagerDuty. Finally, we'll define labels and notification policies to route our alert messages to the proper contact points.

The Grafana alerting system is complex and powerful, so in a sense, we'll only be scratching the surface of its many capabilities. Nonetheless, it should provide a good introduction to many of the key concepts you might need in order to adopt Grafana for your particular needs.

In this chapter, we will cover the following topics:

- Monitoring and observability
- Alerting in Grafana
- Defining alert rules

- Alert messaging to contact points
- Routing alerts with notification policies

# Technical requirements

Tutorial code, dashboards, and other helpful files for this chapter can be found in the book's GitHub repository at `https://github.com/PacktPublishing/Learn-Grafana-10/tree/main/Chapter12`.

# Monitoring and observability

The key to observability is, of course, proper monitoring. Without the ability to monitor, there can be no awareness of the status of your systems and, consequently, no way to react to changes in those systems, be they adverse or otherwise.

In our examples, we will be looking at two kinds of monitoring: an orchestrated computing platform such as Docker Compose or Kubernetes, and a lightweight application such as a web server. We will be using the techniques we demonstrated in the previous chapter to track metrics generated by Telegraf; these principles are the same whether we're talking about small servers or massive compute clouds. But first, let's discuss some key concepts.

## Monitoring processes

When we look at monitoring whether it's on-premises or in the cloud, we tend to see the world from two main perspectives: how the system manages its processes, or the processes themselves. Either you are monitoring how processes are performing in relation to each other on the platform or you're monitoring whether the process is behaving in line with expectation.

In the first case, we only care to monitor processes in terms of how they consume standard system resources such as CPU, memory, or disk space. In the second case, we care about the performance metrics unique to the application itself, whether it's web pages served or data frames visualized.

## Monitoring system resources

The platform itself, regardless of whether it is literally a computer or a virtual abstraction, still must manage a standard array of resources. Among those resources are the following:

- Computational resources in the form of CPUs, GPUs, or any number of the new special-purpose processors for machine learning
- Memory resources, whether they exist in virtual form or in hardware
- Storage resources, such as spinning disks, or solid-state devices

Let's take a closer look at some of these resources and why they might require monitoring attention.

## Monitoring computational resources

Without the CPUs, GPUs, and other processors, computers would just be mostly empty boxes with blinking lights. But while we take computation for granted on a platform, why would we need monitoring?

Like the resources we described previously, computing resources are **bounded**, meaning that they are finite and so must be shared among all the other processes running on the computer. When you run a process on a computer, regardless of how many CPU processing cores it might have, that process is only able to access CPU resources for a short period of time before they must be released for use by other processes.

Depending upon how heavily your processes need to use CPU resources, monitoring them will reveal how much time the processors spend executing your processes as opposed to running other processes, or even its own. Consequently, when you monitor CPU utilization, you will be observing the percentage of time spent doing useful computation. High CPU utilization might be perfectly normal, or it might be an indication of a problem that is preventing work from getting done on time.

Understanding the nature of your computing needs will help to determine whether you should expect to see your computing resources heavily utilized or not. For example, if you have a computational server doing complex simulation work, you might expect that if a steady stream of work is delivered to that server and knowing that simulation software can require a great deal of computing resources, you should then be monitoring for high utilization. Likewise, if you are monitoring an interactive platform, you might only be expecting light utilization, and anything above a lightly loaded CPU might be a cause for concern.

## Monitoring memory resources

Unlike CPU, memory does not always lend itself well to the simplistic notions of high versus low utilization. Memory use can vary widely depending upon the purpose of a process and how well it's been developed. Typically, memory is well managed by modern operating systems so that even with most of their memory in use, computers can still efficiently work with almost no performance degradation.

Common terms you might hear to describe the behavior of operating system memory management are **leaking**, **paging**, **swapping**, or **thrashing**. While memory thrashing is typically considered pathological, sometimes even memory paging or swapping can be considered pathological under certain circumstances. Consequently, careful monitoring of memory resource utilization is still important as memory is still not infinite, and most operating systems will protect themselves by killing processes that are in danger of jeopardizing overall memory management; identifying processes that are misusing memory is thus a key reason for memory monitoring.

### Monitoring storage

Storage monitoring is vital as it is always finite and, unlike memory or CPU, cannot be easily reclaimed once it is truly used up. Storage is often used for tracking state, for cache, for memory mapping, and for process backup. Running out of storage risks catastrophic failure as there is no failover in that case.

Monitoring the state of storage is vital, and so storage monitoring and alerting is often the primary requirement for proper platform observability.

## Monitoring applications

Applications are a little trickier to monitor. While we have very well-understood observability for our compute platforms, monitoring applications and services themselves requires intimate knowledge of these processes. If they provide any observability features, it is often through specific and idiosyncratic APIs. For security reasons, they may require some form of authentication to even access them.

However, there are now efforts underway such as the **Open Telemetry project** to try to craft standards for capturing observability data from software applications. Even so, it will require the cooperation of software developers to modify their code to comply with these initiatives, which means adoption is likely to be slow going.

## Capturing metrics for alerting

For us to properly monitor our CPU resources, we'll need to first capture them. Unfortunately, Grafana does not support the monitoring of Grafana Live data streams, so we'll have to convert them to one of Grafana's supported Data Sources. Luckily, since we are using InfluxDB line protocol, we can store the metrics in an InfluxDB bucket. Telegraf even supports an output plugin for writing directly into InfluxDB. We're going to set that up in the next section.

# Alerting in Grafana

Grafana alerting has evolved significantly over the last few versions to a complex, powerful, and versatile system for combining *monitoring, alerting*, and *notification*. Its power can be a bit intimidating but bear in mind that you may not need every capability in Grafana alerting.

We'll take things step by step, so you can see how the parts fit together. Once you understand the basics, if you run into a more complex observability scenario, you will know how best to extend your own alerting to accommodate it.

Let's start by reviewing how the Grafana alerting works. There are four main components to Grafana alerting: **alert rules**, **labels**, **notification policies**, and **contact points**. We'll go over their roles one by one.

## Alert rules

Alert rules are the trigger mechanism for Grafana alerting. You can have all the metrics you want streaming into Grafana, but if you don't have any alert rules, how would you know when something is wrong? Put simply, alert rules are the conditions that, if met, trigger an alert. However simple that definition may be, defining alert rules can be quite a complex effort.

## Labels

Once alert rules have been defined, labels are metadata Grafana uses to identify different alert rules. In order to define a notification policy, labels are used to match alert rules with their ultimate contact point destination.

## Notification policies

Notification policies are the traffic control for alerting. Notification policies use powerful templating features for setting the content of the messages sent to contact points, and based upon the labels they are matched up with, they determine what messages will go to which contact points.

## Contact points

Contact points integrate Grafana alerting with various supported notification destinations such as email or chat. A contact point is essentially a Grafana plugin that is configured to communicate with a notification destination service.

As you can see each of these four components can seem complex, and lining up all of them to generate even a single message may seem like a daunting task, but a simple alert pipeline can be easily configured using mostly default settings. Let's get started!

# Defining alert rules

Let's start off by talking about how we want to look at triggering alerts. To build an alert, you will need to answer a series of questions in this form:

What *condition* must exist as measured by what *metrics*, and for *how long*?

Let's break this concept down into its constituent parts.

## What condition...

An alert ultimately boils down to a switch: at any given moment in time, the **evaluation interval**, an alert may need to be triggered. How you determine whether the alert should be in a triggered (or **firing**) state is called the **alert condition**. Most of the work you will do in defining an alert condition consists of reducing metrics data to a simple Boolean yes-or-no assertion about whether an alert should be triggered.

Space prevents us from devoting an entire chapter to exploring the possible ways to define alert conditions, but I can offer some heuristics for identifying possible alert conditions:

- Is the condition based upon a threshold? Does the threshold have precursors that would increase the readiness level? For example, when a disk is at 80% capacity, should that trigger a warning alert before a critical one at 95%?

- Look for conditions based upon trends. In these cases, you're looking for values that trend up when they should be down, or down when they should be steady. Classic examples are spiking traffic on a website or rapidly declining disk space. Pay heed to both the *direction* of the trend and the *rate of change*.

- Don't try to anticipate the unexpected, manage it. Don't treat every incident as a requirement to acquire more metrics or define more conditions. Think about your normal state as an envelope of appropriate behavior that should be monitored for anomalies that lie outside that envelope. If your servers' resources normally run at 40% to 50%, don't try to guess what specific threshold might cause performance issues; simply monitor for falling below 40% or rising above 50%.

- Remember to watch for the absence of data; often gaps in data may be the indicator of additional problems. At the very least, it could indicate where additional observability may be necessary.

## What metrics...

To sense whether to trigger an alert, you will need to know something about the state of the world, hence you need to gather the metrics necessary to describe the state of your system sufficiently enough that when you test for the alert condition, you will get an answer that reflects whether the metrics are accurately representing your observations. This is often the trickiest part as sometimes you will need to gather more metrics just to make sure you're properly observing the system state. Here's an admittedly outrageous example of what I mean:

*To protect our coal miners, we've deployed over 250 yellow canaries at various key locations. Each is equipped with radio transmitters delivering information about their current location, level of activity, and respiration. We believe that correctly measuring whether our canaries are in our mines, whether they are still breathing, and if they are still moving, is the best means for determining whether they are alive and are not suffering from the levels of poisonous gas that might affect our miners adversely.*

This is a great description showing how the addition of more metrics makes it possible to derive a good sense of whether the canaries are both alive and in the right parts of the mine. It also points to a potential flaw that we could better describe in this way:

*To protect our miners, we've deployed over 250 sensors capable of detecting and relaying the quantities of three potentially lethal gases (carbon monoxide, carbon dioxide, and methane). Each is tagged and registered with the correct location in the mine.*

The difference between the two shows a trap that you can easily fall into: that of obsessively monitoring second- or third-order effects rather than properly monitoring first-order ones. The lesson is: don't place poor canaries in coal mines and then monitor them for the effects of poisonous gases; directly monitor for the actual gases!

## How long...

Finally, when you have analyzed your metrics for alert conditions, bear in mind the time frame. Do you want an alert on the first sign of trouble, or do you want to wait to see if the condition resolves itself on its own? Think about the effects of generating an alert. Do you want to wake somebody up every 15 seconds, only to say "never mind" after 5? Duration becomes an important characteristic to examine.

With those preliminaries out of the way, let's examine a couple of use cases for monitoring both processes and services. We'll first explore process monitoring by using Telegraf to capture Docker container metrics. We'll build an alert rule to detect when our CPU percentage rises above a certain threshold. Following that, we'll spin up an NGINX web server and again use Telegraf to capture metrics and set up an alert rule to detect when the server goes down.

## Monitoring systems

For us to demonstrate process monitoring, we will use Telegraf's `docker` input plugin to scrape Docker for metrics from our containers and services. More information about the plugin can be found at `https://github.com/influxdata/telegraf/tree/master/plugins/inputs/docker`. Since Grafana alerting doesn't support internal streaming, we'll need to store those metrics in a data source that Grafana alerting does support. Happily, InfluxDB fills the bill, so we just need to add the `influxdb_v2` output plugin to our `telegraf.conf` file.

Before we can update our `telegraf.conf` file though, we'll first need to get an InfluxDB server running. We'll also need to generate an API key for Telegraf so that it can store data in an InfluxDB bucket, and one for Grafana so we can query InfluxDB from a data source. By now, you should be well versed in performing the necessary steps, so I won't need to go into as much detail as in previous chapters.

To get InfluxDB up and running we'll use Docker Compose; here's the relevant section of the `docker-compose.yml` file:

```
influxdb:
    image: "influxdb:latest"
    ports:
        - "8086:8086"
    volumes:
        - "${PWD-.}/influxdb2:/var/lib/influxdb2"
```

To pull the image and start it up, run the following:

```
% docker-compose up –pull missing -d influxdb
```

Open a web browser to http://localhost:8086 and perform the initial setup to set a username and password. Set the **Organization** to LearnGrafana and the **Bucket** to Chapter12.

We need to generate an API token, so go to **Load Data | API Tokens** and clone your user's token. Capture the token to the clipboard and paste it somewhere for future reference.

At this point, we need to set up both the Telegraf docker input plugin and the influxdb_v2 output plugin as well. You can use the InfluxDB + **Create Configuration** tool to generate the appropriate configuration, or you can use this one for the agent and inputs plugin:

```
[agent]
    interval = "1s"
    flush_interval = "1s"


[[inputs.docker]]
  ## Docker Endpoint
  ##     To use TCP, set endpoint = "tcp://[ip]:[port]"
  ##     To use environment variables (ie, docker-machine), set
endpoint = "ENV"
    endpoint = "unix:///var/run/docker.sock"

  ## Set to true to collect Swarm metrics(desired_replicas, running_
replicas)
    gather_services = false

  ## Set the source tag for the metrics to the container ID hostname,
eg first 12 chars
    source_tag = false

  ## Containers to include and exclude. Globs accepted.
  ## Note that an empty array for both will include all containers
    container_name_include = []
    container_name_exclude = []

  ## Timeout for docker list, info, and stats commands
    timeout = "5s"

  ## docker labels to include and exclude as tags.  Globs accepted.
  ## Note that an empty array for both will include all labels as tags
    docker_label_include = []
    docker_label_exclude = []
```

This one is for the `influxdb_v2` plugin:

```
[[outputs.influxdb_v2]]
  ## The URLs of the InfluxDB cluster nodes.
  ##
  ## Multiple URLs can be specified for a single cluster, only ONE of
the
  ## urls will be written to each interval.
  ##     ex: urls = ["https://us-west-2-1.aws.cloud2.influxdata.com"]
    urls = ["http://influxdb:8086"]

  ## API token for authentication.
    token = "<your-token-here>"

  ## Organization is the name of the organization you wish to write
to; must exist.
    organization = "LearnGrafana"

  ## Destination bucket to write into.
    bucket = "Chapter12"
```

Paste in your API token into the config file `token` setting.

You'll also need to make some adjustments to the `docker-compose.yml` to make it possible for Telegraf to access Docker. The Docker socket (as referenced in the `telegraf.conf`) needs to be mapped into Telegraf's Docker container. In our `docker-compose.yml` file, that would look like this:

```
volumes:
    - /var/run/docker.sock:/var/run/docker.sock
```

You will also need to make sure the container runs under both the `telegraf` user and the group that owns the Docker socket file. On Windows and Linux, you can find the `groupid` by running the following command:

```
% stat -c '%g' /var/run/docker.sock
```

The addition to the `docker-compose.yml` will look like this:

```
user: telegraf:<group id>
```

> **Note**
>
> Due to some complications related to how Docker is installed on MacOS, you will need to do things a bit differently. While the `groupid` for `telegraf` does not need to be set in `docker-compose.yml`, the Docker socket file needs to also allow *group* write permissions inside the container. In my case, I needed to use the `chmod` command:
>
> ```
> % docker-compose exec chmod 775 telegraf /var/run/docker.sock
> ```

The final Telegraf service should look like this:

```
telegraf:
    image: "telegraf:latest"
    user: telegraf:<group id>  # not needed on MacOS
    volumes:
        - "${PWD-.}/telegraf/etc/telegraf.conf:/etc/telegraf/
telegraf.conf"
        - /var/run/docker.sock:/var/run/docker.sock
```

Start up the Telegraf container:

```
% docker-compose up --pull missing -d telegraf
```

To confirm you have data, go to **Data Explorer** in your InfluxDB GUI and click on the **Chapter12** bucket. You should see **docker** listed under **_measurement**, indicating the `docker` plugin data is flowing into the bucket and is available as a measurement in InfluxDB.

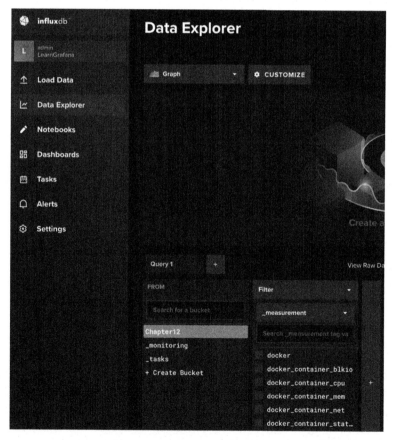

Figure 12.1 – Docker measurements

The last steps are to launch an instance of Grafana and create a new data source that will connect to InfluxDB. We'll first configure a Docker Compose service for Grafana in our `docker-compose.yml` file:

```
grafana:
    image: "grafana/grafana:latest"
    ports:
        - "3000:3000"
    volumes:
        - "${PWD-.}/grafana:/var/lib/Grafana
```

Launch the service and connect to `http://localhost:3000`:

```
docker-compose up --pull missing -d grafana
```

Next, we'll create a data source connection to the InfluxDB database where our data is landing from Telegraf:

1.   Open your browser to the Grafana app and select **Connections | Add new connection** from the main menu.

2.   Search for the InfluxDB data source and select it.

3.   Click on **Add a new data source**. You'll create a new InfluxDB data source with the following settings:

   - **Name**: `InfluxDB`

   - **Query Language**: **InfluxQL**

   - **HTTP | URL**: `http://influxdb:8086`

   - **Custom HTTP Headers | Header**: `Authorization`

   - **Custom HTTP Headers | Value**: `Token <influxdb-api-token>`

   - **Database**: `Chapter12`

Remember to mind the space between the `Token` string and the token itself. You can use the token you generated for your Telegraf output plugin or generate a new one.

Figure 12.2 – InfluxDB data source

If you've configured the data source correctly, Grafana will acknowledge the new measurements corresponding to your `docker` plugin metrics. This would be a good opportunity to familiarize yourself with those different data series in **Explore**.

Now that we have a working data series to query for our alerting, let's create an alerting rule based on the `docker_container_cpu` measurement.

### Alert query

Recalling our earlier rubric for constructing an alert, let's map it into a Grafana alert rule.

We'll start off by setting up a single query that will identify *what metric*, in this case the Docker `docker_container_cpu` measurement. This measurement tracks the various measures of time and other resources the CPU is devoting to containers:

1.  In the main menu, select **Alerting | Alerting rules** and click **+ New alert rule**.

2.  Set the name in the first section, **1 Set alert rule name**, to `docker-cpu`.

3.  Next, we'll set up the query in **2 Define query and alert condition**. Set the data source in Query A to **InfluxDB**.

4.  Click **Options** to the right of the data source dropdown and set the **Time Range** to **now-10m to now**.

5.  Click the pencil icon to the right of the query to switch to raw query mode and enter the following query:

```
SELECT max("usage_percent")
FROM "docker_container_cpu"
WHERE $timeFilter
GROUP BY time($__interval) fill(none)
```

In the query, we're looking at the `docker_container_cpu` metric `usage_percent`, which indicates what percentage of time is devoted to the CPU. We aggregate on the `max` value and fill in blank values with `none`. If data is flowing into InfluxDB, entering the raw query should trigger a graph with the current data stream, as depicted in the following screenshot:

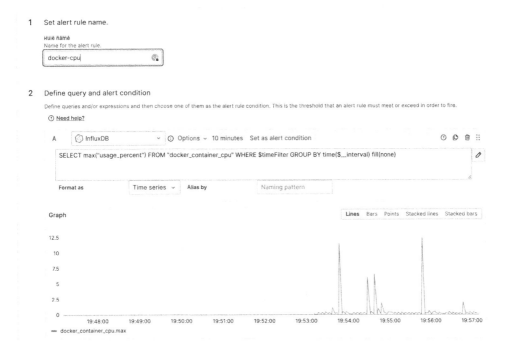

Figure 12.3 – Alert rule query

## Alert conditions

At this point, we do have a data series, but that's insufficient to determine *under what conditions*. We need to reduce the query results to a single value that we will then evaluate to see if an alert should be triggered:

1.  In the **Expressions** section, confirm the type of expression **B** is **Reduce**, because we'll be reducing our threshold series in **A** to a single value.

2.  Set **Input** to **A**. That's our query.

3.  Select **Last** for **Function**. We want to evaluate the latest value at all times.

4.  Set the **Mode** to **Strict**. This mode will accept **non-numerical values (NaN or Not a Number)**, but will trigger an alert downstream if any are detected.

    Finally, we still need to determine whether the single value fulfills the conditions that would generate an alert. Let's set a trigger threshold of 95, which means that we will generate an alert if the service's CPU time is greater than 95%:

5.  Confirm the type of expression **C** is **Threshold**.

6.  Threshold of what? Why, expression **B**, of course. Set **Input** to **B**.

7.  Set the condition to IS ABOVE and the value to 95.

8.  Confirm the **Alert condition** is set in **Threshold** expression **C**.

Figure 12.4 – Alert rule conditions

To check whether your alert rule works, click on **Preview**. You should see an indicator in expression **C** as to whether the condition is met and a visual display of the data series. Unless your machine is heavily loaded, 95% CPU is so high the alert status is most likely indicating a green normal state.

## Alert evaluation behavior

In section **3**, **Set alert evaluation behavior**, the conditions for how we respond to alerts begin to take shape. Here, we store our rule along with other rules that need to be grouped together for logical reasons. We also set the evaluation group of which alerts need to be evaluated during the same interval. Finally, we set the interval of time an alert rule is in violation before we trigger the rule.

Since this is our first and only rule so far, we'll first need to create a folder to store it in. Select **+ New folder** and name it `System Alerts`. Think of the folder as a container, much like a dashboard folder, an organizational feature that allows you to store and assign access control to a collection of alert rules. In fact, the alert rule folders can be found alongside the dashboard folders.

Next, we need to create an evaluation group, a set of alert rules that is evaluated during the same time interval. All alert rules in the same evaluation group are evaluated in sequence during the interval, not simultaneously. Recall that when we set up the alert rule, we set the threshold interval to `10m`, meaning all data over the last ten minutes is run through the expression to check for the alert condition. Don't confuse the alert rule interval with the evaluation rule. The former governs the block of time evaluated for alert conditions; the latter governs how often that evaluation is run.

All alerts must be assigned to an evaluation group. Add alerts by clicking on the drop-down menu. We don't have one yet, so let's create one. We will need to specify the name of the group and its evaluation interval:

1.  Click on **+ New evaluation group**.

2.  Set the name to `cpu` as we will be evaluating CPU time.

3.  Set the evaluation interval to `1m`. You want to set this interval to a period that maintains responsiveness but is long enough that you can perform all the evaluations and not tax your Grafana server. If you later want to change the evaluation group, click on the pencil icon. The following screenshot shows an example of what creating a group looks like:

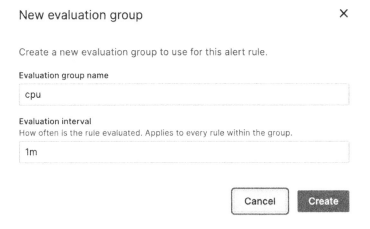

Figure 12.5 – Evaluation group

All members of the same evaluation group will be evaluated sequentially during that minute as well. This can be useful if you need to queue your alerts to run in a specific order or to prevent them from running at the same time.

Finally, we'll need to set the **Pending period value**, the amount of time a violating condition must hold before an alert is triggered. Depending upon your circumstances, you may not want to trigger an alert unless the condition has been maintained for a substantial amount of time. In our case, we'll set it to 5m or five minutes. Here's our evaluation behavior:

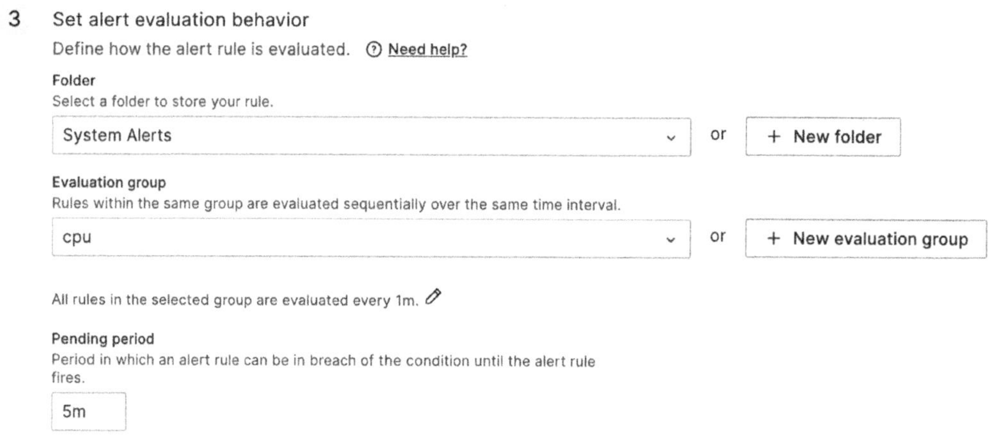

**3    Set alert evaluation behavior**

Define how the alert rule is evaluated.   ⓘ **Need help?**

**Folder**
Select a folder to store your rule.

| System Alerts | ∨ | or | + New folder |

**Evaluation group**
Rules within the same group are evaluated sequentially over the same time interval.

| cpu | ∨ | or | + New evaluation group |

All rules in the selected group are evaluated every 1m. ✎

**Pending period**
Period in which an alert rule can be in breach of the condition until the alert rule fires.

| 5m |

Figure 12.6 – Alert rule evaluation behavior

## Adding annotations

Before we can use our new alert rule, we may need to add specific metadata information to the rule that can be inserted into the alert message payload. These annotations provide detail and richness to the *content* of your alerts and can include a summary, a detailed description, the URL to a runbook of actions to take, other custom annotations, and links to a dashboard and panel created to depict the conditions that triggered the alert.

**Summary**, **Description**, **Runbook URL**, custom annotations, and the dashboard panel link are all stored as template variables for when a notification policy assembles the final message before sending it to the contact point. This is your opportunity to assemble as much information as you think the reader of your alert message needs to address the alert.

In our example, we'll set the summary. The summary is one of several annotations you can attach to an alert rule, which can then be inserted into the message when it's sent to a contact point. Grafana alerting leverages the powerful Golang templating system for message templating, and the annotations are no exception.

While space prevents me from going into much detail on the templating system, I can show you an example of how we could use it. Perhaps we want to indicate in our summary that the CPU percentage is high. While we could indicate in our summary annotation the specific threshold of 95% that we've fallen below, it would be even more useful if we also knew what the actual percentage was.

We can access this in our template from a built-in variable called $value, which corresponds to the values of each of our **B** and **C** expressions. We can get at the value of **B** by using a dotted notation: $value.B. To access the template, we wrap it in double braces.

So, our final summary message could then be set to the following:

**Summary (optional)**: The CPU idle time > 95% [{{ $values.B }}]%

**4    Add annotations**

Add annotations to provide more context in your alert notifications.    ⑦ <u>Need help?</u>

Summary (optional)
Short summary of what happened and why.

```
The CPU idle time > 95% [{{ $values.B }}]%
```

Description (optional)
Description of what the alert rule does.

```
Enter a description...
```

Runbook URL (optional)
Webpage where you keep your runbook for the alert.

```
https://
```

+ **Add custom annotation**        ⊕ **Link dashboard and panel**

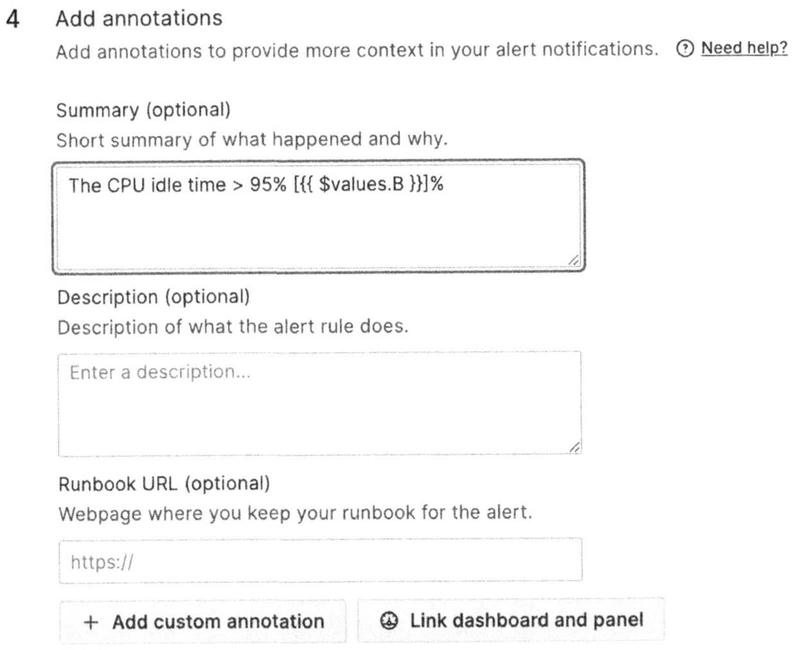

Figure 12.7 – Alert rule summary

All that is left at this point is to configure our notifications by adding special **Labels**. While labels aren't strictly necessary, they will be a useful form of metadata for routing our alerts, so let's investigate adding them now.

## Configuration notifications with labels

Labels are an additional form of metadata that has a few purposes. First, it serves to tie an alert to a specific identifier in order to differentiate it from other alerts. For example, you may want to label an alert with a server or application name so that you are able to trace a common alert to the specific server or application that generated it.

Secondly, it serves as a form of identification for use in a notification policy to direct alerting to various contact points. You may need to label a specific alert with a severity that a notification policy will match to a specific contact point or service in a contact point. Those same labels also apply to silences in case you need to establish a time window to disable a collection of alert rules.

For our case, we'll just add a single severity label. Under **Custom labels**, type `severity` in the key box and `critical` in the value box. Click + **Add label** if you want to add more labels.

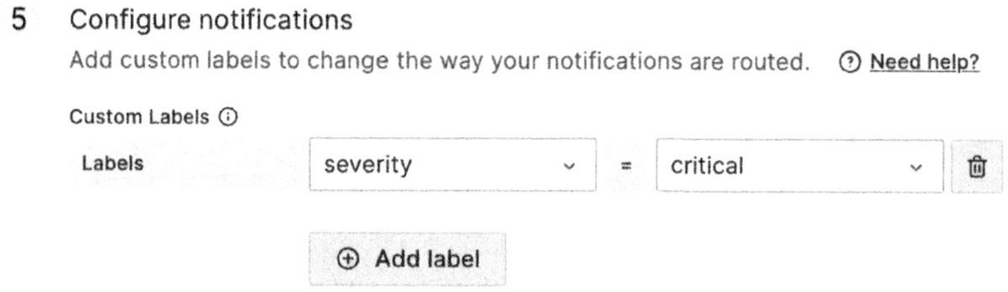

5   Configure notifications
    Add custom labels to change the way your notifications are routed.   ⓘ Need help?

    Custom Labels ⓘ
    Labels            severity          ⌄   =   critical          ⌄   🗑

                        ⊕ **Add label**

Figure 12.8 – Alert rule custom labels

Think about how you might scale up these alerts to cover other relevant CPU metrics. You might find that you need to create several similar rules that are differentiated by metric or by threshold, in which case the metric name or the threshold value itself could become useful labels.

### Multi-dimensional rules

Now, you might be thinking: what if I want to scale up these alert rules to cover all my Docker Compose services? Surely I don't want to create a separate rule for each of them? Well, you don't have to! As a matter of fact, Grafana can not only generate a series of alert rules based on your alert query, but it will also create labels to help you differentiate them in your alert messaging. It does this through something called a **multi-dimensional rule**. What we just created was a single rule, which is what you would expect: a single alert rule that corresponds to a single instance of an alert.

A multi-dimensional rule, by contrast, can generate multiple alert instances based upon the results of the alert query. How does this work? By examining the results of the GROUP  BY in our query, Grafana will then generate an instance and a label for each term in the GROUP  BY. Let's look at our `docker-cpu` alert rule:

1.   Modify the rule query to look like this:

```
SELECT max("usage_percent")
FROM "docker_container_cpu"
WHERE $timeFilter
GROUP BY time($__interval),
    "com.docker.compose.service" fill(none)
```

2.   Press the **Preview** button to see the results of the query.

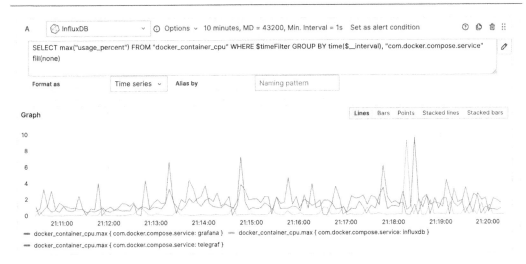

Figure 12.9 – Multi-dimensional alert rule

As you can see, there are multiple datasets, and each one is listed in each of our expressions. If any (or all) of those instances crosses the threshold, it will trigger an alert. Now, how do we take advantage of the labeling? Observe that in an expression, each data series is represented by a key/value pairing of the GROUP BY field and its value in the series.

Each of those key/value pairs is expressed in a label, and that label can be accessed in the template for our summary. Like we did before, we can build a template expression in the summary that references labels using the $labels variable. Normally, you would just access the GROUP BY field in the variable using the dot notation:

```
{{ $labels.com.docker.compose.service }}
```

That won't work if there is a . in the name. However, there is an alternative: using the index template function. The index function takes two parameters, the variable in question and the name of the field in quotes:

```
{{ index $labels "com.docker.compose.service" }}
```

Remember, the entire double-brace template is replaced by the value, so don't worry about the spacing inside. Let's create a new summary value that incorporates what we've learned about both the $labels and the $values variables:

```
CPU usage for Docker Compose service {{
    index $labels "com.docker.compose.service" }
    } is > 95% CPU [{{ $values.B }}]
```

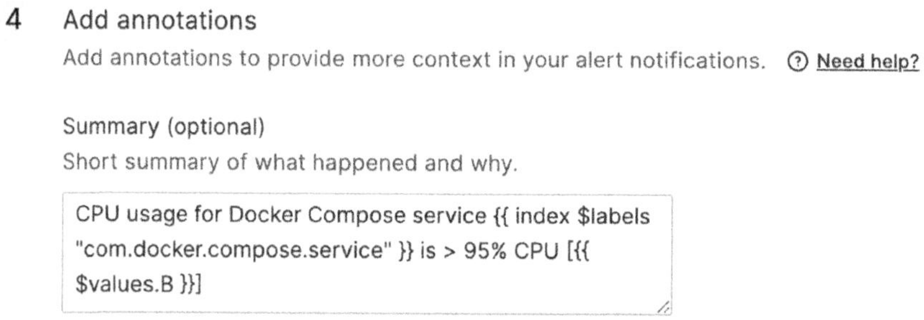

**4**    Add annotations

Add annotations to provide more context in your alert notifications.    ⑦ **Need help?**

Summary (optional)

Short summary of what happened and why.

CPU usage for Docker Compose service {{ index $labels
"com.docker.compose.service" }} is > 95% CPU [{{
$values.B }}]

Figure 12.10 – Template variable in alert rule summary

Click on **Save and exit** to continue.

It's at this point, you might start to wonder about how to evaluate these template expressions to see if they produce the correct messages. Would we have to indefinitely wait for a threshold to be exceeded or to manually trigger an alert to see the message? As it happens, there is indeed a way to observe the evaluated template without triggering an alert:

1.    From **Alerting | Alert rules**, open the alert group you're interested in by clicking the disclosure control on the left of the group as shown by the number *1* in *Figure 12.11*.

2.    Next, open the alert rule by clicking on the disclosure button to the left of the rule itself. This is indicated by the number *2* in *Figure 12.11*.

3.    In this window, you should see each alert rule instance and a description of the summary. If you don't see them, wait a few moments for the evaluation period to pass. If the stated period (1m in our case) passes without an update, you possibly have an error in your summary or other annotation (number *3* in *Figure 12.11*), so you'll want to edit the alert rule and fix any errors.

4.    Open the alert instance you're interested in by again clicking the disclosure button to the left as shown by number *4* in *Figure 12.11*. Directly below the instance, you will see the current summary message with all templates substituted.

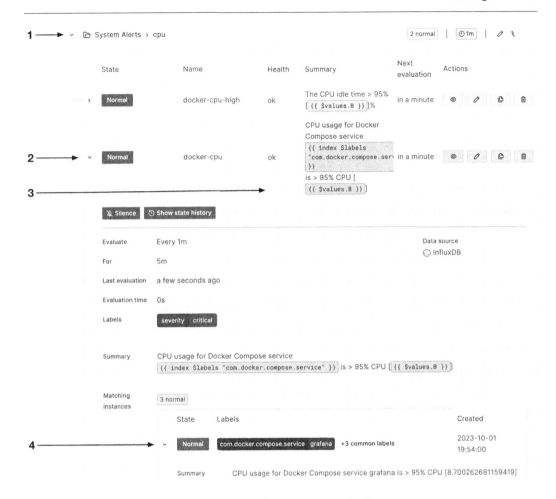

Figure 12.11 – Alert summary evaluation

## Monitoring applications

Now that we've gotten our feet wet with an initial alert rule, let's turn from process monitoring to service monitoring and add an application to monitor for alerting.

We're going to install and launch an instance of NGINX a lightweight open source web server. We don't really care about serving pages, we just want to run the server and gather metrics we can monitor for our alerting purposes. In this case, we want to use Telegraf to continuously extract metrics from the NGINX endpoint and save them in InfluxDB just as we did for the CPU metrics.

## Installing NGINX

Our first task is to set up the Docker Compose configuration with the requisite image, ports, and volume mappings. We'll need to make a tweak to the configuration, so we'll need to map a local configuration file into the container's filesystem, but as we've done before, it should pose no real difficulty.

Here's the `docker-compose.yml` service configuration you'll need:

```
nginx:
    image: nginx
    ports:
        - 8080:8080
    volumes:
        - "${PWD-.}/nginx/html:/usr/share/nginx/html"
        - "${PWD-.}/nginx/default.conf:/etc/nginx/conf.d/default.
conf"
```

This will map a local `default.conf` file into the `/etc/nginx/conf.d` directory in our NGINX container so we can override the built-in configuration. Before we build that configuration, we'll need to configure Telegraf to scrape the NGINX metrics, not unlike what we did with Prometheus many chapters ago.

## Configuring Telegraf

Telegraf has a nice inputs plugin called `nginx`. You can find the configuration information at `https://github.com/influxdata/telegraf/tree/master/plugins/inputs/nginx`. Note this is for the basic open source NGINX not NGINX Plus. We build the configuration with the InfluxDB GUI by going to **Load Data | Telegraf | + Create Configuration**, or go with this:

```
[[inputs.nginx]]
  # An array of Nginx stub_status URI to gather stats.
  urls = ["http://nginx/server_status"]

  # HTTP response timeout (default: 5s)
    response_timeout = "5s"
```

Restart your Telegraf service when you've completed the configuration change. The neat thing is that we will get a new dataset in our existing bucket, and that will translate into a new measurement for Grafana data source to query.

## Configuring NGINX

Next, we need to enable our NGINX metrics with a module called `stub_status`. We just need to configure an endpoint for `stub_status` at `/server_status`, which matches the one specified in the Telegraf configuration.

Here's a configuration file that sets up the endpoint. You should store it in `nginx/default.conf` so the mapped volume exposes it in the container. Start up your NGINX server with this:

```
% docker-compose up --pull missing -d nginx
```

You can check the logs to see that Telegraf is accessing the endpoint:

```
% docker-compose logs -f nginx
...
chapter12-nginx-1  | 172.24.0.4 - - [17/Mar/2023:05:06:08 +0000] "GET
/server_status HTTP/1.1" 200 98 "-" "Go-http-client/1.1" "-"
chapter12-nginx-1  | 172.24.0.4 - - [17/Mar/2023:05:06:09 +0000] "GET
/server_status HTTP/1.1" 200 98 "-" "Go-http-client/1.1" "-"
chapter12-nginx-1  | 172.24.0.4 - - [17/Mar/2023:05:06:10 +0000] "GET
/server_status HTTP/1.1" 200 98 "-" "Go-http-client/1.1" "-"
chapter12-nginx-1  | 172.24.0.4 - - [17/Mar/2023:05:06:11 +0000] "GET
/server_status HTTP/1.1" 200 98 "-" "Go-http-client/1.1" "-"
chapter12-nginx-1  | 172.24.0.4 - - [17/Mar/2023:05:06:12 +0000] "GET
/server_status HTTP/1.1" 200 98 "-" "Go-http-client/1.1" "-"
```

You'll find the data in the InfluxDB `Chapter12` bucket by checking the InfluxDB GUI in Data Explorer. Finally, you can confirm the Grafana data source by going to **Explore** and querying the InfluxDB data source for the `nginx` measurement.

Now that we have our data, let's go ahead and create an alert for it. Click + **New alert rule** to create a new alert rule. In this scenario, we're going to take a slightly different approach. We're going to build a simple dashboard with a single panel for our query. From that panel, we'll generate our alert rule.

### Creating an alert rule from a dashboard panel

Create and save a new dashboard. On the dashboard, create a new panel and open it to edit. Set the time frame to **Last 15 minutes**. Enter the following query:

```
SELECT max("active") FROM "nginx" WHERE $timeFilter GROUP BY time($__
interval) fill(none)
```

The query will check for the number of active connections. Since every poll by Telegraf is an active connection, there should be at least one most of the time. We'll use the active connections as a proxy for determining whether our NGINX server is running. Set the **Title** of the panel to `nginx-active` for reasons that will become obvious later. Click on **Apply** to apply the settings and then on **Save the dashboard**.

Reopen the panel, click on the **Alert** tab, and click on **Create alert rule from this panel**. You should end up back where we were, this time with a new alert rule and our query carried over as the query for the alert rule. We have few more things to set up:

1. Notice the alert rule is named for the dashboard panel you just created.

2. In the **A** query, set **Options | Time Range** to **now-15m to now**.

3. Press *Enter* or *Tab* in the raw query area to confirm that data is visible in the time range.

4. Set the **B Reduce** expression **Input** to **A**, **Function** to **Last**, and **Mode** to **Strict**.

5. Delete the **C Threshold** expression by clicking the trash can icon. We'll replace it with a **Math** expression instead.

6. Click on **Add expression** and select **Math** from the popup menu.

7. Set up the **C Math** expression with a $B < 1 **Expression**. We don't need to specify the **B** expression as our input because we use the $B variable instead.

8. Click on **Set as alert condition** so it is our final expression to evaluate for our alert:

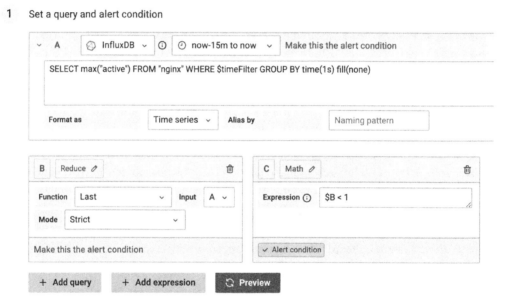

Figure 12.12 – NGINX alert rule query and alert condition

Next, we need to set up further alerting in case NGINX is down and there is no data at all. In section **3**, follow these steps:

1. Under **Folder**, select **+ New folder** and create a new one named `Application Alerts`. Select the **Application Alerts** folder to store this rule.

2. Click **+ New evaluation group** and name it `nginx`. Assign your rule to the new evaluation group. By default, the evaluation time is set to **1m**.

3.  Set the **Pending period** to 5m, if it isn't already.

4.  Open the **Configure no data and error handling** disclosure triangle and set **Alert state if no data or all values are null** to **Alerting**. This triggers an alert if we stop receiving data. Under some circumstances, you might want to use a dedicated heartbeat metric for this purpose.

5.  Here's what our evaluation behavior section should look like:

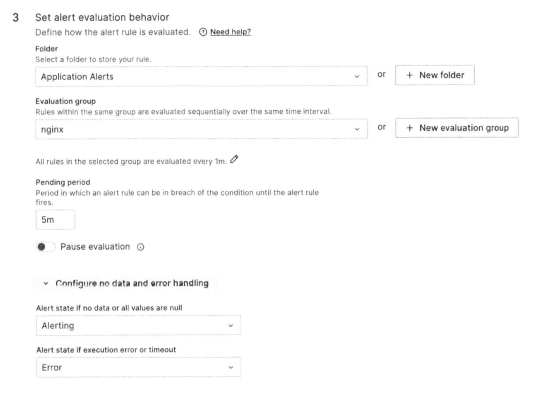

Figure 12.13 – NGINX alert rule evaluation behavior

Finally, we'll need to set our annotations. When it comes to the link to our dashboard panel, the work has already been done for us. We have been gifted two annotations, a UID that links back to the dashboard, and a panel ID for the panel on the dashboard. When the alert fires, the message generated for the contact point will contain a link to the specific panel with the alert rule query.

Go ahead and add a summary that indicates the number of active connections is less than one and save the alert rule. Our annotations section should look like this:

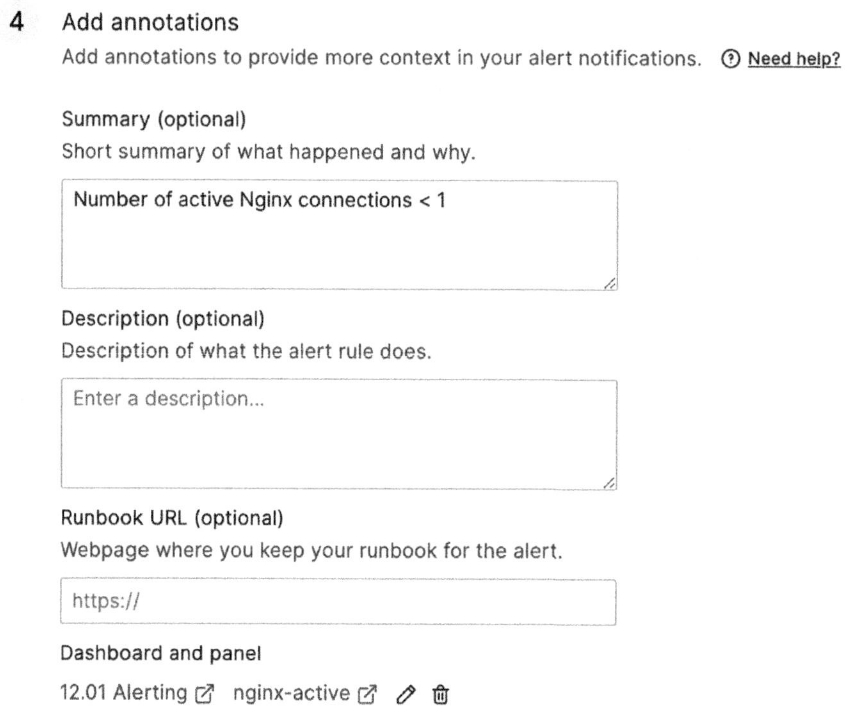

**4    Add annotations**
Add annotations to provide more context in your alert notifications.    ⑦ **Need help?**

Summary (optional)
Short summary of what happened and why.

> Number of active Nginx connections < 1

Description (optional)
Description of what the alert rule does.

> Enter a description...

Runbook URL (optional)
Webpage where you keep your runbook for the alert.

> https://

Dashboard and panel

12.01 Alerting ☐    nginx-active ☐    ✎ 🗑

Figure 12.14 – NGINX alert rule annotations with dashboard UID and panel ID

# Alert messaging to contact points

Before we can establish the notification policies that will direct our alerts to contact points, we should first define our contact points. Grafana supports an ever-growing number of contact points, so to find out more about a specific contact point, consult the Grafana documentation.

We are going to concentrate on three common contact points that cover many typical use cases. We'll use an email contact point to represent the typical use case where email is the destination for all alert messages. The Slack contact point is used when the alert needs to be visible to a defined group, such as the members of a Slack channel. Our final contact point is PagerDuty, a destination for alerts that need to be directed to a specific person or team for potentially immediate action.

## Configuring an email contact point

One of the most common and oldest forms of contact point is simply good old email. Nearly everyone has it, and access to email servers is almost ubiquitous. If you get emails, you can also send them.

To set up an email contact point, we'll first need to gather some information on how to contact and authenticate (if necessary) the **Simple Mail Transfer Protocol** (**SMTP**) email provider we plan to use. We will need to find out the following:

- The SMTP server and port
- The SMTP username and password

Once we've gathered this information, we'll need to modify the Grafana configuration. By default, SMTP is disabled, so we'll need to enable it in the Grafana configuration. One possible way of modifying the configuration is to copy the sample config file into a mapped volume, modify the configuration file, and restart our Grafana server. An easier way, since we're using Docker Compose to provision our containers, is to identify and set environment variables corresponding to the appropriate configuration settings.

Most settings defined in a Grafana configuration file are available as a corresponding environment variable that can be set the following way:

```
GF_SECTION_CONFIGNAME=configvalue
```

`SECTION` is the name of the bracketed section (in uppercase) in the config file, `CONFIGNAME` is the name of the configuration option (in uppercase), and `configvalue` is the configuration value. For example, the following might be in a section of the configuration file:

```
[security]
admin_user = admin
```

That would be overridden with an environment variable such as this:

```
GB_SECURITY_ADMIN_USER=myadmin
```

Armed with that information, and having checked the Grafana documentation at https://grafana.com/docs/grafana/latest/setup-grafana/configure-grafana, we'll need to set four environment variables:

- `GF_SMTP_ENABLED`: "true"
- `GF_SMTP_USER`: "smtp_user"
- `GF_SMTP_PASSWORD`: "smtp_password"
- `GF_SMTP_HOST`: "smtp_host:smtp_port"

You should of course fill in the environment values with your own settings.

> **Warning**
>
> It is at this point that I need to caution you about exposing secure information such as your password in a plaintext file. Do not follow this practice on a production server; this example is intended for educational purposes only!
>
> Both Docker Compose and Kubernetes support the use of encrypted secrets to prevent their exposure in a configuration file such as this one.
>
> For myself, I generated an application-specific password intended for this purpose only, with the understanding that if my computer is compromised, I can easily revoke the password.

This is what your `docker-compose.yml` file should look like after you add the new environment variables:

```
grafana:
    image: grafana/grafana:latest
    ports:
        - 3000:3000
    environment:
        GF_SMTP_ENABLED: "true"
        GF_SMTP_USER: "<smtp_user>"
        GF_SMTP_PASSWORD: "<smtp_password>"
        GF_SMTP_HOST: "<smtp_host>:<smtp_port>"
    volumes:
        - $PWD/grafana:/var/lib/grafana
```

After you've updated `docker-compose.yml`, restart the Grafana server:

```
% docker-compose down
% docker-compose up --pull missing -d grafana
```

Once you've restarted Grafana, you should create a new email contact point:

1.  From the main menu, select **Alerting | Contact points**.

2.  Either click on + **Add contact point** or edit (pencil icon) an existing contact point.

3.  Name the contact point.

4.  Make sure the contact point **Integration** is set to **Email**.

5.  In **Addresses**, enter an email address where you'd like alert messages to be sent.

At this point, you should test the email connection to confirm Grafana can connect to your SMTP server and deliver messages by clicking on the **Test** button.

## Configuring a PagerDuty contact point

While email is certainly traditional and common, when used in the context of an operations or SRE team, it can be pretty limiting. Not everyone consistently reads emails, high-priority messages often get lost among the volume of emails, and email typically doesn't reflect roles and responsibilities. Enter **PagerDuty**, a powerful system for managing the distribution of alerting messages. It's designed to send alert messages to a diverse set of communication mechanisms from email to voice and text to mobile applications.

While it's not in the scope of this book to go through the process of setting up a PagerDuty installation (you can find the docs here: `https://support.pagerduty.com/docs/trial-account-onboarding`), we'll just cover the configuration of a PagerDuty contact point from the perspective of an already-configured installation:

1.  In PagerDuty, click on **Services | Service Directory** to identify the service that you want to direct messages to. In my case, I'll use the **Default Service**.

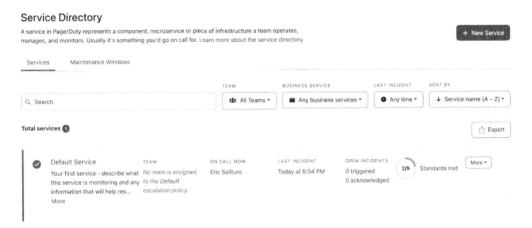

Figure 12.15 – PagerDuty service directory

2.  From the **Service Directory** in PagerDuty, click on the **Default Service** to open it (you may need to click on **Clear All Filters** to see it).

Figure 12.16 – PagerDuty service

3.   Select Integrations from the Integrations tab, next to the Activity tab

4.   Click on **Add an Integration**.

5.   Select the **Events API V2** webhook, as shown in the following screenshot:

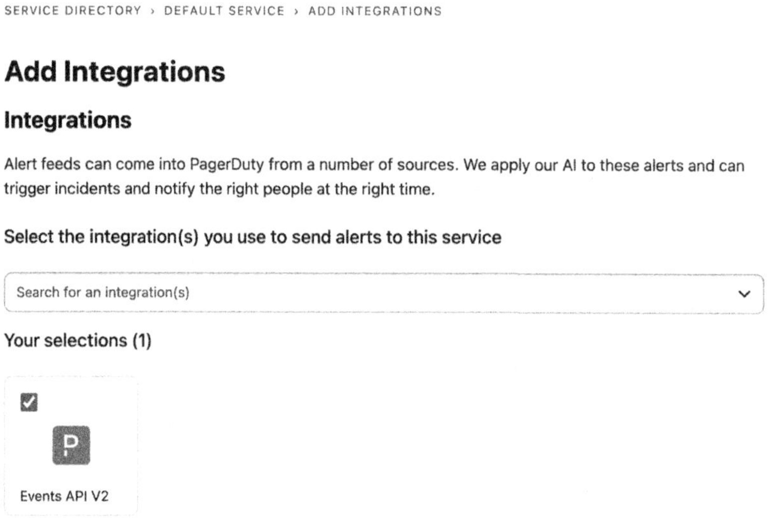

SERVICE DIRECTORY › DEFAULT SERVICE › ADD INTEGRATIONS

## Add Integrations

### Integrations

Alert feeds can come into PagerDuty from a number of sources. We apply our AI to these alerts and can trigger incidents and notify the right people at the right time.

**Select the integration(s) you use to send alerts to this service**

Search for an integration(s)                                            ⌄

**Your selections (1)**

✓

P

Events API V2

Figure 12.17 – PagerDuty Events API integration

6.   Open the integration with the disclosure icon. You should now see an **Integration Key value**. Copy it to the clipboard:

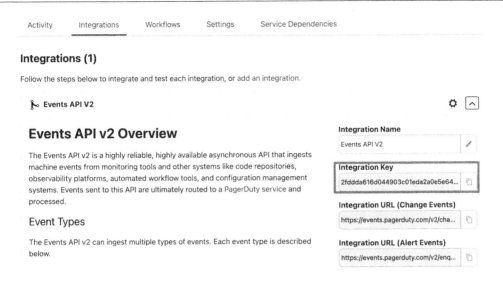

Figure 12.18 – PagerDuty integration key

7.  Now that you have a key, return to Grafana and open **Alerting | Contact points** and do the following:

    I.    Click **+ New contact point**.

    II.   Name your contact point something descriptive like `pagerduty`.

    III.  Set **Integration** to **PagerDuty**.

    IV.   Add your integration key to the **Integration Key** field.

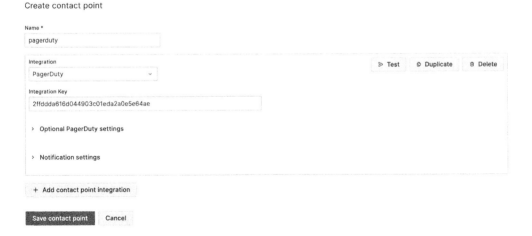

Figure 12.19 – PagerDuty contact point

8.  Click on the **Test** button to send a test alert to your PagerDuty service. You should see the alert fire in PagerDuty. The triggered alert in PagerDuty should look something like this:

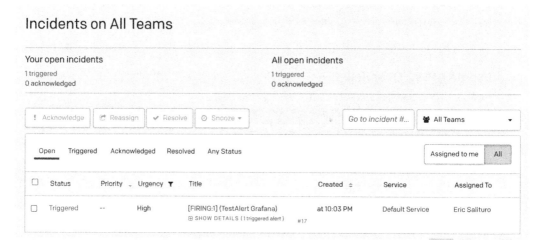

Figure 12.20 – PagerDuty test incident

We only have one last contact point to configure, the Slack contact point.

## Configuring a Slack contact point

Let's now move to our final notification integration, a chat-based one. In a chat application, all participants can see messages and respond to them in real time, and as is often the case, retain the message threads for future reference, especially in situations where participants come into the discussion at later times.

One of the most popular workforce instant messaging systems in the world is Slack; as a platform for managing the kinds of messages generated by observability, it is quite capable. Again, it is beyond the scope of the book to work through the entire process of subscribing to Slack, establishing an environment (called a **workspace** in Slack parlance), or configuring specific channels for observability. We'll assume you've already established a Slack workspace (go to `https://slack.com/get-started#/createnew` to create one).

This section of the chapter will be concerned with integrating a Grafana alerting contact point with Slack. To successfully configure the integration, you will need to have administrative access to Slack as you will be enabling the Slack integration for your workspace. We'll also assume you have permission to create a channel for routing message.

Our first stop is Slack, where we'll create a channel called `#learn-grafana-90-alert`.

Next, we need to create a **Slack application**, which is a special security designation for applications that connect to Slack via the API. Here's the process:

1.  In Slack, from the workspace menu, select **Settings & administration | Manage apps**.

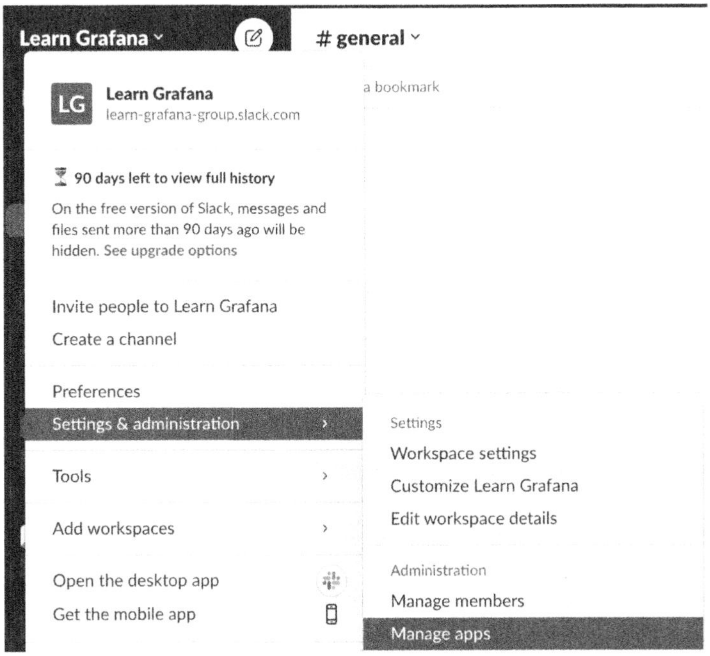

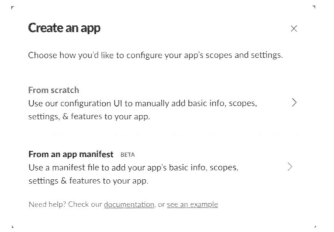

Figure 12.21 – Slack Settings & administration menu

2.  Click **Build** at the top right.

3.  Click the big green **Create an App** button.

4.  Select **From scratch**.

Figure 12.22 – Slack app creation dialog

5.   Set **App Name** to `Grafana Alerting` and select the workspace from the dropdown.

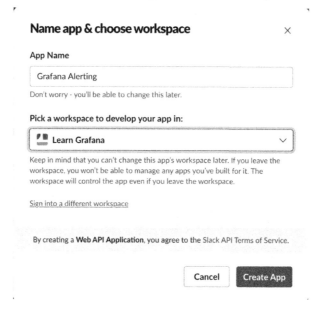

Figure 12.23 – Slack workspace chooser

All you need to do next is to create an incoming webhook, which will bundle the channel for the connection and the Slack authentication in a single URL.

6.   Click on your newly created app. In the **Features** section, select **Incoming Webhooks**.

7.   Enable **Activate Incoming Webhooks**.

8.   Click **Add New Webhook to Workspace**.

9.   Set the name of the channel to the one you created previously.

Figure 12.24 – Slack app channel selection

10. Copy the URL for the incoming webhook to the clipboard.

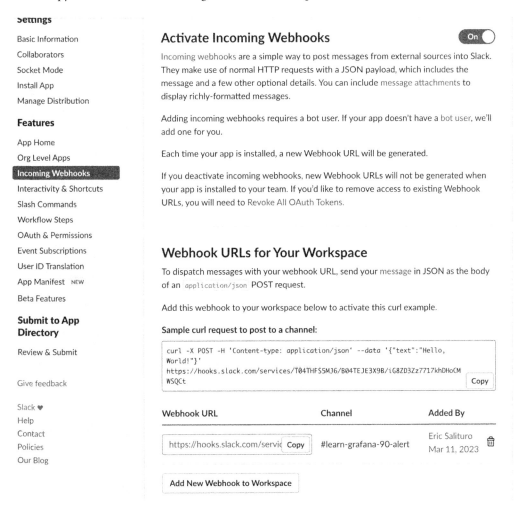

Figure 12.25 – Slack incoming webhooks

11. Now, return to Grafana, select **Alerting | Contact points**, and create a new contact point.

12. Set a name for the contact point, such as `slack`.

13. Set the **Integration** to **Slack**.

14. Since we are sending messages to Slack via webhooks, you can skip the **Recipient** and **Token** settings.

15. Under **Webhook URL**, paste the webhook URL.

Create contact point

Name *

slack

Integration

Slack

▷ Test    ⏷ Duplicate    🗑 Delete

Recipient
Specify channel, private group, or IM channel (can be an encoded ID or a name) -
required unless you provide a webhook

Token
Provide a Slack API token (starts with "xoxb") - required unless you provide a
webhook

Webhook URL
Optionally provide a Slack incoming webhook URL for sending messages, in this
case the token isn't necessary

https://hooks.slack.com/services/T04THFS5MJ6/B04TEJE3X9B/iG8ZD3Zz771

>  Optional Slack settings

>  Notification settings

Figure 12.26 – Slack contact point

16. To test the contact point, click the **Test** button, and select either the **Predefined** message or create a **Custom** one.

17. Check the Slack channel for your message:

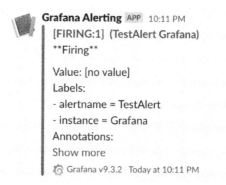

**Grafana Alerting** APP  10:11 PM
[FIRING:1]  (TestAlert Grafana)
**Firing**

Value: [no value]
Labels:
- alertname = TestAlert
- instance = Grafana
Annotations:
Show more
⏱ Grafana v9.3.2 · Today at 10:11 PM

Figure 12.27 – Slack alert test message

That's it for our contact points! We'll need to create notification policies that will route alert messages to these contact points.

# Routing alerts with notification policies

Now that we have our alert rules and our contact points, we're able to link them up using our notification policies. One of the most common notification policies is to match up an alert severity with a particular contact point. That is why we initially set a `severity` label when we created our alert rules.

Now that we have our `severity` label, we can use it in a notification policy, so let's set up such a policy. A notification policy can be as simple or complex as you want. The point is to use the information represented in the labels to determine which contact point(s) should receive your alert. It can be as simple as that.

For example, you may have a situation where you want all your low-severity (informational) incidents to go to an email address, but you want medium-severity (actionable, normal response) incidents to go to Slack or Discord, and your high-severity (actionable, immediate response) incidents to go to PagerDuty. To accomplish that, you'll want to set a label of high, medium, or low severity.

In your notification policy, you then match the label corresponding to the severity with the appropriate contact point:

- **Label**: `Critical severity`, **Contact point**: **PagerDuty**
- **Label**: `Normal severity`, **Contact point**: **Slack**
- **Label**: `Low severity`, **Contact point**: **email**

Let's set that up in practice for our contact points. Go to **Alerting | Notification policies**. If you want all alerts to go to the same contact point, you will set that by editing the default policy. In our case, we'll set the email contact point as our default for archival purposes:

1.  For the **Default policy**, click on the meatballs (3-dot) menu and select **Edit**.
2.  Select your email contact point from the drop-down menu.
3.  Click **Update default policy**.

At this point, you could also adjust the **Group by** options for the **Default policy**. These are the labels that determine which alerts should be treated as being in the same group. **Group by** comes into play as part of the sequencing for alerts. Sequencing is controlled by the **Timing options** section.

The idea behind the alert grouping is to prevent a rapid-fire alerting scenario from overwhelming your contact points with simultaneous, redundant alerts. Imagine a situation where a significant number of servers all go offline due to a networking failure. Each server will generate a single alert, but multiple racks of servers could end up creating hundreds of alerts almost simultaneously. If all the alerts are defined to be in the same group, Grafana will only send a single alert using non-grouping labels to indicate the scope of the alert.

The timing options are configured to protect contact points from an inadvertent **Denial of Service (DoS)** attack by modeling an exponential back-off. The initial alert is sent after 30 seconds, any additional alerts are sent in 5-minute intervals, and any recent alerts don't go out for 4 hours. This assures a reasonable distribution of alerts to minimize cost and avoid service provider **Terms of Service (ToS)** violations.

The key to the group is to make sure you've labeled your alert rules in such a way that if a significant incident were to occur, grouping by the right labels would minimize the number of alerts that need to be sent out, saving on unnecessary and costly redundant messaging.

## Specific routing

Now that we've established the default policy, let's set the policies for our severity labels. Under **Default policy**, click on + **New nested policy** to add a new notification policy.

Under **Matching labels**, do the following:

1. Type severity into the **Label** field.

2. Leave **Operator** as =.

3. Add critical to the **Value** field.

4. Set the contact point to **PagerDuty**.

5. Click **Save policy**.

Here's an example of setting the label in the policy:

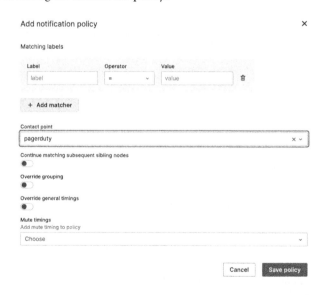

Figure 12.28 – Notification policy

Next, add two more nested notification policies:

- **Matching labels**: `severity = normal` | **Contact point**: **Slack**
- **Matching labels**: `severity = low` | **Contact point**: **email**

Now, it might be the case that you don't want each alert to go to a different contact point; instead, you'd like the policies to be additive, that is, you want only the normal alerts to be sent via email, but the critical alerts to go to all the contact points. That's easy enough: just add additional matchers to each notification policy. Remember to build the policy around the contact point, not the other way around. Ask yourself: what alerts do I want to go to the contact point?

## Mute timings

Space prevents us from going into a lot of detail on mute timings but suffice to say they are useful when you don't want or need an alert to go to a contact point during certain windows of time. Say you don't want normal severity alerts to send email messages during weekends. You first create a mute timing, then assign the mute timing to the notification policy.

Here's how we might do that:

1. Select **Alerting | Notification policies** from the main menu. Click on the **Mute timings** tab.
2. Click on + **Add mute timing**.
3. Under **Name** *, type in `weekends`.
4. Under **Days of the week**, enter `Sat, Sun`.
5. Click **Save**.
6. To assign the mute timing, click the edit box next to the policy with `severity=normal` matching labels.
7. Next to **Mute timings**, select **weekends** from the drop-down.
8. Click **Save**.

Creating this mute timing is depicted in the following screenshot:

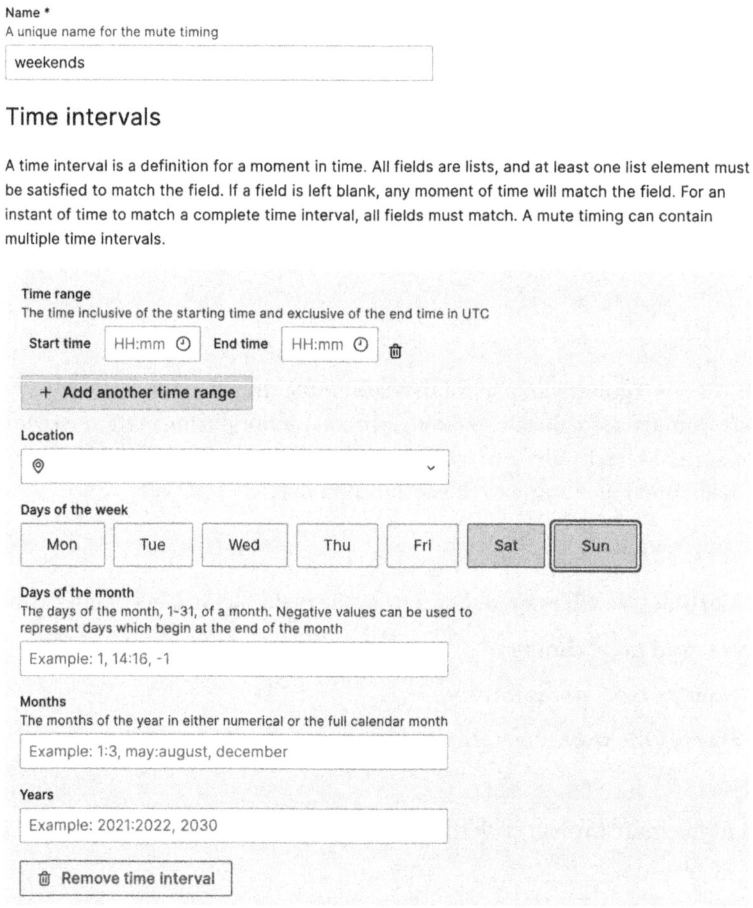

**Name \***
A unique name for the mute timing

weekends

## Time intervals

A time interval is a definition for a moment in time. All fields are lists, and at least one list element must be satisfied to match the field. If a field is left blank, any moment of time will match the field. For an instant of time to match a complete time interval, all fields must match. A mute timing can contain multiple time intervals.

**Time range**
The time inclusive of the starting time and exclusive of the end time in UTC

Start time    HH:mm ⊘    End time    HH:mm ⊘    🗑

+ Add another time range

**Location**

◎                                                      ⌄

**Days of the week**

| Mon | Tue | Wed | Thu | Fri | Sat | Sun |

**Days of the month**
The days of the month, 1–31, of a month. Negative values can be used to represent days which begin at the end of the month

Example: 1, 14:16, -1

**Months**
The months of the year in either numerical or the full calendar month

Example: 1:3, may:august, december

**Years**

Example: 2021:2022, 2030

🗑 Remove time interval

Figure 12.29 – Mute timing

Now you have an end-to-end Grafana alerting system with a couple of alert rules to get you started. Try them out by triggering alerts. You may have to force them by altering the threshold values, so remember to set them back when you finish testing!

## On your own

Grafana alerting is so complex and powerful that a single chapter can hardly do it justice, but this should whet your appetite for exploring even more features. Here are some things you can try out:

- Add a new set of alert rules based on another Docker measurement, such as memory.

- Add additional alert rules to the cpu alert group but with different thresholds of 50% and 10%. Map them into different severity labels.

- Explore the templating system and experiment with how additional annotations can affect the message delivered to the contact point.

- Add more labels and then embed them in annotations or message templates for richer alert messages.

## Summary

This was an extensive chapter, and we covered a lot of ground. Observability is becoming a large, important technology sector and Grafana is keeping up by making its alerting capabilities more powerful and versatile.

In this chapter, we set up monitoring for both Docker and NGINX using InfluxDB as a data source. We created alert rules to query and analyze the data from our monitoring, used expressions to reduce the data to a single value, and created expressions to evaluate that value for violating conditions that might need to trigger an alert. We integrated Grafana contact points with email, PagerDuty, and Slack to receive our alerts with messages that contain annotation data set by our alert rules evaluation behavior. We also established notification policies to route our alert messages to different contact points based on the severity derived from alert rule labels. Finally, we briefly considered how to set up mute timings for when we might want to disable certain alert rules based on the day of the week.

We'll wrap up our tour of observability in the next chapter using Loki to manage log search, which can benefit troubleshooting by linking logs to time-correlated metrics.

# 13
# Exploring Log Data with Grafana's Loki

In this final chapter of *Part 2, Real-World Grafana*, we're going to shift gears a bit. So far, we've been operating under a dashboard-oriented paradigm in terms of how we use Grafana. This is not too unusual since Grafana has always been structured around the dashboard metaphor. The introduction of **Explore** in Grafana 6 brought an alternative workflow – one that is data-driven and, dare I say it, exploratory.

Grafana really shines when working with numerical and some forms of textual data, but what if the data includes substantial amounts of log data? Every day, countless applications disgorge not only standard numerical metrics but also copious text logs. If you've ever enabled debug mode in an application, then you've seen how a few meager kilobytes of information can quickly become a flood of gigabytes worth of repetitive, inscrutable gibberish. Diagnosing a problem by enabling the debugging code is more like the proverbial needle in a haystack as even a few seconds of data spans thousands of lines of text.

The goal of Grafana's **Explore** and other similar tools is to try to get a handle on some of that data by making searching and filtering easier, and by making it possible to associate metrics data with time-correlated log data. It's not enough for **Explore** to provide the ad hoc analysis; it needs to be coupled with data sources that can handle logging and metrics data.

If you are familiar with Elasticsearch, then you'll know this sounds like a description of the ELK stack, which is a combination of Elasticsearch for data storage and search, Logstash for data capture, and Kibana for visualization. Grafana also provides a similar application stack Loki, a project that in their words provides the following (`https://grafana.com/oss/loki`):

> *"...a horizontally-scalable, highly-available, multi-tenant log aggregation system inspired by Prometheus. It is designed to be very cost-effective and easy to operate. It does not index the contents of the logs, but rather a set of labels for each log stream."*

By combining **Loki log aggregation** with **Prometheus metrics** and **Grafana visualization**, Grafana is developing a software suite that rivals the venerable ELK stack.

In this chapter, we'll be covering the following topics:

- Loading system logs into Loki
- Visualizing Loki log data with **Explore**
- Capturing simulated logs generated programmatically and real logs output by Docker
- Querying synchronized logs and metrics in **Explore**

Since our ultimate goal will be to use **Explore** to simultaneously analyze logs and metrics, as in previous chapters, we will be setting up a *pipeline* of several services and getting them to talk to each other. Here's the plan for this chapter:

1. Collect system logs with Promtail, an agent similar in function to Elasticsearch Logstash or Influx Telegraf.
2. Stand up a Loki service as a Grafana data source.
3. Make any transformations to the collected log data to increase its utility in **Explore**.
4. Collect additional logging from the various services in our pipeline, including Grafana.
5. Use Prometheus to scrape the metrics from our services and use an **Explore** feature called **Split** to compare the logs with the time-correlated metrics.

Along the way, we'll be learning about some of the interesting **Explore** features that become available when you use the Loki data source. Let's get started!

# Technical requirements

The tutorial code, dashboards, and other helpful files for this chapter can be found in this book's GitHub repository at `https://github.com/PacktPublishing/Learn-Grafana-10/tree/main/Chapter13`.

# Loading system logs into Loki

To get started, `cd` to the `Chapter13` directory in your clone of this book's repository.

To stand up a Loki logging pipeline, we'll need to set up a series of services in Docker Compose. In our initial deployment, we will set up three services: `loki`, `promtail`, and `grafana`. By now, adding these services to a `docker-compose.yml` file should be familiar and straightforward.

## Networking our services

Before we start up our services, we will want to establish a network that links them all together. All services started from a single `docker-compose.yml` file that shares a common network called `myapp_default`. We will not use the default name and instead define the network name for our service as `loki`. There is no requirement to do this, but it demonstrates how you can link up multiple services to not just one default network but potentially several in a more complex network topology.

This is how we will start off our `docker-compose.yml` file:

```
networks:
    loki:
```

To bind any of our services, we'll need to add a network specification to the service definition, like so:

```
networks:
    - loki
```

We'll see this in action in the next section.

## Installing Promtail

Our first service will scrape logs from our local computer. Similar in function to Telegraf, Promtail serves this purpose in the Loki pipeline. Initially, we will be working with a minimal configuration just to get things up and running, then layer in more specific configurations as we go. The Promtail service configuration looks like this:

```
promtail:
    image: "grafana/promtail:latest"
ports:
    - "9080:9080"
networks:
    - loki
```

First, we pull down the latest version of Promtail and then expose port `9080`. Finally, we must set up a common network called `loki`. This will allow our services to talk to each other. It's not entirely necessary as all services are already linked to a common network by default, but it's helpful to see how you can potentially set up multiple networks in a single `docker-compose.yml` file. Launch the service:

```
% docker-compose up --pull missing -d promtail
[+] Running 1/1
   Container chapter13-promtail-1  Started    0.4s
```

To check for our Promtail service, just query the endpoint with `curl`:

```
% curl -XGET http://localhost:9080/ready
Ready
```

The `Ready` response indicates that our service is up and running.

## Installing Loki

Once we start scraping for logs, Loki will provide the log storage service that the Grafana data source will access to search for and aggregate our logs. Let's have a quick look at the configuration for the Loki service:

```
loki:
    image: "grafana/loki:latest
ports:
    - "3100:3100"
networks:
    - loki
```

In the `Loki` service configuration, we pull the latest Docker image from the repository and expose port `3100`. The `networks` setting links our service to the common network, `loki`. Let's start up our Loki service:

```
% docker-compose up --pull missing -d loki
[+] Running 1/1
   Container chapter13-loki-1  Started          0.6s
```

We'll use `curl` to check for our service readiness:

```
% curl -XGET http://localhost:3100/ready
ready
```

You may see the following message:

```
Ingester not ready: waiting for 15s after being ready
```

It will take the order of a few seconds to a minute to launch. Give it time.

Note that we don't appear to have configured any persistence for either of our services. That's okay for now; the persistence is the logs themselves. Don't worry – we'll add that capability a little later.

## Launching Grafana

This covers our Loki pipeline, so we'll go ahead with our Grafana service, which you should be very familiar with by now:

```
grafana:
    image: "grafana/grafana:${GRAF_TAG-latest}"
ports:
    - "3000:3000"
volumes:
    - "${PWD-.}/grafana:/var/lib/grafana"
```

```
    networks:
        - loki
```

Now, let's launch Grafana:

```
% docker-compose up --pull missing -d grafana
[+] Running 1/1
   Container chapter13-grafana-1   Started      0.6s
   Container chapter13-loki-1      Creating     9.5s
```

Let's configure a Loki data source in Grafana and see what Promtail and Loki have done with our logs.

## Creating a Loki data source

Create a Loki data source in Grafana with these settings:

- **Name**: Loki
- **HTTP/URL**: http://loki:3100

If successful, you should get a message that reads **Data source successfully connected**:

Figure 13.1 – Loki data source

Now that we have a working Loki data source, let's go to **Explore** to see what the data looks like.

# Visualizing Loki log data with Explore

Go to **Explore** and confirm that **Loki** is set as your data source. Welcome to Loki! Things may look a bit different from what you may remember from using **Explore** with other data sources. On the far right of **Kick start your query**, click on **Builder** mode. Let's take a quick tour of some of Loki's UI features:

Figure 13.2 – Loki data source in Explore

The following features are highlighted in the preceding figure:

1.  **Split**: Splits the window into two queries that are side by side. For example, you can put logs on one side and metrics on the other.

2.  **Add to dashboard**: Captures your current query and creates a panel on a dashboard.

3.  **Time frame selection**. Selects the time period for the query.

4.  **Run query**: Use the dropdown to set a continuous refresh rate for the query.

5.  **Live**: This continuously displays the last few loglines matching the query. The button switches to a pause or stop selector.

6.  **Kick start your query**: Offers sample logs and metrics queries to get started.

7.  **Label browser**: Offers sample logs and metrics queries to get started.

8.  **Explain query**: Enables helpful annotations to queries.

9.  **Builder/Code**: Switches from the UI query builder to a simple query code text box.

10. **Query builder**: In **Builder** mode, you can assemble log stream processing pipelines using the LogQL query language, similar to PromQL for Prometheus.

11. **Options**: This sets several options, including overrides for the legend, the log line limit (the default is 1,000 lines), whether the Loki query is over a time range or a point in time, and the resolution of the display corresponding to the query step size.

12. **Add query**: Adds additional queries.

13. **Query history**: Opens the query history selector.

14. **Inspector**: Opens the query inspector, like the one in the panel query.

Let's have a look at the logs. Make sure that you've selected Loki as the data source. Set a **Time range** value that includes the period from when you started up the services in Docker Compose. Under **Label filters**, click on the **Select label** dropdown, and select any of the menu items. Under the **Select value** dropdown, select any item that has been auto-filled. If you don't see anything, don't worry – it just means Promtail's default settings didn't detect any logs.

In this example, we've picked up some logs from a log source or **job** called **varlogs**:

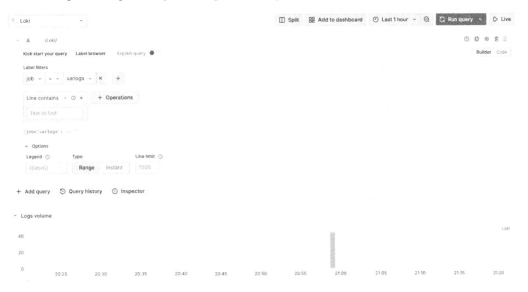

Figure 13.3 – Log query

Note that a LogQL query string is now visible in an area called the **Raw query** section. It should be identical to the query you'd see if you switched to **Code** mode.

Let's open one of the log entries to see how they're processed by Loki:

Figure 13.4 – Log entry

Since these log entries aren't particularly rich – they're just lines of text – Loki is unable to identify any labels other than the ones passed to it from Promtail, `filename`, and the `job` name. Never fear – we're just getting started!

To give you a quick idea of the log metrics capability of Loki, click **Kick start your query**, open **Metric query starters**, and select one of the starters. For example, I selected **Use this query** under **Bytes used by a log stream**, then confirmed I wanted to **Replace query**:

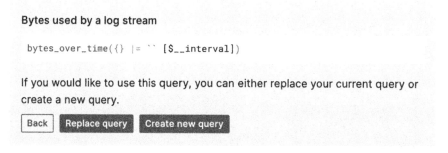

Figure 13.5 – Kickstart metrics query

Clicking **Run query** fires it off. Let's see what the results look like:

Figure 13.6 – Log metrics

Since it's a short data stream generated from a log file, there's only a single data point. Before we move on, let's turn on the **Explain** feature to see how much information it can provide:

Figure 13.7 – The Explain feature

As you can see, Grafana provides extensive documentation to help guide your query designs.

While we were able to sample some readily available logs for Loki, they aren't being consistently delivered in the quantities we would like to have for experimentation purposes. To keep things controllable, we won't depend on our local platform and its variations by operating system, processor, application working set, and so on. Instead, we will *simulate* the logs we need using a logging *generator* that we can completely control.

## Simulating logs with flog

As-is, this is a fairly limited view of Loki's capabilities, largely because we haven't fed it some real logging to work with. Let's fix that by first adding some live logs and then configuring Promtail to scrape them. Taking a cue from the Loki documentation, we'll use an open source logging generator called `flog` to generate fake logging. Next, we'll create a configuration file for Promtail that will scrape those logs in real time.

`flog` is available as a Docker container, so we just need to add it as a service to our `docker-compose.yml` file:

```
flog:
    image: mingrammer/flog:latest
command: -l -d 1
```

The service entry for `flog` is very simple: pull the latest image and run it with the `-l` command-line option for continuous looping, and `-d 1` to run with a delay interval of 1 second so that we don't overwhelm Promtail.

> **Note**
>
> If you are running on an Apple Silicon-based computer, will need to tell Docker to build an image that is supported by Apple Rosetta 2 Intel emulation. You just need to add a platform specification to your `flog` service, like so:
>
> ```
> flog:
>     image: mingrammer/flog:${FLOG_TAG-latest}
>     # uncomment the following line if running on an Apple
> Silicon Mac
>     platform: linux/amd64
>     command: -l -d 1 -f json
> ```

To get an idea of what it can generate, start it up and run the Docker Compose `logs` command with the tail option (`-f`) to see the logs it generates:

```
% docker-compose up --pull missing -d flog
[+] Running 1/1
   Container chapter13-flog-1  Started        0.4s
% docker-compose logs -f flog
chapter13-flog-1  | 176.73.77.191 - - [03/Apr/2023:02:34:43 +0000]
"PUT /compelling/magnetic HTTP/1.0" 502 2314
chapter13-flog-1  | 214.212.27.222 - abshire8143 [03/Apr/2023:02:34:44
+0000] "DELETE /incentivize HTTP/1.1" 205 16657
chapter13-flog-1  | 181.95.51.22 - - [03/Apr/2023:02:34:45 +0000]
"HEAD /best-of-breed/bandwidth HTTP/1.0" 500 18034
chapter13-flog-1  | 126.227.221.120 - trantow4368 [03/
Apr/2023:02:34:46 +0000] "PATCH /mission-critical HTTP/2.0" 401 11849
chapter13-flog-1  | 135.221.239.8 - reinger5263 [03/Apr/2023:02:34:47
+0000] "DELETE /partnerships/partnerships HTTP/2.0" 401 24724
chapter13-flog-1  | 135.186.148.135 - thiel3341 [03/Apr/2023:02:34:48
+0000] "PUT /architect/utilize/e-services/grow HTTP/1.0" 100 26296
chapter13-flog-1  | 198.86.17.203 - bartell2204 [03/Apr/2023:02:34:49
+0000] "HEAD /virtual/rich HTTP/1.0" 403 21582
...
```

By default, Promtail will not know about our new logging, so we'll need to somehow configure it with the necessary information. However, to do that, we'll also need to run and add a configuration file to our `promtail` service container.

## Configuring promtail

First, we need to copy a sample Promtail configuration file (`promtail-config.yaml`) into a local directory before mapping that file into our container. The easiest way to do this is to just download a sample config file from the Grafana Loki *Getting Started* documentation (`https://grafana.com/docs/loki/latest/get-started/#obtain-the-test-environment`):

```
% wget https://raw.githubusercontent.com/grafana/loki/main/examples/
getting-started/promtail-local-config.yaml -O promtail/etc/promtail-
local-config.yaml
```

The `wget` command will save this file as `promtail/etc/promtail-local-config.yml`. This is what the Promtail configuration file looks like:

```
server:
    http_listen_port: 9080
    grpc_listen_port: 0
```

```
positions:
    filename: /tmp/positions.yaml

clients:
    - url: http://loki:3100/loki/api/v1/push
    tenant_id: tenant1

scrape_configs:
    - job_name: flog_scrape
    docker_sd_configs:
        - host: unix:///var/run/docker.sock
        refresh_interval: 5s
    relabel_configs:
        - source_labels: ['__meta_docker_container_name']
        regex: '/(.*)'
        target_label: 'container'
```

While it is beyond the scope of this book to cover Promtail configuration in detail, let's go over this configuration file as it's pretty short. The `server` block sets up Promtail's web server endpoint port, which we exposed in our Docker Compose service configuration. The `positions` block indicates where to store the last-read log file locations in case Promtail is restarted. We'll need to map that into a local file location to persist it. The `clients` block sets the location of our `loki` server to send the logs. By establishing the Docker Compose network as `loki`, we can use it as the hostname for the URL.

`scrape_configs` is where the real work gets done. It specifies where to gather log files, along with a series of **pipeline stages** for further processing, before handing them off to Loki.

Pipeline stages are intended to perform data parsing and transformation, not altogether different than the `filter` section of a Logstash pipeline configuration. Pipeline stages come in four types, each performing different tasks on loglines and passing the results to the next stage:

- **Parsing stages**: Parses the `logline` and `extract` fields from parse matches
- **Transform stages**: Modifies the extracted fields
- **Action stages**: Performs some action with the extracted fields or even the logline itself
- **Filtering stages**: Drops certain stages or loglines

From this configuration, we can see that we will be scraping the Docker socket interface every 5 seconds before passing along the results to a transform stage called `relabel_configs`. In this case, we are going to search for a label attached to the log called `__meta_docker_container_name`. The regular expression, `regex`, matches against the value of that label everything after the slash character. The matched string is given a new label of `container`.

Our new configuration will extract logs from our Docker containers, and label them according to container name. How will that help us find our new logs generated by `flog`? Let's reconfigure our `promtail` service and find out!

## Promtail in Docker Compose

We need to update the `promtail` service in our `docker-compose.yml` file to accomplish a few things:

- We need to map our local Promtail configuration into the container for the `promtail` Docker Compose service

- We also need to update the `promtail` command to launch Promtail and make it use our local configuration file

- We need to map our Docker socket file, `/var/run/docker.sock`, into the container so that Promtail can access it

- Optionally, we want to map local temp directories so that log files can be found and the positions file can persist, even if the container is restarted

Here's the new `docker-compose.yml` service configuration for Promtail:

```
promtail:
image: "grafana/promtail:latest
ports:
    - "9080:9080"
command: -config.file=/etc/promtail/promtail-local-config.yaml
networks:
    - loki
volumes:
    - "${PWD-.}/promtail/etc:/etc/promtail"
    - "${PWD-.}/promtail/tmp:/tmp"
    - /var/run/docker.sock:/var/run/docker.sock
    - /var/log:/var/log
```

Let's stop our service and then start it up with the new configuration:

```
% docker-compose stop promtail
[+] Running 1/1
   Container chapter13-promtail-1   Stopped          0.3s
docker-compose up --pull missing -d promtail
[+] Running 1/1
   Container chapter13-promtail-1   Started          0.6s
```

If everything has gone well, we should be able to return to Grafana **Explore**. Now, when selecting a label under **Label Filters**, we should see (and select) **container**. Clicking on the **Select value** dropdown should now list a set of the following containers, based on the labels derived from our new Promtail configuration:

- `chapter13-grafana-1`

- `chapter13-promtail-1`

- `chapter13-loki-1`

- `chapter13-flog-1`

This answers the question: how do we see the `flog` logs? By selecting `chapter13-flog-1` and clicking on **Run query**, you should now see the results as a graph and a list of log entries:

Figure 13.8 – Flog logs

Alas, when we open one of our log entries, we still don't see much in the way of identifying useful labels, just the container name:

Figure 13.9 – Flog log entry

What we need to see is *structured* logging, such as `logfmt` or JSON. We can adjust the `flog` command to do just that. Modify the command in the `flog` Docker Compose service block so that it looks like this:

```
flog:
    image: mingrammer/flog:${FLOG_TAG-latest}
    platform: linux/amd64
    command: -l -d 1 -f json
```

The command is asking flog to send JSON-formatted output instead. Stop and recreate the container with the new command:

```
% docker-compose stop flog
[+] Running 1/1
   Container chapter13-flog-1  Stopped        0.2s
% docker-compose up --pull missing -d flog
[+] Running 1/1
   Container chapter13-flog-1  Started
```

Checking the log's output shows we are now generating JSON-formatted logs:

```
% docker-compose logs -f flog
chapter13-flog-1  | {"host":"60.111.28.122", "user-identifier":"-",
"datetime":"03/Apr/2023:05:21:47 +0000", "method": "DELETE",
"request": "/e-business/convergence/back-end/robust",
"protocol":"HTTP/1.1", "status":100, "bytes":22594, "referer":
"https://www.nationalvortals.info/e-enable"}
chapter13-flog-1  | {"host":"199.51.180.74", "user-identifier":"-",
"datetime":"03/Apr/2023:05:21:48 +0000", "method": "HEAD", "request":
"/architect/end-to-end/enable/bleeding-edge", "protocol":"HTTP/2.0",
"status":405, "bytes":633, "referer": "https://www.corporateworld-
class.org/monetize/disintermediate/wireless"}
chapter13-flog-1  | {"host":"12.98.181.20", "user-
identifier":"rippin3861", "datetime":"03/Apr/2023:05:21:49 +0000",
"method": "PUT", "request": "/streamline/functionalities",
"protocol":"HTTP/1.0", "status":502, "bytes":3726, "referer":
"https://www.centralone-to-one.net/reintermediate/strategize/
innovative"}
chapter13-flog-1  | {"host":"93.209.28.15", "user-identifier":"-",
"datetime":"03/Apr/2023:05:21:50 +0000", "method": "PUT", "request":
"/e-business/integrate", "protocol":"HTTP/2.0", "status":201,
"bytes":16880, "referer": "http://www.corporateplug-and-play.com/
platforms/visualize/roi/reintermediate"}
...
```

Now, when we refresh our query in **Explore**, we should see those same JSON-formatted logs:

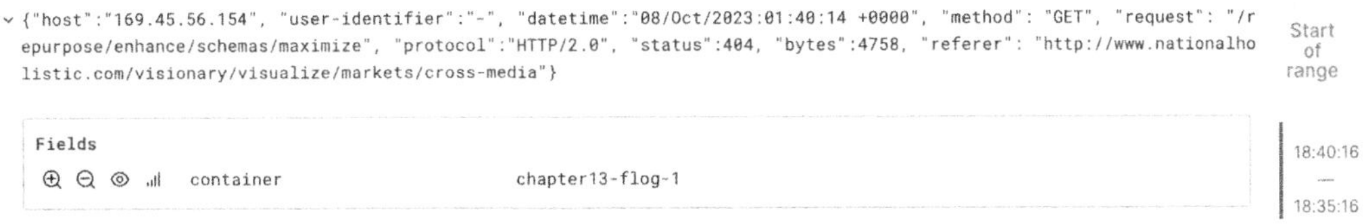

{"host":"169.45.56.154", "user-identifier":"-", "datetime":"08/Oct/2023:01:40:14 +0000", "method": "GET", "request": "/r epurpose/enhance/schemas/maximize", "protocol":"HTTP/2.0", "status":404, "bytes":4758, "referer": "http://www.nationalho listic.com/visionary/visualize/markets/cross-media"}

Start of range

Fields
⊕ ⊖ ◎ ‖  container                    chapter13-flog-1

18:40:16
—
18:35:16

Figure 13.10 – JSON-formatted logs

We need to do one more thing to get Loki to properly detect the fields in our logs. To do that, we need to pass them through a JSON parser. Loki may have already hinted that your query pipeline could use the addition of such a parser. Let's oblige it by adding a JSON parser. Either click on **hint: add json parser** or select + **Operations | Formats | Json**:

Figure 13.11 – JSON-formatted log fields

Now, not only do we have fields, but we also have labels parsed from the logs. Clicking on the magnifying glass with a (+) sign next to one of the labels will add a query for that label to our pipeline:

Figure 13.12 – Log filtering

Already, we can see how powerful Loki and its LogQL query language can be, and we've barely scratched the surface.

From here, we can continue to add label filters to our query to narrow down our search. We can also optimize the display by clicking on the (eye) icons next to only the fields we want to examine.

Next, we're going to look at another option for gathering logs from Docker through the use of a Docker plugin that we can install and connect directly to Loki.

## Alternative Docker log capture

If you are having trouble with the Docker socket method of scraping logs, or for security reasons can't use that method, the folks at Grafana have provided a log driver for Docker that can deliver logs to Loki directly, thus bypassing Promtail entirely. It requires downloading a special Loki log driver for Docker and updating the `docker-compose.yml` file so that it includes driver-specific configuration. To download and install the driver, run the following command:

```
% docker plugin install grafana/loki-docker-driver:latest --alias loki
--grant-all-permissions
```

The plugin installation command will download the latest driver and install it with an alias of `loki` (so that we can access it easily from Docker Compose), with wide-open permissions. To confirm the installation, run the following command:

```
% docker plugin ls
ID NAME DESCRIPTION ENABLED
692bec0b6ade loki:latest Loki Logging Driver true
```

If you get `true` as output, then your plugin loaded properly and is ready to go. More information on the driver can be found in the Loki GitHub repository (`https://github.com/grafana/loki/tree/main/clients/cmd/docker-driver`).

To take advantage of the driver, we'll need to update our `docker-compose.yml` file and reload the containers. For Loki logs, update the service so that it includes a `logging` block:

```
loki:
    image: "grafana/loki:latest"
ports:
    - "3100:3100"
networks:
    - loki
logging:
    driver: loki
    options:
        loki-url: "http://host.docker.internal:3100/loki/api/v1/
push"
```

Here, we're adding a new logging configuration to the service. We reference our driver aliased to `loki` and set the URL the driver needs to send the logs.

You can find the same URL form in the Promtail configuration file. Here's the excerpt:

```
clients:
    - url: http://loki:3100/loki/api/v1/push
```

We configure the logging to set the `--log-opt` command-line option for `docker run`, which launches the container. Information on how to configure containers to use the driver can be found in the following GitHub repository: `https://github.com/grafana/loki/blob/main/docs/sources/clients/docker-driver/configuration.md`.

In case you're wondering why we don't set the host to `loki` (the hostname for the Loki service itself) in the `loki` service configuration, the explanation is a bit tricky. The driver is set by Docker to be on the network for the Docker host itself, not the Docker Compose internal network. Effectively, it is *outside* the network we created for our services. Docker provides a special address for containers to access the internal host network: `host.docker.internal`.

Now that the configuration is out of the way, let's restart our new service stack so that we can access the Docker container logs:

1.  Shut down all our services:

```
% docker-compose down
[+] Running 6/6
 ✓ Container chapter13-promtail-1   Removed        10.2s
 ✓ Container chapter13-grafana-1    Removed         0.3s
 ✓ Container chapter13-loki-1       Removed        31.9s
 ✓ Container chapter13-flog-1       Removed         0.2s
 ✓ Network chapter13_default        Removed         0.1s
 ✓ Network chapter13_loki           Removed
```

2.  Start up the `loki` service first so that the other services have a service to send their logs:

```
% docker-compose up -d loki
[+] Building 0.0s (0/0)                docker:desktop-linux
[+] Running 1/1
 ✓ Container chapter13-loki-1   Started
```

3.  Next, we must run our check to confirm Loki is running:

```
% curl -XGET http://localhost:3100/ready
ready
```

4.  We must set the configurations for the other services in a similar fashion. Here is the `grafana` service:

```
grafana:
    image: "grafana/grafana:latest
    ports:
        - "3000:3000"
    volumes:
        - "${PWD-.}/grafana:/var/lib/grafana"
    networks:
        - loki
    logging:
        driver: loki
        options:
            loki-url: http://host.docker.internal:3100/loki/api/
v1/push
```

5.  Next up is `promtail`:

```
promtail:
    image: "grafana/promtail:${PROMT_TAG-latest}"
    ports:
        - "9080:9080"
    networks:
            loki
    command: -config.file=/etc/promtail/promtail-local-config.
yaml
    volumes:
        - "${PWD-.}/promtail/etc:/etc/promtail"
        - "${PWD-.}/promtail/tmp:/tmp"
        - /var/run/docker.sock:/var/run/docker.sock
        - /var/log:/var/log
    logging:
        driver: loki
        options:
            loki-url: "http:// host.docker.internal
:3100/loki/api/v1/push"
```

6.  Finally, we'll go ahead and set up logging for our `flog` server:

```
flog:
    image: mingrammer/flog:latest
    platform: linux/amd64
    command: -l -d 1 -f json
    logging:
        driver: loki
```

```
        options:
            loki-url: "http://host.docker.internal:3100/loki/api/
v1/push"
```

7.  Remember, if you're changing the configuration files for a service, `docker-compose restart` is sufficient, but if you're changing the service configuration in `docker-compose.yml`, you'll need to recreate the service with `docker-compose up -d`. Start up the rest of the services:

```
erics@blossom Chapter13 % docker-compose up -d grafana promptail
flog
docker-compose up -d
[+] Building 0.0s (0/0)           docker:desktop-linux
[+] Running 4/4
  Container chapter13-promtail-1   Started        0.1s
  Container chapter13-flog-1       Started        0.1s
  Container chapter13-grafana-1    Started
ready
```

Once we've confirmed that the Loki service is up and running, reloading the **Explore** page should reveal new labels corresponding to our additional logs:

Figure 13.13 – Docker logging driver labels

Where did all those labels come from? The Loki logging driver not only delivered the logging for all our containers, but it also set labels based on the Docker container configuration and then parsed them to produce a set of fields. To get the same logs previously delivered by Promtail to Loki, select the `compose_service` label and the `flog` value. You may also need to format the logs through the JSON formatter as before.

While we're here, let's take a quick look at the deduplication feature. **Deduplication** is helpful when you're looking at a stream of logs that are very similar in structure or have large chunks of repetition. **Explore** provides a few deduplication strategies that can reduce logs, depending on what it can safely ignore. To try it out, let's look at Loki's logging capabilities.

Switch from **Builder** mode to **Code**, type in the following query, and click **Run query**:

```
{compose_service="loki"}
```

You should see a well-populated list of log lines, and you might even detect visually similar line clusters. This is because logging code is often repetitive, differing only by a few parameters. Loki can detect these repetitive patterns to reduce entire line clusters down to single representatives.

Bear in mind that **Explore** is not searching for identical lines, rather it is choosing to examine logs after ignoring certain common log fields. There are three methods to choose from:

- **Exact**: Deduplicate logs, ignoring timestamps
- **Numbers**: Deduplicate logs differing only by numerical values
- **Signature**: Deduplicate logs matching similar punctuation and whitespace

Clicking on **Exact** yields the following excerpted results:

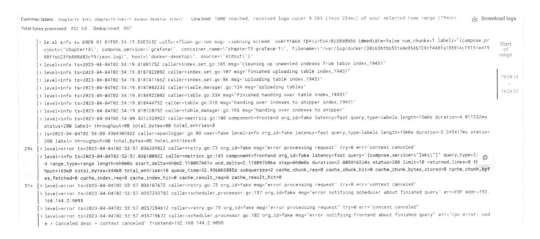

Figure 13.14 – Deduplication

You can see that deduplication has grouped many of the logs, reducing the log count by some 30%.

Now that we've seen the power of Loki log aggregation, let's couple that with Prometheus' metrics to see how we might couple log analysis to metrics.

## Querying logs and metrics with Explore

Adding Prometheus metrics to the mix is relatively simple: we just need to add a new Prometheus service while sending its logs to Loki to be aggregated (why not?). We'll also need to configure Prometheus to scrape the metrics endpoints of our services. We already did this earlier in this book, so it should be no problem for us to configure the scrapers for each service.

First, let's add Prometheus to our Docker Compose:

```
prometheus:
    image: "prom/prometheus:latest"
ports:
    - "9090:9090"
volumes:
    - "${PWD-.}/prometheus/etc:/etc/prometheus"
command: --config.file=/etc/prometheus/prometheus-config.yaml
networks:
    - loki
logging:
    driver: loki
    options:
        loki-url: "http://host.docker.internal:3100/loki/api/v1/
push"
```

Much of the settings are like those for the other services. We pull down the latest image, expose 9090 as our port, connect the loki network, and send logs to Loki. To set up Prometheus metrics scraping of our different services, we must map a local directory for our configuration file (named prometheus-config.yml), then set the prometheus command to read it on startup.

The Prometheus configuration file is based on the one we developed back in *Chapter 4, Connecting Grafana to a Prometheus Data Source*. First, we must set the default scrape interval to 30 seconds:

```
global:
    # How frequently to scrape targets by default.
    scrape_interval:      30s # By default, scrape targets every 30
seconds.
```

We must also set the scrape configuration jobs, one for each service, including Prometheus:

```
scrape_configs:
    # The job name is added as a label `job=<job_name>` to any
timeseries scraped from this config.
    - job_name: 'prometheus'
    static_configs:
        - targets: ['localhost:9090']
    - job_name: 'grafana'
```

```
    static_configs:
        - targets: ['grafana:3000']
    - job_name: 'promtail'
    static_configs:
        - targets: ['promtail:9080']
- job_name: 'loki'
    static_configs:
        - targets: ['loki:3100']
```

We use the service names and exposed ports to set the targets for each job. We don't include `flog` as it's not a true service presenting a metrics endpoint. Start up the new `prometheus` service:

```
% docker-compose up --pull missing -d prometheus
[+] Running 1/1
   Container chapter13-prometheus-1   Started        0.6s
```

You can check the Prometheus service by opening `http://localhost:9090/graph`. Next, we'll need to create a Prometheus data source with the following settings:

- **Name**: `Prometheus`

- **HTTP/URL**: `http://prometheus:9090`

The key portion of the data source should look as follows:

Figure 13.15 – Prometheus data source

If Prometheus is working correctly, you should get a message along the lines of **Data source is working**. Return to **Explore** to have a look at what we've collected. I'm going to use the **Split** feature to compare the log information I gathered with the metrics I've scraped. This particular scenario is meant to be illustrative and was created with the previous version of Grafana. The Grafana 10 interface is virtually identical, so you should have no trouble following along.

First, let's set up a query in **Explore** to examine how our Loki instance is doing:

1.  First, set **Data Source** to **Loki**.

2.  Next, set **Time Range** to the last few minutes or further back in time until we can find some interesting logging data.

3.  Switch to **Code** mode and enter the following query:

    ```
    {compose_service="loki"} | logfmt
    ```

    In this case, quite a few errors have been generated by Loki, possibly due to issues with the flog log lines:

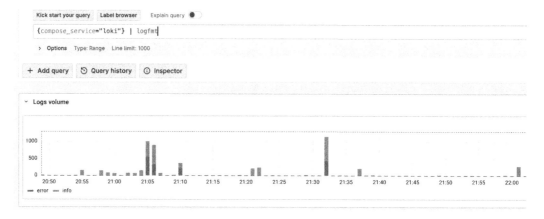

Figure 13.16 – Loki logs

Let's zero in on the error logs only by adding a filter to our query.

4.  Update the query so that it pipes the output of the parser and passes only the messages that specify the error level:

```
logfm{compose_service="loki"} | logfmt | level=`error`
```

Now, all we will see are the logged errors:

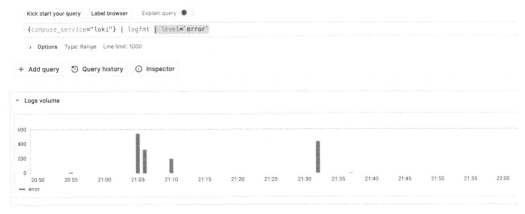

Figure 13.17 – Loki error logs

What we want to do is try to cross-reference these errors to our Prometheus metrics. Can we find metrics that respond at the same time? Can we use those metrics to create an alert that will let us know when the error log levels start climbing?

5.  To get two panes for analysis, click **Split**.

6.  Next, set the right-hand pane data source to **Prometheus**.

7.  Also, make sure you click **Sync all views** (chain link icon) so that you can see the metrics and logs time-correlated.

Much like we did in *Chapter 4, Connecting Grafana to a Prometheus Data Source,* we'll use **Metrics browser** to help us build a query to find metrics that correspond to our error logs:

1.  Start by opening **Metrics browser**.

2.   Type `log` and scroll down to find `loki_log_messages_total` in the list. Clicking on it enters it as a metric. It should then appear under **4. Resulting selector**:

Figure 13.18 – Prometheus selector

3.   Under **2. Select labels to search in**, select **instance** and **level** to make sure you're filtering on a particular Docker instance and log level. The number in parentheses indicates how many options are available.

4.   For **instance**, I selected **loki:3100**, and for **level**, I selected **error**:

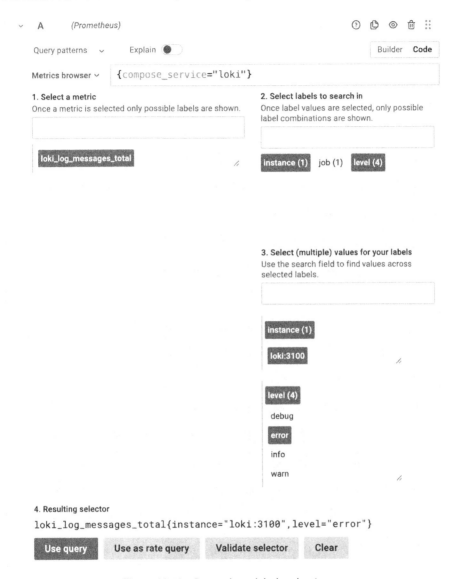

Figure 13.19 – Prometheus labels selection

5. Clicking on **Use query** shows the stairstep pattern of new error logs arriving. We can also see how each jump in the metrics correlates with when Loki registers the error logs:

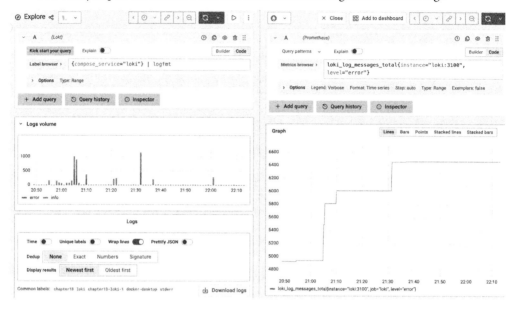

Figure 13.20 – Time linking

Now, we can't develop an alert based on this error log metric because it would trip right after the first error is logged. What we need to do is track when the count of logs *increases*. We're talking about an example of a *rate query*.

6. To get a rate query of log messages, we need to go back and repeat *steps 8* through *11*.

7. But now, instead of clicking on **Use query**, we must click on **Use as rate query** instead.

If you are following along in Grafana 10, you'll get a new metrics query:

```
rate(loki_log_messages_total{instance="loki:3100",level="error"}[$__
rate_interval])
```

Where did `$__rate_interval` come from? In the earlier version of Grafana, **Use as rate query** used `$__interval` as the default time period, which wouldn't generate any data. Checking in the inspector revealed `$__interval` to be about 15s, which is too short a period to yield enough data to evaluate a rate. Manually substituting `$__rate_interval` instead gave `rate` a time period of 1m, which is much larger. Grafana 10 is smarter, and it knows that we need to use `$__rate_interval`:

Figure 13.21 – Rate query

Running the query now shows clear jumps in the rate every time errors are logged. Now, all we need to do is create an alert around these jumps:

1. Click **Add to dashboard** and add it to a dashboard.

2. Next, edit the panel and go to the **Alert** tab.

3.    To generate an alert rule, click **Create alert rule from this panel**:

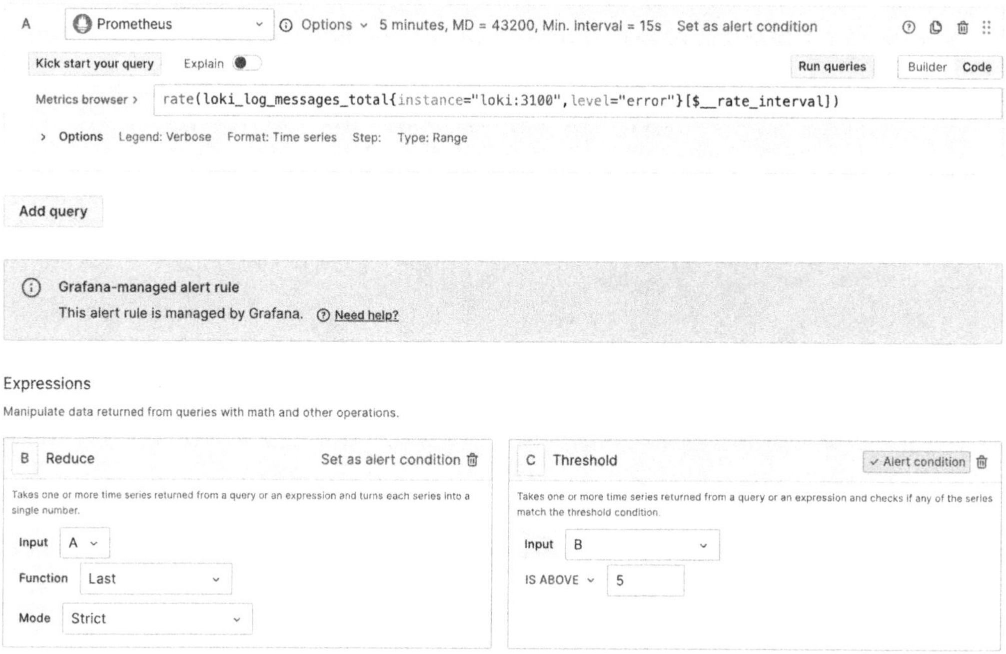

Figure 13.22 – Rate query alert rule

4.    Note that the query has been filled in for you. All you need to do is set a threshold. Based on the history, set the threshold to 5. This means that if Grafana detects more than five errors within `$__rate_interval`, it will trigger an alert.

The rest is just details to be filled out like a normal alert. Since the log spikes only last for a short period, the **Alert** evaluation behavior intervals may need to be tuned so as not to miss the spike as it can be short-lived.

This can be a standard workflow for identifying possible anomalous behavior, capturing it in a dashboard, and finally adding an alert to the existing Grafana Alerting configuration.

## Summary

We've reached the end of *Chapter 13, Exploring Log Data with Grafana's Loki*. In this chapter, we learned how to use **Explore** with the Loki data source to perform ad hoc analysis of logs and aggregated log metrics. We deployed a Loki pipeline to aggregate filesystem log files and the logs generated by our Docker containers. We used Prometheus to collect dozens of metrics about those container services. Finally, using the **Split** feature, we made side-by-side comparisons of both log and service metrics.

With that, we've also reached the end of *Part 2 – Real-World Grafana*. In *Part 3 – Managing Grafana*, we'll step out of our role as an end user of Grafana and into that of an administrator. We'll learn about how to manage dashboards, users, and teams. We'll also learn how to secure the Grafana server by authenticating our users with services such as OAuth2 and LDAP. Finally, we'll explore the rapidly expanding world of cloud monitoring and how Grafana fits into it.

See you soon!

# Part 3 – Managing Grafana

This section is intended to highlight aspects of Grafana beyond building dashboard panels. In these chapters, we'll learn about naming and organizing Grafana's dashboards by organizing them into structured folders, managing users and teams and their permissions to access the dashboards and folders in a Grafana organization, leveraging external authentication services such as LDAP, Okta, and Oauth, and connecting to cloud provider metrics and logging into AWS, Google Cloud, and Microsoft Azure.

This part comprises the following chapters:

- *Chapter 14, Organizing Dashboards and Folders*
- *Chapter 15, Managing Permissions for Users, Teams, and Organizations*
- *Chapter 16, Authenticating Grafana Logins Using LDAP or OAuth 2 Providers*
- *Chapter 17, Cloud Monitoring AWS, Azure, and GCP*

# 14
# Organizing Dashboards and Folders

Welcome to the first chapter of *Part 3, Managing Grafana*. By now, you've created some awesome dashboards. Maybe you've even set up valuable alerts with some of those dashboards, and now you're in the enviable position of being your team's Grafana guru. That great honor will be accompanied by great responsibilities. You're now the de facto manager of your Grafana server and all the requisite administrative tasks that come along for the ride.

In this section of the book, we'll cover some of the more common aspects of Grafana management, from keeping your dashboards tidy to managing and authenticating your users and teams, to monitoring your applications in the cloud. In *Part 2, Real-World Grafana*, we used various realistic scenarios to drive the descriptions and the associated exercises. In this section, we will present the material in a more straightforward how-to style, and along the way, cover use cases, tips, and guidelines.

We'll start by looking at some strategies for managing the broad but common problem of dashboard proliferation in this chapter, then proceed through more esoteric problems such as user management (*Chapter 15, Managing Permissions for Users, Teams, and Organizations*) and authentication using services such as Okta and LDAP (*Chapter 16, Authenticating Grafana Logins Using LDAP or OAuth 2 Providers*) before ultimately culminating in a survey of current cloud monitoring integrations such as AWS and Azure (*Chapter 17, Cloud Monitoring AWS, Azure, and GCP*).

By the end of this chapter, not only should you have a good understanding of the run-of-the-mill aspects of managing dashboards, compiling them into playlists, and cataloging them on dashboard panels, but you should have learned about strategies for naming dashboards, organizing them into folders, and managing your site as it scales up.

In this chapter, we will have a look at the following topics:

- Managing dashboards and creating folders

- Starring and tagging dashboards

- Building and running dashboard playlists

- Cataloging dashboards in the Dashboard list panel visualization

- Duplicating dashboards

> **Info**
>
> Tutorial code, dashboards, and other helpful files for this chapter can be found in this book's GitHub repository at `https://github.com/PacktPublishing/Learn-Grafana-10/tree/main/Chapter14`.

Let's get started!

# Managing dashboards and folders

By now, you've probably created at least a handful of dashboards, if only to work through the examples in this book. Ideally, you're well on your way to creating many more, along with other members of your team, unit, and even your entire company. What you'll quickly find – if you haven't already – is that you've ended up with a number of dashboards in various stages of development and potentially connected to a number of data sources, all of them lying around in the dashboard display.

Conceptually, Grafana provides four classification schemes aimed at helping you identify dashboards to satisfy common organizational needs. The first is what I call a **significance-based** scheme, which identifies the most important dashboard through a **starred** or **favorited** designation. The second is a **structure-based** scheme, which places dashboards into an arbitrary hierarchical structure of folders. The third scheme is a **nomenclature-based** scheme, or the naming convention by which we determine how best to name dashboards. The fourth and final scheme is **semantic-based** in that we attach labels or tags to dashboards, giving them whatever meaning we might desire.

Let's first look at how to name a dashboard, while also keeping in mind good practices for doing so. After that, we'll go into how to organize dashboards into folders.

## Naming a dashboard

Here's how to name (or rename) a dashboard:

1. Open the dashboard.
2. Select the gear icon for dashboard settings.
3. Make sure the **General** item is selected on the side menu.
4. Type a name into the **Name** field.
5. Click on **Save dashboard**.
6. Click on **Close** to return to the dashboard.

Here's an example of editing the name of the dashboard and setting it to `My Excellent Dashboard`:

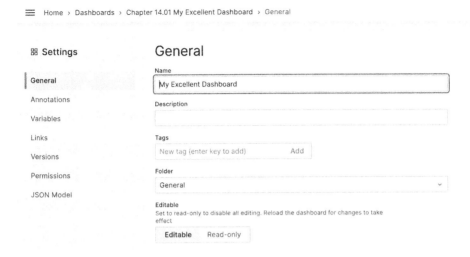

Figure 14.1 – Editing a dashboard name

Whenever you make a change to the dashboard settings, remember to make the long UX journey to the right-hand side of the page and click on **Save dashboard**. If you return to the dashboard without saving the change, there is always the possibility that Grafana won't catch it when you try to load a different one.

## Dashboard naming tips

The first opportunity you will get to organize your dashboards is when you first create and then save your dashboard. At that point, you will be forced to decide about what you want to name it. A lot of people, me included, will be much more interested in building the dashboard than coming up with a proper name. Unfortunately, that tendency leads to a lot of `Dashboard 1`, `Dashboard 2`, and `Dashboard 4 copy` dashboards.

These less-than-creative names fail for a couple of reasons: they don't describe the content of the dashboard either to your future self or to your audience, or they tend to collide with other lazily named dashboards. Here are a few of my opinionated suggestions for constructively naming them:

- **Do use a name that accurately describes the contents of the dashboard**: A few examples are `Total CMMR Income From Region 2`, `Server Room Climate Monitors`, and `Minneapolis 311 Calls-Real Time`.

- **Do try to adhere to some form of naming convention so that they are easy to scan in lists**: For example, `"Financial Analysis, SEC Model 2012-10, Daugherty"`, `"Sales Profile, Refreshed Customers AUNZ, Jones"`. Here, we're placing the broadest scope of the dashboard first, followed by a more specific description, followed by the owner. You might also do this with tagging and folders, but it does make it quicker to find the dashboard from a lengthy list.

- **Do consider using template variables to combine dashboards that differ by a single variable**: Such as a department, business unit, or region, rather than name multiple similar dashboards with specific names.

- **Don't try to encode a hierarchical dashboard structure by naming convention**: For example, `Global Sales-Regional-NE Texas` and `Global Sales-Regional-SW Texas`. Place the dashboards into nested folders and set up labels to reflect the tiers of your hierarchy.

- **Don't try to use the name for version control**: For example, `Housing Analysis 2021. v22`. Grafana tracks all dashboard saves, and you can always revert to an earlier version from the **Dashboard settings | Versions** page. Remember to add a comment to your saves so that you know what the version change is about.

These suggestions should not be interpreted as requirements; you might find it easier to do some of these but not others. You may not even have to ability to implement the kind of naming conventions you'd like. However, if you do have the opportunity to set up standards, try to maintain them as consistently as possible. It's better to try and maintain some level of control with a few outliers as opposed to an unmanageable free-for-all that you are forced to clean up later. Now that we have some best practices for naming our dashboards, let's find out how to further organize them into folders.

## Working with dashboard folders

After naming the dashboards, arranging them into specific folders is the next mechanism for keeping things organized and tidy. Not only do folders keep your dashboards in some form of structured storage, but they also provide a means by which you can establish access controls to your dashboards. We'll discuss access control in more detail in the next chapter.

In the meantime, let's go over some common folder-related tasks:

- Creating dashboard folders
- Adding dashboards to folders
- Deleting folders

Finally, we'll also go over some tips for keeping dashboards and folders tidy and manageable.

## Creating a dashboard folder

The easiest way to organize dashboards is to corral them into folders. But how do we create folders? It's easy:

1. Select **Dashboards** from the main menu, then select **New | New folder** from the drop-down menu.

2. On the **Create a new folder** page, type the folder's name into the **Folder name** field.

3. Click **Create**, as shown here:

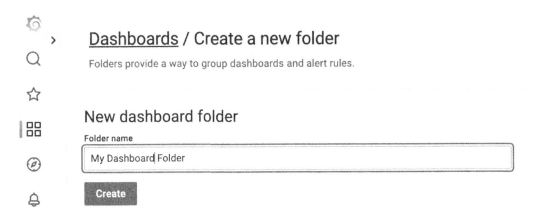

Figure 14.2 – Creating a new folder

After creating a new folder, you will land on the **Dashboards** tab of the dashboard folder management page, as shown in the following screenshot:

Figure 14.3 – Dashboard folder management

Once you've created a folder, you'll want to put something in it. We'll cover adding dashboards to a folder next.

### Adding dashboards to a folder

When a folder is created, by default it is in the `General` folder. You can always move it from there, provided you have the proper permissions.

There are two methods for adding a dashboard, **dashboard-centric** and **folder-centric**.

The dashboard-centric method places a single dashboard in a folder by editing it:

1. Load a dashboard and open its **Settings**.

2. Select the **General** page, if you aren't already looking at it.

3. Select a dashboard folder from the **Folder** dropdown.

4. Save the dashboard by clicking **Save dashboard**. If you return to the dashboard without saving, the location will appear to have changed, but it may not persist if you open a different dashboard.

5. Click **Close** to return to the dashboard and confirm the new dashboard location in the dashboard navigation menu.

Selecting the folder from the dropdown can be seen in the following screenshot:

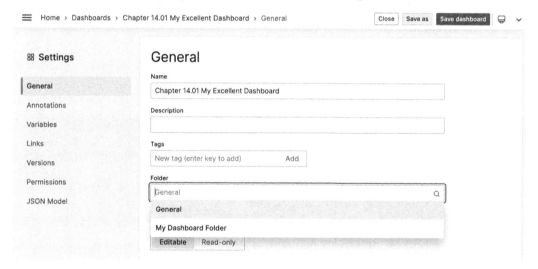

Figure 14.4 – Setting the dashboard folder

The folder-centric method collects one or more dashboards and moves them into a designated folder:

1. Select **Dashboard** from the main menu.

2. If one doesn't already exist, create a new one by selecting **New | New Folder**.

3. Check the boxes next to the dashboards you wish to place into the folder.

4.  Click **Move**.

5.  Select the folder from the **Choose Dashboard Folder** pop-up dialog.

Here's what a dashboard move to another folder looks like:

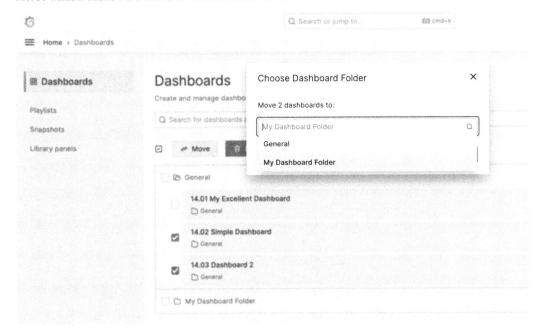

Figure 14.5 – Dashboard move to a folder

This method is clearly the one to use if you need to move a lot of dashboards around. What if you get tired of your folder? Next, we'll find out how to delete a folder.

## Deleting folders

In Grafana, deleting folders is a high-risk operation, so do it with the utmost caution because deleting a folder also deletes its contents. Follow these steps to delete a folder:

1.  Select **Dashboard** from the main menu.

2.  Click the box next to the folder to delete.

3.    Click **Delete**. You will see a warning if the folder contains dashboards:

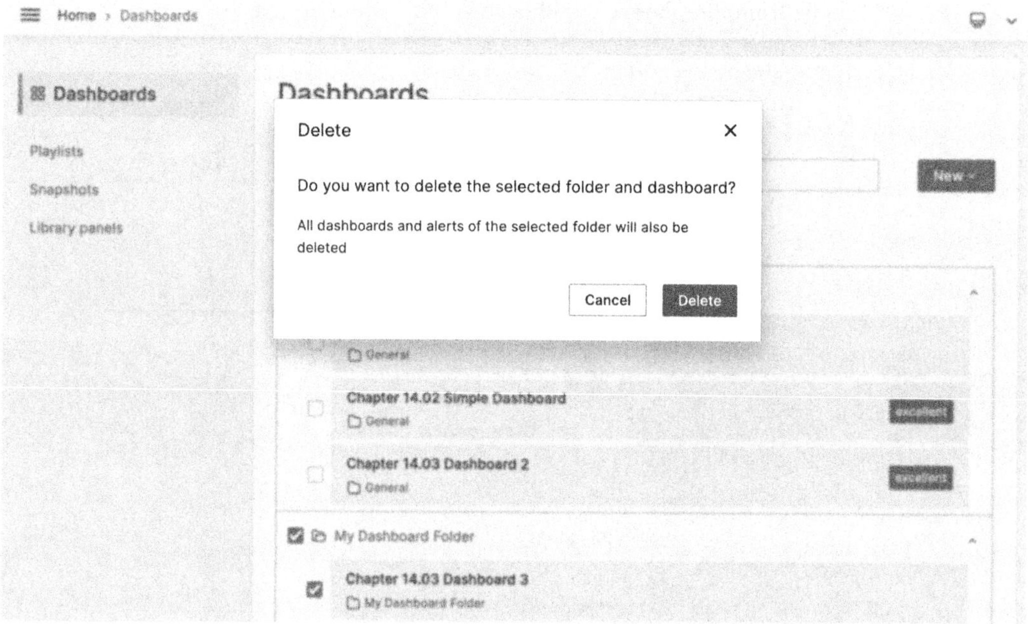

Figure 14.6 – Dashboard deletion warning

This is a very risky procedure, so you may want to consider tagging (with a **Delete** tag, for example) the dashboards you want to delete and evacuating everything else from the folder before deleting it.

## Tips to manage dashboard folders

Here are a few suggestions when it comes to managing dashboard folders:

- **Do** embrace folders, opting for depth over breadth. Fewer top-level folders will make it easier to find and work with dashboards.

- **Do** think about the overall folder structure for your dashboards and settle for the one that offers the most utility. If you have a larger organization, it might be better to create a folder structure that partitions by department or business unit, and then allow each to create their own hierarchies. Alternatively, you might be a member of a small team that creates dashboards within an ongoing set of projects, perhaps with a folder devoted to each project.

- **Don't** redundantly embed hierarchy in folder names; for example, `A/Project A-Database Queries/Project A-Database Queries-Queries per Server`. Just name each folder and dashboard for its place in the hierarchy since the *navbar* breadcrumbs will depict the hierarchy; that is, `Project A/Database Queries/Queries per Server`.

- **Don't** duplicate dashboards into multiple folders. This approach will prove to be a maintenance nightmare. If you are tempted to put the same dashboard into multiple folders by performing duplication, consider tagging the dashboard with multiple tags instead, or consider the possibility of using template variables if the dashboard is minimally altered after being placed in the different folders.

In the next section, we'll look at starring and tagging dashboards.

# Starring and tagging dashboards

Our previous sections mostly dealt with the key structural aspects of a dashboard: the name and its location in a specific folder. We will now turn to more semantic aspects, ones that are best described in terms of dashboard metadata, namely dashboard stars and labels. As we saw in *Chapter 10, Working with Advanced Dashboard Features and Elasticsearch*, dashboard tags may prove useful when linking dashboards, but that's not the case for tags or stars, as we're about to find out.

## Marking dashboards as favorites

Starred dashboards are mostly useful for when you want to highlight certain dashboards as important or otherwise memorable to you. They can be for bookmarking frequently accessed dashboards or for marking dashboards as needing some kind of special attention.

Starring dashboards is even easier than tagging:

1.  Load up a dashboard.

2.  Click the star icon to **Mark as favorite**, as shown in the following screenshot:

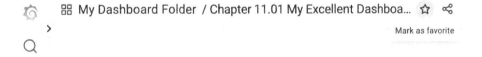

Figure 14.7 – Starring a dashboard favorite

This is pretty inefficient if you want to star several dashboards at one time, so it's better to star them from a **Dashboard list** panel visualization instead:

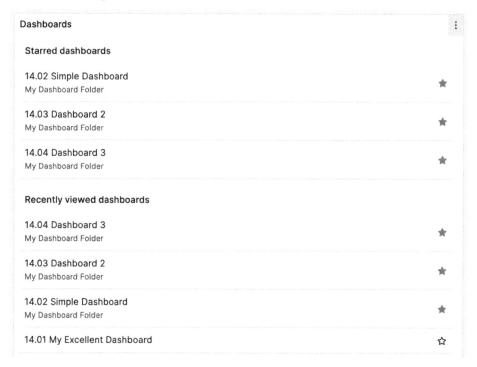

Figure 14.8 – Quickly selecting favorites from Dashboard list panel

Starring a dashboard will place it under the starred side menu item, so you do want to reserve that for the most used/important dashboards. Otherwise, you should rely on dashboard tagging.

## Tagging dashboards

Dashboard tags are vastly more powerful than stars. For example, you can tag each dashboard with any number of tags. These tags can be leveraged for many important functions, including grouping, searching, and filtering. We saw tags in action when we created dashboard links back in *Chapter 10, Working with Advanced Dashboard Features and Elasticsearch*.

You will find dashboard tags used in several places:

- Dashboard links
- **Dashboards** page
- **Dashboards | Playlists** page
- **Dashboard list** visualization panel

Let's go over the common tag tasks, namely adding and deleting tags.

### Adding tags

Currently, there is only one mechanism for adding tags to a dashboard:

1. Open a dashboard for editing.

2. Select the dashboard's settings gear icon.

3. Make sure you're viewing the **General** page.

4. Type the tag name into the field.

5. Click **Add** to add one or more tags.

6. Click **Save dashboard**.

7. Click **Close** to return to the dashboard.

Here, we're adding the tag called `excellent`:

Figure 14.9 – Dashboard tagging

Refer to *Chapter 10, Working with Advanced Dashboard Features and Elasticsearch*, for details on how to use tags to link dashboards. As we've seen, tags are very useful, but creating them can be tedious as they can only be added on a per-dashboard basis. Sadly, deleting them isn't much easier.

### *Deleting tags*

Unfortunately, there is no explicit mechanism for managing tags, either to create them or to delete them. If you want to get rid of a tag, you will need to go through every tagged dashboard and delete it manually.

What if you need to continuously cycle through a series of dashboards? Perhaps you have an operational dashboard that shows several cycling dashboards, or you have a running demo of dashboards to show off for stakeholders or customers. This is where playlists come in.

# Building and running dashboard playlists

A dashboard playlist is a selection of dashboards that can be played in a looped sequence. Any dashboard can appear in such a playlist. A playlist consists of one or more dashboards displayed in a sequence, separated by a specified interval. They're typically used to create an automated display cycle of dashboards for unattended venues such as kiosks or operation centers.

## Creating a playlist

Before we can start running a playlist, we'll need to create one. The **Playlists** page can be found under the **Dashboards** main menu. Follow these steps:

1.  Under **Dashboards** on the main menu, select **Playlists**.
2.  Click **New Playlist**.
3.  Set a **Name** for the playlist. You will not be able to save the playlist until you set the **Name**.
4.  Set the time **Interval** between dashboards.
5.  Select a dashboard from the **Add by title** drop-down menu to add a dashboard to the playlist. You can also add tagged dashboards by selecting tags from the **Add by tag** drop-down menu. The number next to the tag represents the number of dashboards with the tag.
6.  Using the six-dot drag handle, drag and drop dashboards in the **Dashboards** list to adjust the playlist display order for the dashboards.
7.  Click **Save** to commit your changes.

Here is an example of the playlist page after selecting a dashboard for the playlist:

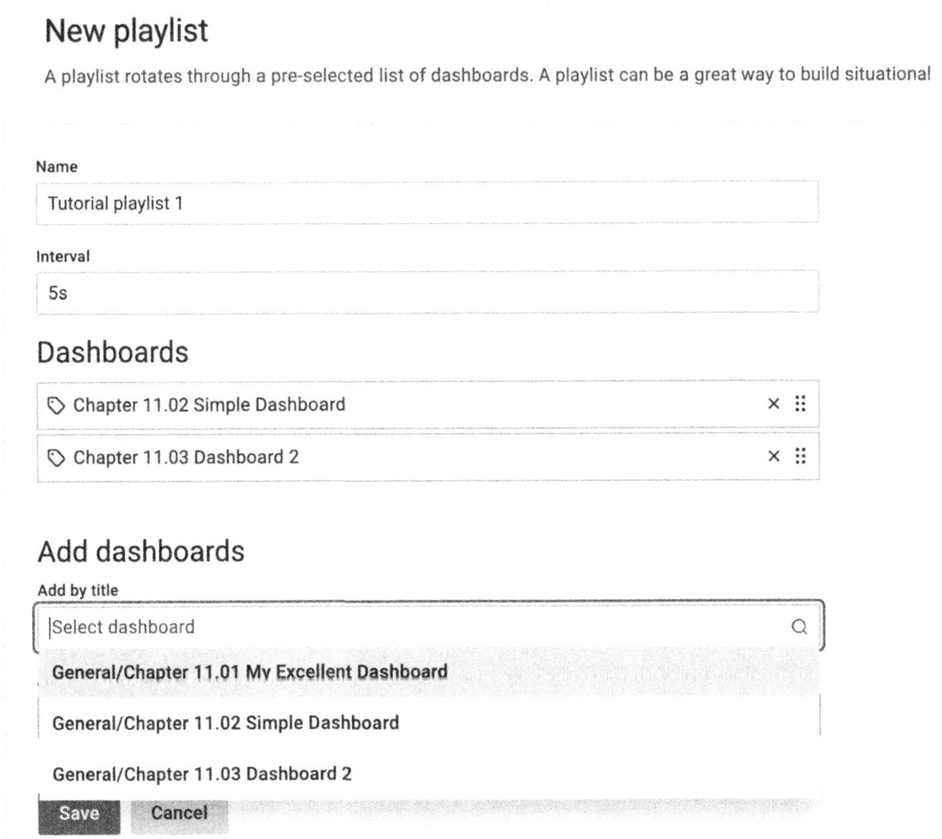

## New playlist

A playlist rotates through a pre-selected list of dashboards. A playlist can be a great way to build situational

**Name**

Tutorial playlist 1

**Interval**

5s

## Dashboards

| 🗁 Chapter 11.02 Simple Dashboard | ✕ ⠿ |
|---|---|
| 🗁 Chapter 11.03 Dashboard 2 | ✕ ⠿ |

## Add dashboards

**Add by title**

| Select dashboard | Q |
|---|---|

General/Chapter 11.01 My Excellent Dashboard

General/Chapter 11.02 Simple Dashboard

General/Chapter 11.03 Dashboard 2

Save    Cancel

Figure 14.10 – Creating a dashboard playlist

As the number of dashboards grows, it could become more difficult to find dashboards for playlists, so consider naming conventions, tags, or stars so that you can filter on them when you create or edit playlists.

In the next few sections, we'll go into a little more detail about how to run playlists, especially in their various display modes. These modes are designed to hide the user interface controls depending on how much interaction you will have with the dashboards running in the playlist.

## Displaying a playlist

Now that you've set up a playlist, it's time to play it. Here's how to run a playlist:

1. From the **Dashboard** side menu, select **Playlists**.

2. Click **Start playlist**, then select the appropriate mode from the dialog:

   - **Normal**

   - **TV**

   - **Kiosk**

   Here is an example of the dialog for selecting the playlist **Mode**:

Figure 14.11 – Start playlist dialog

These modes correspond to the three view modes controlled by **Cycle view mode**, which can be found at the top of the dashboard. Let's look at each one to see how they differ.

## Displaying playlists in normal mode

In **Normal** mode, the navigation bar, row, and panel controls are all visible. Clicking the hamburger tribar on the top left still reveals the main menu. The standard dashboard controls are replaced with playlist controls. Following is a look at the controls in the top navigation bar between the breadcrumbs and the time range controls:

Figure 14.12 – Normal playlist mode controls

From left to right, the playlist controls are as follows:

- **Left fast forward icon**: Goes to the previous dashboard in the playlist
- **Stop playlist**: Stop the playlist from playing
- **Right fast forward icon**: Goes to the next dashboard in the playlist

Normal mode is useful if you still want to access the UI. Accessing items in the main menu will stop the playlist.

## Displaying playlists in TV mode

**TV** mode is similar to **Normal** mode in that the menus, top navbar, row, and panel controls are still visible. TV mode will activate after 1 minute of inactivity; this is useful when you need to grab control for a moment, but then have the playlist return to playing when you step away for a period of time.

The following capture shows a TV mode dashboard. Note the panel scaling and arrangement, as well as the various dashboard controls:

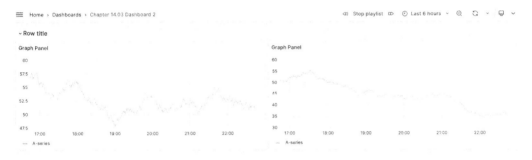

Figure 14.13 – TV mode

If you really want a clean display that only shows off your dashboard panels, then you want **Kiosk** mode. Let's look at Kiosk mode.

## Displaying playlists in Kiosk mode

If you need to run a playlist unattended with no visible controls, select either of the Kiosk modes. In this mode, all the controls including the side menu are hidden.

In either Normal or TV playlist modes, you can immediately switch to Kiosk mode by clicking on the small monitor icon at the top right. To return to the previous mode, hit the *Esc* key.

## Displaying playlists with auto fit panels

Both TV mode and Kiosk mode feature alternates that include the *autofit* option. Autofitting causes the dashboard panels to automatically stretch or shrink to fill the entire screen space, depending on how much larger the display screen is compared to the original dashboard layout.

For example, here's a simple dashboard with two panels in TV mode:

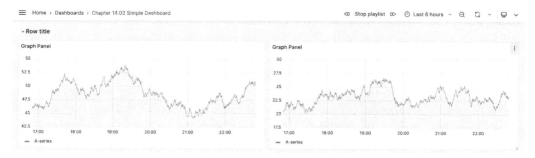

Figure 14.14 – Dashboard in TV mode

Here is the same dashboard in TV mode (with autofit):

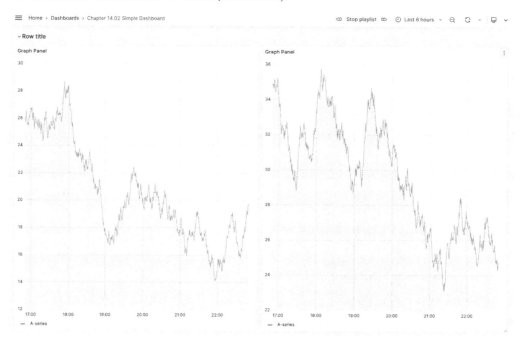

Figure 14.15 – Dashboard in TV mode with autofit

Typically, you'll want to use autofit not when you have a couple of panels you want to stretch to fit, but rather when you have a few extra panels you want Grafana to squeeze onto the screen. This can prove to be helpful when the screen size of your display is a bit different than the one you use to lay out your dashboard.

To give you an idea of how flexible autofit can be, here is the graph portion of a dashboard in Normal layout mode:

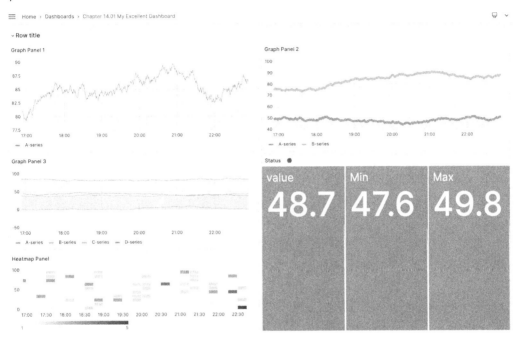

Figure 14.16 – Dashboard in Normal mode

And here's the same portion of the dashboard in Kiosk mode (with autofit panels):

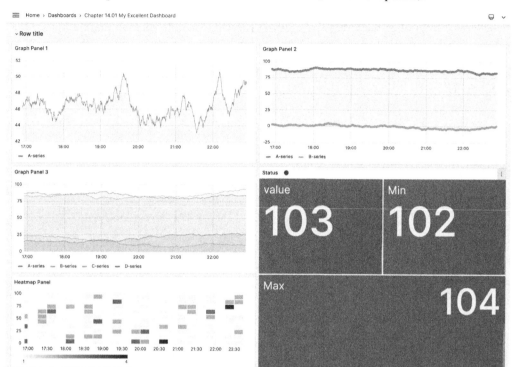

Figure 14.17 – Dashboard in Kiosk mode with autofit

As you can see, Grafana adjusted the size of each panel to squeeze all the panels onscreen.

## Editing a playlist

On the **Playlists** page, clicking on **Edit playlist** will open an **Edit Playlist** page, which is similar in structure to the **New Playlist** page. Here, you can do the following:

- Change the **Name**
- Set the **Interval**
- Delete dashboards by clicking the × icon
- Change the dashboard display order using drag and drop
- Add dashboards by using the drop-down menu under **Add by title**, or by selecting a tag from the drop-down menu under **Add by tag**

That covers basic dashboard playlist features. Now, let's move on to another helpful dashboard management feature: a panel visualization designed solely to display a catalog of dashboards!

# Exploring the Dashboard list panel

If you've taken a look at the **Home** dashboard, then you're already familiar with the dashboard list panel visualization. You can set the dashboard list visualization for any panel by selecting it from the visualization dropdown in edit mode. It typically displays starred dashboards (for quick reference) and a list of recently visited dashboards. It can also be configured with several more options. Let's open it up and see what else we can configure it to do.

## Setting Dashboard list panel options

In the **Dashboard list** section of the panel edit pane are the following settings and descriptions:

- **Include current time range**: Carries over the current time range to the selected dashboard
- **Include current template variable values**: Carries over the current template variable settings to the selected dashboard
- **Starred**: Enables display of starred dashboards
- **Recently viewed dashboards**: Enables display of recently viewed dashboards
- **Search**: Enables display of the results of the **Search** section
- **Show headings**: Enables the display of headings for each option mentioned previously
- **Max items**: Sets the maximum number of items displayed of each type

The first two switches control whether the current time range and template variables carry over into the dashboards selected from the list. The next three switches enable and disable the display of starred, recently viewed, and search results. The last two control whether headings are displayed and how many dashboards can be displayed at one time.

The **Query**, **Folder**, and **Tags** settings can be combined into a search filter that allows you to specify a static list of dashboards that will always be displayed, as opposed to the **Starred** and **Recently viewed** dashboards, which are dynamically generated:

- **Query**: Searches for dashboards matching the string, partial matches included
- **Folder**: Includes all dashboards within a folder
- **Tags**: Includes all dashboards matching tags

Setting multiple search fields will return results that match all the fields. If you want to expand the search as wide as possible, be sure to set **Folder** to **All**.

Here's an example showing many of the options, including **Search**, that are enabled:

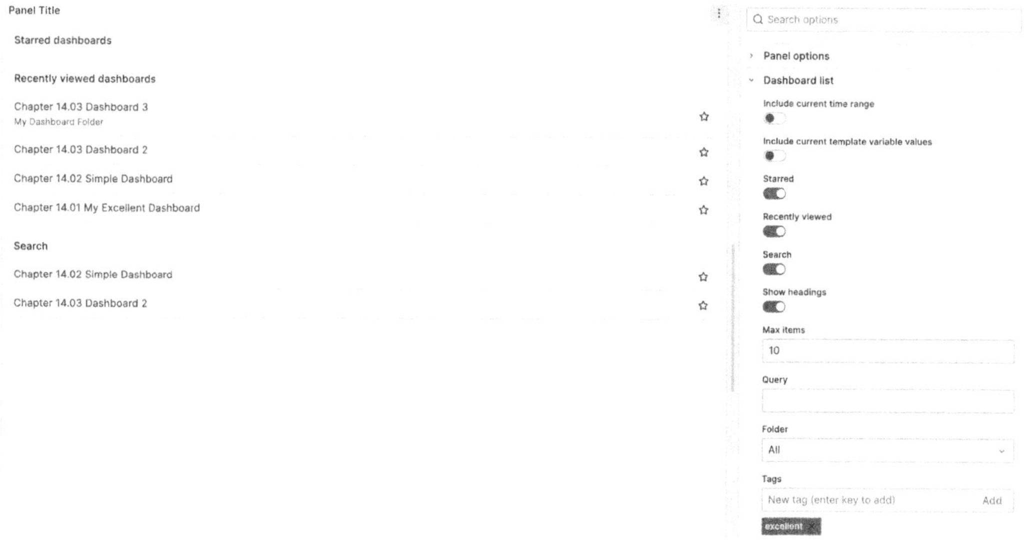

Figure 14.18 – Dashboard list visualization options

If you want to get a feel for how the **Dashboard list** panel works, play with the one on the **Home** dashboard or just create your own!

One of the trickier aspects of working with popular or useful dashboards is how to duplicate them for use in other contexts, without creating a maintenance headache. We're going to discuss a couple of the safer strategies next.

# Duplicating dashboards

If you want to experiment with changes to a dashboard or you want to propagate a dashboard to another organization or even another server, there are two ways to duplicate or copy a dashboard.

## Internal dashboard duplications

If you just want to create another version of the dashboard for experimentation or to stage prior to putting it into production, use the **Save as** option at the top of the dashboard **Settings** page. Remember, you can always roll back changes to an existing dashboard from the **Versions** page under dashboard **Settings**.

Here's how to copy a dashboard to a new name:

1. Open the dashboard settings.

2.  Instead of clicking **Save dashboard**, click on **Save as**. That will bring up a new dialog where you can pick a name for the copy of the dashboard:

3.  Set the name and optionally the folder. Set the tags if you'd like to keep the existing tags.

Figure 14.19 – Copying a dashboard

4.  Click **Save**.

Alternatively, if you are just concerned about making irreversible changes, you can save a copy at the current version, sometimes called a **checkpoint**, then roll back if you need to. The process goes something like this:

1.  Make a change to a dashboard to enable a save point.

2.  Go to the dashboard **Settings** and click **Save dashboard**.

3.  In the **Details**, note the save is a checkpoint.

4.  Click **Save**.

Make the changes you want to experiment with, and at the point you feel like you need to roll back, make a save. This will give you a new checkpoint that is different from the previous one, otherwise the changes will just be on the previous save. Here's a quick glimpse of how to revert a dashboard to an earlier save:

1.  To roll back, open the dashboard **Settings** and go to the **Versions** page.

2.    Click the **Restore** button to restore the older version:

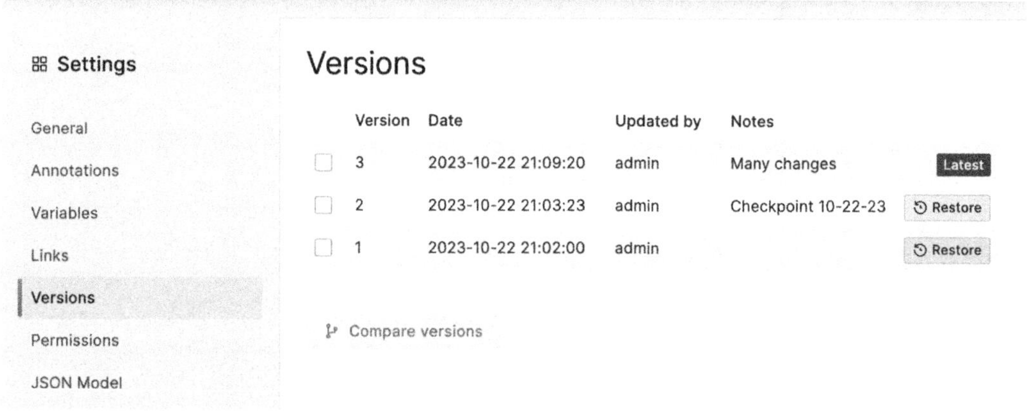

Figure 14.20 – Dashboard version control

## External dashboard duplications

This is all fine if you are sticking to your own Grafana organization. However, if you need to make a copy of a dashboard to be used outside your current organization, you'll want to export a dashboard, then import it from within the other organization.

As we discussed previously in *Chapter 10, Working with Advanced Dashboard Features and Elasticsearch*, the **Export** tab can accessed from the **Share** modal that pops up when you click the sharing icon. If you don't plan to connect the dashboard to a data source accessible to both organizations, you'll want to enable **Export for sharing externally**.

If you plan to do this frequently, consider putting the exported dashboards under some form of revision control, such as GitHub. Bear in mind that these actions will potentially increase your dashboard maintenance burden as any changes you make to the original dashboard might also need to be propagated to your duplicated dashboards as well. Have a system in mind for dealing with these scenarios, or things could get unmanageable quickly!

## Summary

This was a relatively easy introduction to some of the concepts involved in Grafana management. In this chapter, we looked at how to name dashboards and folders, as well as some strategies for creating folders, and looked at starring and tagging dashboards and how they can be useful for grouping and filtering dashboards. Then, we created some dashboard playlists, a common function if you are creating dashboard presentations. We looked at how the **Dashboard list** panel can be configured to help create catalogs of dashboards, especially by leveraging the search option and tags. Finally, we discussed strategies for duplicating dashboards.

The intention here wasn't to reveal especially esoteric Grafana concepts – in fact, you may have already been working with some of the features we highlighted in this chapter. The goal was to get you to shift your thinking to a more operational viewpoint, one that often must take into account the potentially competing needs of different stakeholders. In other words, if you become responsible for your Grafana operations, you won't be able to build dashboards, name them whatever you like, and put them anywhere:

- You might need to consider what happens if you update a dashboard someone else is using without telling them

- When you move dashboards into folders, you might need to communicate to the users that the dashboards they regularly use may have moved

- You might need to consider how to maintain and update dashboards used in different Grafana organizations

Just managing the dashboards on a moderately-sized server instance can be a challenging task, not necessarily for technical reasons, but for the inevitable social-political circumstances that arise when multiple groups must share a common resource.

It may not always be easy, but if you face these challenges head-on and engage your user community with transparency, continual improvement, and good humor, your experience will surely be a rewarding one. Good luck!

In the same vein of handling the challenge of managing asset entities such as dashboards and folders, in the next chapter, *Chapter 15, Managing Permissions for Users, Teams, and Organizations*, we'll take on the challenge of managing actor entities such as users and teams, especially when it comes to managing simply *who accesses what*.

# 15
# Managing Permissions for Users, Teams, and Organizations

In this chapter, we'll be taking a closer look at how to manage users, teams, and organizations with respect to controlling access to Grafana resources, such as dashboards, folders, or data sources. Throughout the course of this book, you've probably been logging into your site as the sole admin user, which is fine for a server limited to a local computer used almost exclusively for learning. However, it would be a completely unsuitable setup for a server supporting even a handful of users.

If you are responsible for managing your Grafana site, you'll soon be dealing with new users, and with every new user comes the inevitable question, *how much access should I allow this user?* You could set up every user with full admin permissions to do anything and everything, but what if they accidentally delete something important? What if they inadvertently create a panel that accesses a data source containing sensitive records? Conversely, if you deny all your users any permissions other than the essentials, what if they need to fix another user's dashboard and you're not available?

It would be beyond the scope of this book to offer a complete checklist of all the possible scenarios that you must consider before endeavoring to establish a secure, healthy Grafana environment, so we'll try to do the next best thing – give you the ability to understand how users and permissions work in Grafana, as well as how they come together to give you the flexibility to adapt your configuration to suit your specific needs.

In this chapter, we'll look at how to add users to a Grafana site, as well as how to manage the permissions for our users. Once we've addressed the fundamentals for user permissions, we'll learn how grouping users into teams can be a useful strategy for managing permissions on a larger scale. Finally, we'll look at how to partition a Grafana site into organizations that each have independent users, data sources, and dashboards, making it possible to offer the security benefits of isolation without the need to maintain multiple servers.

In this chapter, we will cover the following topics:

- Understanding key permission concepts

- Adding users

- Setting permissions

- Establishing teams

- Administering users and organizations

Let's get started!

# Understanding key permission concepts

Before we can delve into the specifics of adding users or setting their permissions, we need to cover some fundamental security concepts that are built into Grafana. Once you understand the terminology, it will be easier to piece together how these concepts interact to produce a coherent framework to govern user access.

## Organizations

You may not have been aware of it, but for the entire time we've been learning about Grafana, we've been working inside an entity that Grafana refers to as an **organization**. Much like our universe is a single entity unto itself, this default organization, or **org** for short, can have its own teams, data sources, dashboards, dashboard folders, and so on. These types of resources cannot be accessed from or shared with any organization. Grafana lets you create as many organizations as you want, and while each one is completely independent of the others, users can be members of more than one organization.

## Users

Obviously, anyone needing access to a Grafana site must also have some kind of account. Within Grafana, these accounts are called **users**. In *Chapter 16, Authenticating Grafana Logins Using LDAP or OAuth 2 Providers*, we'll look at common user authentication mechanisms used in larger enterprises, but for now, we'll use regular password logins. A user can belong to multiple organizations and, once logged in, can easily switch between them.

## Roles

To determine what a user can do within a given organization, each user is assigned a role. Grafana provides three typical user roles and one special role. The typical user roles are called **Viewer**, **Editor**, and **Admin**:

- **The Viewer role**: This is basically a *read-only* role in that it can't do anything except see dashboards and folders, but it can't edit them

- **The Editor role**: This can only create and edit dashboards, alerts, and folders
- **The Admin role**: This can do everything within an organization, including adding and modifying users, teams, data sources, and plugins

The special role is called **Super Admin**, and it has ultimate power over the entire site, including the ability to administer both users (including other Super Admins) and organizations.

## Teams

To make it easier to manage the permissions for larger groups of users, Grafana includes a grouping of users called a **Team**. Within an organization, users can be assigned to teams, which may have their own permission settings. Depending on how those permissions are set, membership in a Team can even elevate the access level for a user above its defined organizational role.

With these concepts in mind, let's learn how to add new users to a Grafana site.

# Adding users

While it might seem perfectly reasonable to use and manage a simple Grafana tutorial server with a single admin user, it would be impractical, if not irresponsible, to try to do the same for a Grafana site with more than a couple of people. With that in mind, you should go ahead and establish independent user accounts for anyone who plans to access your site. It will also be your responsibility to add and delete those user accounts, set their roles, and establish what those users will be able to access within those roles.

> Tip
> Initially, you probably logged in with the default admin user, which is installed with every Grafana instance. That user has full administrative privileges and, unless you changed it, an insecure password. This is not at all secure, so before you even add a single user, be sure to reset the password to one of your own choosing.

## Adding users – by invitation only

Out of the box, Grafana only provides a single mechanism to add users – via an administrative invitation. This is generally for good security reasons, especially if your site happens to be exposed to the internet. Generally, it's better to be in the position of controlling who can request access to your site when you must proactively reach out to prospective users. Grafana makes it easy to create those accounts and send off the invitations. It also tracks all invitations so that you can send out reminders or even retract them.

To be able to invite a new user, you will need to have an account with an admin organization role. Log in and go to **Administration | Users** in the main menu. After selecting the **Organization users** tab, you will be presented with a listing of all user accounts within your organization. To invite a new user, simply click **Invite** and submit the form (as shown in *Figure 15.1*). You can set either a username (for a local user) or an email address. The name is optional but helps to keep track of who your users are. You can choose from one of three roles – that is, **Viewer**, **Editor**, or **Admin**, but it is often safer to select the most restrictive role, **Viewer**.

By toggling the **Send invite email** switch, you can send an email invitation, provided you have entered a valid email address. If you plan to send email invites, you will need to configure the **Simple Mail Transfer Protocol** (**SMTP**) on your Grafana server to send emails. Refer to *Chapter 12, Monitoring Data Streams with Grafana Alerts*, for more information on how to set up SMTP with the docker-compose.yml environment variables.

Here is a typical invitation:

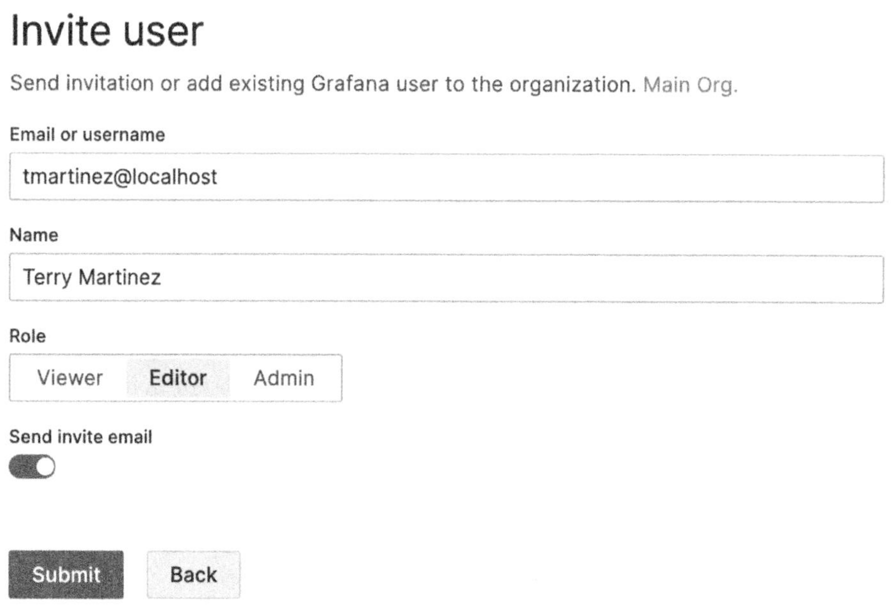

## Invite user

Send invitation or add existing Grafana user to the organization. Main Org.

Email or username

> tmartinez@localhost

Name

> Terry Martinez

Role

> Viewer    **Editor**    Admin

Send invite email

⬤○

[ Submit ]    [ Back ]

Figure 15.1 – A new user invitation

Once you've set up a new user invitation, you can see all your invited users in the **Pending Invites** tab. If you want to manually share an invitation link via another method, such as a text message or Slack, click **Copy Invite** to place the URL on the clipboard for pasting:

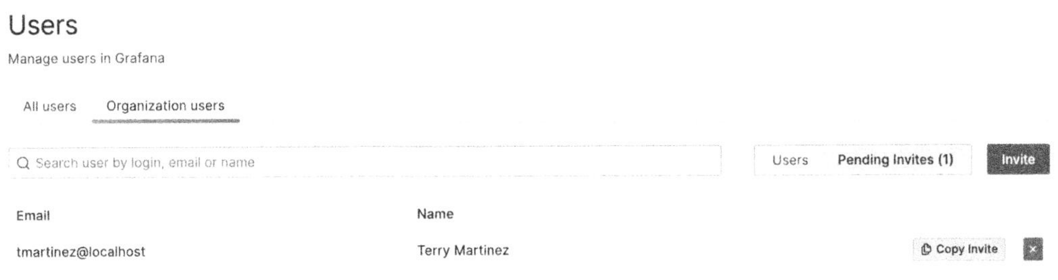

Figure 15.2 – Pending Invites

This is an example of what a user might see when following the link:

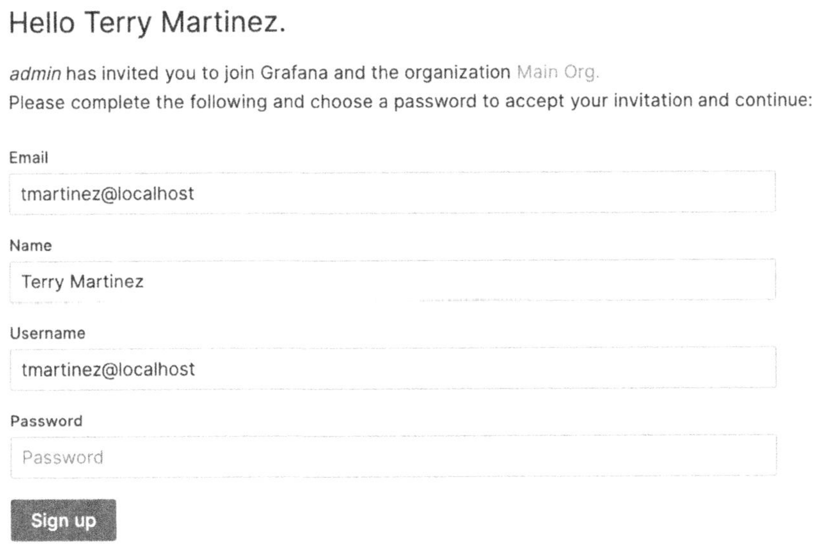

Figure 15.3 – An example invitation

To get to this page, just click on **Copy Invite** next to the name, and paste the URL into a browser. The same URL is embedded in the email message, so all they need to do is add a password and click **Sign up**, and they're in!

> **Tip**
> If, at any point, you decide you want to revoke an active or invited user, just click the red **x** symbol in either the **Users** tab or the **Pending Invites** tab.

## Adding users – a self-service model

If you are in a situation where you don't necessarily need to be manually adding users to your site, and you have relative confidence that you can trust your user community, you can modify your Grafana server configuration to allow users to add themselves. Bearing in mind that you may not want to make this change without consulting your IT security team first, here's how to do it.

First, you will need to modify the `users` configuration setting for `allow_sign_up` from the default `false` to `true`. If you were editing the configuration file (`conf/grafana.ini`) for your Grafana server, it would look like this:

```
[users]
allow_sign_up = true
```

Since we are using Docker Compose to set our configuration, we'll use an environment variable instead. As discussed previously in *Chapter 12, Monitoring Data Streams with Grafana Alerts*, any setting in the configuration file can be mapped to a corresponding environment variable in this way:

```
GF_<SectionName>_<KeyName>
```

The variable must be capitalized as well. In this case, the environment variable should be `GF_USERS_ALLOW_SIGN_UP`. This is what our `docker-compose.yml` file looks like:

```
services:
    grafana:
            image:  "grafana/grafana:latest"
            ports:          - "3000:3000"
            environment:        - GF_USERS_ALLOW_SIGN_UP=true
            volumes:        - "${PWD-.}/grafana:/var/lib/grafana"
```

Shut down your Grafana service (if one is running) and then start it back up:

```
% docker-compose down
[+] Running 2/2
    Container chapter15-grafana-1     Removed        0.2s
    Network chapter15_Removed         0.0s
% docker-compose up -d
[+] Running 2/2
    Network chapter15_default         Created        0.0s
    Container chapter15-grafana-1     Started        0.3s
```

When you open the landing page for Grafana, you should see a subtle difference. There is now a **New to Grafana?** prompt and a **Sign up** button:

Figure 15.4 – Self-sign up

Clicking the **Sign up** button presents the user with a form they need to submit before they can be granted access. By default, all new users are set to the **Viewer** role, which is the role with the most restrictive settings. That default can be changed by altering the `auto_assign_org_role` user configuration setting (the `GF_USERS_AUTO_ASSIGN_ORG_ROLE` environment variable).

Now that we've added users, we'll need to manage what level of access they have to Grafana. You probably want every user to be able to create and edit dashboards, but maybe you don't want them to also be able to delete them by mistake. That's where permissions come in.

## Setting permissions

While you can grant a role to every user for the purpose of ultimately restricting their access to your Grafana site, you also need the ability to determine what parts of the site are ultimately accessible to users with those different roles. Happily, Grafana allows users with admin privileges to specify access levels for dashboards and folders.

## Setting organization roles

First off, let's simply set the user's organization role. It's a straightforward process, and one that you probably followed when you first invited a user:

1.  Go to **Users** under **Administration** in the main menu.

2.  Select the **Organization users** tab.

3.  Set a **Role** for the user in the dropdown. This is what the **Users** tab page might look like with a handful of users:

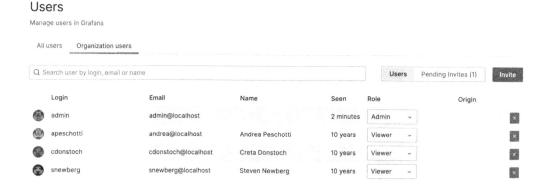

Figure 15.5 – The Organization users tab

Once we've set the role for the user, we can either allow the default roles to be applied to folders or choose whether we want to add specific roles to the folder.

## Setting folder permissions

Now that we've established roles for our users, we can set the access controls for our dashboards and folders. Typically, the default permissions for a folder directly map into the roles, as we described previously:

*   The **Admin** role can *administer* the folder

*   The **Editor** role can *edit* the folder

*   The **Viewer** role can *view* the folder

Here's what those typical folder permissions look like:

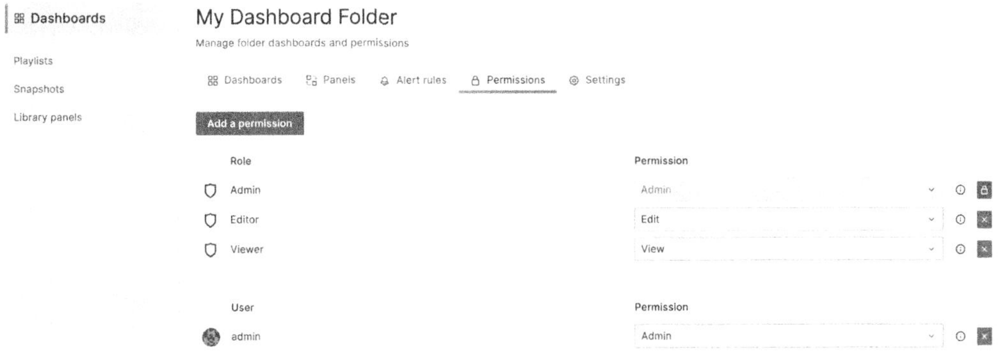

Figure 15.6 – The dashboard folder permissions

You can either modify the permissions for those roles or set additional permissions. It's easy to alter the existing permissions for a folder:

1.  From the main menu, select **Dashboards**.
2.  Hover over the dashboard folder you wish to configure and click **Go to folder**.
3.  Select the **Permissions** tab.
4.  Select a new permission for the given role from the dropdown.

To add a new permission, you will need to specify whether the permission applies to a user, team, or role (for lack of a better term, let's call it a **permission target type**); the specific user, team, or role (the **permission target**); and the permission itself:

1.  From the **Dashboards** page, go to a dashboard folder.
2.  Go to the **Permissions** tab.
3.  Click **Add a permission**.
4.  Select the permission target type (**User**, **Team**, or **Role**) from the drop-down menu.
5.  Select the permission target from the dropdown.
6.  Select the permission (**View**, **Edit**, or **Admin**) from the drop-down menu.
7.  Click **Save**.

Permission target types can be a single user, a team (if you've created a team for your organization), or everyone with either the viewer or editor roles. Let's walk through a quick example for an example folder called My Dashboard Folder:

1.  Go to My Dashboard Folder.

2.  Select the **Permissions** tab.

3.  Click **Add a permission**.

4.  Select **User** from the dropdown, and then select the user from the dropdown – in this case, **apeschotti**.

5.  Select the **Edit** permission from the dropdown.

6.  Click **Save**.

Here's what our example looks like while editing the user:

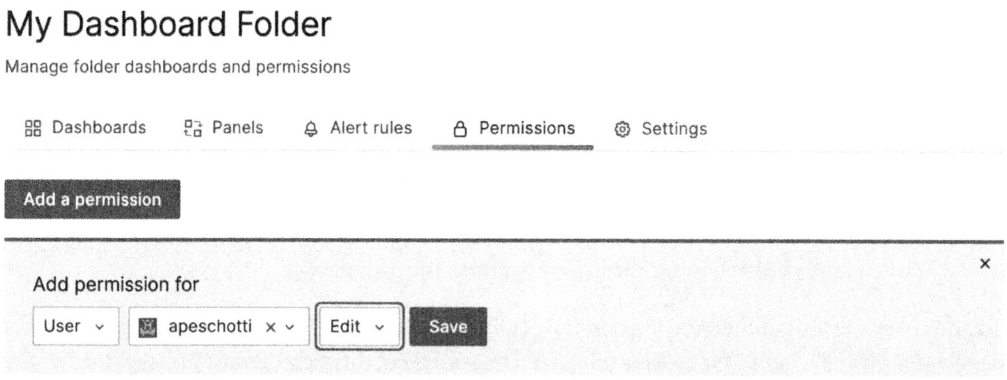

# My Dashboard Folder

Manage folder dashboards and permissions

&#9783; Dashboards      &#9783; Panels      &#9760; Alert rules      &#128274; Permissions      &#9881; Settings

<kbd>Add a permission</kbd>

---

Add permission for                                                                                                                    ×

| User  ∨ |   &#128100; apeschotti  × ∨ |   | Edit  ∨ |   Save |

Figure 15.7 – Setting the dashboard folder permissions

And that's all there is to assigning folder permissions. The workflow for dashboards is quite similar, so let's look at it now.

## Setting dashboard permissions

Like folders, dashboards can also be assigned permissions, but with an additional subtlety – dashboards can inherit permissions from folders. The process of editing permissions on a dashboard is quite like how you alter the existing permissions for a folder:

1.  Open a dashboard.

2.  Click the settings (gear) icon.

3. Go to the **Permissions** tab.

4. Select a permission from the dropdown.

Again, to add a new permission, you will need to specify the permission target type, the permission target, and the permission, as follows:

1. Open a dashboard.

2. Click the settings (gear) icon.

3. Go to the **Permissions** tab.

4. Click **Add a permission**.

5. Select the permission target type (**User**, **Team**, or **Role**) from the dropdown.

6. Select the permission target from the dropdown.

7. Select the permission (**View**, **Edit**, or **Admin**) from the dropdown.

8. Click **Save**.

Permission target types can be a single user, a team (if you've created a team for your organization), or everyone with either the viewer or editor roles. Let's walk through a quick example of a hypothetical dashboard called Simple Dashboard:

1. Open Simple Dashboard.

2. Click the settings (gear) icon.

3. Select the **Permissions** tab.

4. Click **Add a permission**.

5. Select **User** from the dropdown.

6. Select the **snewberg** user from the dropdown.

7. Select the **Admin** permission from the dropdown.

8. Click **Save**.

Here's what our example looks like:

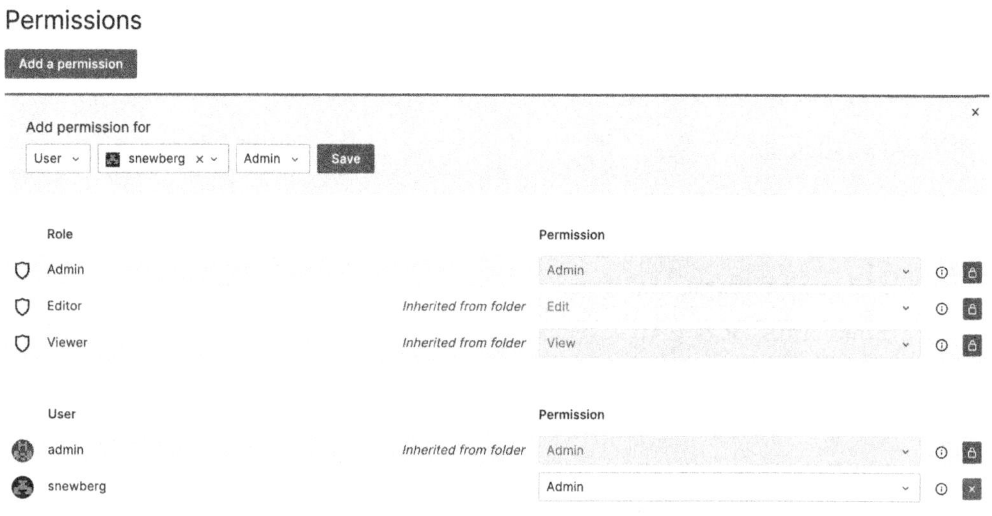

## Permissions

Add a permission

Add permission for                                                                                                   ×

[ User ˅ ]  [ 🖼 snewberg  × ˅ ]  [ Admin ˅ ]  [ Save ]

| Role | | Permission | |
| --- | --- | --- | --- |
| 🛡 Admin | | Admin | ˅  ⓘ 🔒 |
| 🛡 Editor | *Inherited from folder* | Edit | ˅  ⓘ 🔒 |
| 🛡 Viewer | *Inherited from folder* | View | ˅  ⓘ 🔒 |

| User | | Permission | |
| --- | --- | --- | --- |
| 👤 admin | *Inherited from folder* | Admin | ˅  ⓘ 🔒 |
| 👤 snewberg | | Admin | ˅  ⓘ ✕ |

Figure 15.8 – Setting dashboard permissions

Note how the other existing permissions are inherited from the enclosing folder's permissions. To override those inherited permissions, you'll need to first click the blue lock icon.

With that, we've covered setting up permissions for users, but doing so for several users can quickly become tedious. Because of that, Grafana has another role level that can encompass a collection of users called a Team. Next, we'll look at how to set up a team, as well as how to assign permissions at the team level.

# Establishing teams

Above a user, a Team forms the next level of a kind of hierarchy of role class. While every user is assigned a permission level (**Viewer**, **Editor**, or **Admin**), you can also assign each user to a team, which can then have its own permission settings. The first thing we'll need to do is add a team.

## Setting up a team

Setting up a team and adding users requires a user with the organization role of admin. To create a team, follow these steps:

1.  Go to **Administration | Teams** from the main menu.
2.  Click **New team**.
3.  Enter the name of the team and an optional **Email** contact.

4.  Click **Create**, as shown in the following screenshot:

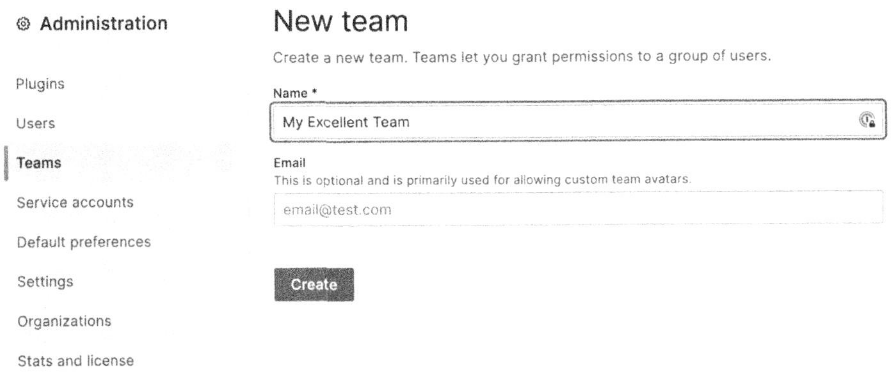

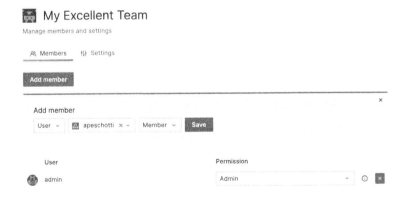

Figure 15.9 – A new team creation

Once you've created a team, you can add users as members of the team, as follows:

1.  Go to **Administration | Teams** from the left sidebar.

2.  Select the team you wish to add members to.

3.  Click **Add member**.

4.  Select the role type from the drop-down menu.

5.  Select a member from the drop-down menu.

6.  Set the role for the member from the drop-down menu.

7.  Click **Save**.

The following screenshot shows what adding a team member looks like:

Figure 15.10 – Adding a team member

Now that we've added a team, we'll learn about how to set various preferences for the team, including its email address, home dashboard, and UI theme.

### Team members

From the **Teams** page, go to the **Members** tab to manage the team's members:

- If you need to delete a team member, simply click the red **x** icon next to the user's entry on the team's page

- If you need to delete a team, click the red **x** icon character next to the team entry on the **Teams** page

### Team settings

From the **Team** page, go to the **Settings** tab to change the team settings. These settings will apply to any member of the Team. This is what you should know:

- Under **Team Details**, you can rename the team and change its email address

- Under **Preferences**, you can set things such as the **UI Theme**, **Home Dashboard**, **Timezone**, **Week start**, and **Language** settings

> Info
> Changing the team settings will override the organization preference settings.

## Permission rules

By now, you may worry that the myriad combinations of organization, teams, users, and roles, not to mention the various dashboard and folder permissions, are so complex that planning or troubleshooting access control issues might become intractably difficult. Nothing could be further from the truth! Grafana determines access control with some simple rules. First, permissions are defined in four layers:

- The organizational role (**Admin**, **Editor**, or **Viewer**)

- Team membership (**Member** or **Admin**)

- Direct permission assignment on dashboards, folders, and data sources

- **Super Admin** enabled

When permissions in more than one layer are defined, the highest permission setting prevails, according to two rules:

- The **Organization Admin** role cannot be overruled

- Lower specific permissions can be overruled by higher general permissions

What this means practically is that setting users to stricter permissions (**Viewer**, for example) has no effect if an organization's permission for a dashboard is looser (**Admin**, for example). If you need to strictly control access to a particular resource, make sure to remove any general permission settings for the resource. The best way to learn the implications of these rules is to experiment with different combinations of settings firsthand. Give it a try!

Someone will need to establish and manage Grafana users and organizations. That is the role of the Super Admin, as that role must operate above the organizational level. Let's look at the practical aspects of administering both users and organizations in Grafana.

# Administering users and organizations

There are two major tasks that can only be performed by a user with the Super Admin role – the management of users and the management of organizations. When you logged into your brand-new Grafana site as admin, you were really logging in as a super admin, and as a super admin, you have the ability to create users and organizations. Managing users and organizations is accomplished through a special **Server Admin** page, which can only be accessed by super admins from the left sidebar

First, let's look at how to create new users. Previously, we discussed the idea that the only way to add new user accounts is to invite someone or (with a configuration change) allow users to add themselves. Those restrictions only apply to organizations and organizational Admins. As it turns out, there is yet another way – if you're a Super Admin.

## Managing users

If you have several users to add to your site and you need to assign them to different organizations, it might be more efficient to simply add them manually. You can add users and assign them passwords from the **Administration | Users** page, all without the need to go through the process of sending out invites and waiting for the response. Here's how to create a new user:

1. From the main menu, go to **Adminstration | Users**. Confirm you are on the **All users** tab.

2. Click **New user**.

3. Fill in at least the **Name** and **Password** details, as indicated by the asterisks (*). The other settings can be set by the user after they've logged in.

As you're creating a user, this is what the **New user** page typically looks like:

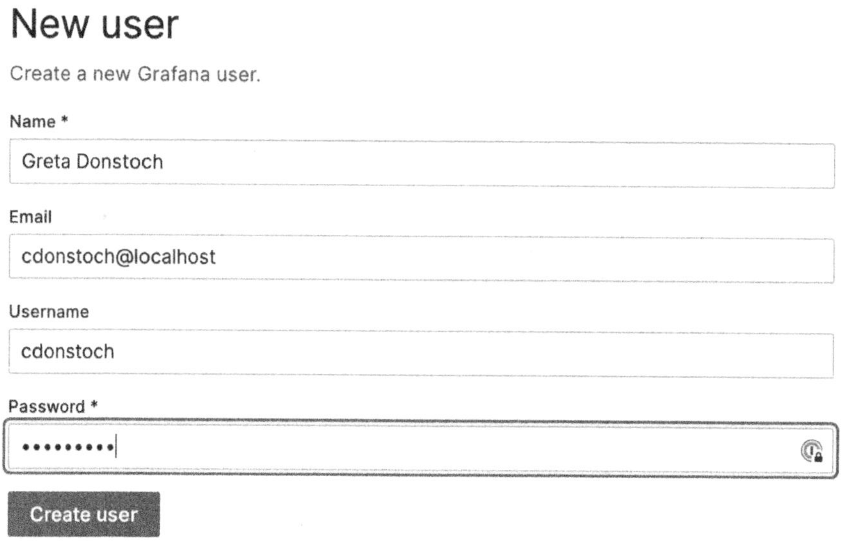

# New user

Create a new Grafana user.

Name *

Greta Donstoch

Email

cdonstoch@localhost

Username

cdonstoch

Password *

•••••••••

Create user

Figure 15.11 – Adding a new user

Now, let's look at how to modify a user:

1.  From the main menu, select **Administration | Users**. Confirm you are on the **All users** tab.

2.  Click on a user.

3.  Edit the user information by clicking **Edit** next to the item. You can edit the user's name, email, username, and password. The remaining items will be covered shortly.

Continuing down the user's page, let's look at disabling or deleting the user.

## Disabling or deleting a user

First, we'll look at how we manage the user account. Under **User information**, we can disable or delete the account, as follows:

-   To delete the user, select **Delete User**

-   If you only want to block the user without deleting, select **Disable User**

Now, let's look at elevating a user to **Super Admin**.

## *Elevating a user to Super Admin*

You might be wondering how to go about giving another user the **Super Admin** role. You can only do this if you're a Super Admin yourself. We can elevate a user to **Super Admin** under **Permissions | Grafana Admin**, as follows:

1.  Select **Change**.

2.  Select **Yes** from the toggle.

3.  Finally, select **Change** to confirm.

Let's move on down, we'll next learn how to set the user's organization membership.

## *Setting user organization membership*

As a Super Admin user, you can control organizational membership at a global level, which means you can add, remove, and set the role of the user for any organization. To add a user to an organization, follow these steps:

1.  Under **Organizations**, select **Add user to organization**.

2.  Select an organization from the dropdown.

3.  If necessary, select a role from the dropdown.

4.  Click **Add to organization**. Here is an example:

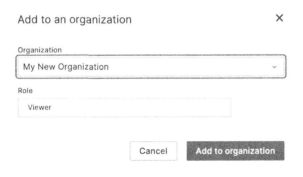

Figure 15.12 – Adding a user to an organization

To change the user's role within an organization:

1.  Next to the organization in question, select **Change role**.

2.  Select the new role from the dropdown.

3.  Click **Save**.

Finally, to remove a user from an organization, follow these steps:

1. Select **Remove from organization**. Bear in mind that a user must be a member of at least one organization.

2. Click **Confirm removal**.

You can get a lot of user account management accomplished from this one page. On the other hand, you can easily affect a lot of users, so be careful when assigning Super Admin permissions.

## Organization admin and Super Admin roles

It might seem a little head-spinning to try to keep track of the differences between an Admin operating at the organization level and a Super Admin acting at the Server Admin level. What if you set the organization role of the only Admin user to Editor? Can you lock yourself out of an organization, or completely out of Grafana for that matter?

Fortunately, Grafana has some safety in place to keep you from getting stuck. While organizational Admins can set Admin permissions, Super Admins can set both organizational Admins and Super Admins.

Super Admins can, of course, downgrade a role, but not in such a way as to reduce the number of Super Admins to zero. Any such attempt will trigger an error message. That way, you, as a Super Admin, can't inadvertently lock yourself out of your ability to administer your own site.

Likewise, each organization must also have at least one user at the Admin level. Any attempt to eliminate all Admins in an organization will also trigger an error. This is to prevent the only Admin from locking themselves out of their organization.

## Managing organizations

The other major task performed by Super Admins is managing organizations. But why might you want to set up more than one organization in the first place? While it isn't necessary to establish multiple organizations on a single Grafana site, there are cases where you may want to establish independent Grafana sites, each with its own data sources, dashboards, and so on, but you don't want to spin up multiple servers.

For example, you may have restrictions on who can access proprietary or sensitive information, and you don't want the members of one organization accessing the data sources of another. You may have specific accounting constraints that determine which plugins a particular organization has access to.

While it is simple enough to spin up another Grafana instance in this case, it is much easier, from a management perspective, to have a single deployment that's partitioned into multiple organizations. This way, you can provision data sources and plugins more easily, and the Grafana UI makes it easy to quickly switch from one organization to another. You can easily assign users to multiple organizations and grant them roles specific to the organizations they are members of.

## Creating a new organization

We'll start by creating a new organization. You will need to be logged in as a user with the Super Admin role:

1.  From the left sidebar, go to **Organizations** under **Administration**.
2.  Click + **New org**.
3.  Fill in the **Organization name** field.
4.  Select **Create**.

That's all there is to it! You will be automatically switched to the new organization, where you can then set the preferences for the organization.

To delete an organization, simply click the red (×) icon next to the organization. This is an irreversible operation, so heed the scary-looking dialog box that pops up for confirmation.

## Switching between organizations

As a Super Admin, you can not only switch to a different organization you are a member of but also switch to any organization, simply by selecting the organization from the drop-down menu at the left of the search bar, at the top of the window. Once you have set your current organization, you can then change its name, the default preferences, and the preferences set for all organization members. Here's how.

## Renaming and setting an organization's default preferences

To rename or set a organization's default preferences, follow these steps:

1.  To rename the current organization, go to **Administration | Default preferences** from the main menu.
2.  Change the organization name in the textbox.
3.  Click **Update organization name** to confirm the change.

Alternatively, you can edit the name of any organization from the **Organizations** page simply by selecting the organization you want to rename, changing the name in the text box, and clicking **Update**.

To change the default preferences for an organization, follow these steps:

1.  Under **Preferences**, additionally set or change the **Interface Theme**, **Home Dashboard**, **Timezone**, **Week start**, and **Language** settings.
2.  Click **Save**.

Any user can override the default settings for themselves by editing them on their **Profile** page.

> **Tip**
> The **Home Dashboard** drop-down menu will be filled in with any of the organization's starred dashboards.

That completes an overview of the management of Grafana's users, teams, and organizations. Let's summarize what we learned in this chapter.

## Summary

In this chapter, we covered many common tasks faced by a Grafana admin. First, we took a closer look at users, teams, and organizations and saw how roles can be mapped to permissions for dashboards, folders, and data sources. Then, we learned how organization admins can manage both users and teams. Finally, we examined how the Super Admin role can create new users and organizations.

Don't worry if it's difficult to visualize all the possibilities afforded by the Grafana permission model. It may be that, for now, you have no need to establish multiple organizations, specify permissions on specific dashboards or folders, or even assemble users into teams. However, as your site grows in complexity, you may find that access control issues present themselves, and you may want to come back to this chapter. Concepts that seem a little abstract right now may have concrete relevance in the future.

Throughout the course of this book, we've been using a simple password-based authentication scheme for our Grafana server, but there are a number of powerful external authentication systems available. In the next chapter, we'll take a look at a few of them. These systems are important for integrating your Grafana authentication with that of a larger organization so that users have a seamless experience, regardless of whether they are logging into their email, chats, conferences, or even Grafana.

# 16

# Authenticating Grafana Logins Using LDAP or OAuth 2 Providers

In the previous chapter, when delving into how to manage users and teams, we briefly examined the options for adding and authenticating users. We also looked at how Grafana can group user memberships into teams, allowing for more granular control over permissions to resources such as dashboards, panels, and data sources. Out of the box, Grafana provides a very straightforward authentication scheme based on authenticating against a user/password pair. New users can either be created under this scheme or they can add themselves (with a minor configuration change). Grafana provides more than a couple of variations of this mechanism, with varying levels of complexity and security.

However, the use of these methodologies is not considered ideal. In many corporate environments, user access must be strictly tracked and integrated with numerous systems, including administration and the IT department. Authentication models must provide robust security against any potential threat; they may need to scale to hundreds – if not thousands – of users. In these circumstances, Grafana's native authentication would be inadequate for the task and, depending on the corporate environment, may not pass the required security reviews.

A solution to these issues can be found in a dedicated external service capable of storing users and their credentials and supporting state-of-the-art protocols for authenticating them. These **authentication services** work to offload most of the drudgery of maintaining user access lists, groups, authentication tokens, and so on. They tend to provide some or all of the following important features:

- **Single sign-on (SSO)**: Authenticates the user once so that they can access many platforms
- **Universal directory services**: Tracks users, groups, credentials, and contact information
- **Adaptive multi-factor authentication**: Verifies login with a personal confirmation
- **User life cycle management**: Initiates, suspends, and terminates user accounts

In the following sections, we'll look at how Grafana can integrate with the locally deployed **OpenLDAP** directory service. As an alternative, we will look at three external authentication services that provide authentication through the **OAuth 2** standard. We'll start with GitHub, where many software-driven organizations and individuals may already have accounts. We'll follow that with a look at Google, which many enterprises will have access to through their **G Suite application stack**. Finally, we will wrap things up with the **Okta** dedicated authentication service provider. The following topics will be covered in this chapter:

- Authenticating with OpenLDAP
- Authenticating with GitHub
- Authenticating with Google
- Authenticating with Okta

## Authenticating with OpenLDAP

Let's start with one of the more venerable authentication schemes available today: **Lightweight Directory Access Protocol (LDAP)**, originally developed in the early 1990s. While it is often used to store user information for authentication purposes, it can also serve all kinds of directory information, including user groups, hostnames, network addresses, and even office addresses and phone numbers.

In this section, we'll set up a simple directory using the OpenLDAP implementation and configure Grafana to bind to the OpenLDAP server to look up users and teams. This process can be a little bit complicated, but we'll go through it step by step. It is beyond the scope of this book to go through the details of setting up and maintaining a production LDAP directory, but I will endeavor to explain things in some detail as we go along. If you are looking to integrate your Grafana server with an existing LDAP installation, this should give you a feel for what is involved.

To set up an LDAP authentication server, follow these steps:

1. Download and install an OpenLDAP server.
2. Configure Grafana to bind to the LDAP server.
3. Test to confirm whether Grafana can connect to LDAP.
4. Add a user to the LDAP directory.
5. Perform an LDAP lookup from within Grafana.

We'll start by downloading and configuring an open source LDAP server called **OpenLDAP**.

# Setting up an OpenLDAP server

We will use Docker Compose to download an image of the OpenLDAP implementation of LDAP, which is available from `osixia`. Information about how to work with this Docker image can be found on GitHub at `https://github.com/osixia/docker-openldap`. Our Docker Compose file will ultimately contain two services: one for LDAP and the other for Grafana. The full `docker-compose.yml` file is available in this book's GitHub repository in the `Chapter16` directory.

Here's the first part of the LDAP service:

```
ldap:
  image: osixia/openldap
```

Here, we're just downloading the image from `osixia`. Once we have downloaded the image, we'll need to open port `389`. If you enable support for **Transport Layer Security** (**TLS**) connections, you'll need to open port `636`. For demonstration purposes, we'll connect to our LDAP server over an unsecured connection:

```
    ports:
      - 389:389
```

By default, the `osixia` Docker image has a predefined organization and domain, but we'd like to override that with our own. We can do that with a couple of environment variables:

```
    environment:
      LDAP_ORGANISATION: "My Grafana Company"
      LDAP_DOMAIN: "grafana.org"
```

Finally, we need to create volumes to serve two purposes – if we want to persist our LDAP directory database and so that we can access the container's internal filesystem to add our own files. We'll need this capability later when we add a user.

Once we've created `docker-compose.yml`, we can go ahead and launch it to get the LDAP server up and running:

```
% docker-compose up --pull missing -d ldap
[+] Running 11/11
  ldap 10 layers
  [...]    0B/0B      Pulled       39.1s
    83c5cfdaa538 Pull complete          3.6s
    b7185bbc69c9 Pull complete              3.7s
    5aad93bf369a Pull complete       3.8s
    3908fcbd6300 Pull complete              4.4s
    2ec0882530ef Pull complete           4.5s
    96ac4bb6da11 Pull complete        4.5s
```

```
    735dc1ab9556 Pull complete            6.3s
    7e5bbbe3d89a Pull complete        6.3s
    b00b9df2d406 Pull complete        6.3s
    0cad5ac09677 Pull complete            6.4s
[+] Running 2/2
  Network chapter16_default    Created    0.1s
  Container chapter16-ldap-1   Started    1.1s
```

To confirm whether we have a running installation, we can carry out a simple query:

```
% docker-compose exec ldap \
        ldapsearch -x -w admin \
          -H ldap://localhost \
          -b dc=grafana,dc=org -D "cn=admin,dc=grafana,dc=org"
```

That's a gnarly-looking command, but it's not too bad if we break it down:

- The first line, docker-compose exec ldap, indicates that we're going to run a command inside the ldap container.

- The next line is the ldapsearch command. The -x option indicates that we want to use simple authentication by using -w as the option and admin as the password.

- You might be able to guess that -H ldap://localhost is the option for passing the server address (called ldapuri) – in this case, for opening a connection to a ldap server on localhost.

- The -b dc=grafana,dc=org option indicates the search base for our query, a kind of *root* in our LDAP search hierarchy. We are searching the domain or dc for grafana.org, which we specified in our LDAP_DOMAIN environment variable when we configured our service.

- Lastly, -D "cn=admin,dc=grafana,dc=org" specifies our search term; this is called a **distinguished name**. Think of it as encoding the admin@grafana.org login name, built by combining the common name (cn) and the two domain names (dc).

If your server is running, you should get results that look something like this:

```
# extended LDIF
#
# LDAPv3
# base <dc=grafana,dc=org> with scope subtree
# filter: (objectclass=*)
# requesting: ALL
#

# grafana.org
```

```
dn: dc=grafana,dc=org
objectClass: top
objectClass: dcObject
objectClass: organization
o: My Grafana Company
dc: grafana

# search result
search: 2
result: 0 Success

# numResponses: 2
# numEntries: 1
```

You should see an entry – one matching an organization of `grafana.org`. If you don't see these results, ensure your server is running in Docker Compose. Now, let's go ahead and set up our Grafana server.

## Configuring Grafana to use LDAP

For our Grafana server, we'll use the same Docker Compose service we've used throughout this book, but with one small change. As with the LDAP service, we will create an additional volume mapping to a local directory so that we can install a file in the container's filesystem. In the case of Grafana, we'll be installing a couple of necessary configuration files to enable proper LDAP support on our server.

Let's walk through our Grafana Docker Compose service. The first few lines are pretty much identical to a typical service:

```
grafana:
    image: grafana/grafana:latest
ports:
  - "3000:3000"
```

Following those lines is our first big change. We're going to tell Grafana to look for a configuration file in `/etc/grafana/grafana.ini`:

```
environment:
  GF_PATHS_CONFIG: "/etc/grafana/grafana.ini"
```

To access the file outside the container, we'll need to create a volume mapping. We'll create two – the usual one for persisting our Grafana data and one for the `config` file:

```
volumes:
  - $PWD/grafana/data:/var/lib/grafana
  - $PWD/grafana/etc:/etc/grafana
```

Finally, we'll make the `ldap` service a dependency for our `grafana` service:

```
depends_on:
  - ldap
```

Now that we've set up our service, we'll need to add two configuration files. The first file is called `grafana.ini` and is used to override the default configuration, much like how we used environment variables in previous chapters. We could do the same in this case, but since we will be installing an additional file, we might as well go ahead and use the `grafana.ini` file. Our `grafana.ini` file is based on an example provided by Grafana and looks like this:

```
[auth.ldap]
# Set to `true` to enable LDAP integration (default: `false`)
enabled = true

# Path to the LDAP specific configuration file (default: `/etc/
grafana/ldap.toml`)
config_file = /etc/grafana/ldap.toml

# Allow sign-up should be `true` (default) to allow Grafana to create
users on successful LDAP authentication.
# If set to `false` only already existing Grafana users will be able
to login.
allow_sign_up = true
```

It's pretty straightforward and, with all the comments, self-explanatory. From what we can see in this file, we need to install a second file in `/etc/grafana` called `ldap.toml`. This file will describe how Grafana will communicate with the LDAP server.

Our `ldap.toml` file also comes from the Grafana documentation, albeit with a couple of changes so that we can use it in the Docker container context. Here's an excerpt of the file (the full file can be found in the `Chapter16` folder in this book's GitHub repository at `https://github.com/PacktPublishing/Learn-Grafana-10/blob/main/Chapter16/ldif/new-user.ldif`):

```
[[servers]]
# Ldap server host (specify multiple hosts space separated)
host = "ldap"
```

The first change we've made is to set `host = "ldap"` so that our Grafana server can talk to the `ldap` server container. Next, for this tutorial, we'll need to disable TLS/SSL:

```
use_ssl = false
```

This is inadvisable for a production environment, but for demonstration purposes, it will be fine. Finally, we need to set the bind password so that Grafana can authenticate with the LDAP server. The default for the OpenLDAP Docker image is `admin`:

```
bind_password = "admin"
```

You should create a `grafana/etc` directory in your current directory and copy the files there (if they aren't already), then launch your `grafana` service:

```
% docker-compose up -d grafana
Creating network "ch13_default" with the default driver
Creating ch13_ldap_1 ... done
Creating ch13_grafana_1 ... done
```

Since the `ldap` service is a dependency on the `grafana` service, it will also launch (if it isn't already running). Let's check out our Grafana server to confirm that it can connect to our LDAP server.

## Securing the bind password

Now, having a free-text password in your configuration file is not a good practice, so let's devote a little extra effort to fixing that. First, let's change the `bind_password` entry so that it redirects to an external environment variable. This way, we can set the variable's value at service launch:

```
bind_password = "${LDAP_BIND_PASSWORD}"
```

We could set the environment variable in our `docker-compose.yml` file like this:

```
  grafana:
...
    command:
      export LDAP_BIND_PASSWORD="admin"
```

That's not much better than leaving it in the original configuration file – we just moved the password text from one configuration file to another. A better solution is to store our password in a Docker Compose secret. To do that, we need to take care of three things:

1.  We need to store the password in a secret file, which we'll call `ldap_admin_secret.txt`.

2.  We need to create a secret in our `docker-compose.yml` file that points to our secret.

3.  We need to reference the secret when we set the password environment variable.

The first thing we must do is create the secret file and add the password to it. Next, we must update our `docker-compose.yml` file by adding the following secret:

```
secrets:
  ldap_admin_secret:
    file: ./ldap_admin_secret.txt
```

Make sure the path is relative to the `Chapter16` directory. The secret will be named `ldap_admin_secret`. Keep this in mind for later.

Finally, update the grafana service in our docker-compose.yml file to the following:

```
grafana:
  image: grafana/grafana:latest
  ports:
    - "3000:3000"
  environment:
    GF_PATHS_CONFIG: "/etc/grafana/grafana.ini"
  volumes:
    - "${PWD-.}/grafana/data:/var/lib/grafana"
    - "${PWD-.}/grafana/etc:/etc/grafana"
  depends_on:
    - ldap
  secrets:
    - ldap_admin_secret
  command:
    ['/bin/sh', '-c', 'export LDAP_ADMIN_PASSWORD=$$(cat /run/
secrets/ldap_admin_secret) ; source /run.sh']
```

By default, the path to a secret in a Docker Compose container is /run/secrets/<secret_name>, which we are referencing in the entrypoint command – this sets LDAP_BIND_PASSWORD to the contents of the secret file. It's just replacing the existing entrypoint command with a new one that invokes a shell to run two commands: one copies the password stored in the secret file, while the other runs the *real* entrypoint command.

You might have noticed that we're still not quite secure, are we? We are still storing our password in free text (and in a GitHub repository). We'll create a .gitignore file and store the name of our password file in it:

```
ldap_admin_secret.txt
```

This is not too bad for security. The file won't be checked into GitHub, the content of the file itself is only made available to the Docker service as a secret, and the container only gets it as an environment variable at runtime. It's not potentially visible to anybody along its journey from a local file to Grafana.

## Testing the Grafana configuration

From a browser, log in as a Grafana admin and navigate to **Authentication** under **Administration**. You'll find that the currently **Configured authentication** method is indeed **LDAP**:

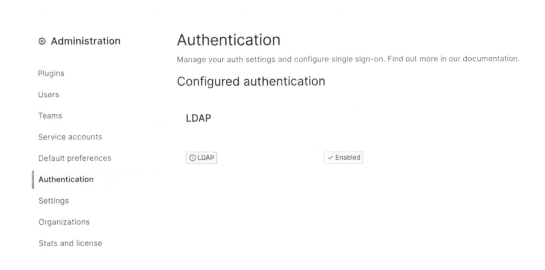

Figure 16.1 – LDAP configuration enabled

Click on the **LDAP** box. If Grafana was successful in binding to your LDAP server, you should see a page showing a check next to port 389, indicating a successful connection to your LDAP server:

Figure 16.2 – Successful LDAP connection

Searching for a user won't yield anything as we don't have any users in LDAP. So, let's add one.

## Adding a user to OpenLDAP

For our server to truly be useful for authentication, we'll need to add user accounts. Before we proceed, however, we need to take note of something. When we add a user to LDAP, we need to make sure the entry fields we add to the directory will be understood by Grafana – that is, when Grafana does an

LDAP lookup for a user, it knows what fields in the response to look for to satisfy itself. We can find this list at the bottom of our `ldap.toml` file:

```
[servers.attributes]
member_of = "memberOf"
email =   "email"
```

This is a list of Grafana user fields and their corresponding entries in an LDAP entry. Armed with this information, we can set up a user, making sure we include the appropriate fields. We use the `ldif` format for the file, which will be named `new-user.ldif`. Here's the file I've created for a user:

```
dn: cn=myuser,dc=grafana,dc=org
changetype: add
givenName: My
sn: User
cn: myuser
uid: cn
uidNumber: 14583102
gidNumber: 14564100
homeDirectory: /home/myuser
objectClass: top
objectClass: posixAccount
objectClass: inetOrgPerson
userPassword: {SHA}kd/Z3bQZiv/FwZTNjObTOP3kcOI=
mail: myuser@grafana.org
```

As you can see, I've included the name, surname, username, and email, and tagged these properties with the appropriate field names. The SHA-encoded user password I created using an LDAP command-line tool – `slappasswd` – is provided alongside the OpenLDAP installation in the container:

```
% docker-compose exec ldap \

        slappasswd -h {SHA} -s mypassword
{SHA}kd/Z3bQZiv/FwZTNjObTOP3kcOI=
```

Next, we'll copy this file into a directory we've created that's visible to the container (`slap.d`, for example):

```
% mkdir -p slapd.d/assets/test
% cp ldif/new-user.ldif slapd.d/assets/test
```

Finally, we must run the `ldapadd` command to inform our LDAP server of the new user:

```
% docker-compose exec ldap \
      ldapadd -x -w admin \
           -H ldap://localhost \
```

```
          -D "cn=admin,dc=grafana,dc=org" \
          -f /etc/ldap/slapd.d/assets/test/new-user.ldif
adding new entry "cn=myuser,dc=grafana,dc=org"
```

Let's break this command down:

- In our first line, we invoke a command inside our `ldap` service container

- In the second line, we invoke the `ldapsearch` command, which we will simply authenticate (`-x`) with the password (`-w`), `admin`

- In the next line, we indicate the URI for the LDAP server with the `-H` option

- Finally, we use the `-D` option to pass the bind account name (`admin@grafana.org`)

Following these boilerplate options is the option (`-f`) for the path to the LDIF file (as seen from inside the container). Remember that in `docker-compose.yml`, we volume-mapped our local `slapd.d` directory to `/etc/ldap/slapd.d` inside the container.

## Looking up a user in Grafana

Now that we have a user in our LDAP, let's confirm that Grafana sees the user. On the **Authentication** page, click on the **LDAP** box and enter our new user, `myuser`, in the **Username** box under **Test user mapping**. You should see the following results:

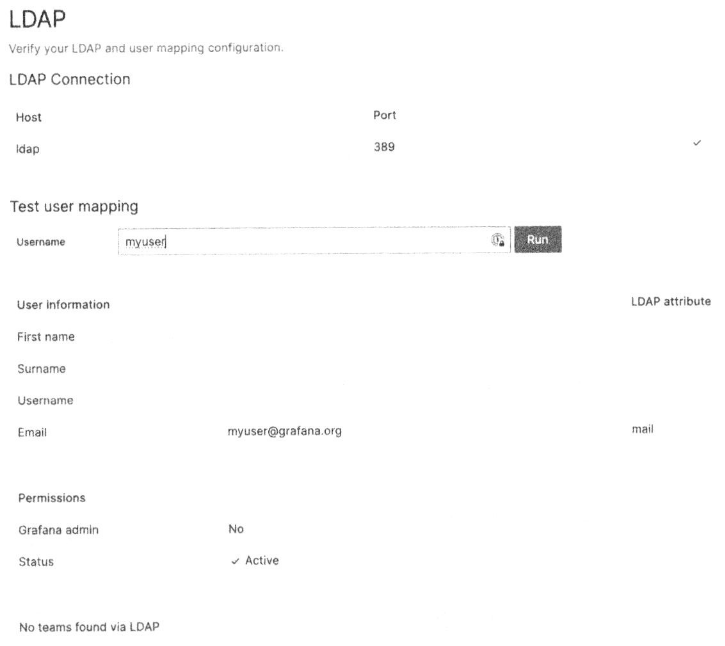

Figure 16.3 – LDAP test user mapping

Note how the Grafana fields are filled in from the corresponding fields in our LDAP entry. However, there's a bunch of information left out that we know we included in the LDAP user entry we created. We need to map more of that data using the `servers.attributes` configuration option in our `ldap.toml` file. It looks like we should be able to map the following fields into counterparts in our LDAP entry:

- **First Name**
- **Surname**
- **Username**
- **Email**

We just need to include those and their LDAP counterpart fields in the `servers.attributes` section:

```
name = "givenName"
surname = "sn"
username = "cn"
email =   "mail"
```

Remember to restart your Grafana server. Now, when you query for a user, you should see the mapped fields filled out, as shown in the following screenshot:

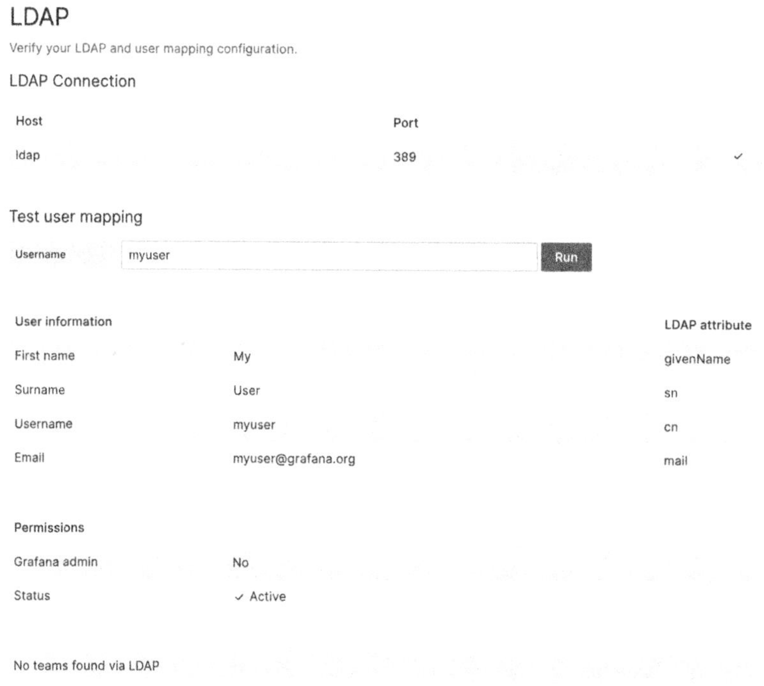

## LDAP

Verify your LDAP and user mapping configuration.

### LDAP Connection

| Host | Port | |
|------|------|---|
| ldap | 389 | ✓ |

### Test user mapping

| Username | myuser | Run |
|----------|--------|-----|

| User information | | LDAP attribute |
|------------------|------|----------------|
| First name | My | givenName |
| Surname | User | sn |
| Username | myuser | cn |
| Email | myuser@grafana.org | mail |

| Permissions | |
|-------------|---|
| Grafana admin | No |
| Status | ✓ Active |

No teams found via LDAP

Figure 16.4 – LDAP test user mapping with fields filled in

There you have it! Try logging into your Grafana server with our new user account to confirm that Grafana is authenticating against the username and password stored in LDAP.

Now that we've examined how to internally host an authentication server, we'll move on and look at how to perform external third-party authentication using the OAuth 2 protocol standard.

# Authenticating with OAuth 2

Now that we've covered our local LDAP authentication, we'll cover three examples that all use the OAuth 2 authentication standard. It is beyond the scope of this book to go into detail about the OAuth 2 standard but suffice to say it represents one of the most popular industry standards for application authentication. To use OAuth 2 to provide Grafana authentication, rather than running a lookup service, we will leverage external providers. We will look at three different popular services, each providing similar setup techniques but serving slightly different audiences.

In each case, we'll go through the typical workflow for registering the Grafana application to secure a known key, then configuring Grafana to use the key to perform the necessary trusted authentication after a user has logged into a provider account.

Without going into the specifics, the process for each implementation of OAuth 2 is relatively consistent:

1. Register both Grafana's login page URL and a special redirect URL for the provider to send properly authenticated users.

2. Return a client ID and a client secret. These work like Grafana's username and password with the provider.

3. Configure Grafana with the appropriate provider information, including the client ID and secret.

4. Restart Grafana so that it picks up the new configuration.

> **Note**
> The instructions presented here are valid at the time of writing but may be subject to change.

## GitHub OAuth 2 authentication

First, we'll look at Grafana authentication via GitHub, a common site for organizations working in the software space. We'll need to create an authorized OAuth 2 application for Grafana to talk to. In each of the following examples, we'll assume you are registering on behalf of a Grafana server at `http://localhost:3000`. Obviously, for a production server, you'll want to use an actual host and domain name; for our purposes, it will suffice to work with our local server. Follow these steps:

1. Log into GitHub using the account that will be responsible for the application.

2. From your user account menu, navigate to **Settings** | **Developer Settings**.

3.  Select **OAuth Apps**. You'll be presented with the following screen:

Figure 16.5 – GitHub OAuth Apps

4.  Click on **Register a new application**.

5.  Fill in the following fields and click on **Register application**:

    • **Application name**: Grafana

    • **Homepage URL**: http://localhost:3000

    • **Authorization callback URL**: http://localhost:3000/login/github:

## Register a new OAuth application

**Application name** *

    Grafana

Something users will recognize and trust.

**Homepage URL** *

    http://localhost:3000

The full URL to your application homepage.

**Application description**

    Application description is optional

This is displayed to all users of your application.

**Authorization callback URL** *

    http://localhost:3000/login/github

Your application's callback URL. Read our OAuth documentation for more information.

☐ **Enable Device Flow**

Allow this OAuth App to authorize users via the Device Flow.
Read the Device Flow documentation for more information.

    Register application       Cancel

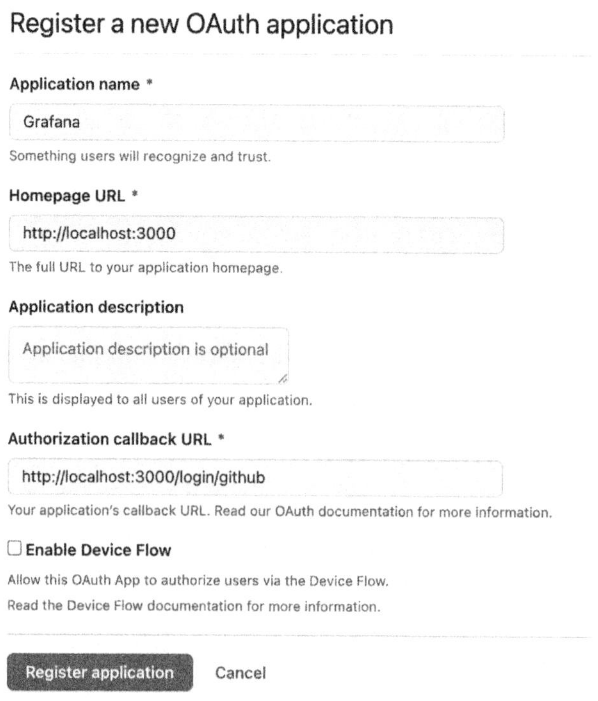

Figure 16.6 – GitHub – Register a new OAuth application

6.  Copy and retain the client ID and client secret for the Grafana configuration. You'll find them on the application page:

Figure 16.7 – GitHub client ID and secrets

7.  Now, add the following lines to your `grafana.ini` file (making sure to comment out any other auth.* sections):

```
[auth.github]
enabled = true
```

```
allow_sign_up = true
client_id = <CLIENT_ID>
client_secret = <CLIENT_SECRET>
scopes = user:email,read:org
auth_url = https://github.com/login/oauth/authorize
token_url = https://github.com/login/oauth/access_token
api_url = https://api.github.com/user
team_ids =
allowed_organizations =
```

Of course, you'll want to fill in your own client ID and client secret. After making your edits to the `grafana.ini` file, restart your Grafana server. When you open `http://localhost:3000`, you should see the Grafana login page with the option to sign in with GitHub.

Moving on from GitHub, next, we'll look at authentication via Google, a provider that's common with many enterprises that depend on Google for office applications, such as Gmail and the G Suite of tools.

## Google OAuth 2 authentication

Compared to GitHub, Google has a much more elaborate system, but if your Grafana users are part of your G Suite account, this is a good way to provide them with access. After some initial steps that involve configuring an OAuth consent page, getting a client ID and client secret is simple:

1.  Go to `https://console.developers.google.com/apis/credentials`. If this is your first time accessing this area, you may have to accept Google's Terms of Service to proceed:

Figure 16.8 – Google – Credentials

2. Create a project if you don't already have one. For our example, we'll call it `grafana`:

New Project

Project name *
grafana                                                                          ❓

Project ID: grafana-386023. It cannot be changed later.  EDIT

Organization *
learngrafana.net                                                         ▾    ❓

Select an organization to attach it to a project. This selection can't be changed later.

Location *
⊞ learngrafana.net                                                      BROWSE

Parent organization or folder

CREATE    CANCEL

Figure 16.9 – Creating a new Google project

3. Once you've created the project, you'll be returned to the **Credentials** page. Select **+ CREATE CREDENTIALS | OAuth client ID**:

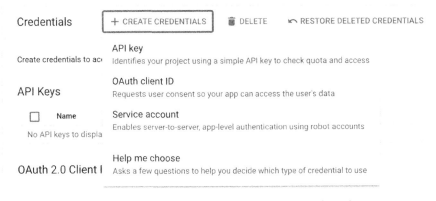

Credentials    + CREATE CREDENTIALS    🗑 DELETE    ↶ RESTORE DELETED CREDENTIALS

Create credentials to ac∙

API Keys

☐  Name

No API keys to displa

OAuth 2.0 Client I

API key
Identifies your project using a simple API key to check quota and access

OAuth client ID
Requests user consent so your app can access the user's data

Service account
Enables server-to-server, app-level authentication using robot accounts

Help me choose
Asks a few questions to help you decide which type of credential to use

Figure 16.10 – Creating Google OAuth client ID credentials

4. You'll be required to fill out an OAuth consent page. This configures the page that you will see when you attempt to sign in using Google. Since this is an internal application, you only need to fill out the following minimal information:

- **App name**: Grafana

- **User support email**: `<email address>`:

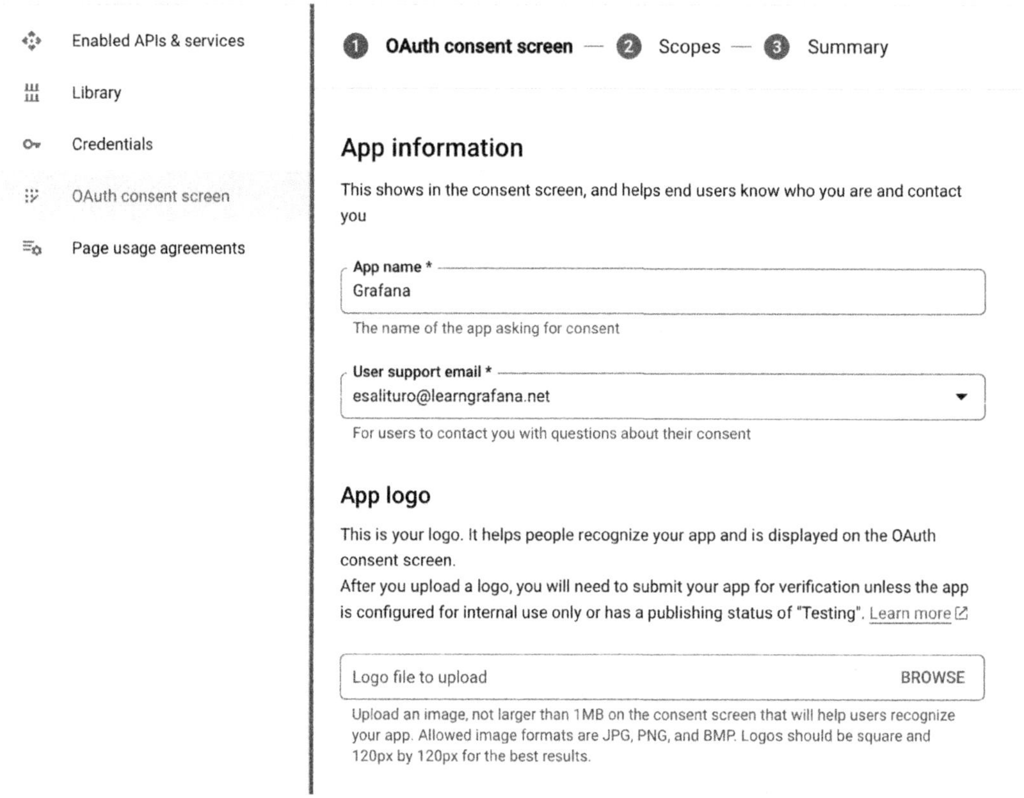

Figure 16.11 – OAuth consent screen

5.  After saving the consent screen configuration, you can finally do what you came here for – create an OAuth client ID. Under **Authorized JavaScript Origins**, click on + **Add URI** and add `http://localhost:3000` in the **URIs 1 \*** textbox.

6.  Under **Authorized redirect URIs**, click on **+ Add URI** and add `http://localhost:3000/login/google` in the **URIs 1** * textbox. Your form should look something like this:

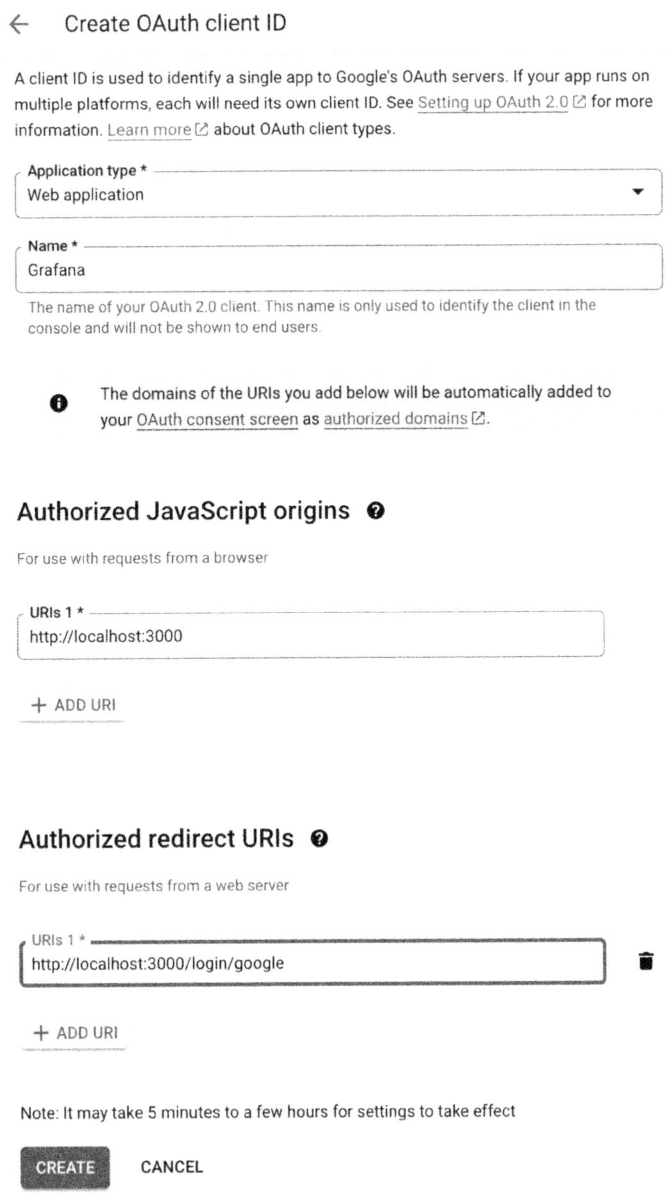

Figure 16.12 – Create OAuth client ID

7.  Click **Create**. You should now have an OAuth ID created with a client ID and a client secret. You'll need those for the Grafana configuration, so you should either click on the two copy icons and save the client ID and client secret to a file, or click on **DOWNLOAD JSON** to save the credentials:

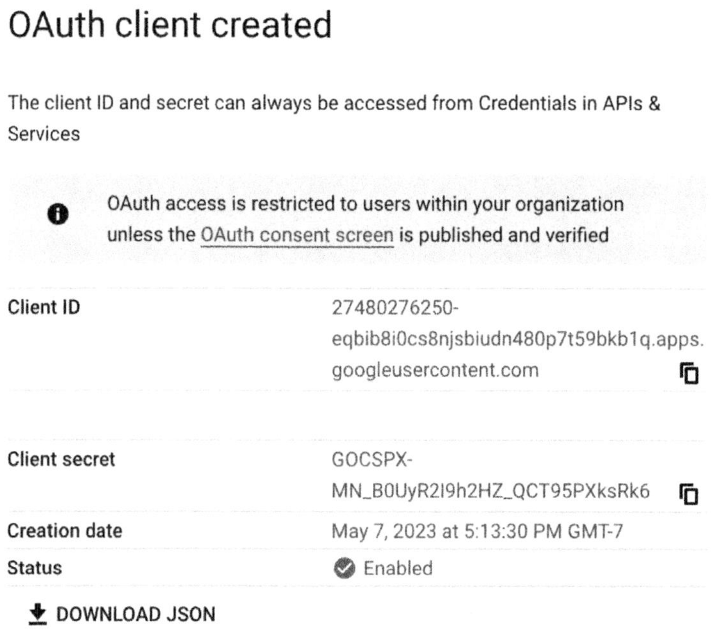

## OAuth client created

The client ID and secret can always be accessed from Credentials in APIs & Services

ℹ  OAuth access is restricted to users within your organization unless the OAuth consent screen is published and verified

| | |
|---|---|
| Client ID | 27480276250-eqbib8i0cs8njsbiudn480p7t59bkb1q.apps.googleusercontent.com |
| Client secret | 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 |
| Creation date | May 7, 2023 at 5:13:30 PM GMT-7 |
| Status | ✅ Enabled |

⬇ DOWNLOAD JSON

Figure 16.13 – OAuth client created

Next, we'll set up the configuration on the Grafana side. Edit `grafana.ini`, making sure to comment out any other auth.* sections, and add the following lines:

```
[auth.google]
enabled = true
client_id = 27480276250-
    laq6jp99jqbqgfiked0d7kq3js9umld7.apps.googleusercontent.com
client_secret = eFUVWK2EgnqXHUcy-FDendOP
scopes = https://www.googleapis.com/auth/userinfo.profile
    https://www.googleapis.com/auth/userinfo.email
auth_url = https://accounts.google.com/o/oauth2/auth
token_url = https://accounts.google.com/o/oauth2/token
allowed_domains =
allow_sign_up = true
```

Fill in your own client ID and client secret. If you want new users to be able to self-register with Google OAuth, make sure `allow_sign_up` is set to `true`. Restart your Grafana server; you should now have a Google sign-in option on your Grafana startup screen:

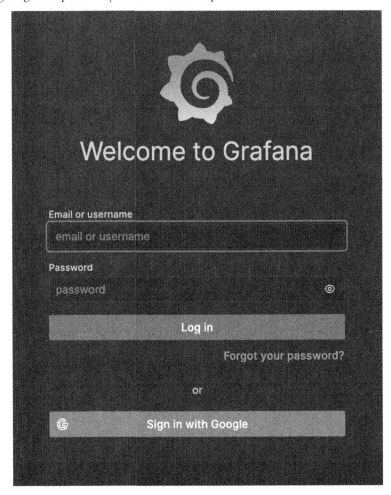

Figure 16.14 – Grafana – Sign in with Google

Finally, we'll look at authentication with Okta, a full-service provider that is well-known for providing SSO solutions.

## Authenticating with Okta

Okta is a well-known authentication provider for enterprises. The process is very similar to Google, but it only requires you to register your application with Okta to generate a client ID and secret. To generate the appropriate secrets, you'll need to sign up for a developer account. Once you've logged into your Okta developer account, follow these instructions:

1.  From the **Dashboard** area, open **Applications**, select **Applications**, and click on **Create App Integration**:

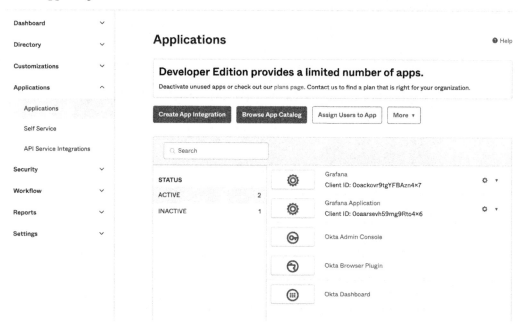

Figure 16.15 – Okta – the Applications menu

2. Select **OIDC – OpenID Connect** for **Sign-in method** and **Web Application** for **Application type**, then click **Next**:

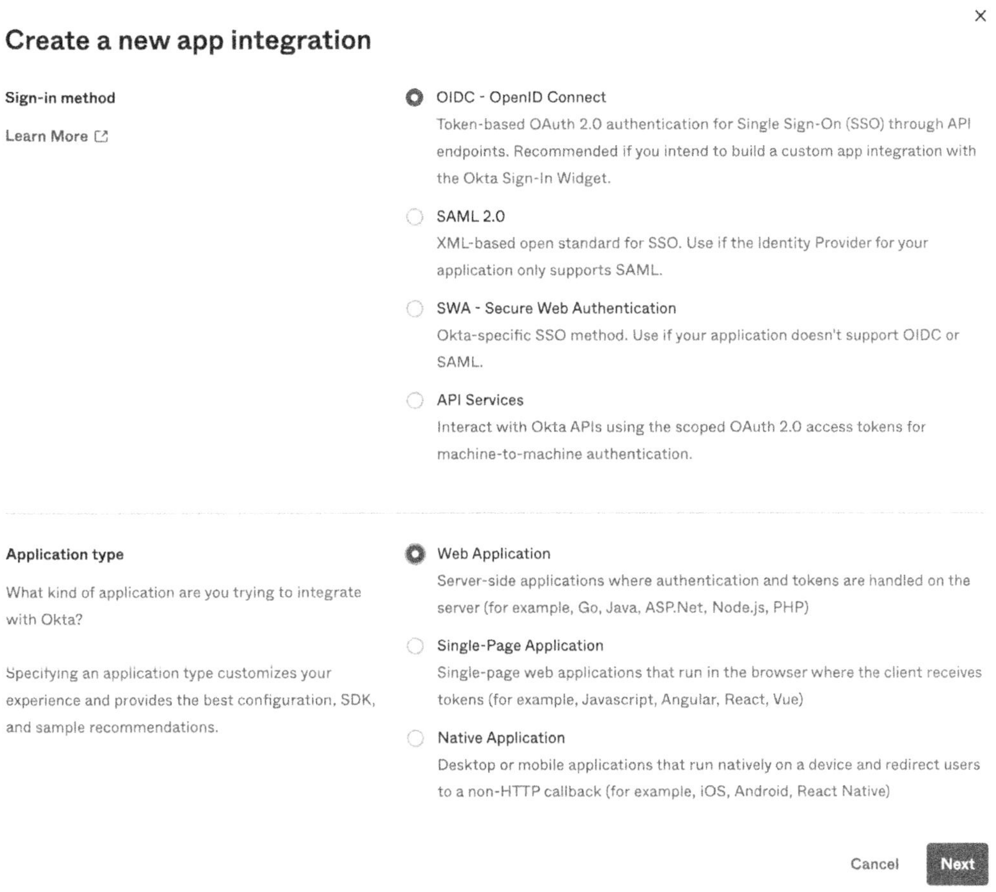

## Create a new app integration

×

| | |
|---|---|
| **Sign-in method** | ⦿ OIDC - OpenID Connect |
| Learn More ↗ | Token-based OAuth 2.0 authentication for Single Sign-On (SSO) through API endpoints. Recommended if you intend to build a custom app integration with the Okta Sign-In Widget. |
| | ○ SAML 2.0 |
| | XML-based open standard for SSO. Use if the Identity Provider for your application only supports SAML. |
| | ○ SWA - Secure Web Authentication |
| | Okta-specific SSO method. Use if your application doesn't support OIDC or SAML. |
| | ○ API Services |
| | Interact with Okta APIs using the scoped OAuth 2.0 access tokens for machine-to-machine authentication. |

| | |
|---|---|
| **Application type** | ⦿ Web Application |
| What kind of application are you trying to integrate with Okta? | Server-side applications where authentication and tokens are handled on the server (for example, Go, Java, ASP.Net, Node.js, PHP) |
| | ○ Single-Page Application |
| Specifying an application type customizes your experience and provides the best configuration, SDK, and sample recommendations. | Single-page web applications that run in the browser where the client receives tokens (for example, Javascript, Angular, React, Vue) |
| | ○ Native Application |
| | Desktop or mobile applications that run natively on a device and redirect users to a non-HTTP callback (for example, iOS, Android, React Native) |

Cancel    Next

Figure 16.16 – New app integration settings

3. On the **New Web App Integration** form, under **General Settings**, fill in the following fields and click **Done**:

- **App integration name**: `Grafana`
- **Sign-in redirect URIs**: `http://localhost:3000/login/okta`

- **Sign-out redirect URIs**: `http://localhost:3000:`

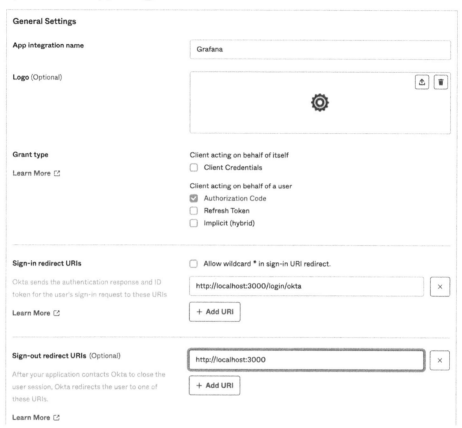

Figure 16.17 – New Web App Integration – General Settings

4.   Under **Trusted Origins**, set **Base URIs** to `http://localhost:3000:`

Figure 16.18 – App integration – Trusted Origins

5.   Finally, under **Assignments**, set **Allow everyone in your organization to access** for **Controlled access** and accept the recommended defaults for **Enable immediate access**. Click **Save** to continue:

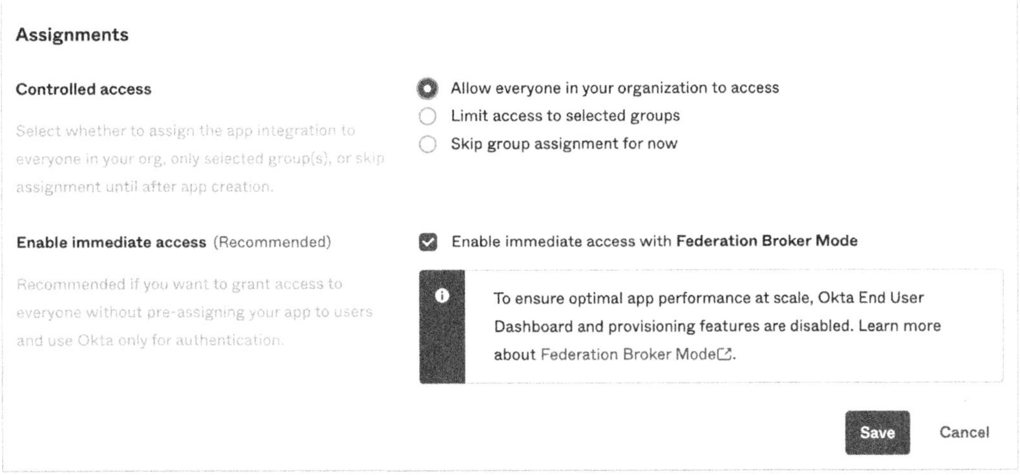

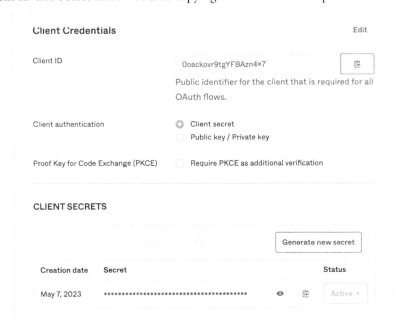

Figure 16.19 – App integration – Assignments

6.   On the next page, on the **General Settings** tab, you'll find a **Client Credentials** box with both **Client ID** and **Secret** fields. You'll be copying them in the next step:

Figure 16.20 – Okta client ID and secret

7.  Add the following configuration lines to your `grafana.ini` file (making sure to comment out any other auth.* sections):

```
[auth.okta]
name = Okta
icon = okta
enabled = true
allow_sign_up = true
client_id = 0oackq4tx6ivAX4w04x7
client_secret = vwYpfG6OW-Bmm3d9b-eRVsPRZA0v0xK_FCukKXBK
scopes = openid profile email groups
auth_url = https://dev-670643.okta.com/oauth2/v1/authorize
token_url = https://dev-670643.okta.com/oauth2/v1/token
api_url = https://dev-670643.okta.com/oauth2/v1/userinfo
allowed_domains =
allowed_groups =
role_attribute_path =
```

8.  You'll need to add your client ID and secret from the previous step. You'll also need to include your Okta tenant ID under `auth_url`, `token_url`, and `api_url`. Typically, this can be found at your Okta URL: `https://<tenant-id>.okta.com/`.

9.  Restart your Grafana service; you should have the option to sign in with Okta on the Grafana login screen:

Figure 16.21 – Grafana – Sign in with Okta

10. If you are currently logged into Okta, clicking on **Sign in with Okta** will sign you into Grafana.

That completes our tour of three popular OAuth 2 providers. Well done! This is by no means the full list of authentication services Grafana integrates with. You'll want to check out the Grafana documentation for the full list.

## Summary

We certainly covered a lot of ground in this chapter. First, we learned how to install and configure an OpenLDAP server and integrate it with Grafana to provide authentication lookup. Then, we walked through the process of registering Grafana with three different OAuth 2 providers: GitHub, Google, and Okta. If you want full control of all aspects of user lookup for authentication, then LDAP is certainly a viable solution. If you'd rather have authentication handled securely by a third-party provider, especially if it integrates with other user management systems in your organization, then an external OAuth provider is probably a better solution.

Yet, after all of this, we have only touched on a few of the ever-growing number of authentication options available for Grafana, so consult the Grafana documentation for more details.

In this chapter, we took a small step in integrating Grafana authentication with external cloud services. In the next (and final) chapter, *Chapter 17, Cloud Monitoring AWS, Azure, and GCP*, we will make a giant leap into the cloud. We will configure Grafana data sources to monitor cloud services, such as Amazon CloudWatch and Google Cloud Monitoring. We'll also tackle the process of setting up your cloud account to work with Grafana, as well as installing data sources and dashboards that are specially designed to query Amazon AWS metrics and logging. If you have any services running in the cloud, you should check this chapter out!

# 17

# Cloud Monitoring AWS, Azure, and GCP

In this final chapter of *Learn Grafana 10.x*, we'll take a brief look at Grafana's cloud integration capabilities. Grafana treats cloud monitoring as just another data source, so adding monitoring features to your cloud deployments is not much more than filling in a few fields in a data source configuration. Most of the work lies on the provider side as you will need to spend some time on cloud console pages registering applications and generating authentication credentials.

Once you have completed the walk-throughs for each cloud provider, you should have a good idea of how to navigate parts of a cloud services management console. You will be able to create the policies, service accounts, and credentials necessary to link Grafana with cloud providers. Armed with these credentials, you should have no trouble configuring future cloud monitoring data sources.

Then, once you have access to a vast variety of cloud monitoring data resources and you start to put monitor dashboards together, you will start gaining insights into how your cloud services are performing. Over time, you may even want to establish Grafana alerts, similar to the ones we studied in *Chapter 12, Monitoring Data Streams with Grafana Alerts*.

It's beyond the scope of this book to cover cloud technology, nor does it allow for a survey of all cloud platforms in the industry. We will, however, review offerings from the three largest cloud providers – that is, Amazon, Microsoft, and Google.

> **Note**
> The workflows and user experiences depicted in this chapter were accurate at the time of writing, but the cloud space is fast-moving and ever-changing, so things may look a little different by the time you get your hands on this book. Check with Grafana and your cloud provider for the most current information.

We'll assume that, before proceeding with this chapter, you have already established accounts with one or more of these cloud service providers and that you also have the requisite administrator permissions to provision resources and manage user accounts, application registries, and access roles.

The following topics will be covered in this chapter:

- Configuring an AWS CloudWatch data source
- Configuring a Microsoft Azure Monitor data source
- Configuring a GCM data source

With this in mind, let's get started with one of the first big cloud players: **Amazon Web Services** (**AWS**).

## Configuring an AWS CloudWatch data source

This section assumes that you have an AWS account with administrative privileges. You'll also need to be logged into the **AWS Management Console** so that you can work through these steps. The basic process is straightforward:

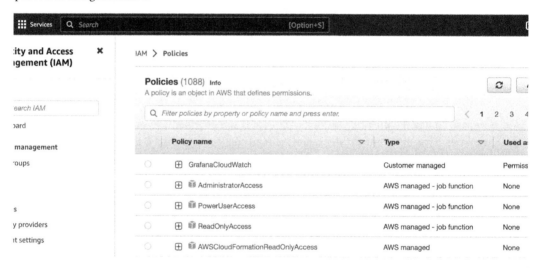

Figure 17.1 – AWS IAM service

We will be creating a policy that allows Grafana to use the AWS CloudWatch API to get metrics data. Grafana has helpfully supplied a basic set of policies to help us access both CloudWatch metrics and logs. Here's the JSON version of the policy:

```json
{
    "Version": "2012-10-17",
    "Statement": [
        {
            "Sid": "AllowReadingMetricsFromCloudWatch",
            "Effect": "Allow",
            "Action": [
```

```
                "cloudwatch:DescribeAlarmsForMetric",
                "cloudwatch:DescribeAlarmHistory",
                "cloudwatch:DescribeAlarms",
                "cloudwatch:ListMetrics",
                "cloudwatch:GetMetricData",
                "cloudwatch:GetInsightRuleReport"
            ],
            "Resource": "*"
        },
        {
            "Sid": "AllowReadingLogsFromCloudWatch",
            "Effect": "Allow",
            "Action": [
                "logs:DescribeLogGroups",
                "logs:GetLogGroupFields",
                "logs:StartQuery",
                "logs:StopQuery",
                "logs:GetQueryResults",
                "logs:GetLogEvents"
            ],
            "Resource": "*"
        },
        {
            "Sid": "AllowReadingTagsInstancesRegionsFromEC2",
            "Effect": "Allow",
            "Action": [
                "ec2:DescribeTags",
                "ec2:DescribeInstances",
                "ec2:DescribeRegions"
            ],
            "Resource": "*"
        },
        {
            "Sid": "AllowReadingResourcesForTags",
            "Effect": "Allow",
            "Action": "tag:GetResources",
            "Resource": "*"
        }
    ]
}
```

To create the policy, follow these steps:

1.  Select **Policies** from the left-hand menu and click **Create policy**:

Figure 17.2 – Create policy

2.  On the **Create policy** page, select the **JSON** tab and replace the contents of the textbox with the preceding JSON blob of code.

3.  Click **Review policy**. If the JSON text was entered correctly, you should now see three services affected by the policy: **CloudWatch**, **EC2**, and **Resource Group Tagging**. Go ahead and name your policy something descriptive, such as `GrafanaCloudWatch`:

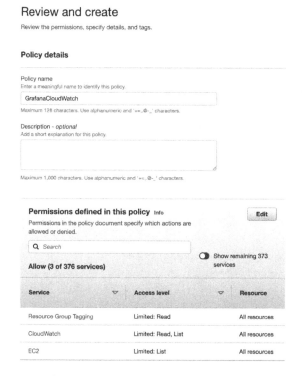

Figure 17.3 – Reviewing policy permissions

4.  Click **Create policy** to confirm the policy's creation.

You should now see a banner confirming the policy's creation.

## Creating the user

Now that you've created a policy, you will need to assign the policy to a user. We'll create a specific user for this policy, named grafana:

1.  From the IAM service page, select **Users** from the left-hand side menu and click **Add user**.

2.  On the **Add user** page, set the following details and click **Next** to continue:

    • Select **User details** | **User name**: grafana

    • Select **AWS access type** | **Access type**: **Programmatic access**:

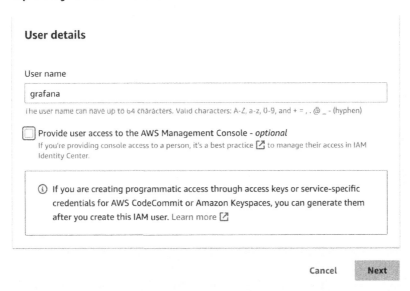

Figure 17.4 – User details

3.  On the **Set permissions** page, select **Attach existing policies directly**.

4.  Type grafana into the search box to find the **GrafanaCloudWatch** policy and check it. Click **Next** to continue.

5.   Confirm the following and then click **Create user** to proceed:

- **User details** | **User name**: `grafana`
- **Permissions summary** | **Name**: **GrafanaCloudWatch**
- **Permissions summary** | **Type**: **Customer managed**
- **Permissions summary** | **Used as**: **Permissions policy**:

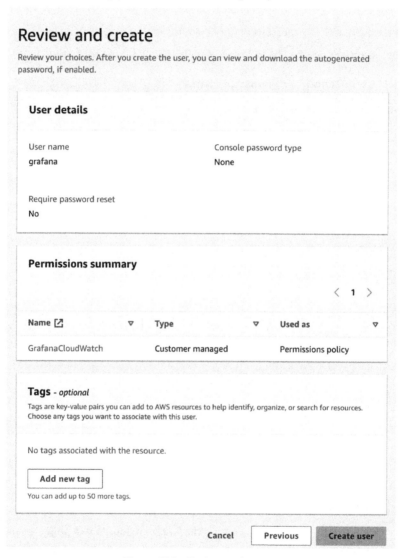

Figure 17.5 – Review and create

If you missed the part where we downloaded the credentials CSV file, don't worry. You can always generate a new one (illustrated as follows):

1. From the **Identity and Access Management (IAM)** left-hand menu, select **Users**.

2. Click on the **grafana** user to load the **Summary** page.

3. Select the **Security credentials** tab.

4. Under **Access keys**, click **Create access key** to generate a new credential.

5. From the **Access key best practices & alternatives** page, select **Application running outside AWS** and click **Next** to continue:

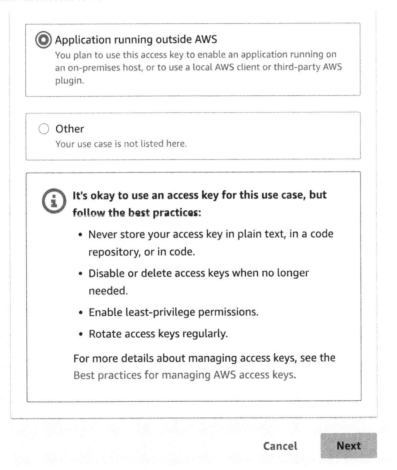

Figure 17.6 – Selecting an application running outside AWS for the access key

6.  Click **Download .csv file** to save the credentials file, as illustrated here:

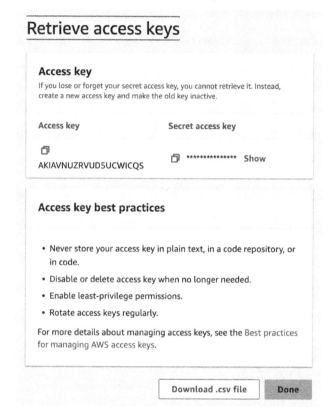

Figure 17.7 – Retrieve access keys

Now that you have a CSV file containing the necessary credentials, you should have everything you need to configure our CloudWatch data source.

## Configuring a new Grafana connection for AWS CloudWatch

Once you have configured AWS with a user (grafana) with the proper policy (**GrafanaCloudWatch**), you'll need to set up a CloudWatch data source within Grafana so that you can gather metrics via the CloudWatch API:

1.  We will use a docker-compose.yml file with the following contents to start up a Grafana server:

    ```
    services:
      grafana:
    ```

```
image: "grafana/grafana:latest"
ports:
  - "3000:3000"
volumes:
  - "${PWD-.}/grafana:/var/lib/grafana"
```

2.  Start up the `grafana` service by running the following command:

    ```
    % docker-compose up -d --pull missing grafana
    ```

3.  Under **Connections** on the main menu, select **Add new connection**.

4.  Search for `CloudWatch` and select it.

5.  Click on **Add new data source**.

6.  You have a couple of options regarding how to configure the data source with the credentials for the Grafana user:

    *   Launch Grafana with the `AWS_ACCESS_KEY_ID` and `AWS_SECRET_ACCESS_KEY` environment variables

    *   Load a credentials file located in `~/.aws/credentials`

    *   Hardcode the credentials into the data source itself

    In this case, we are going with the third option. In a production setting, you probably want to manage the user credentials so that you can rotate them regularly, without having to reconfigure the data source all the time. However, we are going with the easy path for now, so we'll just fill in the fields from our CSV file.

7.  Fill in the fields as follows:

    *   **Authentication Provider**: **Access & secret key**

    *   **Access Key ID**: (from the CSV file)

    *   **Secret access key**: (from the CSV file)

    For the **Default** region, you'll want to check what region you've specified for CloudWatch. Go to the **CloudWatch** service from **Management Console** and check the pull-down menu at the top right, between the **User** and **Support** menus. It should indicate a geographic region when you select the menu. The bold selection indicates your default region. In our case, I have set **Default Region** to **us-east-2**:

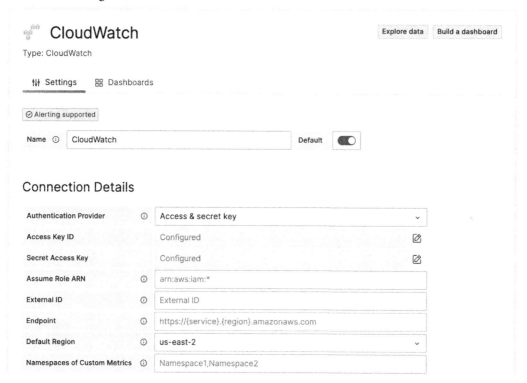

Figure 17.8 – CloudWatch data source

8.   Click **Save & test**. If everything worked as planned, you should see a green **Data source is working** indicator:

Figure 17.9 – CloudWatch data source access confirmation

From here, you can start monitoring CloudWatch services by creating a dashboard panel and selecting your CloudWatch data source in the query.

To get you started, the data source configuration page includes a **Dashboards** tab (as depicted in *Figure 17.8*), where you can download sample dashboards to monitor several popular Amazon AWS services, including the following:

- Amazon EC2
- Amazon EBS
- AWS Lambda
- Amazon RDS
- CloudWatch Logs

Each dashboard you download contains panels specifically tailored to monitor the service in question. To get started, simply select your data source from the **Data source** template variable dropdown. Try them out!

Now, let's move on and look at our next cloud provider: Microsoft and its Azure cloud service.

## Configuring a Microsoft Azure Monitor data source

The next stop in our tour of the big cloud providers takes us to Microsoft Azure. The Azure Monitor data source supports four different services:

- **Azure Monitor**
- **Azure Log Analytics**
- **Application Insights**
- **Application Insights Analytics**

Fortunately, you can configure Azure to allow the data source to access all four services.

As you may recall from *Chapter 16, Authenticating Grafana Logins Using LDAP or OAuth 2 Providers*, to generate OAuth2 client IDs and secrets, we needed to register our Grafana server as an *application* with the cloud service. The process for Microsoft Azure is very similar:

1. Copy your **Tenant ID** from **Microsoft Entra ID**.
2. Register a new application for the Grafana data source and establish its proper role.
3. Generate a **Client ID** value and secret for authentication from Grafana.
4. Create and configure the Azure Monitor Grafana connection with the **Tenant ID** and **Client** credentials.

Start by creating or signing into your Microsoft Azure account. You'll also need to create a subscription – the free **Basic level** subscription is sufficient for this tutorial. We'll start from the Azure portal.

## Registering the Grafana application

The first task is to register a new application so that we'll be able to generate the application client ID and secret. Under **Azure Services**, go to **Microsoft Entra ID**. Then, follow these steps:

1. The first thing you will notice is the **Tenant ID** value for **Default Directory**. Copy the ID and save it somewhere for later use. You can even paste it into the Azure Monitor data source if you want to skip ahead.

2. From the left-hand menu, select **App registrations** and click **+ New Registration**.

3. Fill in the following details (see the following screenshot):

   - **Name**: Grafana

   - Select **Accounts in this organizational directory only (Default Directory only - Single tenant)**

   - **Redirect URI**: **Web** | http://localhost:3000

4. Click **Register** to complete the registration process:

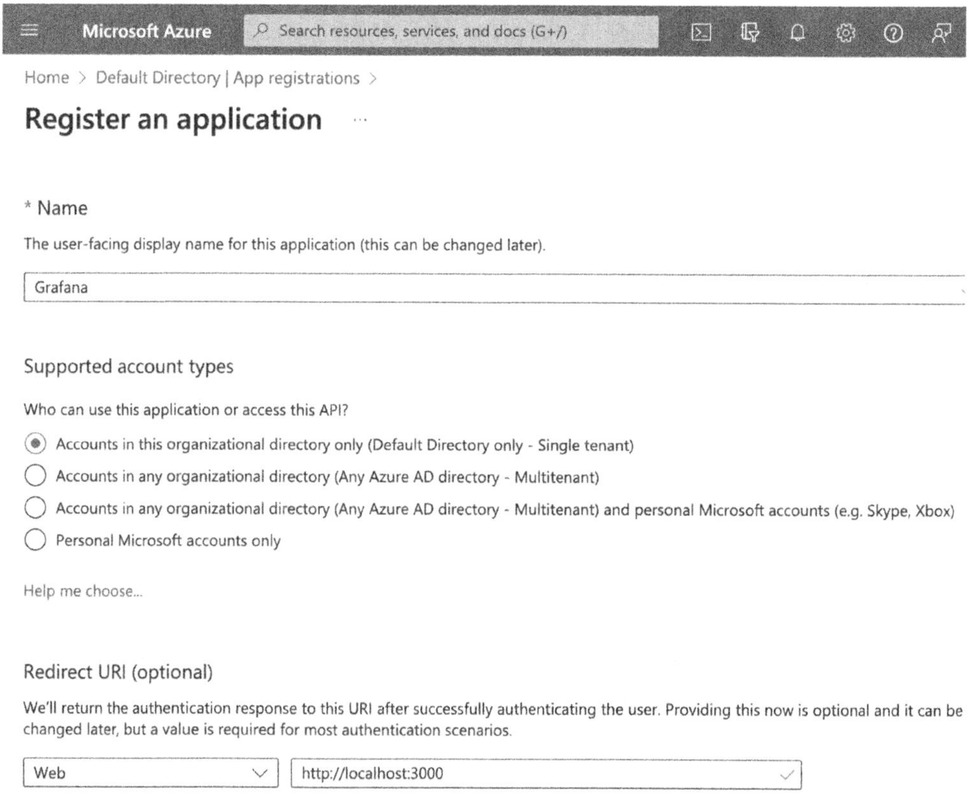

Figure 17.10 – Azure application registration

**Redirect URI** is the link back to the application after authentication. Unlike the examples in *Chapter 16, Authenticating Grafana Logins Using LDAP or OAuth 2 Providers*, we aren't authenticating a user of Grafana; here, we are authenticating Grafana as an application with Azure.

## Setting the application role

Once we have an application, we'll need to set the role for it. This will dictate what level of access the data source can have. We'll set our permissions at the subscription level as that's the easiest way to do things. Follow these steps:

1. Go to the Azure portal and search for `Subscriptions`.

2. Click on the appropriate subscription. In my case, it's called **Azure Subscription 1**.

3. Select **Access control (IAM)**.

4. Click + **Add** and, from the drop-down menu, select **Add role assignment**:

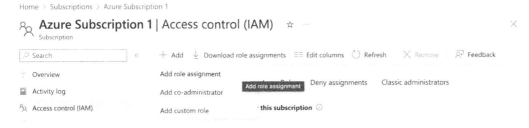

Figure 17.11 – Add role assignment

5. Under the **Role** tab on the **Add role assignment** page, type `reader` into the search box and select **Reader** from the displayed list of roles. Click **Next** to continue to the **Members** tab:

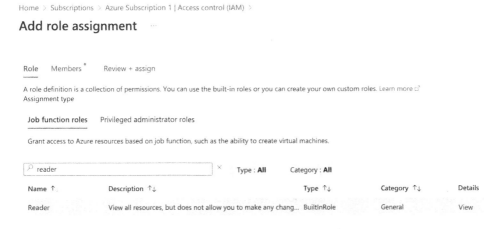

Figure 17.12 – Assigning the Reader role

6. On the **Members** tab, confirm that **Selected role** is **Reader**. Next to **Members**, click + **Select members**.

7. Under **Select**, in the search box, type grafana to find the registered **Grafana** application, and click **Select** to confirm this:

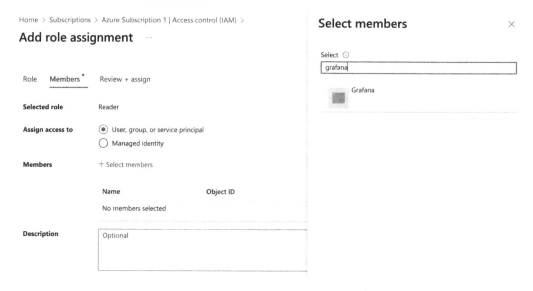

Figure 17.13 – Adding the Grafana member

8. Click **Review + Assign** to add Grafana as **Reader**.

If you haven't already captured the tenant ID and client ID, you can find them by going back to **Home | Microsoft Entra ID** and selecting **App registrations**. Clicking on your registered **Grafana** application should reveal both the **Directory (tenant) ID** and the **Application (client) ID** details. We only need to generate our application client secret and we'll be almost done!

## Generating application secrets

In much the same way as we did in *Chapter 16*, *Authenticating Grafana Logins Using LDAP or OAuth 2 Providers*, we're going to generate an application client secret. Follow these steps:

1. Make sure you're on your Grafana **Overview** page, which you can reach via **Home | App Registrations**.

2. From the left-hand menu, select **Certificates & secrets**.

3. Under **Client secrets**, click + **New client secret**.

4. Fill out the form as follows and click **Add** (see the following screenshot):

- **Description**: `Grafana Client Secret`

- **Expires: Recommended 180 days (6 months)**:

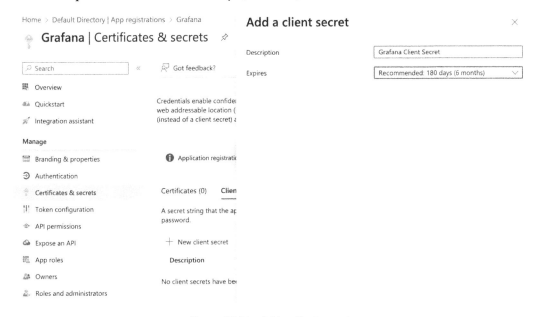

Figure 17.14 – Add a client secret

5. Click the copy icon next to the Grafana client secret's **Value** field for the generated key and paste it somewhere where you can access it for our next task.

You should now have the requisite information to begin configuring an Azure Monitor data source.

## Configuring a new Grafana connection for Azure Monitor

Gather the generated credentials and get ready to connect Grafana to Microsoft Azure Monitor. You did copy your **Tenant ID**, **Application** (client) **ID**, and **Client secret**, right?

1. Return to Grafana and, under **Connections**, select **Add new connection**.

2. Search for and select **Azure Monitor** and fill in the following details:

- **Name**: `Azure Monitor`

- **Azure Cloud: Azure**

- **Directory (tenant) ID**: `<Tenant_ID>`

- **Application (client) ID**: `<Application_ID>`

- **Client Secret:** `<Client Secret>`

3.    Click **Load subscriptions** and select the appropriate subscription from the menu.

> **Note**
>
> If you get an error, go back to **Certificates & secrets** and confirm that you copied **Value** for the Grafana client secret, not the secret ID.

At this point, you should be able to click **Save & test** and get an indication of which services the data source was able to contact. Don't be alarmed by the error message – we will enable the failed services momentarily:

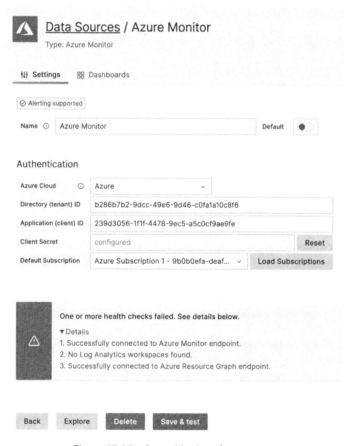

Figure 17.15 – Azure Monitor data source

The service that it's complaining about in check #2 is for Azure Log Analytics. To pass all the checks, we need to establish a Log Analytics workspace. **Azure Log Analytics**, like **Google Cloud Monitoring**, allows you to query and perform analytics on your application cloud logs.

# Configuring Azure Log Analytics

To proceed with the rest of this exercise, you'll need to create a Log Analytics workspace if you don't already have one. This process is relatively straightforward but it will involve provisioning some Azure resources, which may potentially cause you to incur additional costs, so feel free to skip this section if that is a concern.

I am including it to complete the Azure data source provisioning section; it will prove useful if you have an interest in querying and analyzing Azure cloud application log data. To proceed, follow these steps:

1. From the Azure portal, search for or select **Log Analytics Workspaces**.

2. Click + **Create** to add a new workspace.

3. Fill in the following details (see the following screenshot):

   - **Project details**:

     - **Subscription**: Select a subscription from the drop-down menu

     - **Resource group**: Create a new group or select one from the drop-down menu

   - **Instance details**:

     - **Name**: Create a name for the provisioned instance

     - **Region**: Select a region from the dropdown:

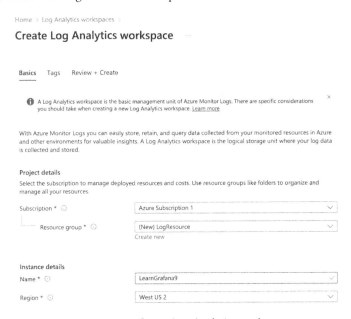

Figure 17.16 – Create Log Analytics workspace

4.  Click **Review + Create**; then, after validation, click **Create** to deploy the Log Analytics workspace. The final deployment should look something like this:

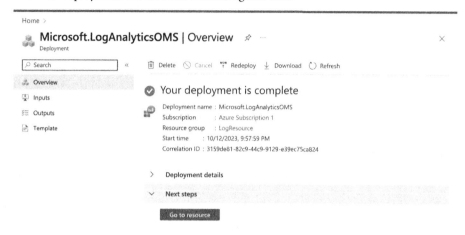

Figure 17.17 – Azure Log Analytics deployment

You should now be able to return to your **Azure Monitor** data source and click **Save & Test** to confirm the configuration for Azure Log Analytics. It should now give you a green success indicator:

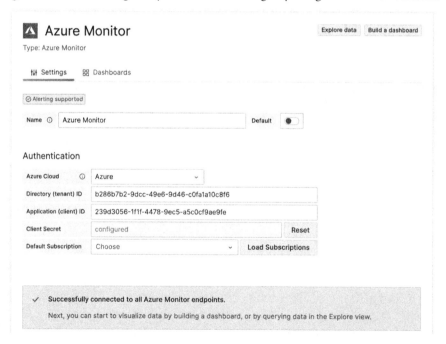

Figure 17.18 – Full Azure data source support

From here, you can go to the **Dashboards** tab to import various dashboards for monitoring your Azure cloud instance. Among the sample dashboards are the following options:

- **Azure / Alert Consumption**
- **Azure / Insights / Applications**
- **Azure / Insights / Applications Test Availability Geo Map**
- **Azure / Insights / Cosmos DB**
- **Azure / Insights / Data Explorer Clusters**
- **Azure / Insights / Key vaults**
- **Azure / Insights / Networks**
- **Azure / Insights / SQL Database**
- **Azure / Insights / Storage Accounts**
- **Azure / Insights / Virtual Machines by Resource Group**
- **Azure / Insights / Virtual Machines by Workspace**
- **Azure / Resources Overview**

If you have a new Azure cloud instance, you probably won't have many or even most of these services installed to monitor on one of the sample dashboards. However, the **Resources Overview** dashboard should be functional even with a minimal subscription.

Let's move on to our last cloud provider: **Google Cloud Platform** (**GCP**). We'll be connecting to **Google Cloud Monitoring** (**GCM**), Google Cloud's system for monitoring, alerting, and logging in GCP. The Grafana data source provides example dashboards for monitoring Google Cloud Functions, **Google Cloud Environment** (**GCE**) VMs, Cloud SQL, and more.

## Configuring a GCM data source

Our last stop on our tour of cloud providers is GCP and its GCM service. We'll go through the procedure to connect the GCM data source. The process for connecting a local data source with GCM involves only a few steps:

1. Enable the relevant monitoring APIs.
2. Create a service account with appropriate permissions.
3. Generate a **JSON Web Token** (**JWT**).
4. Load the JWT into the GCM data source configuration.

To get started, log in to your Google Cloud console and select the appropriate project. It is in this project that we'll define our service account. This will be the only one our data source can access. You will need to create a separate data source for each GCP project you want to monitor.

## Enabling a Google Cloud API

After selecting your project, use the left-hand menu to navigate to **APIs & Services**. Then, follow these steps:

1. Select + **Enable APIs and Services**.
2. Use the search box to locate **Stackdriver Monitoring API** and then select it.
3. Enable the API.
4. Go back to the **APIs & Services** dashboard and, again, select + **Enable APIs and Services**.
5. This time, search for `Cloud Resource Manager API` and select it.
6. Enable the API.

Once you have enabled the API, you should be able to create a service account with the necessary permissions to access it.

## Creating a Google service account

Go back to the **APIs & Services** dashboard and navigate to **Credentials**. Follow these steps:

1. Click + **CREATE CREDENTIALS** and select **Service account** from the drop-down menu:

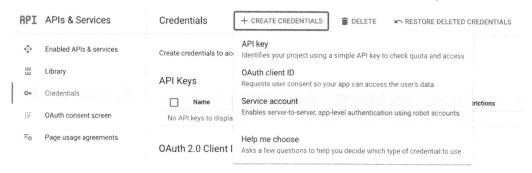

Figure 17.19 – Google Cloud – creating a service account

2. Fill in the following fields (fill them in at your discretion) and click **CREATE AND CONTINUE** (see the following screenshot):

   • **Service account name**: Grafana Data Source

- **Service account description**: `Service account for Grafana Stackdriver data source` (or something similarly descriptive):

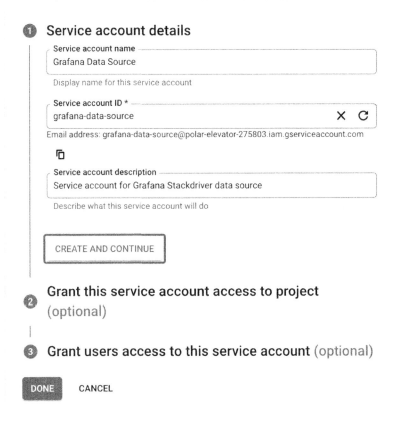

Figure 17.20 – Specifying service account details

3. Now, add the **Monitoring Viewer** role, using the search box to locate it, and then click **Continue**.

4. Skip the optional **Grant users access to this service account** step and click **Done**.

5.  To create the necessary credentials, go to the **Credentials** page. Under **Service accounts**, you should see your new service account. Click on it to go to the **Service account details** page:

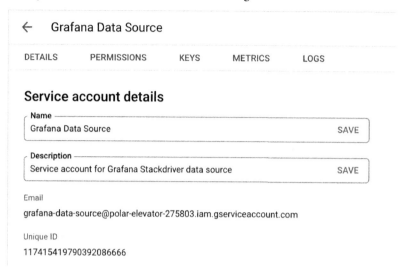

Figure 17.21 – Service account details

6.  Click on the **KEYS** tab, click on **ADD KEY**, and select **Create new key**:

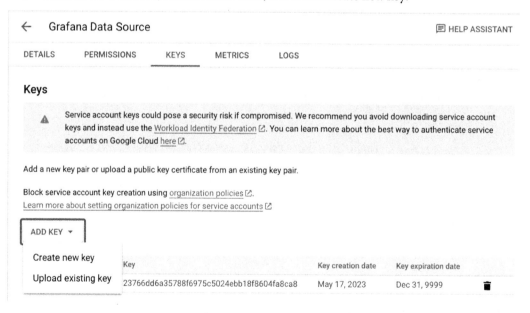

Figure 17.22 – Create new key

7. Leave **JSON** selected and click **CREATE**. You'll get a confirmation popup that specifies the name of the JWT key file; a JSON file will be downloaded:

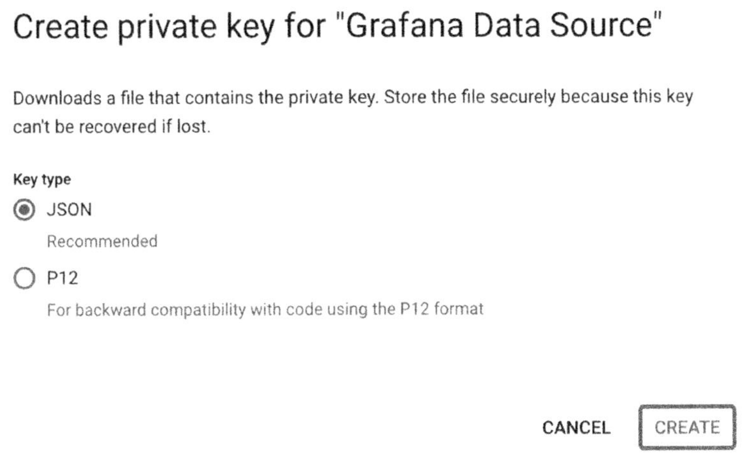

## Create private key for "Grafana Data Source"

Downloads a file that contains the private key. Store the file securely because this key can't be recovered if lost.

**Key type**

◉ JSON
   Recommended

○ P12
   For backward compatibility with code using the P12 format

CANCEL     | CREATE |

Figure 17.23 – JSON key type

Locate the JSON file containing your credentials for the next steps.

## Configuring a new Grafana connection for GCM

Now that you have the necessary JWT credentials, there's not much more involved. Back in Grafana, go to **Connections** | **Add new connection** and follow these steps:

1. Search for and select **Google Cloud Monitoring**.

2. Click **Add new data source**.

3. Fill in the following details:

   - **Name**: `Google Cloud Monitoring`

   - **Authentication** | **Authentication Type**: **Google JWT File**

4. Drop your JSON JWT file into **Drop the Google JWT file here**.

5. If the key was parsed correctly, you should see the contents of **Project**, **Client Email**, and **Token URI**.

6.  Click **Save & Test** to confirm that you have a valid connection to Google Cloud:

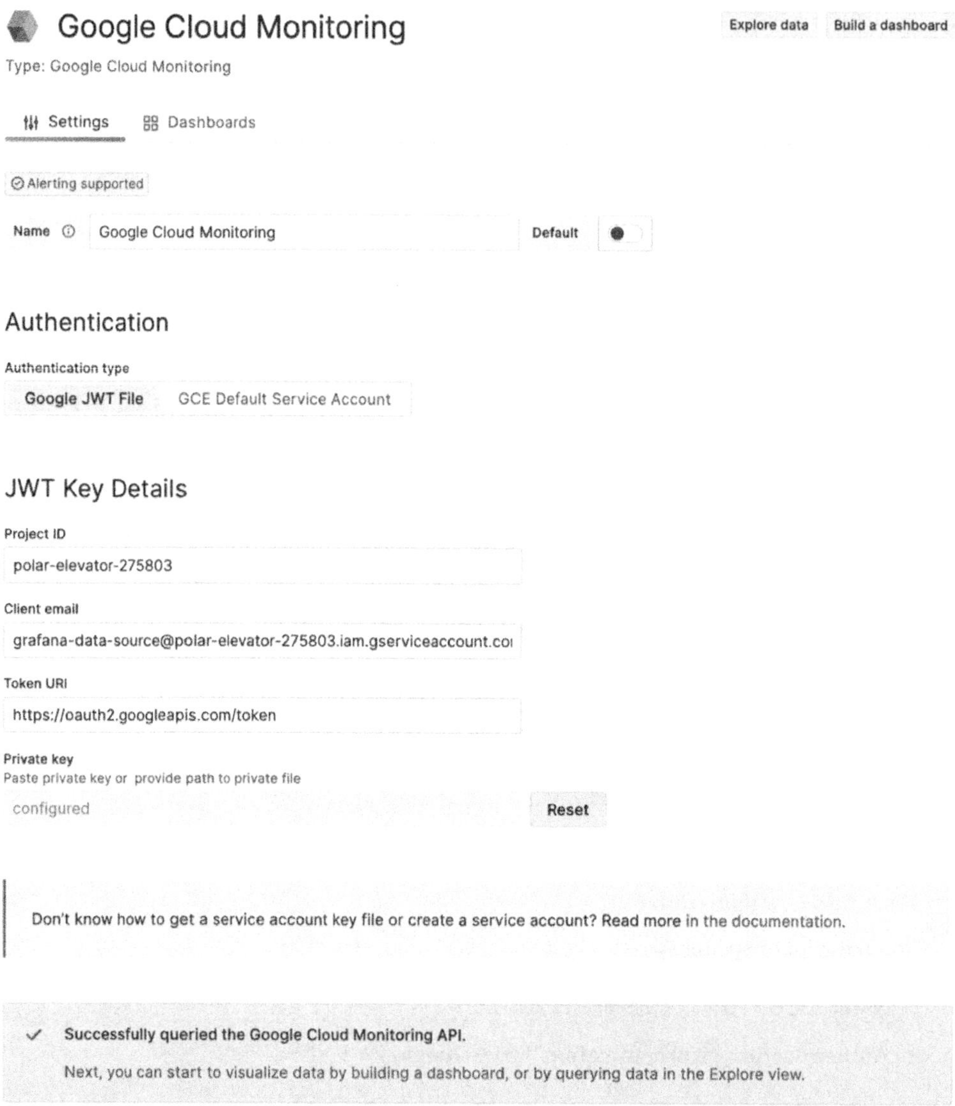

Figure 17.24 – GCM data source

And we're done! From here, you should check the **Dashboards** tab to see the set of dashboards available for import. Here is a list of sample dashboards provided with the GCM data source:

- **Data Processing Monitoring**
- **Cloud Functions Monitoring**
- **GCE VM Instance Monitoring**
- **GKE Prometheus Pod/Node Monitoring**
- **Firewall Insights Monitoring**
- **GCE Network Monitoring**
- **HTTP/S LB Backend Services**
- **HTTP/S GCP Load Balancer Monitoring**
- **Network TCP Load Balancer Monitoring**
- **MicroService Monitoring**
- **Cloud Storage Monitoring**
- **Cloud SQL Monitoring**
- **Cloud SQL(MySQL) Monitoring**

While you may not have many of the services installed, you can see that many commonly used Google services are covered by these dashboards. As with the previous data sources, these sample dashboards can provide valuable insights into the creation of dashboards. Open them up, examine how the queries are set up, step through how the graph is styled, then copy it and make it yours. Good luck!

## Summary

In this chapter, we covered Grafana integrations for three of the world's biggest cloud providers. Grafana currently provides built-in data sources for Amazon CloudWatch, Azure Monitor Logs, and Google Cloud Monitoring. While each service can have its own interfaces of varying complexity, the procedures are remarkably similar. They consist mainly of registering an application (or application service account), assigning a role to enable or restrict the application permissions, and generating a client ID and secret. Once you have the secrets, it's only a matter of plugging them into the data source.

Not only have we reached the end of this chapter, but we've reached the end of this book! I hope you found the previous chapters as informative and enjoyable to read as it was for me to write them. By the time you read this, Grafana 10 will have undoubtedly experienced several feature releases beyond the initial rollout and will only continue to grow in terms of its versatility. May your understanding grow as well. Good luck!

# Index

## Symbols

# Other Books You May Enjoy

If you enjoyed this book, you may be interested in these other books by Packt:

**Alteryx Designer Cookbook**

Alberto Guisande

ISBN: 9781804615089

- Speed up the cleansing, data preparing, and shaping process
- Perform operations and transformations on the data to suit your needs
- Blend different types of data sources for analysis
- Pivot and un-pivot the data for easy manipulation
- Perform aggregations and calculations on the data
- Encapsulate reusable logic into macros
- Develop high-quality, data-driven reports to improve consistency

**Splunk 9.x Enterprise Certified Admin Guide**

Srikanth Yarlagadda

ISBN: 9781803230238

- Explore Splunk Enterprise 9.x features and usage
- Install, configure, and manage licenses and users for Splunk
- Create and manage indexes for data storage
- Explore Splunk configuration files, their precedence, and troubleshooting
- Manage forwarders and source data into Splunk from various resources
- Parse and transform data to make it easy to use
- Extract fields from data at search and index time for data analysis
- Engage with mock exam questions to simulate the Splunk admin exam

## Packt is searching for authors like you

If you're interested in becoming an author for Packt, please visit `authors.packtpub.com` and apply today. We have worked with thousands of developers and tech professionals, just like you, to help them share their insight with the global tech community. You can make a general application, apply for a specific hot topic that we are recruiting an author for, or submit your own idea.

## Share Your Thoughts

Now you've finished *Learn Grafana 10.x*, we'd love to hear your thoughts! Scan the QR code below to go straight to the Amazon review page for this book and share your feedback or leave a review on the site that you purchased it from.

https://packt.link/r/1-803-23108-4

Your review is important to us and the tech community and will help us make sure we're delivering excellent quality content.

# Download a free PDF copy of this book

Thanks for purchasing this book!

Do you like to read on the go but are unable to carry your print books everywhere?

Is your eBook purchase not compatible with the device of your choice?

Don't worry, now with every Packt book you get a DRM-free PDF version of that book at no cost.

Read anywhere, any place, on any device. Search, copy, and paste code from your favorite technical books directly into your application.

The perks don't stop there, you can get exclusive access to discounts, newsletters, and great free content in your inbox daily

Follow these simple steps to get the benefits:

1. Scan the QR code or visit the link below

https://packt.link/free-ebook/9781803231082

1. Submit your proof of purchase
2. That's it! We'll send your free PDF and other benefits to your email directly

Printed in Great Britain
by Amazon

39068625R00302